RESEARCH IN ACCOUNTING REGULATION

Supplement 1 • 1997

SPECIAL TENTH ANNIVERSARY
INTERNATIONAL EDITION

RESEARCH IN ACCOUNTING REGULATION

SPECIAL TENTH ANNIVERSARY INTERNATIONAL EDITION

Volume Editor: LARRY M. PARKER
Weatherhead School of Management
Department of Accountancy
Case Western Reserve University

Consulting Editor: GARY JOHN PREVITS
Weatherhead School of Management
Case Western Reserve University

SUPPLEMENT 1 • 1997

JAI PRESS INC.

Greenwich, Connecticut *London, England*

55 Old Post Road, No. 2
Greenwich, Connecticut 06830

JAI PRESS LTD.
38 Tavistock Street
Covent Garden
London WC2E 7PB
England

ISBN: 0-7623-0338-7
ISSN: 1052-0457

Transferred to digital printing 2006

CONTENTS

EDITOR'S NOTE

BOOK REVIEWS

LIST OF CONTRIBUTORS

Simon Archer	University of Surrey
Donald F. Arnold, Sr.	Union College
Richard A. Bernardi	State University of New York at Plattsburgh
Robert Bloom	John Carroll University
Carrie Bloomer	Financial Accounting Standards Board
Kevin Carduff	Case Western Reserve University
Frank L. Clarke	University of New Castle, Australia
Marilynn Collins	John Carroll University
Graeme W. Dean	University of Sydney
Joselito G. Diga	Australian National University
Ruth W. Epps	Virginia Commonwealth University
Timothy J. Fogarty	Case Western Reserve University
Lorraine Gilbert	Case Western Reserve University
Richard M. Goligoski	Deloitte & Touche, LLP
Sylwia Gornik-Tomaszewski	Baldwin-Wallace College
Pei-Gin Hsieh	Case Western Reserve University
Khondkar E. Karim	Monmouth University
Rifaat A.A. Karim	Accounting and Auditing Organization for Islamic Financial Institutions
Heidi Hylton Meier	Cleveland State University

R. Narayanaswamy	Indian Institute of Management Bangalore
Belverd E. Needles, Jr.	DePaul University
Khursheed Omer	University of Houston, Downtown
Anne J. Rich	Quinnipiac College
Shahrokh M. Saudagaran	Santa Clara University
Mark A. Segal	University of South Alabama
Philip H. Siegel	Monmouth University
Sudarwan	Office of Accounting Jakarta, Indonesia
Gu Liang Tang	Beijing Institute of Business
Yunwei Tang	Shanghai University
Wanda A. Wallace	College of William and Mary
Michele L. Wingate	University of Colorado at Denver
Arthur R. Wyatt	University of Illinois, Urbana-Champaigne

MAIN PAPERS

THE IMPACT OF CAPITAL MARKET DEVELOPMENTS ON ACCOUNTING REGULATORY POLICY IN EMERGING MARKETS:
A STUDY OF ASEAN

Shahrokh M. Saudagaran and Joselito G. Diga

ABSTRACT

The heterogeneous, often conflicting, interests which accounting must cater to has engendered continuing discussions on various normative aspects of accounting policy (Demski 1973; Cyert and Ijiri 1974; Buckley 1980). The absence of definitive criteria for making choices requires those involved in accounting policy determination to exercise their own value judgments in making choices (May and Sundem 1976; Beaver 1981). Although the policy dimensions of accounting extend to several areas, the role of accounting in the context of domestic capital markets has garnered most of the attention. The extant research focuses on the industrialized countries in Europe, North America and Australasia. Research outside these geographical areas

Research in Accounting Regulation, Supplement 1, pages 3-48.

ISBN: 0-7623-0338-7

has been sparse. This study examines whether and to what extent the accounting policies formulated in five Southeast Asian countries respond to the structure and demands of their capital markets.

Based on the extant literature, we distinguish between macro-user and micro-user oriented accounting systems. We find the relationship between capital markets and financial accounting systems in ASEAN to be subtle and complex, rather than direct as suggested in prior contingency-based accounting research. The hypothesis that a country's dominant source of finance is a major determinant in whether the accounting system is macro-user of micro-user oriented finds cautious and qualified support. A more accurate depiction in ASEAN is that the capital markets, as shaped by a configuration of historical, political and economic factors, provided one of the necessary conditions for cultivating accounting policies in each country. The historical origins of capital markets in ASEAN is found to be a particularly relevant factor. The effects of colonization have permeated not only the nature and content of extant legislation but, more fundamentally, the conditions in which capital markets developed in these countries. These findings support the view the "spheres of influence" have and will continue to strongly impact accounting developments in countries with emerging markets such as those in ASEAN.

INTRODUCTION

The policy implications of accounting in a domestic and transnational context have been the subject of increasing attention (Burchell et al. 1980; Bromwich and Hopwood 1983; Meek and Saudagaran 1990). The heterogeneous, often conflicting, interests which accounting must cater to have engendered continuing discussions on various normative aspects of accounting policy (Demski 1973; Cyert and Ijiri 1974; Buckley 1980). Moreover, the absence of definitive criteria for making choices requires those involved in accounting policy determination to exercise their own value judgments in making choices (May and Sundem 1976; Beaver 1981). Currently, most of the extant research dealing with the policy aspects of accounting focuses on the United States and the United Kingdom, and to a lesser extent, other industrialized countries in Europe and Australasia. Research outside these geographical areas has generally been sparse.

This paper attempts to address the dearth in this research by analyzing the experience of the countries in the Association of Southeast Asian Nations (ASEAN) in an effort to better understand the impact of capital markets on the accounting systems of emerging economies. ASEAN is currently comprised of seven countries with diverse political, economic, legal, and cultural environments. Formed in 1967, ASEAN has emerged as an important economic and political entity. With a combined gross domestic product in excess of U.S.$600 billion in 1995 and a population of 432 million, it represents a market greater than those of countries belonging to the European Union (EU) and to the North American Free Trade Agreement (NAFTA). Yet surprisingly, there is very little in the international accounting literature on the ASEAN countries. The aim of this paper is to determine whether, and to what extent, the accounting policies formulated in these countries respond to the structure and demands of their capital markets. The analysis here will be confined to the original five members of the group: Indonesia, Malaysia, the Philippines, Singapore, and Thailand. These five countries have more developed banking and securities market sectors relative to those in Brunei and Vietnam—the other two members of ASEAN. In comparison, the basic institutional and regulatory frameworks for capital markets in Brunei and Vietnam, the two most recent ASEAN members, are less developed and are currently in the process of being established.[1]

This paper provides evidence regarding the subtle, yet pervasive and enduring, impact that domestic capital markets have on the development of accounting systems in countries such as those in ASEAN. In particular, we find that developments in securities markets, more so than the banking sector, are intertwined with changes in the accounting systems of these countries. Accounting, however, appears to be both a cause and effect of changes in domestic capital markets. On the one hand, demands arising from capital markets provide a rationale for adopting particular forms of accounting. Reciprocally, accounting is perceived as a prerequisite for the growth of domestic capital markets.

The remainder of the paper is structured as follows. In the second section, we analyze the role of accounting in the context of domestic capital markets. Specifically, we discuss the policy implications of adopting either a macro-user or micro-user oriented accounting system, the two main classes of accounting systems supported in extant comparative accounting research. The third section provides an overview of accounting systems in ASEAN countries. We attempt to locate accounting systems in ASEAN within the framework of macro-user and micro-user oriented systems by examining previous classificatory research, as well as the broad aims of accounting in these countries expressed in their legislation and accounting standards. In the fourth section, we examine whether, and to what extent, capital markets in ASEAN influenced their accounting systems. A distinction is made between the importance of the banking sector and the securities markets vis-à-vis the development of accounting in each country. Finally, the fifth section draws some conclusions and highlights areas for further research.

POLICY IMPLICATIONS OF ACCOUNTING AND CAPITAL MARKETS

Accounting and the Nature of Domestic Capital Markets

A country's capital market encompasses the part of its financial sector that is involved in the mobilization and intermediation of private savings, and the allocation of medium and long-term financial resources for investments in the country

Table 1. Organization and Elements of Capital Markets

	Non-securities Markets	Securities Markets
Instruments	Loans	Equity (shares of stock)
	Mortgages Leases	Equity equivalents (convertible bonds or debentures)
	Sale and Lease-back	Debt securities (bonds or debentures
		Financial derivatives (options and futures)
Institutions	Central Banks	*Primary Market*
	Development Banks	Corporate Government Issuers
	Specialized Banks (e.g. Import-Eport)	Investment, Merchant Banks
	Commercial Banks	Brokers, Dealers
	Savings Banks	Securities Regulatory Bodies
	Insurance Companies	Debenture Trustees
	Pension & Employee Provident Funds	Venture Capital Firms
	Leasing Companies	
		Secondary Market
		Over-the-Counter Markets
		Stock Exchanges
		Brokers, Dealers
		Clearance & Settlement Agencies
		Transfer Agents & Mutual Funds

Source: ADB (1986).

(Asian Development Bank [ADB] 1986). From an economic policy perspective, a country's capital market is considered a crucial infrastructural requirement for promoting economic development, particularly in its roles of mobilizing domestic and international financial resources and allocating scarce capital resources efficiently to their most productive uses (ADB 1986, 1995; World Bank 1989, 1990, 1993).

A capital market consists broadly of a securities market and a non-securities market, each category encompassing different instruments and institutions (see in Table 1). The distinction between securities and non-securities markets is essential in understanding the specific context in which accounting operates in various countries. Previous comparative accounting research suggests that accounting depends, in part, on the relative importance and level of development of a country's securities and non-securities markets (Choi 1973; Pratt and Behr 1987; Cooke and Wallace 1990; Alexander and Archer 1995). An analysis of differences in the way domestic capital markets are organized can therefore provide insights into the role of accounting in different national settings.

Domestic capital markets can be differentiated according to their level of financial development (Frankel 1993). A country's level of financial development, in turn, can be determined by analyzing the principal sources of long-term capital for domestic enterprises (Fry 1993) (see Figure 1). In rudimentary economies, the main sources of long-term capital are informal or "curb" markets, that is, small-scale moneylenders or sources known personally to the borrower. As the scale and scope of economic activities expands, however, enterprises require capital in amounts that are generally far in excess of what a small group of individuals can supply. Financial institutions that "intermediate" between savers and borrowers emerge to address the need for large amounts of long-term capital. At the next stage of development, the domestic financial system becomes even more sophisticated, with enterprises able to raise capital directly by issuing their own securities to the public. It is in this context that secondary markets for corporate securities play a facilitating role by allowing investors to diversify their risk and increase the liquidity of their investments (World Bank 1990). Arguably, the level of development of financial systems is indicated not by the actual size of the securities markets or banking sector per se, but rather by the importance of various sources of long-term capital (Frankel 1993). In some countries, the banking sector remains the dominant source of finance for large-scale corporate activities, despite the presence of comparatively large stock markets. For example, Japan has a large securities market (second only to the United States in terms of market capitalization) but bank finance remains by far the most important source of long-term capital for Japanese enterprises (Choi and Hiramatsu 1987). The government also usually plays an active role in allocating domestic credit in countries whose financial systems are dominated by the banking sector (ADB 1986; World Bank 1990). Finally, the cutting edge of financial sophistication characterize financial systems that offer a variety of risk-management instruments, otherwise known as "financial derivatives." In these countries, financial risk associated with investing in corporate securities can be managed and tailored to various levels of risk preferences through the use of various financial derivative instruments. The availability of these financial instruments, in turn, attracts a greater number of investors to participate in the financial market (Ghon Rhee et al. 1990; Frankel 1993).

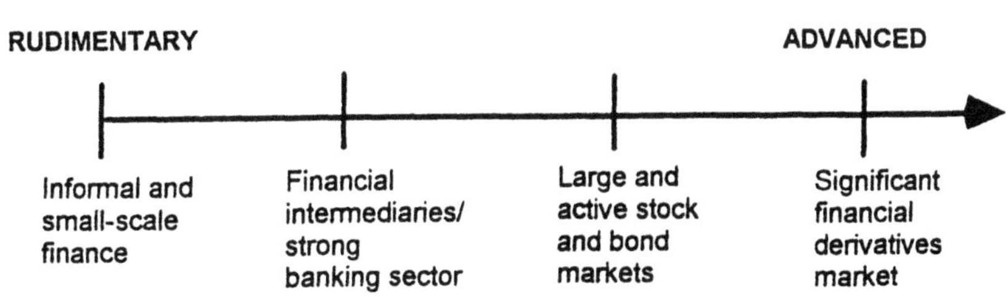

Figure 1. Level of Development of Capital Markets

Financial accounting, in its role of providing information for economic decision making, is central to the process of allocating financial resources in capital markets. In the non-securities sector, financial accounts provide an important basis for lending decisions of financial institutions in most countries, including those in ASEAN (Leftwich 1983; Skully 1986; *Financial Times* 1993). As a matter of policy, financial institutions require borrowers to furnish detailed financial information as part of the loan extension process to evaluate the relative credit risk of prospective and existing borrowers.

Conversely, financial reporting requirements are essential for the adequate oversight and supervision of banks and financial institutions in most countries (World Bank 1990). Financial institutions are usually required to submit to government agencies (and in some cases, publish in major newspapers) their financial statements as part of discharging their accountability requirements. Regulatory requirements for banks and financial institutions (e.g., Basle Accord requirements with respect to capital adequacy) are often based on accounting information furnished by these enterprises (World Bank 1989).

Extensive evidence exists also that accounting reports are relevant to investors' buy and sell decisions on corporate securities (Foster 1980; Beaver 1981). The importance of accounting reports for stock market investors has been demonstrated through multicountry capital market studies and in surveys of financial statement users (Choi and Levich 1990; Bhushan and Lessard 1992). The link between accounting information and well-developed securities markets is a particularly crucial policy matter for less developed countries (LDCs) aiming to attract increased capital flows to develop their economies (Enthoven 1977; Ndubizu 1984; Rozeff 1990; Larson 1993; Hossain et al. 1994; Sedaghat et al. 1994). As indicated by Walter (1993, 15), "The nature and extent of information production and disclosure is central to equity market development and the ability to attract cross-border flows. . . . The stronger and more independent the information infrastructure, the more attractive an emerging market will be to foreign equity investors."

The emerging consensus that financial accounting is important for the efficient operation of capital markets has permeated policymaking at the national and international levels. The regulation of corporate financial reporting is a pervasive phenomenon worldwide (Lev 1988; Cooke and Wallace 1990). At an international level, organizations such as the International Accounting Standards Committee (IASC) and the International Organization of Securities Commissions (IOSCO) are concerned with ensuring an adequate supply of reliable and relevant financial information necessary for cross-border financial transactions (Chandler 1992; IASC 1993). Moreover, multilateral lending institutions such as the World Bank and the Asian Development Bank (ADB) are at the forefront of recommending to LDCs the need to ensure a robust accounting system to enhance the development of their financial systems (ADB 1986, 1995; World Bank 1989, 1990, 1993).

Notwithstanding the emerging consensus regarding the importance of having an adequate domestic accounting system, the debate over which form of financial reporting system is most appropriate for a country is far from settled. The extent and persistence of diverse financial reporting regulations and practices worldwide attests to different views on what constitutes "proper accounting" (Ndubizu 1984; Hove 1986; Gray and Roberts 1991). A significant stream of research in comparative international accounting has sought to address such issues from a contingency perspective, aiming to explain current features of accounting systems in terms of various "contingent" economic, political, and sociocultural variables (Radebaugh 1975; Cooke and Wallace 1990; Doupnik and Salter 1995).[2] Results of these studies, however, are far from conclusive and suggest the need for an in-depth understanding of the impact of specific factors, such as domestic capital markets, on accounting policy development.

Policy Choices in Accounting

Accounting policy here refers to making choices with respect to the broad aims established for accounting, the institutional framework for setting and implementing accounting regulations, detailed accounting rules, and corporate accounting practices. The aim of analyzing financial accounting systems from a policy perspective is to determine the nature, rationale, and process of making choices from among alternative courses of action. The pertinent policy issues in regard to specific accounting elements are summarized in Table 2.[3]

The relative scope and importance of policy decisions increases as one climbs the accounting policy hierarchy. Decisions regarding the broad aims of financial accounting have a profound and long-term impact on the institutional basis, specific accounting rules, and accounting practices in a country. Also, the available

Table 2. Hierarchy of Accounting Policies

Element of Accounting	*Accounting Policy Issues*
Broad aims of financial accounting	• What should be the *aim* of financial accounting in terms of the user orientation of the accounts? • What should be the role of financial accounting in regard to capital markets, fiscal (tax) policy and macroeconomic planning policy?
Institutional setting for accounting regulation	• Which approach(es) to *formulating* accounting regulation should be adopted? • Which approach(es) to *enforcing* accounting regulation should be used?
Specific accounting rules and requirements	• Which specific *disclosure* and *measurement* rules should be adopted and to whom should these rules apply?
Corporate accounting practices	• Which specific *disclosure* and *measurement* methods will be used in presenting the company's accounts?

Table 3. Accounting in a Macro-user and Micro-user Oriented Environment

Functional Core	*Role in Macro-user Oriented*	*Role in Micro-User Oriented*
Capital Markets	Accounting helps ensure "financial stewardship" that is, non-dissipation of assets and protection of creditors.	Accounting provides relevant and reliable information about an enterprise's "true" state of economic well-being.
Taxation	Accounting plays a primary role; no difference between tax accounting and financial accounting methods.	Accounting plays an indirect and supportive role; tax accounting and financial accounting methods differentiated clearly.
National economic planning	Accounting: • ensures the effect of government economic policies are reflected in enterprise accounts • provides inputs for industry or national accounting reports.	Accounting plays an incidental role. Government relies indirectly, if at all, on enterprise accounts in preparing national or industry economic plans.

alternatives increase significantly as one descends the hierarchy. There are significantly more options, for example, in regard to specific accounting practices compared to types of institutional arrangements for regulating accounting.[4] In regard to the broad aims of accounting, we assert that two general preferences have been demonstrated thus far. One is to emphasize the usefulness of the accounting system for private sector users (i.e., capital markets) and the other is for government users (i.e., tax or economic planning).[5]

In this study, we specifically examine the broad accounting aims with respect to domestic capital markets. The broad aims of financial accounting, as used here, correspond to the "core of functional claims" (Burchell et al. 1980, 9-10) attributed to accounting systems which include, among others, providing information for decision making, assisting in enforcing institutional accountability and stewardship, providing a means for calculating tax liabilities of enterprises, and contributing to management of the macro economy.

Countries can be compared based on the relative importance attached to particular roles of accounting in society. On this basis, prior research supports strongly a dichotomisation between a macro-user oriented and a micro-user oriented accounting system (Mueller 1968; Nobes 1983, 1984; Doupnik and Salter 1993).[6] The differences between these two systems in relation to the main roles of accounting in society are outlined in Table 3.

As indicated in Table 3, the overall difference between the two systems relates to the intended users of accounting information. In macro-user oriented systems, government agencies, particularly tax and economic planning agencies, are the principal users of accounting reports. In comparison, a diverse set of capital providers is perceived to be the most important user group of accounting reports in micro-user oriented systems.

Differences between the two systems are also quite pronounced with respect to the role of accounting in capital markets. In countries that have adopted micro-user oriented accounting systems, the goal of accounting has traditionally been to provide "true and fair" or "fairly presented" financial statements. The notions of true and fair and fairly presented are associated generally with the need to provide adequate and reliable financial disclosures and the use of accounting methods that reflect the "economic substance" rather than the "legal form" of transactions.

In comparison, the goal of providing fairly presented accounts has not been acknowledged explicitly in countries with macro-user oriented accounting systems.[7] The traditional aim of accounting, particularly in regard to providers of long-term capital, has been to guard against the surreptitious dissipation of assets (Nobes 1983, 1984; Bloom and Naciri 1989; Alexander and Archer 1995). This goal was supposedly attained through the use of "conservative" accounting measurement methods that understated reported assets and profits of the enterprise (Emenyonu and Gray 1992).

The contrasting goals of accounting in the context of domestic capital markets indicate fundamentally different assumptions between macro-user and micro-user oriented accounting systems in regard to the role of accounting in effective corporate governance (Benston 1982; Macdonald and Beattie 1993; Tricker 1994). In micro-user oriented environments, the role of accounting is viewed in terms of providing a reliable benchmark for evaluating management performance. A major determinant of management's performance is maintaining an adequate track record of earnings performance and cash or dividend flows. In view of the incentives for management to bias reported results, there is a perceived need for "neutral and unbiased" accounting methods that could mitigate potential conflicts of interests between enterprise managers and owners (Cyert and Ijiri 1974; Watts and Zimmerman 1978). Conversely, debates regarding the "economic consequences" of accounting have raised the possibility that accounting methods could be adopted in order to promote specific desired effects, for example, boosting spending on research and development to increase enterprise competitiveness (Solomons 1978, 1983; Cooper and Keim 1983). The dominant view, however, is that accounting should remain for the most part insulated from wrangling over potential beneficial or adverse economic consequences. Otherwise, the neutrality and, hence, credibility of accounting reports would suffer (FASB 1978; Dyckman 1988; Solomons 1991).[8]

In contrast, in most macro-user oriented accounting systems in continental Europe—such as France, Germany, and Sweden—the role of accounting is viewed in terms of contributing *intentionally* toward enterprise stability and continuity (Alexander and Archer 1995). This view is mediated by conditions prevalent in these countries. First, institutional creditors often play a significant role in corporate governance in these countries, through representation in the enterprise's board of directors and executive management or through a system of cross-ownerships between borrowing and lending enterprises (Macdonald and Beattie 1993;

Tricker 1994). Prudent accounting methods contribute to dampening possible management hubris in distributing dividends perceived to be detrimental to creditors and providing "rock bottom" asset values that do not overstate the security potential of assets in case of liquidation. Moreover, the entitlements of a wider set of corporate stakeholders appear to be well recognized in continental Europe and in Japan (Choi and Hiramatsu 1987; Meek and Gray 1989). The requirements of government agencies (primarily tax and economic planning agencies) and employees (including management) are ranked of the same, if not greater, importance as capital providers.[9] The enterprise is viewed as helping to guarantee long-term, if not lifetime, employment and as contributing toward national economic goals.[10] In this environment, neutrality in accounting procedures is subordinated to the goal of influencing deliberately the behavior of enterprise agents toward certain predefined goals, an arrangement deemed unacceptable (because it leads to "biased" accounts) in micro-user oriented accounting systems.

There is little evidence that these polar views of the role of financial accounting in countries can be reconciled in the short term. There is one school of thought which believes that deliberate efforts toward accounting harmonization can reduce the gap regarding the broad aims of countries (Choi and Levich 1990; Bhushan and Lessard 1992; Beresford 1995). Even in the European Union (EU), where the greatest visible progress toward regional accounting harmony has arguably been achieved, there remain substantial differences in terms of the broad aims of accounting and, consequently, the methods and practices among countries (Emenyonu and Gray 1992; Nobes 1993). Evidence suggests that accounting differences are, to a significant extent, perpetuated by underlying differences in these countries' capital markets (Choi and Hiramatsu 1987; Pratt and Behr 1987; Bloom and Naciri 1989; Alexander and Archer 1995). Whereas the United Kingdom and the United States, for example, have had a long tradition of active securities markets, Germany and France (two of the largest economies in the EU) have, in general, relied on bank finance as a source of industrial capital. An intriguing, albeit unexplored, dimension in comparative accounting research is the extent to which these differences in customary sources of capital—that is, securities markets versus banks—is itself a reflection of more enduring ideological and cultural characteristics in a country.[11]

ACCOUNTING SYSTEMS IN ASEAN COUNTRIES

In this section, we analyze the features of ASEAN accounting systems to determine the broad aims of accounting in each country. We also attempt to locate the accounting systems in ASEAN countries within the classificatory framework of macro-user and micro-user oriented systems. The discussion here comprises three aspects. First, we examine extant comparative accounting research to determine how ASEAN countries have been classified. Then, we consider the broad aims of accounting as expressed in domestic legislation and statutes. Finally, we analyze the contribution of domestic accounting standards in explicating the role of accounting in each country.

Comparative Research in Accounting

In general, there are few references to ASEAN in extant comparative accounting research. Among the analytical classification research, the pioneering work of Mueller (1968) did not specifically mention any of the ASEAN countries as reflecting any of the four patterns or approaches to accounting development. Nobes (1984) mentions the Philippines as having a micro-based accounting system influenced heavily by the United States. Berry (1987) also classifies the Philippines as being under the U.S.-influenced, micro-business practice systems. In addition, Berry (1987) classifies Malaysia and Singapore as falling under the U.K.-influenced, micro-business practice systems. The empirical test conducted by Doupnik and Salter (1993) of the Nobes and Berry classificatory frameworks supported the classification of Malaysia and Singapore as part of the U.K.-influenced countries. Surprisingly, they also found the Philippines to be U.K.-influenced rather than U.S.-influenced. Thailand's accounting system was found to resemble the French-influenced accounting systems of Belgium, Egypt, Liberia, Panama, Saudi Arabia, and the United Arab Emirates. None of the preceding studies included Indonesia.

In terms of the statistically derived classifications, Frank (1979) included Singapore as part of the U.K.-influenced group while the Philippines was included in the U.S.-influenced group. Nair and Frank (1980) obtained results consistent with most analytical studies, finding Malaysia and Singapore to be part of the U.K. group and the Philippines part of the U.S. group.

In general, except for the findings of Doupnik and Salter (1993), the ASEAN countries were identified closely with particular clusters, specifically, Malaysia and Singapore as part of the U.K.-influenced group, and the Philippines as one of the U.S.-influenced countries. Prior research suggests, therefore, that accounting systems in Malaysia, the Philippines, and Singapore have adopted a micro-user perspective. In contrast, the accounting system in Thailand adopted a macro-user oriented approach. No information on Indonesia was available from these studies.

Aims Expressed in Statutes and Legislation

As in most other countries, various forms of legislation underpin financial accounting in ASEAN countries. This legislation deals principally with company laws and statutes on securities issuance and exchange (Maolanond and Nobuyuki 1985). The pertinent accounting-related laws in ASEAN are summarized in Table 4.

Table 4. Legislation Affecting Financial Accounting in ASEAN

	Indonesia	*Malaysia*	*Philippines*	*Singapore*	*Thailand*
Company Law	Limited Company Law, 1995	Companies Act, 1965 (as ammended)	Corporation Code, 1980 (National Law No. 68)	Companies Act, 1967 (as amended)	Public Limited Company Act, BE 2535 (1992)
Securities and Exchange Law	Presidential Decree No. 53 (Capital Market Law) of 1976	Securities Industry Act, 1983 (as amended)	Revised Securities Act, 1982	Securities Industry Act 1992 (as amended)	Securities and Exchange Act, BE 2535 (1992)
Accounting Law for Companies	None	None	None	None	Account Act, BE 2515 (1972)

Company Law

Limited liability companies represent the most important legal form of organization in the ASEAN countries in terms of the scale and diversity of their economic activities. Company laws have been enacted in each ASEAN country to regulate the formation, operation and dissolution of limited liability companies. These laws contain provisions on various aspects of corporate activities, including:

- Incorporation or formation of companies;
- Corporate governance structures (corporate charter, by-laws, directors, and officers);
- Rights and obligations of shareholders, particularly minority shareholders;
- Methods of raising capital;
- Corporate dissolution, liquidation, reconstructions, mergers, and takeovers; and
- Accounts and audit.

In terms of financial reporting requirements, companies in ASEAN are mandated generally to maintain adequate accounting records and to prepare and submit financial statements on a regular basis to users, particularly to capital providers. In addition, a public company is required to furnish a prospectus before it can issue corporate debt or equity securities. Given their ability to raise funds from the general populace, public companies straddle the requirements of both company laws and securities laws. Consequently, more demanding financial reporting regulations have generally applied to public companies in ASEAN, including requirements to:

- Furnish quarterly or semi-annual financial statements;
- Publish financial statements in a large newspaper; and
- Provide additional schedules and details of accounts to users and government entities.

Among ASEAN countries, however, differences exist as to the degree of detail contained in the legal provisions and on specific provisions relating to public companies. Table 5 highlights these distinctions among the company laws of ASEAN countries. Several patterns can be discerned from this table. First, the requirements and guidelines pertaining to financial accounts are similar in Malaysia and Singapore. In both countries, sufficient accounting records are required to enable "true and fair" financial statements to be prepared and audited. Both also require group accounts to be prepared by all enterprises. Moreover, fairly detailed disclosure requirements for the balance sheet and profit-and-loss accounts are specified in a Ninth Schedule of each country's company law.

Table 5. Company Law Requirements Concerning Financial Reports

	Indonesia	*Malaysia*	*Philippines*	*Singapore*	*Thailand*
Financial statements to be prepared	Balance sheet Income statement Directors' report	Balance sheet Profit and loss account Directors' report Statutory Declaration by managing director Group of consolidated statements	Balance sheet Income statement Notes	Balance sheet Profit and loss accounts Statement of cash flows Directors' report Group of consolidated statements	Balance sheet Profit and loss account Directors' report
Guidelines for preparing financial statements	None speficied	Must provide true and fair view Comply with Ninth Schedule of Companies Act	None specified	Must provide a true and fair view Comply with Ninth Schedule of Companies Act	Comply with Ministerial Regulations
To whom should financial statements be submitted	All shareholders Registrar of Companies	All shareholders Appointed auditor Registrar of Companies	All shareholders Securities and Exchange Commission	All shareholders Appointed auditor Registrar of Companies	All shareholders Registration Department of Ministry of Commerce
Accounting system requirements	None specified	None specified	None specified	Must maintain adequate system of Internal control Audit committee required for listed companies	
Specific disclosure requirements	None specified	Ninth Schedule of Companies Act	None specified	Ninth Schedule of Companies Act	None specified

Table 6. Comparison of 'Conceptual Frameworks" in ASEAN

	Indonesia	*Malaysia*	*Philippines*	*Singapore*	*Thailand*
USERS	None specifically mentioned	Investors, employees, lenders, suppliers and trade creditors, customers, governments and their agencies, public	Owners, creditors, suppliers, tax authorities, employees, customers, regulatory agencies, financial analysts, stock exchanges, lawyers, financial press, trade associations, labor unions	Investors, employees, lenders, suppliers and trade creditors, customers, governments and their agencies, public	Shareholders, investors, creditors, employees government agencies, public
BASIC FINANCIAL STATEMENTS	Balance sheet, income statement Statement of changes in financial position Notes to financial statements	Balance sheet, income statement Statement of changes in financial position Notes to financial statements	Balance sheet, income statement Statement of retained earnings State of changes in financial position	Balance sheet, income statement Statement of changes in financial position Notes to financial statements	Balance sheet, income statement Statement of retained earnings, Statement of changes in financial position, Notes and supplementary statements
BASIC ACCOUNTING ASSUMPTIONS	Going concern, accounting period, monetary measurement, exchange rates, accrual concept	Accrual basis of accounting, going concern	Going concern, time periods, monetary measurement, acrrual, exchange prices, approximation and judgment, substance over form, articulated financial statemments, general purpose	Accrual basis of accounting, going concern	Going concern, consistency, accual, adequate disclosure

(continued)

Table 6. (Continued)

	Indonesia	*Malaysia*	*Philippines*	*Singapore*	*Thailand*
LIMITATIONS OF FINANCIAL STATEMENTS	Historical, general purpose, estimates and jugment, materiality, conservatism, economic substance over legal form, technical terms and audience knowledge, flexibility in accounting methods, qualitative information	Timeliness, costs versus benefits, balance between qualitative characteristics	Historical, general purpose, money terms, measurement bases, accrual, estimates and judgment, classificantion and summarization, varifiability, conservatism, substance over form, technical terms, audience knowledge	Timeliness, costs versus benefits, balance between qualitative characteristics	Conservatism, economic substance over legal form, materiality
SCOPE OR APPLICABILITY OF CF	• All financial statements should follow principles	• Basis for developing standards • Assist in forming audit opinion • Assist users in interpretation	• Basis for guiding future development of financial accounting	• Basis for developing standards • Assist in forming audit opinion • Assist users in interpretation	• Must be adhered to by all enterprises required to prepare financial statements under Ministerial Regulation No. 2 (BE 2519)
REPORTING ENTITY	Individual company defined by its economic control rather than legal definition	An enterprise for which there are users who rely on financial statements as major source of financial information	"The specific business enterprises" from an economic perspective	An enterprise for which there are users who rely on financial statements as major source of financial information	Not defined

Within ASEAN, the company laws of Malaysia and Singapore provide relatively more stringent and detailed requirements concerning enterprise financial accounting. In contrast, the laws in Indonesia, the Philippines, and Thailand are much less detailed in that they only require that certain financial statements be prepared and disseminated to users and government agencies, without specifying any rules on the preparation of financial statements.

These patterns reflect colonial links and historical associations. Malaysia and Singapore, both former British colonies, modeled their company laws on the U.K. Companies Act 1948 and the Australian Uniform Companies Act 1961 (Pillai 1984; CCH 1990). Subsequent amendments to the Malaysian and Singapore company laws have not altered the fundamental requirements to provide "true and fair view" financial statements.

In comparison, the financial accounting requirements in the company laws of Indonesia, the Philippines, and Thailand are of a more general nature. They also represent different origins and influences. In Indonesia, the principal law on companies until 1995 was the rather antiquated Commercial Code of 1848 based on the early Dutch Commercial Code.[12] The financial accounting provisions of this early law were quite general, specifying only that any person carrying on a business activity must keep records sufficient to allow determination of that person's financial rights and obligations (Samidjo 1985). However, the early code did not specify how this was to be accomplished. In practice, however, although the accounting requirements of the Indonesian commercial code were not specific, most Indonesian companies prepared financial statements to satisfy the requirements of government agencies, such as the Foreign Investment Board (known by its Indonesian acronym "BKPM"), and institutional creditors.[13]

The Philippine Corporation Code of 1980 required registered corporations to maintain records of all business transactions, minutes of meetings of stockholders and the board of directors, and stock registry books. Some of the provisions of the current Code were based on the financial reporting provisions of the Corporation Law of 1906, promulgated by the Philippine legislature working under the U.S. colonial administration (De Leon 1990). The Code stipulated that a company was obligated to furnish stockholders with financial statements, including a balance sheet and profit-and-loss account, duly audited and signed by a Certified Public Accountant (§75). In addition, the financial statements were required to show "in reasonable detail [the company's] assets and liabilities and the results of its operations" (§75). The task of formulating detailed financial reporting requirements for registered corporations, however, was delegated to the Philippine Securities and Exchange Commission, the government agency that concurrently administers the country's securities law.

In Thailand, the earliest legislation governing companies was the Civil and Commercial Code, Book III (1914 as amended in 1929). This law stipulated that "true accounts" must be maintained of the "sum received and expended by the company for each receipt and expenditure" and of the "assets and liabilities of the company." In addition, the Code required companies to maintain certain books of accounts, including a cash book, journal, ledger, and stock-in-trade account. The British notion of "true accounts" reflected the early influence of the U.K. Companies Act 1908 in the drafting of the Thai legislation (Maolanond and Nobuyuki 1985). The Thai commercial legislation also drew upon the German commercial code, particularly provisions dealing with safeguarding creditors. For example, the Code emphasized the need for an audit of a company's balance sheet to ensure sufficient reserve against possible bankruptcy while being silent regarding an income statement audit (ICAAT 1973). The Thai Code was similar to Indonesian and Philippine company legislation in that it did not specify detailed financial accounting requirements. This task was delegated to the Thai Ministry of Commerce, which issued regulations in 1976 governing the financial reporting of companies.

The company laws in the five ASEAN countries were instrumental in sustaining conditions for improved corporate accounting practices by underscoring the importance of keeping adequate accounting records and mandating the preparation and distribution of financial statements. Only the company laws of Malaysia and Singapore, however, have enshrined the micro-user oriented focus of accounting implicit in the notion of "true and fair view" accounts. In comparison, corresponding legislation in Indonesia, the Philippines, and Thailand did not specify whether the accounting system ought to be macro-user or micro-user oriented. Nonetheless, the financial reporting systems in these countries feature varying degrees of a micro-user orientation. Private sector groups, particularly professional accounting bodies, have played a significant role in delineating the broad aims of accounting in these countries, thus filling the vacuum left by less than specific company law requirements.

Securities Market Law

Similar to their company laws, the securities regulations in ASEAN reflected foreign influences based on historical and economic ties. Modern securities laws in ASEAN were enacted mostly during the 1960s and 1970s at a time when the economies of the ASEAN countries were experiencing profound structural changes (Maolanond and Nobuyuki 1985). Distinct patterns are discernible, however, in terms of the structure and content of these countries' securities regulations.

The Malaysian and Singapore Securities Industries Acts share significant similarities, particularly regarding provisions on accounting and auditing requirements. These similarities reflect the common origin of their legislation. Both were patterned after the Securities Act of New South Wales of Australia. These laws mirror the close linkages between the securities markets in both countries. Until 1973, the stock markets of Malaysia and Singapore were unified (and known as the Stock Exchange of Malaysia and Singapore), although trading floors were located in each country. Even after each country set up its own stock exchange, a significant amount of cross-listing of companies and transborder investment activity still occurred between them.[14]

In comparison, significant diversity exists in the securities market laws of Indonesia, the Philippines, and Thailand. In Indonesia, the securities market legislation was based on a law enacted shortly after the country's independence from the Netherlands. The Stock Exchange Law of 1952 was promulgated to facilitate the trading of Dutch corporate securities in the Jakarta Stock Exchange. In the mid-1970s, a series of government-led reforms resulted in creating two government bodies that would influence significantly capital market development in the country. One was the Capital Market Executive Agency (Bapepam), which acted as the supervisory agency for developing the securities market. The second was PT (Persero) Danareksa, a national investment trust company, which was formed to encourage small investors to participate in the fledgling Indonesian capital market. These reforms enhanced significantly the operation of securities markets in Indonesia (Skully 1984; SEACEN 1989).[15]

Philippine securities law, promulgated in 1936 during the U.S. colonial era, was patterned after the U.S. Securities Act 1933 and the Securities and Exchange Act 1934 and created a Philippine version of the U.S. Securities and Exchange Commission (SEC). Revisions of the law were made in 1982. While maintaining the principles and aims of the original legislation, the Revised Securities Act (1982) addressed areas not covered by the original law, including detailed requirements on the financial statements to be prepared and information to be disclosed by public corporations. In addition, it also specifically empowered the Philippine SEC to determine appropriate accounting standards for all public companies in the country.

In Thailand, the first securities legislation was enacted in 1974 on the basis of a study commissioned by the World Bank on how the country's securities markets should be organized. The study, conducted by Professor Sidney Robbins of Columbia University (who was also former Chief Economist of the SEC), recommended a system patterned after the U.S. securities markets (Maolanond and Nobuyuki 1985). General supervisory powers over the country's securities markets were exercised by the Securities Exchange of Thailand when a new law, the Securities and Exchange Act of 1992, transferred those powers to the Thai SEC. Since 1992, public companies have also been required to prepare and submit audited annual accounts and quarterly financial statements to their shareholders and the Thai SEC. As in the Philippines, the Thai SEC was empowered specifically to determine the nature and scope of financial reporting after consulting with the Thai Board of Auditing Practice (a separate agency under the Thai Ministry of Commerce).

Analysis of extant securities laws in ASEAN reveals a similar dichotomization between the U.K.-influenced countries (Malaysia and Singapore) and the non-U.K. group (Indonesian, the Philippines, and Thailand). Compared to their counterparts in ASEAN, securities laws in Malaysia and Singapore were focused more narrowly on regulating stockbroking businesses. In contrast, the securities laws in

Indonesia, the Philippines, and Thailand legislated procedures regulating both stockbrokers and publicly held companies. Moreover, the securities legislation in Malaysia and Singapore did not address aspects of financial accounting by public companies, probably in order to avoid duplicating the provisions in their company laws. In comparison, the securities law in Indonesia, the Philippines, and Thailand clarified the statutory basis of government agencies for regulating corporate accounting practices. The three ASEAN securities regulators—Bapepam (Indonesia), the Philippine SEC, and the Thai SEC—have all been given specific authority to establish appropriate accounting regulations in their respective countries. Similar mandates were not given to securities regulators in Malaysia and Singapore.

The impact of these differences in securities laws has been significant in ASEAN. The absence of a designated securities agency with authority to set accounting regulation in Malaysia and Singapore effectively signaled their governments' tacit approval to private sector groups, particularly the accounting profession in each country, to participate actively in determining accounting regulations. The Registrars of Companies, which are the government agencies responsible for implementing the company laws in these countries, were concerned mainly with ensuring compliance with detailed company law provisions, not with setting accounting standards.[16] In comparison, the potential for a more interventionist, government-determined policy for financial accounting has been set by securities legislation in Indonesia, the Philippines, and Thailand. In these countries, the securities regulators have been granted statutory powers to determine appropriate accounting standards. In practice, however, the securities regulators in these countries have generally delegated to professional accounting bodies the task of setting accounting standards, a state of affairs resembling those in industrialized countries with micro-user oriented accounting systems such as the United Kingdom and the United States. The evolution of securities laws in the non-U.K. influenced groups also indicates that securities markets served as the primary rationale for regulating accounting practices in these countries.

Accounting Law

Consistent with the continental European influence on its accounting regulatory practices, Thailand is unique among ASEAN countries in enacting legislation aimed at regulating the accounting practices of companies. The Thai Account Act of 1939 was promulgated to regulate corporate accounting practices and required all limited companies, partnerships, and persons engaged in business covered by Ministry of Commerce regulations to maintain detailed accounts. Provisions of this law were patterned after the German Stock Corporation Law of 1937 which, in turn, was enacted following widespread corporate failures in Germany during the 1920s and 1930s (Alexander and Archer 1995). One of the principal motivations of the Thai legislation, similar to the original German law, was to protect adequately creditors in the case of corporate bankruptcies. The law therefore enshrined the notion of "prudence" as the dominant principle governing accounting in Thailand.

A revised Account Act of 1972 was promulgated in order to rectify perceived inadequacies in the original law. Once more, the revisions reflected modifications in the German Stock Corporation Law made in 1965. The revisions called for restricting opportunities for asset under valuations through the use of methods such as secret reserves. Similar to the original law, however, the new Thai Account Act maintained notions of prudence and creditor protection as important principles of preparing accounts. The new law also required all companies and businesses registered with the Ministry of Commerce to submit audited financial statements annually. A subsequent law was promulgated in 1976 to provide more detailed guidelines implementing the Account Act. These regulations are administered by Thailand's Ministry of Commerce. Despite subsequent developments in the company law and securities legislation in Thailand, the Account Act has had an enduring influence on its accounting regulation and practice. In particular, Thailand is the only ASEAN country that has enshrined notions of prudence and conservatism in its accounting regulations (ICAAT 1993).

Aims Expressed In Accounting Standards

The perceived roles of accounting can also be discerned from the pronouncements of authoritative bodies in financial accounting. A principal characteristic of accounting regulation in ASEAN is that private sector groups play a strong, in most cases dominant, role in defining the nature and scope of financial accounting in these countries.

Objectives of Financial Accounting

The extant accounting standards in ASEAN are of relatively recent origin. Most of these standards have been formulated by professional accounting bodies in each country in the 1970s and 1980s. A review of accounting standards as of the end of 1993 shows the statement of aims for accounting in each country. As indicated below, ASEAN accounting standards are virtually unanimous in underscoring the usefulness of financial accounting for economic decision making, as a tool for making rational decisions regarding the allocation of financial and other resources. The adoption of a "decision-usefulness" objective in ASEAN represents a shift from the more traditional function of accounting as serving mainly a "financial stewardship" function (Cyert and Ijiri 1974; Buckley 1980; Beaver 1981; Benston 1982):

Indonesia

In principle the purpose of Financial Accounting and Financial Statements is to make available financial information regarding a company that will be used by interested parties as material for consideration in making economic decision" (PAI, Art. 1).

Malaysia and Singapore

The objective of financial statements is to provide information about the financial position, performance and changes in financial position of an enterprise that is useful to a wide range of users in making economic decisions" (adopted from IAS Framework for the Preparation of Financial Statements, ¶12).

Philippines

The basic purpose of financial accounting and financial statements is to provide quantitative financial information about a business enterprise that is useful to statement users, particularly owners and creditors, in making economic decisions. This purpose includes providing information that can be used in evaluating management's effectiveness in fulfilling its stewardship and other managerial responsibilities" (SFAS 1, §C, ¶1).

Thailand

Accounting is a service activity which provides financial information about an enterprise for the purpose of economic decision making" (FAS 1, ¶2).

In general, the statements of aims were defined broadly in order to accommodate a wide range of potential users, except perhaps in the Philippines where the aims appear to focus on the needs of investors and creditors. This difference reflects the close association between Philippine and U.S. accounting concepts. Unlike comparable statements of accounting aims in Australia, Canada, New Zealand, or the United Kingdom, the U.S. statement of aims focuses on the information needs of investors and creditors (FASB 1978; Mathews and Perera 1996).[17] Other users mentioned in the statements of aims of ASEAN countries include shareholders, creditors, employees, suppliers, tax authorities and other government agencies, and the general public. Notably absent in these pronouncements is a statement that enterprise accounts could be used to provide statistics for macroeconomic planning, a purpose that is emphasized in countries that adopt some form of general accounting plan (Alexander and Archer 1995; Baydoun and Willett 1995). While the aims of financial accounting in ASEAN do not preclude the use of financial accounting for macro-user purposes, they imply strongly that the intended users of accounting information are decision-makers (micro-users) dealing with a particular enterprise.

Conceptual Frameworks of Accounting

A conceptual framework of accounting has been defined as "a coherent system of interrelated objectives and fundamentals that can lead to consistent standards and that prescribes the nature, function, and limits of financial accounting and financial statements" (FASB 1976, 2). Conceptual frameworks appear to be associated uniquely with countries that embrace a micro-user oriented accounting system. Countries such as Australia, Canada, New Zealand, the United Kingdom, and the United States, in particular, are at the forefront of developing and adopting their own particular versions of conceptual frameworks (Mathews and Perera 1996). IAS also contain a conceptual framework for financial accounting (IASC 1993). More similarities than differences characterize extant conceptual frameworks in countries with micro-user oriented accounting systems. Most conceptual frameworks contain:

- A statement of aims or objectives of financial accounting;
- Targeted users of financial statements;
- Financial accounting statements that ought to be issued;
- Qualities and characteristics of "good" financial accounting;
- Limitations of financial statements;
- Scope of applicability of conceptual framework;
- Definition of "reporting entity;"
- Definition and basis of recognizing financial statement elements; and
- Measurement of financial statement elements and concept of capital maintenance

Following the model of a conceptual framework used in these countries (i.e., a framework that includes most, if not all, the above mentioned contents), only Thailand does not currently have a conceptual framework similar to those that exist in other countries with micro-user oriented systems. Malaysia and Singapore adopted wholly the IASC "Framework for the Preparation and Presentation of Financial Statements" (IASC 1993; ICPAS 1994; MACPA 1993; MIA 1993). While this framework does not have mandatory status in either country, it provides a reference point for developing and adopting accounting standards in both countries. The Philippines patterned its conceptual framework (Statement of Financial Accounting Standard No. 1, "Basic Concepts and Accounting Principles Underlying Financial Statements of Business Enterprises") on the U.S. APB Statement No. 4 dating to 1970 (ASC 1988). The Indonesian conceptual framework (Indonesian Accounting Principles, Part 1—Principles, 1984) also drew from APB Statement No. 4, although in a much more abbreviated form. Thailand has not developed nor adopted a conceptual framework as comprehensive as those that currently exist in other ASEAN countries. Rather, a Statement of Fundamental Accounting Assumptions (Financial Accounting Standard No. 1) provides definitions of accounting terms and conventions applicable to Thai companies (ICAAT 1993). While these accounting concepts are similar to those found elsewhere in ASEAN, unlike the conceptual frameworks of the other countries, the Thai version included both macro and micro-user oriented elements of accounting. Table 6 provides an analysis of particular aspects of "conceptual frameworks" in ASEAN.

As indicated in Table 6, the "conceptual frameworks" in Indonesia and Thailand are substantially less detailed than those found in Malaysia, Singapore and the Philippines. The Indonesian framework, for example, does not discuss the various

Table 7. Comparison of Qualitative Characteristics in ASEAN Standards

Qualitative Characteristics	*IND*	*MAL*	*PHI*	*SIN*	*THA*
Relevance	•	•	•	•	
Materiality	•	•	•	•	•
Reliability	•	•	•	•	•
Fredom from bias/neutrality	•	•	•	•	•
Comparability/consistency	•	•	•	•	•
Understandability	•	•	•	•	
Recognition of substance over form	•	•	•	•	•
Decision usefulness					
Cost/benefit		•		•	
Predictive value					
Feedback value					
Timeliness	•	•	•	•	
Verifiability	•		•		
Representational faithfulness		•		•	
Completeness	•	•	•	•	•
Objectivity					
Accuracy					
Uniformity					
Conservatism/Prudence	•	•	•	•	•

Source: IAI (1989); MIA (1993); MACPA (1993); ASC (1988); ICPAS (1994)
Table design adopted from Mathews and Perera (1996).

users of financial statements. The Thai framework is notably silent with respect to issues of asset definition, recognition and measurement.

Indications of the broad financial accounting aims can also be discerned from the qualitative objectives or characteristics of accounting mentioned in each country. Table 7 compares these qualitative characteristics in ASEAN conceptual frameworks. Consensus is apparent in such characteristics as materiality, reliability, neutrality, comparability, substance over form, completeness, and conservatism or prudence. It is interesting that Thai accounting standards adhere to the notion of "economic substance over legal form" when legal requirements to follow some tax regulations for financial accounting purposes contradict this principle. It is probable that Thai accounting standards communicate the views of the accounting profession but do not necessarily reflect those of the regulators. Thailand also stands apart from other ASEAN countries in endorsing a conservative or prudent bias in accounting measurement. Thai standards emphasize that "conservatism is to be applied in preparing financial statements when a matter of uncertainty is involved . . . [also] conservatism concept is applied when there are more than one possible alternative of accounting practices." Accountants are recommended to

Table 8. Relative Importance of Commercial Banking and Securities Markets in ASEAN*

	Indonesia		*Malaysia*		*Philippines*		*Singapore*		*Thailand*	
	1980	*1994*	*1980*	*1994*	*1980*	*1994*	*1980*	*1994*	*1980*	*1994*
Total assets of commercial banks (US $ billions)	16	90	15	70	18	34	78	115	15	153
Stock market capitalization (US $ billion)	.07	47	12.4	199	3.5	56	24.4	135	1.2	132
Bond market capitalization (US $ billion)	nil	9	7	40	0.2	25	4	45	0.2	14
Ratio of bank assets to securities market capitalization	229	1.6	0.8	0.3	4.9	0.4	2.7	0.6	10.7	1.1

Note: *All figures are as of end of year.

Source: SEACEN (1991); World Bank (1994); IFC (1994) and (1990); FEER (1995).

choose the one [method] that will present assets and profits at the lower rate. The rule, in short, is "anticipate no profits but recognize all losses, charge as expenses in case of doubt" (FAS No. 1, ¶9, quoted in ICAAT 1993). This is reflected, for example, in Thai requirements to provide a legal reserve from reported profits.

While it has been suggested that conceptual frameworks provide a logical and consistent guide to formulating accounting standards, it is not apparent yet how these conceptual frameworks would contribute to accounting standard-setting in ASEAN. What is clear, however, is that ASEAN professional accounting bodies have followed the lead of their counterparts elsewhere, particularly accounting bodies in industrialized countries with micro-user oriented accounting systems (e.g., Australia, Canada, New Zealand, United Kingdom, United States), which have introduced their own versions of conceptual frameworks. Overall, the existence of these conceptual frameworks in ASEAN characterize these countries' accounting systems as:

- Emphasizing decision-usefulness as an important function of accounting;
- Institutionalizing the flexibility in measurement and disclosure that is characteristic of financial reporting in these countries; and
- Signaling the important role played by professional accounting bodies in shaping accounting development in these countries.

CAPITAL MARKET DEVELOPMENT AND ACCOUNTING SYSTEMS IN ASEAN

The preceding analysis of the broad aims of accounting in ASEAN suggests, in general, an orientation toward micro-users of accounting information. In this section, we discuss the nature and level of development of capital markets in ASEAN as a basis for understanding the role of accounting in the context of these countries' capital markets. Analysis of ASEAN capital markets requires consideration of the rapid, often profound, changes occurring in the financial systems of these countries. These changes stem from the economic dynamism of countries such as Malaysia, Singapore, and Thailand, which have been catapulted into the ranks of newly industrialized countries (NICs) or near-NICs (World Bank 1993). Even among the less industrialized economies of Indonesia and the Philippines, changes in national financial systems have been significant, particularly in the 1980s and 1990s (Andersen 1993). Notwithstanding these developments in their financial systems, the analysis here indicates that the broad aims of accounting take on an enduring character which persists despite changes in each country's capital markets.

In order to highlight the nature and scope of capital markets in ASEAN, we reviewed the relative importance of each country's banking sector and securities markets. Table 8 compares the size of the commercial banking sector to the securities market in each country as of 1980 and 1994. The table shows that as of the 1980 year-end, the size of the commercial banking sector far exceeded the capitalization of securities markets (stock and bond markets) in ASEAN, except for Malaysia. However, by the end of 1994, the situation had been mostly reversed, with securities markets exceeding banking assets in importance, except in Indonesia and Thailand where the banking sectors remained dominant. Between 1980 and 1994, the trend pointed unequivocally toward a reduction in the importance of commercial banks as a source of corporate capital vis-à-vis the securities markets. In most instances, the reduction has been dramatic. Indonesia, for example, reduced the ratio of total bank assets to total securities market capitalization from 229 times in 1980 to only 1.6 times in 1994. Somewhat less remarkable, albeit still substantial, reductions were registered in all ASEAN countries particularly Thailand and the Philippines. Among the five ASEAN countries, Malaysia and Singapore had the most well-developed securities markets since the early 1980s. However, the most spectacular growths in securities markets were experienced in Indonesia and Thailand, which managed to increase the sizes of their securities markets 800-fold and 100-fold, respectively, over the 14-year period beginning in 1980. These developments will be analyzed here in terms of the underlying nature of financial systems in these countries. The analysis will be separated into the development of the banking sector and the securities markets in ASEAN.

Banking Sector

Historically, banks have been the preferred source of capital for business and industry in ASEAN. The banking systems of these countries were established and developed during the colonial era to cater mainly to the commercial interests of the colonizing country (Skully 1984, 1985; SEACEN 1989). The Dutch East Indies Company and the British East Indies Company, both worldwide trading entities at that time, first established rudimentary banking systems in Indonesia and Malaysia/Singapore, respectively. In the Philippines, the Spanish colonial administrators provided a relatively extensive array of banks and financial institutions in the islands as early as the 18th century, a system further developed by the U.S. colonial government in the early 1900s. Thailand had developed its own banking system, patterned after European (mainly British and German) models in the 19th century.

Two patterns of development are discernible with respect to the modern banking systems in ASEAN. The first pattern involves countries that largely, and to a certain extent still, maintain an oligopolistic banking sector controlled by a handful of domestic banks. Countries belonging to this category are Indonesia, the Philippines, Thailand, and to a lesser degree, Malaysia (Skully 1984; Robison 1986; Hewison 1988; Frankel 1993). The second category includes only Singapore, a country that liberalized its financial sector early in its postindependence period to encourage foreign financial institutions to play a major role in the country's financial system (Edwards 1987).[18] These different patterns of development had a significant influence on the development of capital markets and, consequently, of financial accounting systems in these countries.

Among the countries with oligopolistic banking systems, Indonesia and Malaysia featured a strong government presence in the banking sector. In Indonesia, the dominant sources of capital until the late 1980s were five government-owned commercial banks, which together controlled more than half of total banking sector assets. Essentially, the banks were called upon to carry out the government's credit policies with respect to channeling funds to certain preferred economic sectors and enterprises (Robison 1986; Andersen 1993). The other half of the banking sector was controlled mainly by private commercial banks owned or associated with prominent Indonesian family-owned conglomerates. Reforms carried out in the 1980s and 1990s sought to reduce the dependence on these government-owned financial institutions.[19]

Malaysia also has a tradition of strong government participation in banking (Skully 1984; SEACEN 1989). The two largest commercial banks in the country, Bank Bumiputra Malaysia Bhd. and Malayan Banking Bhd., were both established in the 1960s, around the time of the country's independence from Britain, in order to carry out the government's mandate with respect to the financial system. In particular, these two banks were instrumental in assisting the government's New Economic Policy (NEP) in the 1970s aimed at reducing the wealth gap between major ethnic groups in the country.[20] Compared to Indonesia, Malaysia had a significantly longer history of active securities markets, a system carried forward from the British colonial era. Moreover, foreign banks were allowed to establish operations in the country in the 1970s way ahead of comparable developments in Indonesia.

The banking systems in the Philippines and Thailand differ from their counterparts in Indonesia and Malaysia in that these have traditionally been dominated by private sector interests rather than the government (Hewison 1988; SEACEN 1989). Apart from the Philippine National Bank, established in the early 1900s to serve as the government's depository, commercial banking has firmly been in the hands of Filipinos of ethnic Chinese and Spanish descent.[21] Until the mid-1990s, the Philippine banking system was restricted significantly to foreign interests, causing some to charge that the system was being operated as a cartel (Kunio 1985; Frankel 1993). In comparison, Thai commercial banking has traditionally been controlled by Thais of ethnic Chinese descent. The rest of the commercial banking sector is controlled by the Thai government, the Royal family, and the military (Hewison 1988). As in Indonesia and the Philippines, strong links between banks and certain commercial-industrial conglomerates were maintained in Thailand (McVey 1992).[22]

Qualitatively, the banking system in Singapore stands apart from the rest of ASEAN. The principal difference is that foreign-owned banks play an economically significant, if not dominant, role in the country (Edwards 1987; SEACEN

1989; *Financial Times* 1993). The expanded role of foreign banks in Singapore is consistent with the open and deregulated economic policy pursued by the Singapore government early in its postindependence history (World Bank 1993). There are a few large domestic banks owned by the government (e.g., Development Bank of Singapore) and domestic interests (e.g., Overseas Union Bank).

The historical predominance of banks as a source of capital for ASEAN companies suggests that the financial accounting system should have evolved toward a more macro-user and creditor-oriented system (Nobes 1984; Emenyonu and Gray 1992). Prior to the mid-1980s, it was not feasible for ASEAN companies, apart from those in Malaysia and Singapore, to raise any sizable amount of capital through issuing corporate securities. Results of the analysis are therefore inconsistent with earlier findings that the broad aims of accounting in ASEAN suggest mainly micro-user oriented accounting systems, such as those found in the United Kingdom and the United States. Prima facie, it appears easy enough to attribute this to the pervasive impact of each country's colonial history (Radebaugh 1975; Hove 1986). Nonetheless, this explanation is not inherently satisfactory given the growing realization, particularly in the comparative international accounting literature, of the contextual importance of the financial environment in explaining the nature of the accounting system (Nobes 1984; Pratt and Behr 1987; Bloom and Naciri 1989; Meek and Saudagaran 1990). While recognizing therefore that colonial influences established the foundations for the accounting system, an important research task is to examine postindependence conditions that sustained and/or altered the context in which accounting operates.

The analysis here reveals that despite the traditional dominance of the banking sector in ASEAN, the securities markets have provided the more important impetus for shaping accounting in ASEAN. One reason is the relative degree of information asymmetry existing in the banking sector compared to securities markets. As in Germany and Japan, it is common practice among ASEAN companies to have interlocking directorships and common ownerships between lending and receiving institutions (Kunio 1985; Robison 1986; ADB 1986; Hewison 1988; McVey 1992).[23] The dominant commercial and industrial enterprises in ASEAN are associated mainly with large family/clan-based conglomerates or government-owned networks of firms. The banks themselves are often part of this corporate network, explaining the degree of insider knowledge they possess of the companies receiving the loans. In such an environment, there are few incentives encouraging firms to adopt stringent accounting policies, particularly with respect to accounting disclosures (Choi 1973; Enthoven 1977; Pratt and Behr 1987; Bloom and Naciri 1989; Meek and Gray 1989).[24]

Securities Markets

As early as the 1960s, securities markets competed with financial intermediaries as an important source of corporate finance in Malaysia and Singapore and, to a

Table 9. Size of ASEAN Stock Markets*

	Indonesia		*Malaysia*		*Philippines*		*Singapore*		*Thailand*	
	1980	*1993*	*1980*	*1993*	*1980*	*1993*	*1980*	*1993*	*1980*	*1993*
Stock Market capitalization (US $ billion)	0.06	33	12	220	3.5	40	24	133	1.2	131
Turnover (US $ billion)	0.01	22	2.6	154	0.6	7	3.7	82	0.3	87
Number of listed companies	6	174	182	410	195	180	103	178	77	347
Stock market capitalization/GDP (per cent)	0.08	23.2	50.6	338.5	9.9	74.1	219	280.6	3.8	110.5

Note: *All figures are as of end of year.

Source: IFC Emerging Stock Market Factbook (1994) and (1990); IMF Financial Statistics.

lesser extent, the Philippines (Skully 1984, 1985; SEACEN 1989; *Financial Times* 1993). In comparison, securities markets were virtually nonexistent or insignificant in Indonesia and Thailand during the 1960s. The revolution in corporate financing occurred during the late 1970s and early 1980s, particularly in Indonesia and Thailand, in terms of the growing importance of securities markets as a source of long-term capital. Changes in the size and activity levels of ASEAN stock markets between 1980 and 1993 are summarized in Table 9.

As shown in Table 9, the most explosive growth in market capitalization, turnover, and listing activity occurred in Indonesia and Thailand, two countries that had traditionally been strongly dependent on bank finance. Even after recognizing the growing importance of securities markets in ASEAN, it is useful to analyze these recent trends in terms of their historical antecedents. We submit that the early origins of securities markets in ASEAN explain, in part, the preference for a micro-user oriented accounting system articulated in Malaysia, Singapore, and the Philippines. In contrast, Indonesia did not indicate a clear preference for a micro-user oriented system until later in the 1970s. Thailand historically had been oriented toward a macro-user oriented accounting system.

In most of the ASEAN countries, except Thailand, the foundation of the modern commercial sector and capital markets were created during each country's colonial period (Skully 1984; Rowley 1987; SEACEN 1989). In Indonesia, the Association of Securities Traders of Indonesia was established by Dutch merchants in Jakarta as early as 1912, followed by similar associations in Surabaya and Semarang, two of Indonesia's largest cities, in 1924. These informal stock exchanges catered to the Dutch business community and investors who, at that time, controlled the industrial, trading, and agricultural activities in Indonesia. The stock exchanges were closed during World War II and Indonesia's struggle for independence against the Dutch. They reopened in 1952, principally to raise capital to rebuild the country's economy, and continued to operate until 1958, when the nationalization of Dutch companies and expulsion of Dutch nationals halted stock exchange operations. The stock exchanges remained moribund until the 1970s, when government reforms facilitated the stock market's revival.

In comparison, British sharebroking firms were established in the Straits Colony/Malaya (present-day Malaysia and Singapore) in the 1870s (Skully 1984; Rowley 1987; SEACEN 1989). It was not until the 1900s, however, that the rapid development of stock exchange infrastructure took place. At the turn of the century, numerous tin mining and plantation companies, mostly British-owned, were established in the colony, and the trading of shares of these companies occurred, albeit on an informal basis. A rudimentary form of regulatory framework was established after the 1929 stock market crash in the United States. This was the Singapore Stockbrokers' Association, established in June 1930 by foreign, mainly British, merchants. This agency became the forerunner of the present Kuala Lumpur Stock Exchange and Stock Exchange of Singapore. As in other ASEAN countries, trading activities were halted during the World War II. The stock exchange was formalized in May 1960 when the Malayan Stock Exchange was established, although the extant arrangement of having two trading floors located in Kuala Lumpur and Singapore continued. These two trading floors were integrated by telephone links and, despite the separation of Malaysia and Singapore in 1965, operated essentially as a unified stock exchange. It was only in 1973, following the termination of the currency interchangeability agreement between Malaysia and Singapore, that separate stock exchanges were established in both countries.

In the Philippines, the first stock exchange, called the Manila Stock Exchange, was established in August 1927. During the U.S. colonial era and shortly thereafter, this stock exchange was a prominent focus of financing activity in the country and, according to some accounts, for a long time this was the premier stock market in the region (Rowley 1987). It was not until the early 1970s that the Hong Kong Stock Exchange, currently the region's largest, overtook the Manila Stock Exchange in terms of market capitalization and turnover. Throughout this period, the Manila Stock Exchange was dominated by U.S. companies and stockbroking agencies. A second stock exchange, the Makati Stock Exchange, was established in 1956 in what was to become the country's financial district. Until 1993, the two exchanges competed with each other for transactions, although listing and other requirements in the two exchanges were unified early in the 1970s. In 1992, these two stock exchanges merged to form the Philippine Stock Exchange.

In Thailand, the first stock exchange was established in 1962 by a small group of merchants. Known as the Bangkok Stock Exchange, Ltd., the organization was registered first as a limited partnership and subsequently as a limited company. It was organized principally for the benefit of a few professional brokers and dealers and at its height in 1975 traded only in 36 listed companies (Rowley 1987). In comparison with extant stock exchanges in Malaya and the Philippines, the Bangkok Stock Exchange was small and, for the most part, dormant. It was not until the mid-1970s, with the active participation of the Thai government, that the stock market in Thailand grew into one of the largest stock markets in the region. Prior to this, there was little incentive for Thai companies to raise capital through a public issuance of securities. Bank capital was readily available to prominent family-owned companies (which also owned the major commercial banks) that controlled the large industrial conglomerates in the country (Hewison 1988).

This analysis of securities markets in ASEAN discloses certain patterns which explain, in part, the predisposition of the countries toward a micro- or macro-user oriented accounting system. In the case of Indonesia, Malaysia, the Philippines, and Singapore, the fledgling stock markets were controlled and operated principally for the benefit of colonial economic interests in each country. Prior to these countries' political independence, a reasonably strong tradition of private capital, albeit controlled by foreign interests, had already been established (Kunio 1987; McVey 1992). Accounting systems used in the colonizing countries were introduced to support American, British, and Dutch commercial interests in these countries.[25] By the time each country achieved political independence, the accounting system introduced during the colonial era was already well-established in the country's economic framework. This was particularly the case for Malaysia, the Philippines, Singapore, and to a lesser extent, Indonesia.

The evolution of Indonesia's political economy after the Dutch era, however, requires a separate analysis. Unlike other ASEAN countries that were colonized, the postcolonial transition in Indonesia was tumultuous and traumatic rather than smooth and conciliatory. Several years of armed conflict against the Netherlands immediately preceding independence resulted in a strong anti-Dutch sentiment in Indonesia, culminating in the confiscation of Dutch commercial assets and expulsion of Dutch nationals in the 1950s. The radical postcolonial transformation of Indonesian society had a significant impact on the Indonesian accounting system. In particular, the transformation led to the subordination and eventual replacement of the Dutch accounting system by an accounting system patterned after that of the United States (Yunus 1988).[26]

The experience of Thailand also differentiates it from other ASEAN countries in that the Thai stock market is of relatively recent origin compared to other ASEAN countries. The stock market did not play a significant role in raising long-term capital until the 1970s, when government intervention led to the establishment of the Stock Exchange of Thailand. Even in the 1970s, the contribution of the stock market was pale in comparison with other sources of long-term capital.

Overall, with respect to their securities market development, ASEAN countries can be categorized into *early developers* (Malaysia, the Philippines, and Singapore) and *late bloomers* (Indonesia and Thailand). The early developers evidenced a continuity of the importance of securities markets and colonial-era accounting systems well into each country's postindependence history. This continuity facilitated and reinforced a preference for a micro-user oriented accounting system early in these countries' history. In contrast, no counterweight existed to the dominance of banks and financial institutions among the "late bloomers." The financial environment was conducive to adopting a macro-user oriented accounting system, dominated by or operated for the benefit of government users. Reflective of the underlying environment, accounting regulation in Thailand has traditionally preferred a more conservative, creditor-oriented, and tax-driven accounting system similar broadly to the accounting systems in Japan and Germany. During the 1960s and 1970s, Indonesia hardly had any government regulation dealing with corporate financial accounting, apart from the broad requirements for certain types of companies (i.e., foreign joint ventures and those receiving loans from government-owned financial institutions) to submit audited annual accounts (Yunus 1988).

Nonetheless, as securities markets gained in importance as a source of capital in countries such as Indonesia and Thailand, corporate financial accounting correspondingly became a key policy issue in these countries. The evolution of the Thai and Indonesian financial environments also indicates that the accounting systems in these countries would gradually come to resemble the micro-user oriented accounting systems that exist in Malaysia, the Philippines, and Singapore. Recent developments in accounting regulations in Indonesia and Thailand will therefore need to be understood against the background of their securities market developments. In particular, both countries have moved toward regimes requiring more extensive financial disclosures and adherence to accounting measurement standards widely accepted in the United Kingdom and the United States.[27] The strong regulatory endorsement of International Accounting Standards (IAS) for domestic use in Indonesia and Thailand in the late 1980s and early 1990s (Malaysia and Singapore adopted IAS as early as the 1970s) affirms further the decisive shift toward a micro-user oriented accounting system.[28] Several conditions in ASEAN countries would favor such a transformation in their accounting systems.

The first are the views of international agencies such as the World Bank and the Asian Development Bank, which continue to influence the policy debates in the ASEAN countries. In its report on capital market developments in the Asia-Pacific region, the ADB (1995) stated that "accounting information is an essential element of infrastructure for a financial system" (p. 229). For its part, the World Bank (1989, 90) stresses that "in developing countries, accounting and auditing practices are sometimes weak, and financial laws and regulations do not demand accurate and timely financial reports. Developing an effective accounting and auditing profession is essential for building efficient financial markets." The World Bank is currently engaged in a long-term project to upgrade accountancy skills in Indonesia (Yunus 1988).[29]

In an earlier report, the ADB (1986) signaled its preference for a micro-user oriented accounting system as follows:

> Without adequate accounting, auditing and financial reporting, it is not possible to determine the true position and profitability *of an enterprise. Thus, in the absence of any of these, finance can be misallocated and investors can be misled. Furthermore, without* uniform reporting requirements and generally-accepted principles and standards, it is not possible to make comparisons between one company and another. In sum, adequate accounting and auditing are at the heart of a properly-functioning financial system" (pp. 52-54, emphases added).

Note that the ADB report appears to support a true economic picture view, similar to existing arrangements in most micro-user oriented systems. While the term "uniformity" appears to suggest a macro-user oriented system, the term needs to be understood in the context of preparing "generally accepted principles and standards" that focus on the decision needs of investors and creditors. Moreover, the ADB (1986) study endorsed an enhanced and more professional role played by accounting professions in ASEAN, similar to existing arrangements in countries such as the United Kingdom and the United States.[30] The World Bank also supports strongly a micro-user oriented view of accounting. In its guidelines for project-based financial reporting, the World Bank requires its borrowers to adopt particular accounting policies, including "adequate disclosure in the financial statements of all material information" and "a *true and fair view* of financial performance and status presented by the financial statements" (World Bank 1982, §2.05, emphasis added).

Another factor encouraging the shift toward a micro-user oriented system is the substantial demand for corporate information from investors, stock brokers and financial analysts. ASEAN countries, in particular, represent increasingly popular destinations of domestic and foreign institutional investment (Clark 1994; IFC 1994; Price 1994). In 1993, there were already 99 funds managed outside ASEAN that focused specifically on securities in Indonesia, Malaysia, the Philippines, and Thailand. In addition, several dozen international investment firms have established operations in the ASEAN markets (Price 1994; *FEER* 1995).

Moreover, the demand for more stringent financial accounting standards could only be bolstered by perceived regulatory inadequacies (Rowley 1987). For example, the rapid growth of the Indonesian securities markets in the late 1980s led to a pressure for increased regulation:

> [F]ears began to be expressed by a number of analysts about the [Indonesian stock] market's underlying weaknesses, including the use of dubious accounting methods and the lack of a code of ethics among local brokerage firms, and the absence of adequate supervision by the regulatory authorities (*Financial Times* 1993, 92).

Instances of fraud involving faulty financial reporting have increased pressure to tighten supervision of securities market operations. Prominent examples of securities market breaches related to financial reporting can be cited from each ASEAN country:

- In Indonesia, the near collapse of a major commercial bank, Bank Summa, owned by a prominent family revealed substantial undisclosed obligations of the bank. In another case, a listed company, Argo Pantes, reported a significantly inflated earnings figure prior to its listing. Six weeks later, after its stocks were being actively traded, the company reported a corrected earnings figure that was 65% lower than the earlier reported figure (*Financial Times* 1993).
- In Malaysia and Singapore, the collapse of Pan Electric Industries, a company listed in both the Kuala Lumpur and Singapore Stock Exchanges, in 1985 effectively brought the two exchanges to an unprecedented three-day closure. It was subsequently discovered that the company had substantial undisclosed liabilities in its financial statements (Rowley 1987).
- In Thailand, one of the country's leading finance companies listed on the Stock Exchange of Thailand, Raja Finance, went bankrupt in the late 1970s, leading to a collapse in the Thai market. Once more, the extent of the company's liabilities was not properly disclosed in its accounting reports (Rowley 1987).
- The Philippines has not yet had a large-scale corporate collapse affecting the stock exchange. Nonetheless, problems in financial accounting even among

listed companies still exist. For example, a major listed company had to restate its reported earnings of U.S.$2.2 billion in the first nine months of 1991 to a full-year loss of U.S.$5.7 million in 1991 due to "clerical errors" (Walter 1993). The ADB (1995) issued a guarded assessment of accounting in the country:

> Under Philippine [financial accounting] practice, much depends on the willingness of the firm to disclose pertinent information about itself and the project. Therefore, audited financial statements are as good as the amount and quality of information provided by the firm. In this environment, the problem of asymmetric information persists (p. 227).

In summary, the coalescing of several factors favored strongly the adoption of micro-user oriented accounting systems in ASEAN despite the traditional dominance of the banking sector in these countries. These factors included the influence on domestic policy exerted by multilateral lending institutions such as the ADB and World Bank, the perceived information demands associated with growing securities markets, and apparent regulatory lapses related to erroneous financial reporting. The policy of most ASEAN governments of allowing strong private sector participation in developing financial accounting policy also assured that professional accounting bodies in these countries, receptive as they were to influences from the United Kingdom and the United States, could further promote a micro-user oriented view of accounting in their respective countries.

CONCLUSIONS AND AREAS FOR FURTHER RESEARCH

This paper has argued that the broad aims of accounting are linked closely to the development of each country's capital markets. The capital markets provide the context as well as rationale for the existence of financial accounting systems in a country. Based on the extant comparative accounting literature, we distinguished between macro-user and micro-user oriented accounting systems. A macro-user oriented system was described as being attuned to government uses of accounting information whereas a micro-user oriented system emphasized the information needs of individual investors and creditors. We examined, in the context of accounting policy developments in five ASEAN countries, the proposition that macro-user oriented systems were associated more with bank-dominated capital markets while micro-user oriented systems were linked to capital markets with strong securities sectors.

The relationship between capital markets and financial accounting systems was found to be subtle and complex, rather than direct as suggested in prior contingency-based comparative accounting research. The hypothesis that a country's dominant source of finance was a major determinant in whether the accounting system would be macro-user or micro-user oriented found cautious and qualified support in ASEAN. A more accurate depiction in ASEAN is that the capital markets, as shaped by a configuration of historical, political, and economic factors, provided one of the necessary conditions for cultivating accounting policies in each country.

The historical origins of capital markets in ASEAN was found to be a particularly relevant factor. The effects of colonization have permeated not only the nature and content of extant legislation but, more fundamentally, the conditions in which capital markets developed in these countries. On one hand, ASEAN countries with an early history of dependence on securities markets were found to be strongly micro-user oriented in their broad accounting aims. These countries include Malaysia, Singapore, the Philippines, and to a lesser extent, Indonesia. In comparison, the absence of a colonial tradition in Thailand resulted in an amalgamation of macro- and micro-user oriented elements of accounting at different institutional levels. In general, these findings support the view that "spheres of influence" have and will continue to have a strong influence on accounting developments in ASEAN countries (Seidler 1967; Previts 1975; AAA 1977; Frank 1979).[31]

Another important variable mediating the influence of capital markets on accounting policies was the government's attitude with respect to private sector organizations participating in accounting policy development. In general, ASEAN governments sanctioned the strong participation of professional accounting bodies in accounting standard setting. In turn, professional accounting bodies in these countries have endorsed and continue to support a micro-user oriented perspective of accounting. The accounting orientation is apparent in pronouncements and conceptual frameworks developed by these professional bodies. Government approval has generally been tacit in nature, implied by the free hand given to professional bodies to formulate accounting policies, albeit with the possible threat of veto if standards are deemed unacceptable.[32] Paradoxically, the securities laws in Indonesia, the Philippines, and Thailand provided originally for a more interventionist role for government bodies in determining financial accounting policies (Saudagaran and Diga 1997).

Finally, it was found that securities markets were a more important source of accounting system changes in ASEAN compared to the banking sector. In particular, the growth of securities markets in ASEAN spurred direct government involvement in regulating these markets to respond to increasing demands for a more transparent corporate financial reporting regime. Despite the traditional reliance on banks as a source of corporate funds, relatively rapid growth in the securities markets of ASEAN countries has resulted in a clear shift toward a micro-user oriented regime of accounting. One implication of this analysis is our prediction that as ASEAN capital markets continue to become more sophisticated, their accounting systems will tend to converge or harmonize toward a micro-user oriented system.

The analysis here suggests several areas for further research regarding the link between capital markets and accounting policy development. The first relates to examining closely the impact of the globalization of financial markets on the accounting systems of countries (Bromwich and Hopwood 1983; Saudagaran 1991; Saudagaran and Biddle 1995; Beresford 1995). To a substantial extent, the growing interdependence among financial markets has already occurred despite the diversity of accounting regimes worldwide (Choi and Levich 1990). However, increasing pressures to reduce the barriers to capital could heighten the debate over global accounting harmonization (Biddle and Saudagaran 1991). If so, then the development of global capital markets could become a strong rationale for harmonizing accounting systems toward a micro-user oriented perspective. The ongoing efforts of the IASC to gain support for its accounting standards from IOSCO suggests the centrality of global capital markets in the debate over accounting harmonization (Wallace 1990; Chandler 1992).[33] The role of IASC could then be to facilitate the transition of countries with traditionally macro-user focused accounting systems into ones more attuned to the information needs of investors and creditors.

Even before accepting the actual or intended benefits of harmonization, however, the tradeoffs associated with adopting either a micro-user or macro-user accounting orientation need to be analyzed and debated thoroughly (Enthoven 1977; Rivera 1989; Larson 1993; Sedaghat et al. 1994). The policy recommendations of influential multilateral lending institutions such as the ADB and the World Bank tend to support a micro-user oriented accounting system in the context of facilitating the growth of emerging capital markets (ADB 1986, 1995; World Bank 1982, 1989, 1990). Currently, there are two conflicting positions with respect to the role of accounting policies in economic LDCs. The first is that micro-user oriented accounting systems are a prerequisite for the development of domestic capital markets, a position endorsed by the above mentioned multilateral institutions. Others, however, contend that the micro-user oriented accounting view is inappropriate, even harmful, for the financial market developments of LDCs (Ndubizu 1984; Hove 1986; Larson 1993; Baydoun and Willett 1995).[34] Larson (1993), for example, found evidence that the adoption of IAS was associated with lower levels of economic development in LDCs.[35] The policy implications of alternative accounting models have not yet been explored thoroughly, particularly for LDCs.

A further line of research would be to examine comparatively the roles of governments and private sector organizations in shaping the development of accounting systems in their countries. The proposition that accounting systems are "determined" solely, or even principally, by historical accidents, such as a country's prior colonial experience, should be subject to a more critical analysis including testing the "spheres of influence" argument in other geographic regions. Research on accounting policy should focus on the factors and conditions responsible for maintaining and transforming accounting systems over time. These factors are linked closely to the various roles that accounting systems play with respect to different groups in society. Only by adopting a clear policy perspective, we believe, will research be able to understand the contemporary rationale and impact of accounting systems in the context of societies in which they are located.

NOTES

1. Brunei joined ASEAN in 1984 shortly after its independence from the United Kingdom. Vietnam became an ASEAN member in 1995. At present, both countries do not have domestic securities markets.

2. As stated by Doupnik and Salter (1995), the aim of contingency-based research in comparative international accounting is to arrive at a "general model" that could explain and predict patterns of accounting systems worldwide on the basis of specific environmental factors.

3. The notion of "accounting policy" in this paper is a broad one that encompasses choices with respect to different elements of an accounting system. In contrast, the term "accounting policy" is used in some studies in the context of accounting measurement and disclosure rules and/or practices adopted by reporting enterprises (cf. May and Sundem 1976; Buckley 1980; Foster 1980; Beaver 1981; Lev 1988).

4. Studies that compare the alternative approaches to accounting regulation in industrialized countries include Puxty et al. (1987), Bloom and Naciri (1989), and Gorelik (1994).

5. This view is supported by empirical evidence from comparative international accounting research.

6. Mueller (1968) first suggested four patterns of accounting development. His four patterns could be reduced, however, into two categories depending on the user bias of the accounting system: (1) macroeconomic/uniform accounting, and (2) microeconomic/independent discipline. These categories were subsequently defined by Nobes (1983, 1984) and Berry (1987) and supported statistically in the study by Doupnik and Salter (1993).

7. The European Community's (EC) Fourth Directive on Company Law (Art. 2) states that "the annual accounts shall give a true and fair view of the company's assets, liabilities, financial position and profit or loss". Apparently, the United Kingdom insisted that the phrase be inserted in the directive primarily "to protect the traditional framework of UK accounting" (Higson and Blake 1993, 110). Despite the presence of the "true and fair" requirement in the company laws of all EC member countries, evidence suggests that continental European countries have largely maintained intact their macro-user oriented accounting systems. For a discussion, see Nobes (1993).

8. As emphasized by FASB (1978, ¶107): "Neutrality in accounting is an important criterion by which to judge accounting policies, for information that is not neutral loses credibility." The same view is expressed by Solomons (1991): "If accounting is to retain any credibility—and without credibility it is worthless—its guiding light must be neutrality in financial reporting" (p. 294).

9. It is common practice in continental Europe, for example, to have representatives from labor unions or workers' councils to sit as members of the company's board of directors. France has specifically required enterprises to publish an annual *bilan social* ("social balance sheet") to report on matters relevant to employees.

10. The most notable example of this practice is the system of accounting for untaxed reserves in Finland, Germany, and Sweden, where companies are allowed to make appropriations of their pretax profits in order to "stabilize" future earnings. The government sanctions this practice to allow companies to smooth their reported earnings according to their respective business cycles (see Alexander and Archer 1995).

11. Hofstede (1987), for example, identified at least four models of economic organization wherein the Anglo-U.S. model is portrayed as a *village market* where the ultimate and optimal mode of control was believed to be through market forces. In comparison, the French model was described as a *pyramid* with a strict hierarchy and set of rules, while the German model was that of a *well-oiled machine* organized around rules but where hierarchical positions mattered less. ASEAN countries,

such as Indonesia and Singapore, were depicted as following the *family* model of organization of having an undisputed leader but few formal rules. These different perspectives on economic organizations suggest varied roles for accounting in these societies.

12. The new Indonesian Limited Company Law (*Undang Perseroan Terbatas*) was promulgated only in March 1995. Compared to the original Indonesian Commercial Code 1848, the new law covers a greater number of areas including the formation of companies, directors' duties and liabilities, and financial reporting requirements. The new Indonesian law is broadly similar also to company laws in the United States.

13. The Indonesian Foreign Investment Law required foreign joint venture companies (referred to as "PMA") to submit audited financial statements to the Foreign Investments Co-ordinating Board. The government also required companies that received loans from government-owned financial institutions to furnish regular accounting reports.

14. Separate exchanges were established in 1973 following the termination of the currency interchangeability agreement between Malaysia and Singapore. In 1990, the Malaysian government also prohibited Malaysian companies from listing in the Singapore stock exchange.

15. It was not until 1987, however, following additional securities market reforms that the Indonesian stock market turned into one of the fastest growing emerging stock markets in the world.

16. In both Malaysia and Singapore, professional accounting bodies have traditionally established accounting standards, although without specific and official mandates from their respective governments.

17. SFAC 1 (¶34) states: "Financial reporting should provide information that is useful to present and potential *investors and creditors* and other users in making rational investment, credit, and similar decisions".

18. The strategy of the postindependence Singapore Government led by Lee Kuan Yew was to establish the former colony as the foremost trading center in the region. As such, barriers to foreign investment were removed. Currently, there are more than 200 commercial and merchant banks operating in Singapore, most of which are foreign owned. Singapore is also considered one of the region's most sophisticated financial centers.

19. Reforms in the Indonesian financial sector focused on two aspects. First, the banking sector was deregulated to reduce the level of dependence on the government-owned banks. Second, the securities markets were revived to make them a more attractive source of corporate capital. See Andersen (1993) for details on these reforms.

20. The NEP was an "affirmative action" program implemented by the Malaysian government in 1970 primarily to boost the chances of Bumiputras (i.e., indigenous Malays) in the country to engage in economically productive undertakings. It was contemplated to address increasing resentment among the Bumiputras, by far the largest ethnic group, that they were being disadvantaged against the Chinese and Indians, the two other large groups, in economic affairs. The NEP was a cornerstone of government policy until the late 1980s.

21. The situation in the Philippines is similar to that in Indonesia, Malaysia, Singapore, Thailand, and Vietnam. In each country, the ethnic Chinese own a disproportionately large share of commercial and industrial enterprises. For a discussion of the economic importance of the ethnic Chinese in ASEAN, see McVey (1992).

22. The model of large-scale conglomerates in ASEAN resembles, in part, the Japanese *keiretsu* system, which consists of a network of firms bound together by long-term agreements, interlocking directorships, and cross-ownerships. A major difference, however, is that ASEAN conglomerates are more clearly associated with particular prominent business families or clan groups, similar to the arrangement described by Hofstede (1987).

23. Unless one or the other is government-owned or operated, both are controlled by the same family or clan group (see McVey 1992).

24. According to the ADB (1986, 1995) and World Bank (1989, 1990), the predominance of these corporate networks provides a disincentive to many of the large firms' listing on a stock exchange. Public listing would subject these firms to increased scrutiny and dilute the control enjoyed by current owners.

25. Among the other Southeast Asian countries, the British commercial system was introduced in Brunei and Burma while the French system dominated colonial Vietnam, Cambodia, and Laos. Thailand, having never been colonized, drew upon a variety of sources in designing its own commercial system.

26. The establishment of close links between Indonesian and U.S. educational institutions was a pivotal source of change as it served to introduce U.S. accounting ideas to the country. See the discussion in Yunus (1988).

27. Substantial evidence suggests that IAS, which have been adopted in Indonesia and Thailand, incorporate accounting methods that are widely accepted in the United Kingdom and United States (Wallace 1990; Chandler 1992). It has been suggested that IAS, in fact, strongly reflect accounting methods in the United Kingdom and the United States to a greater extent than those in continental Europe (Hove 1989; Rivera 1989).

28. Thailand began selectively adopting IAS as domestic accounting standards in 1987; Indonesia signaled support for IAS for domestically listed companies in 1994. In both instances, the shift toward IAS was related ostensibly to the need to further develop each country's stock markets.

29. The World Bank project is coursed through the Indonesian Co-ordinating Agency for Accountancy Development (CAAD) and focuses on technical training to create the required corps of Indonesian accountants. Most of the training programs are provided by the Big Six' accounting firms which are well-represented in Indonesia.

30. According to the ADB (1986) study, the ASEAN-4 (Indonesia, Malaysia, Philippines, and Thailand) need to strengthen considerably their accounting profession by establishing and enforcing generally accepted accounting principles, auditing standards, and uniform financial reporting requirements. The ADB also recommended the strengthening of the institutional capacity of professional accounting bodies in the following roles: (1) training; (2) testing; (3) certification and licensing; (4) establishing uniform accounting and auditing standards; and (5) developing, in conjunction with other relevant parties, requirements as to types, forms, and content of financial statements. According to ADB, the accounting profession should be self-governing, with clear responsibility for setting and monitoring standards and enforcing professional discipline among its members.

31. The AAA (1977) identified five "zones of influence," an approach which argues that accounting systems follow particular dominant national models: British, French\Spanish\Portuguese, German\Dutch, United States, and Communist. Similar groupings have also been suggested by Seidler (1967), Previts (1975), and Frank (1979).

32. A similar situation exists to a significant extent in other micro-user oriented countries where private sector bodies, not necessarily the accounting profession, formulate accounting standards. In the United States, for example, both Congress and the SEC have the right to "veto" standards promulgated by the FASB if these are deemed to be unacceptable. See related discussions in Solomons (1978, 1983), Puxty et al. (1987), Bloom and Naciri (1989), and Gorelik (1994).

33. IOSCO indicated qualified support for the efforts of the IASC to develop internationally acceptable accounting standards. The ongoing project of the IASC to reduce the number of options found in IAS (ED 32—International Comparability Project) was linked to the possibility of obtaining IOSCO support.

34. Baydoun and Willett (1995) point out that much of the literature questioning the appropriateness of "Western" accounting systems for LDCs do not clarify which aspects of foreign accounting systems are detrimental to economic development of LDCs.

35. Whether or not this was because of the impact of the accounting system is difficult to discern, however, because of the number of possible confounding variables not covered in the study (see Larson 1993).

REFERENCES

Accounting Standards Council (ASC). 1988. *Compilation of Statements of Financial Accounting Standards Nos. 1-18*. Manila: Accounting Standards Council.

Alexander, D., and S. Archer. 1995. *The European Accounting Guide*. London: Academic.

American Accounting Association (AAA). 1977. Report of the 1975-76 Committee on International Accounting Operations and Education. *Accounting Review* 52(Supplement): 65-132.

Andersen, P.S. 1993. Economic growth and financial markets: The experience of four Asian countries. In *Finance and the International Economy*, ed. R. O'Brien. New York: Oxford University Press for The Amex Bank Review.

Asian Development Bank (ADB). 1986. *Capital Market Development in Selected Developing Member Countries of the Asian Development Bank*. Manila: ADB.

Asian Development Bank. 1995. *Asian Development Outlook 1995*. Manila: Oxford University Press for the Asian Development Bank.

Baydoun, N., and R. Willett. 1995. Cultural relevance of Western accounting systems to developing countries. *Abacus* 31(1): 67-92.

Beaver, W.H. 1981. *Financial Reporting: An Accounting Revolution*. Englewood Cliffs, NJ: Prentice-Hall.

Benston, G. 1982. An analysis of the role of standards in enhancing corporate governance and social responsibility. *Journal of Accounting and Public Policy* 1(1): 5-17.

Beresford, D. 1995. International capital markets: Converging on the horizon. *Finance & Treasury* (September 11): 3-7.

Berry, I. 1987. The need to classify worldwide accountancy practices. *Accountancy* 100(October): 90-91.

Bhushan, R., and Lessard, D.R. 1992. Coping with international accounting diversity: Fund managers' views on disclosure, reconciliation, and harmonization. *Journal of International Financial Management and Accounting* 4(2): 149-165.

Biddle, G.C., and S.M. Saudagaran. 1991. Foreign stock listings: Benefits, costs, and the accounting policy dilemma. *Accounting Horizons* 5(3): 69-80.

Bloom, R., and M.A. Naciri. 1989. Accounting standard setting and culture: A comparative analysis of the United States, Canada, England, West Germany, Australia, New Zealand, Sweden, Japan and Switzerland. *International Journal of Accounting* 24(1): 70-97.

Bromwich, M., and A.G. Hopwood. 1983. Some issues in accounting standard setting: An introductory essay. In *Accounting Standards Setting: An International Perspective*, eds. M. Bromwich and A.G. Hopwood. London: Pitman.

Buckley, J. 1980. Policy models in accounting: A critical commentary. *Accounting, Organizations and Society* 5(1): 49-64.

Burchell, S., C. Clubb, A.G. Hopwood, J. Hughes, and J. Nahaphiet. 1980. The roles of accounting in organizations and society. *Accounting, Organizations and Society* 5(1): 5-27.

Chandler, R. 1992. The international harmonization of accounting: In search of influence. *International Journal of Accounting* 27(3): 222-233.

Choi, F.D.S. 1973. Financial disclosure in relation to the European capital market. *International Journal of Accounting* 9(1): 54-66.

Choi, F.D.S., and K. Hiramatsu. 1987. *Accounting and Financial Reporting in Japan*. Wokingham, U.K.: Van Nostrand Reinhold.

Choi, F.D.S., and R.M. Levich. 1990. *The Capital Market Effects of International Accounting Diversity*. Homewood, IL: Dow Jones-Irwin.

Clark, R.A. 1994. ASEAN equity markets: The role of ASEAN securities markets in development. *Journal of Asian Business* 10(1): 25-43.

Commerce Clearing House (CCH). 1990. *Guide to Company Law in Malaysia & Singapore* Singapore: CCH Asia.

Cooke, T.E., and R.S.O. Wallace. 1990. Financial disclosure regulation and its environment: A review and further analysis. *Journal of Accounting and Public Policy* 9(1): 79-110.

Cooper, K., and G.D. Keim. 1983. The economic rationale for the nature and extent of corporate financial disclosure regulation: A critical assessment, *Journal of Accounting and Public Policy* 2(3): 189-205.

Cyert, R., and Y. Ijiri. 1974. Problems of implementing the Trueblood Objectives Report. *Journal of Accounting Research* 12(Supplement): 29-42.

De Leon, H.S. 1990. *The Corporation Code of the Philippines—Annotated Edition.* Manila: Rex.

Demski, J. 1973. Choice among financial reporting alternatives. *Accounting Review* 49(2): 221-232.

Doupnik, T.S., and S.B. Salter. 1993. An empirical test of a judgmental international classification of financial reporting practices. *Journal of International Business Studies* 24(1): 41-60.

Doupnik, T.S., and S.B. Salter. 1995. External environment, culture, and accounting practice: A preliminary test of a general model of international accounting development. *International Journal of Accounting* 30(3): 189-207.

Dyckman, T.R. 1988. Credibility and the formulation of accounting standards under the Financial Accounting Standards Board. *Journal of Accounting Literature* 7: 1-30.

Edwards, A. 1987. *Singapore: A Guide to the Structure, Development and Regulation of Financial Services.* London: Economist.

Emenyonu, E.N., and S.J. Gray. 1992. EC accounting harmonization: An empirical study of measurement practices in France, Germany and the UK. *Accounting and Business Research* 23(89): 49-58.

Enthoven, A.J.H. 1977. *Accountancy Systems in Third World Economies.* Amsterdam: North-Holland.

Far Eastern Economic Review (FEER). 1995. Focus: Asian capital markets (July 27): 37-59.

Financial Accounting Standards Board (FASB). 1976. *Scope and Implications of the Conceptual Framework Project.* Stamford, CT: FASB.

Financial Accounting Standards Board. 1978. *Statement of Financial Accounting Concepts No. 1: Objectives of Financial Reporting by Business Enterprises.* Stamford, CT: FASB.

Financial Times. 1993. *Banking in the Far East 1993: Structures and Sources of Finance.* London: Financial Times Business Information.

Foster, G. 1980. Accounting policy decisions and capital market research. *Journal of Accounting and Economics* 2(1): 29-62.

Frank, W.G. 1979. An empirical analysis of international accounting principles. *Journal of Accounting Research* 16(2): 593-605.

Frankel, J.A. 1993. Recent changes in the financial systems of Asian and Pacific countries. Center for International And Development Economics Research Working Paper No. 93-031, University of California at Berkeley.

Fry, M. 1993. Financial opening and monetary control in Pacific Basin developing countries. In *Financial Opening: Policy Issues and Experiences in Developing Countries*, eds. H. Reisen and B. Fischer, 143-165. Paris: OECD.

Ghon Rhee, S., R.P. Chang, and R. Ageloff. 1990. An overview of equity markets in Pacific-Basin countries. In *Pacific-Basin Capital Markets Research*, eds. S. Ghon Rhee and R.P. Chang, 81-100. Amsterdam: North Holland.

Gorelik, G. 1994. The setting of accounting standards: Canada, the United Kingdom, and the United States. *International Journal of Accounting* 29(2): 95-122.

Gray, S.J., and C.B. Roberts. 1991. East-West accounting issues: A new agenda. *Accounting Horizons* 5(1): 42-50.

Hewison, K. 1988. The structure of banking capital in Thailand. *Southeast Asian Journal of Social Science* 16(1): 81-91.

Hofstede, G. 1987. The cultural context of accounting. In *Accounting and Culture: Plenary Session Papers and Discussants' Comments from the 1986 Annual Meeting of the AAA*, ed. B.E. Cushing, 1-11 Sarasota, FL: American Accounting Association.

Hossain, M., L.M. Tan, and M. Adams. 1994. Voluntary disclosure in an emerging capital market: Some empirical evidence from companies listed on the Kuala Lumpur Stock Exchange. *International Journal of Accounting* 29(4): 334-351.

Hove, M.R. 1986. Accounting practices in developing countries: Colonialism's legacy of inappropriate technologies. *International Journal of Accounting* 21(1): 81-100.

Hove, M.R. 1989. The inappropriateness of international accounting standards in less developed countries: The case of International Accounting Standard Number 24—Related party disclosures—Concerning transfer prices. *International Journal of Accounting* 24(2): 165-179.

Institute of Certified Accountants and Auditors of Thailand (ICAAT). 1973. *Accounting Profession in Thailand.* Bangkok: ICAAT.

Institute of Certified Accountants and Auditors of Thailand (ICAAT). 1993. *Accounting Standards Nos. 1-24.* Bangkok: ICAAT.

Institute of Certified Public Accountants of Singapore (ICPAS). 1994. *Statements of Accounting Standards.* Singapore: ICPAS.

International Accounting Standards Committee (IASC). 1993. *International Accounting Standards.* London: IASC.

International Finance Corporation (IFC). 1980-1994 (various years). *Emerging Stock Markets Factbook.* Washington, DC: IFC.

Kunio, Y. 1985. *Philippine Industrialization: Foreign and Domestic Capital.* Singapore: Oxford University Press.

Larson, R.K. 1993. An empirical investigation of the relationships between international accounting standards, equity markets and economic growth in developing countries. Unpublished Ph.D. dissertation, University of Utah.

Leftwich, R. 1983. Accounting information in private markets: Evidence from private lending agreements. *Accounting Review* 58(1): 23-42.

Lev, B. 1988. Towards a theory of equitable and efficient accounting policy. *Accounting Review* 63(1): 1-23.

Macdonald, N., and A. Beattie. 1993. The corporate governance jigsaw. *Accounting and Business Research* 23(91A): 304-310.

Malaysian Association of Certified Public Accountants (MACPA) 1993. *Members Handbook.* Kuala Lumpur: MACPA.

Malaysian Institute of Accountants (MIA) 1993. *Members Handbook.* Kuala Lumpur: MIA.

Maolanond, P., and Y. Nobuyuki. 1985. *Corporation and Law in ASEAN Countries: A Case Study of Thailand.* Tokyo: Institute of Developing Economies.

Mathews, M.R., and M.H.B. Perera. 1996. *Accounting Theory & Development,* 3rd edition. Melbourne: Thomas Nelson.

May, R., and G.L. Sundem. 1976. Research for accounting policy: An overview. *Accounting Review* 51(4): 743-763.

McVey, R. 1992. *Southeast Asian Capitalists.* New York: Cornell Southeast Asia Program.

Meek, G.K., and S.J. Gray. 1989. Globalization of stock markets and foreign listing requirements: Voluntary disclosures by continental European companies listed on the London Stock Exchange. *Journal of International Business Studies* 20(2): 296-314.

Meek, G., and S. Saudagaran. 1990. A survey of research on financial reporting in a transnational context. *Journal of Accounting Literature* 9: 145-182.

Mueller, G.G. 1968. Accounting principles generally accepted in the United States versus those generally accepted elsewhere. *International Journal of Accounting* 3(2): 91-103.

Nair, R.D., and W.G. Frank. 1980. The impact of disclosure and measurement practices on international accounting classifications. *Accounting Review* 55(3): 426-450.

Ndubizu, G.A. 1984. Accounting standards and economic development: The Third World in perspective. *International Journal of Accounting* 19(2): 181-196.

Nobes, C.W. 1983. A judgemental international classification of financial reporting practices. *Journal of Business Finance and Accounting* 10(1): 1-19.

Nobes, C.W. 1984. *International Classification of Financial Reporting.* Beckenham, UK: Croom Helm.

Nobes, C.W. 1993. The true and fair view requirement: Impact on and of the Fourth Directive. *Accounting and Business Research* 23(93): 35-48.

Pillai, P.N. 1984. *Companies and Securities Handbook: Singapore and Malaysia.* Singapore: Butterworths.

Pratt, J., and G. Behr. 1987. Environmental factors, transaction costs, and external reporting: A cross-national comparison. *International Journal of Accounting* 22(2): 1-24.

Previts, G.J. 1975. On the subject of methodology and models of international accounting. *International Journal of Accounting* 10(2): 1-12.

Price, M.M. 1994. *Emerging Stock Markets: A Complete Investment Guide to New Markets around the World.* New York: McGraw-Hill.

Puxty, A.G., H.C. Willmott, D.J. Cooper, and A. Lowe. 1987. Modes of regulation in advanced capitalism: Locating accountancy in four countries. *Accounting, Organizations and Society* 12(3): 273-291.

Radebaugh, L.H. 1975. Environmental factors influencing the development of accounting objectives, standards, and practices in Peru. *International Journal of Accounting* 11(1): 39-56.

Rivera, J.M. 1989. The internationalization of accounting standards: Past problems and current prospects. *International Journal of Accounting* 24(4): 320-341.

Robison, R. 1986. *Indonesia: The Rise of Capital.* Sydney: Allen & Unwin.

Rowley, A. 1987. *Asian Stockmarkets: The Inside Story.* Hong Kong: Far Eastern Economic Review.

Rozeff, M.S. 1990. Stock market regulation in the Pacific basin: Lessons from U.S. experience. In *Pacific-Basin Capital Markets Research*, eds. S. Ghon Rhee and R.P. Chang, 417-428. Amsterdam: North Holland.

Samidjo, Pengantar Hukum Indonesia. 1985. *Introduction to Indonesian Law.* Bandung: C.V. Arminco.

Saudagaran, S.M. 1991. The SEC and the globalization of financial markets. In *Research in Accounting Regulation*, Vol. 5, eds. G.J. Previts, L. Parker, and R.K. Eskew, 31-53. Greenwich, CT: JAI Press.

Saudagaran. S.M., and G.C. Biddle. 1995. Foreign listing location: A study of MNCs and stock exchanges in eight countries. *Journal of International Business Studies* 26(2): 319-342.

Saudagaran, S.M. and G.J. Diga. 1997. Accounting regulation in ASEAN: A choice between the global and regional paradigms of harmonization. *Journal of International Financial Management and Accounting* 8(1): 1-32.

Schweikart, J.A. 1985. Contingency theory as a framework for research in international accounting. *International Journal of Accounting* 21(1): 89-98.

Sedaghat, A.M., T. Sagafi-nejad, and G. Wright. 1994. Economic development and securities markets in developing countries: Implications for international accounting. *International Journal of Accounting* 29(4): 297-315.

Seidler, L.J. 1967. International accounting: The ultimate theory course. *Accounting Review* 42(4): 775-781.

Skully, M.T. 1984. *Financial Institutions and Markets in Southeast Asia: A Study of Brunei, Indonesia, Malaysia, Philippines, Singapore and Thailand.* London: Macmillan.

Skully, M.T. 1985. *ASEAN Financial Co-operation: Developments in Banking, Finance and Insurance.* New York: St. Martin's Press.

Skully, M.T. 1986. *Merchant Banking in ASEAN: A Regional Examination of its Development and Operations.* Singapore: Oxford University Press.

Solomons, D. 1978. The politicization of accounting. *Journal of Accountancy* 14(6): 65-72.

Solomons, D. 1983. The political implications of accounting and accounting standard-setting. *Accounting and Business Research* 13(49): 107-118.

Solomons, D. 1991. Accounting and social change: A neutralist view. *Accounting, Organizations and Society* 16(3): 287-295.

South East Asian Central Banks Research and Training Centre (SEACEN). 1989. *The Development of Capital Markets in the SEACEN Countries*. Kuala Lumpur: SEACEN.

Tricker, R.I. 1994. *International Corporate Governance: Text, Readings and Cases*. New York: Prentice-Hall.

Wallace, R.S.O. 1990. Survival strategies of a global organization: The case of the International Accounting Standards Committee. *Accounting Horizons* 4(2): 1-22.

Walter, I. 1993. Emerging equity markets: Tapping into global investment flows. *ASEAN Economic Bulletin* (1): 1-19.

Watts, R., and J. Zimmerman. 1978. Towards a positive theory of the determination of accounting standards. *Accounting Review* 53(1): 112-134.

World Bank. 1982. *Guidelines for Financial Reporting and Auditing of Projects Financed by the World Bank*. Washington, DC: International Bank for Reconstruction and Development.

World Bank. 1989. *World Development Report 1989*. New York: Oxford University Press for the International Bank for Reconstruction and Development.

World Bank. 1990. *Financial Systems and Development*. Washington, DC: International Bank for Reconstruction and Development.

World Bank. 1993. *The East Asian Miracle: Economic Growth and Public Policy*. Washington, DC: Oxford University Press for the International Bank for Reconstruction and Development.

Yunus, H. 1988. *History of Accounting in Developing Nations: The Case of Indonesia*. Birmingham, UK: University of Birmingham.

U.S. STOCK MARKET REACTION TO PRELIMINARY EARNINGS ANNOUNCEMENTS AND SEC FORM 20F OF FOREIGN FIRMS

Ruth W. Epps

ABSTRACT

This research examines the information content of financial reports of foreign firms listed on U.S. stock exchanges. The financial reporting events analyzed in the study are foreign firms' preliminary earnings announcements and Securities and Exchange Commission (SEC) filings. Emphasis is placed on the effect of disclosure sequence and firms' reporting environments on abnormal stock returns. Foreign firms announce their preliminary earnings a few months earlier than the SEC filings, which the firms file close to the statutory filing date of 180 days after the fiscal year-end. However, the U.S. stock markets' reaction to the SEC filings is significant when the SEC filings occur in the absence (or in advance) of preliminary earnings announcements, indicating the impact of information arrival sequence on the market.

Research in Accounting Regulation, Supplement 1, pages 49-74.

ISBN: 0-7623-0338-7

Foreign firms' reporting environments also have a significant impact on the U.S. stock markets.

INTRODUCTION

This study examines how the U.S. stock markets respond to foreign firms' earnings disclosures when the reporting event occurs in different sequences. Foreign firms have the following three major financial reporting events: (1) preliminary earnings announcement in a press release (PEA), (2) SEC Form 20F filing, and (3) annual reports to shareholders (ARS). Foreign firms can report earnings under: (1) foreign GAAP, (2) U.S. GAAP, or (3) both foreign and U.S. GAAPs (financial statements that are prepared under either foreign or U.S. GAAP but reconciled to the other GAAP). Earnings in the PEA are based on the domicile country GAAP (foreign GAAP), while earnings in the 20F and ARS are based on either U.S. GAAP or foreign GAAP with the disclosure of material departure from U.S. GAAP. The PEA event usually precedes the 20F and ARS filing events, but on some occasions the reporting events occur in other sequences (for example, the PEA follows the 20F or ARS). Also, some foreign firms do not have the reporting events of PEA or ARS.

This study analyzes firms' reporting lags (intervals between the fiscal period end and financial reporting date) to determine whether there are any systematic reporting patterns. The study also examines squared market model prediction errors to determine the information content of foreign firms' financial reporting. Financial reporting of foreign firms differs from domestic firms' in the following areas:

1. The preliminary earnings announcements in the media are usually based on foreign GAAP;
2. Foreign firms file a 20F that is less stringent than a 10K for U.S. firms regarding the filing date, disclosure level, and GAAP application; and
3. Filing of quarterly reports and annual reports to shareholders are not required as part of foreign reporting practice.[1]

Previous studies report that the PEA is an information relevant event. However, the studies report mixed results about whether the 20F filing has an information content, warranting further study. One major methodological weakness of previous event studies is that they did not consider the effect of different event sequences on the markets. The present study expands the previous studies by taking different sets of reporting event sequence into consideration. Additionally, to observe the effect of foreign firms' financial reporting environments on the U.S. stock market reaction, the present study partitions the sample data according to firm characteristics and domicile country. The sample firms are identified by nationality, and the national reporting practices are classified into the groups suggested in the comparative accounting practices research.[2] Firm size, industry classification, and stock exchange listing are used to control for the firm-specific information environments.

PREVIOUS RESEARCH

Several studies have applied the earnings-return framework by Ball and Brown (1968) to examine the information content of transnational financial reports. Most studies regress the earnings of financial reporting events on stock returns in either short windows or long windows.

Some studies (Meek 1983, 1991; Frost and Pownall 1994)[3] reported that foreign firms' earnings announcements are value-relevant to U.S. investors. However, the studies report no significant information content of SEC 20F filings. The studies find that foreign firms file the SEC 20F close to the statutory filing date of 180 days after the fiscal year-end, indicating that the 20F is not a timely report.

Other studies (McQueen 1993; Amir, Harris, and Venuti 1993) reported that foreign firms' 20F filing may be an information-relevant event. The studies find a significant association between security returns and U.S. GAAP earnings in 20F. The studies also find that some of specific 20F components are value-relevant.

The mixed results regarding the 20F may be due to a methodological weakness of previous studies that did not incorporate an earnings event sequence. Pope and Rees (1992) report that the U.S. GAAP reconciliations in the 20F are transitory, suggesting that the refinement of an empirical model can be achieved by conditioning the 20F on prior disclosures. Recent studies (Meek 1991; Pope and Inyangete 1992; Hall, Hamao, and Harris 1994; Frost and Pownall 1994) also find that the stock market reaction to financial reporting events is influenced by firm's financial reporting environments such as firm size and trading frequency. Hence, in the present study, the U.S. stock market reaction to foreign financial reports is contingent upon event sequences and reporting environments.

RESEARCH METHOD

Cross-national accounting differences may affect the decisions of financial information users (investors). The SEC has concerns about the extent of influence the accounting differences may have on the investment in foreign stocks listed on the U.S. markets.

Annual financial reporting events of the foreign firms listed on the U.S. stock exchanges are preliminary earnings announcements (PEAs), Form 20F filing, and annual reports to shareholders (ARSs). Normally, during these reporting events, earnings or nonearnings information becomes available to the stock markets.

Empirical evidence on the information content of these financial reporting events is of interest in the present study.

Research Question

The research question addressed in the study is: Do the U.S. stock markets have unusual security returns in response to foreign firms' earnings disclosures occurring in different sequences?

The foreign firms' earnings disclosures may affect the U.S. stock exchanges, depending on the information content a specific GAAP earnings disclosure conveys to investors. Foreign firms are required to prepare the SEC filings based on U.S. GAAP (or foreign GAAP with a reconciliation to U.S. GAAP). The PEAs and ARSs are voluntary disclosures, but the SEC Form 20F, equivalent to the SEC 10K for U.S. domestic firms, is a mandatory disclosure.[4] United States investors are expected to respond differently to the foreign GAAP earnings information, depending on their ability to decipher the different measurement rules across nations. The greater the ability of the U.S. investors to decipher the differences, the less information content (value) the U.S. GAAP earnings disclosure (20F) is likely to convey to investors.

Foreign firms have different combinations of annual financial reporting events. The sequence of the public reporting events may have an impact on the investors' stock valuation. The earliest reporting event is likely to have the greatest influence on the stock market, while the influence of subsequent reporting events is likely to be diminished. The preliminary earnings announcements (PEAs) normally precede the Form 20F and ARSs. However, the PEAs may follow the Form 20F and ARSs in some instances. Also, some foreign firms do not have the reporting event of PEAs or ARSs. Different sequences of earnings reporting events or absence of certain reporting events can be expected to provide explanations for unusual security returns associated with the release of earnings information.

Hypotheses and Empirical Model

The present study collected the dates of foreign firms' PEA and SEC filings. Using the event dates, the reporting lags (the number of days after the fiscal year-end that firms announce preliminary earnings and file 20F or ARS with the SEC) were computed. Most foreign firms file only a 10K, 20F, or ARS, and the filed document is then used to represent the other two documents not filed. The SEC filing manual codifies this multiple-purpose filing under the code name of "ARK."

Disclosure date availability and sequence allow the following three basic partitions: PEA and 20F/ARK available; only PEA available; and only 20F/ARK available. The PEA and 20F/ARK partition has the following two sequences of information arrival: the PEA date precedes the 20F/ARK filing date; and the 20F/ARK filing date precedes the PEA date. Hypothesis 1, stated in the null form, is:

Hypothesis 0-1. Foreign firms have no systematic pattern of financial reporting lags.

To detect any systematic reporting lag patterns, medians and interquartile ranges were analyzed for the partitioned foreign firms. The analysis of medians and interquartile ranges was expected to provide evidence on the financial reporting behavior of the foreign firms listed on U.S. stock exchanges. The analysis addresses the question of whether foreign firms use the reporting events to release "good" news early or "bad" news late (Easton and Zmijewski 1993). For example, if foreign firms have a tendency to file the 20F very close to the statutory filing date—that is, 180 days after the fiscal year-end—then the 20F is not likely to be used as a firm's strategy for releasing financial information. In this example, the other events, such as the PEA, are likely to be used as a firm's financial reporting strategy.

To examine whether foreign firms' operating environments are associated with reporting behavior, the study partitioned the sample according to national origin of foreign firms, stock exchange listing, firm size (total sales), and industry classification.[5] The Spearman correlations are computed to assess the associations of the partitioned variables with reporting lags. The secondary hypotheses for the partitioning, stated in the null form, are:

Hypothesis 0-1a. Foreign firms have no systematic pattern of financial reporting lags when they are partitioned according to nationality.

Hypothesis 0-1b. Foreign firms have no systematic pattern of financial reporting lags when they are partitioned according to stock exchange listing.

Hypothesis 0-1c. Foreign firms have no systematic pattern of financial reporting lags when they are partitioned according to firm size.

Hypothesis 0-1d. Foreign firms have no systematic pattern of financial reporting lags when they are partitioned according to industry classification.

Market Reaction to Financial Reporting Events

The market reactions were measured by the unusual security returns associated with the reporting events. The security return of the event period was compared to that of the control period. Hypothesis 2, stated in null form, is:

Hypothesis 0-2. There are no significant unusual security returns around the foreign firms' financial reporting events conditioned on the disclosure sequences.

Hypothesis 0-2 was tested by analyzing the squared market model prediction errors. Easton and Zmijewski (1993) provide the following four-step test procedures:

1. The first step estimates the daily market model for each observation and calculates the market model prediction errors (PE) for the event period. These prediction errors are used to calculate average prediction errors for all firms for each event date.
2. The second step calculates standardized squared market model prediction errors (SSPE) for daily and multiple-day return windows.
3. The third step estimates *z*-statistics.
4. The final step evaluates the *z*-statistic. A positive *z*-statistic indicates that the event period SSPE is higher than expected.

The following one-factor market model was used to estimate each firm's normal returns over the five-year sample period:[6]

$$R_{it} = \alpha_i + \beta_i R_{mt} + \varepsilon_{it}$$

where: R_{it} = *Center for Research in Security Prices (CRSP) return for firm i* on day *t*;

R_{mt} = return on the CRSP equally-weighted market index;

α_i, β_i = U.S. market model parameters for firm i;[7]

e_{it} = *random disturbance for firm i* on date *t*, assumed to be independently and identically distributed (iid) with mean zero and variance σ^2.

In the model, the ($\alpha_i + \beta_i R_{mt}$) represents a firm's expected return, and the (ε_{it}) is the prediction error. For each firm, the standard errors of the estimation period and the event period are calculated.[8] Dividing the prediction error by the standard error generates a standardized prediction error for a particular security on a given day. The choice of return windows is arbitrary. The present study performed sensitivity analysis, varying the length of the holding period from one to seven days. Thus, the present study uses a both one-day return and a multiple day return. The market model parameters are estimated over a 201-day trading period from day t = –199 to t = 1 (where day t = 0 is the day of firms' reporting event date). The length of the estimation period is also arbitrary, involving a tradeoff between "the benefits of a longer period (an improved prediction model) and the cost of a longer period (model parameter instability)" (Peterson 1989, 38).

The present study partitions the reporting events based on the availability and sequence of event dates in the same manner as it partition the observations for analyzing reporting lags. The sequence of the PEA and 20F/ARKS disclosure dates allows the following partitions:

1. Three ways for PEA announcement dates: PEA precedes 20F/ARK; 20F/ARK precedes PEA; and 20F/ARK unknown (PEA only).
2. Three ways for 20F/ARK filing dates: PEA precedes 20F/ARK; 20F/ARK precedes PEA; and PEA unknown (20F/ARK only).

Additionally, the following secondary hypotheses, stated in the null form, are tested:

Hypothesis 0-2a. There are no unusual security returns around the event period for the sample firms partitioned according to firm size.

Hypothesis 0-2b. There are no unusual security returns around the event period for the sample firms partitioned according to stock exchange listing.

Hypothesis 0-2c. There are no unusual security returns around the event period for the sample firms partitioned according to share type.

Hypothesis 0-2d. There are no unusual security returns around the event period for the sample firms partitioned according to international accounting system clusters.

Hypothesis 0-2e. There are no unusual security returns around the event period for the sample firms partitioned according to nationality.

Sample Data

The sample firms consist of foreign firms whose common stock shares or American Depository Receipts (ADRs) were traded on the New York Stock Exchange (NYSE), the American Stock Exchange (AMEX), and the National Association of Securities Dealers Automated Quotation System (NASDAQ). Foreign firms are defined as the firms incorporated outside the United States. Using the 1994 COMPUSTAT data base and the annual editions of each stock exchange's Fact Book,[9] foreign firms were identified.

The sample period consisted of five years, 1988 through 1992. The five-year limitation was imposed because some data, such as the SEC filing dates, were collected manually. The foreign firms had to meet the following selection criteria in order to be included in the research sample:

1. Have SEC filing data available from the Disclosure Incorporation's microfiche for the period 1988 through 1992;
2. Have security return data available on CRSP tape for the sample period; and
3. Have preliminary earnings announcements available from the Wall Street Journal Index.

Table 1. Distribution of Sample Firms

Countries	*Number of Firms*	*Stock Exchanges*	*Number of Firms*	*Two-digit SIC Code*	*SIC Number*
Australia	8	New York	47	10	3
Bermuda	3	American	14	12	1
Cayman Islands	2	NASDAQ	34	13	1
Denmark	1			20	6
England	27			23	2
Finland	1			24	1
France	2			26	1
Greece	1			27	2
Hong Kong	2			28	10
Ireland	3			29	3
Israel	6			30	1
Italy	4			32	3
Japan	15			33	5
Netherlands	6			35	7
Norway	2			36	10
Philippines	4			37	4
Scotland	1			38	7
South Africa	1			42	1
Spain	1			44	3
Sweden	5			45	2
				47	1
				48	5
				49	1
				50	1
				53	2
				61	1
				64	1
				67	3
				70	1
				73	4
				78	1
				87	1
Total firms	95	Total firms	95	Total firms	95

A total of 95 foreign firms met the selection criteria. These firms constitute the sample for the analysis of the reporting lags and prediction errors. Table 1 presents a distribution of countries, stock exchanges, and industries in the sample.

For the country distribution, firms from England (27) and Japan (15) represent 44% of the total sample firms. Hence, the analysis includes the effect of country-specific representation on the result. Most foreign firms in the sample (72 out of 95) are listed on either NYSE (47) or NASDAQ (34). NYSE and AMEX have

Table 2. Annual PEA and 20F/ARK Reporting Lags

	Reporting Lag from FYE to PEA			*Reporting Lag from FYE to 20F/ARK*			
Sequence of Disclosure	*Mean*	*Std.*	*Median*	*Mean*	*Std.*	*Median*	*Total Number of Observations*
Both PEA and 20F/ARK Dates Known							
PEA precedes 20F/ARK	73.2	33.9	68.0	160.1	34.2	178.0	386
25% quartile			57.0			133.0	
75% quartile			82.0			182.0	
20F/ARK precedes PEA	138.0	63.5	139.0	106.1	54.5	119.0	10
25% quartile			90.0			85.0	
74% quartile			176.0			133.0	
Either PEA or 20F/ARK Dates Unknown							
PEA dates only	67.9	24.4	66.0				54
25% quartile			55.0				
75% quartile			79.0				
20F/ARK dates only				163.1	35.3	179.0	97
25% quartile						150.0	
75% quartile						182.0	
All Observations	73.1	34.0	68.0	160.1	35.6	178.0	547
25% quartile			57.0			136.0	
75% quartile			82.0			182.0	

Key: FYE: fiscal year-end.
PEA: preliminary earnings announcement date on the Wall Street Journal.
20F/ARK: SEC Form 20F/ARK filing date on the Disclosure Inc.'s microfiche.
Number of observations: number of obeservations for each partition.
Std.: Standard deviation.

common characteristics, such as listing requirements. Hence, the analysis of stock exchange effect focuses on difference between NYSE/AMEX and NASDAQ firms, by grouping 14 AMEX firms with NYSE firms.

SEC Filing Dates

The SEC filing dates were obtained from Disclosure Incorporation's microfiche. The SEC provides the filings to Disclosure Inc. for public distribution. When the SEC receives a filing from a firm, it stamps a "received" date on the cover and notifies the public by recording on the Work Load File. Hence, the "received" date represents the earliest date that the public can have access to the filings in the SEC's public reference room. The SEC "on file" date is the latest date the SEC filing is publicly available. Public access lag between "receipt" date and "on file" date averages approximately five days for 10K filings (Easton and Zmijewski 1993). For Disclosure Inc., the "date received," is the date which the company records on the cover page when it receives the filings for processing from the SEC. Several event studies report that the "date received" is a proxy for the publicly available date of the SEC filings. Easton and Zmijewski (1993) found that the lag between the SEC onfile date and the Disclosure Inc. "date received," which is used in the present study, averaged zero for 10K reports. For the study period, 1988 through 1992, the sample firms generated 295 observations for the SEC filing event. One hundred and seventy-two (172) of the observations represent actual 20F filings, and the other 123 observations represent the ARK event.

The PEA dates were available from the Wall Street Journal Index (WSJI). The WSJI dates were verified by reference to the specific issue of the Wall Street Journal (WSJ). A total of 252 PEA observations were generated by the sample firms.

ANALYSIS OF THE RESULTS

The summary statistics of the reporting lags for PEA and 20F/ARK are presented in Table 2. The mean PEA reporting lag for all observations is 73.1 days with a median of 68.0 days and a standard deviation of 34.0. The mean reporting lag for all 20F/ARK observations is 160.1 days with a median of 178.0 and a standard deviation of 35.6. These results are consistent with the findings reported by Meek (1983, 1991). Firms tend to announce PEA a few months ahead of the 20F/ARK filings, which are filed close to the statutory filing date of 180 days after the fiscal year-end.

When the sample observations are partitioned according to the sequence of disclosure dates, the reporting lags for PEA and 20F/ARK are consistent across the partitions. When PEA precedes 20F/ARK, the median reporting lag for 20F/ARK is 178 days and the median reporting lag for PEA is 68 days. Similarly, in the situation where only 20F/ARK dates are known, the reporting lag for 20F/ARK is

Table 3. Reporting Lags Across Partitions: Nationality and Stock Exchange

	Reporting Lag from FYE to PEA			Reporting Lag from FYE to 20F/ARK			
Partition Variables	*Mean*	*Std.*	*Median*	*Mean*	*Std.*	*Median*	*Number of Observations*
Country							
Australia	58.3	26.4	54.5	158.7	26.7	173.5	36
Carribean:							
Bermuda, Cayman Island	85.9	7.7	85.5	142.1	39.1	128.0	17
Great Britain:							
England, Scottland, Ireland	73.3	27.0	68.0	143.0	41.5	136.0	183
Northern Europe:							
Denmark France, Netherlands	70.3	26.2	72.0	167.1	37.9	181.0	60
Southern Europe:							
Italy, Greece, Spain	92.7	45.2	87.0	176.6	11.5	180.5	34
Far East:							
Japan, Hong Kong, Philippines	69.7	48.9	58.0	164.9	31.9	176.0	123

(continued)

Table 3. (Continued)

	Reporting Lag from FYE to PEA			*Reporting Lag from FYE to 20F/ARK*			
Partition Variables	*Mean*	*Std.*	*Median*	*Mean*	*Std.*	*Median*	*Number of Observations*
Scandinavian: Norway, Sweden, Finland	73.1	26.6	67.0	175.4	21.9	181.0	48
Israel:	75.7	24.7	81.0	158.8	14.6	181.5	37
Stock Exchange							
New York	69.3	29.4	65.0	151.4	35.3	172.0	270
American	75.8	33.5	79.0	171.4	35.8	181.0	71
NASDAQ	78.6	39.8	74.0	168.0	33.2	180.0	201

Key: See Table 2.

Table 4. Association of Reporting Lags with Firm's Reporting Environments—Correlation Analysis

Stock Exchange	*NYSE*	*AMEX*	*NASDAQ*	*Size (Sales)*
20F/ARK Coefficient	−0.2397	0.1647	0.1444	−0.1771
p-value	0.0001	0.0045	0.0131	0.0023
PEA Coefficient	−0.2039	0.0805	0.1541	−0.2766
p-value	0.0011	0.2025	0.0144	0.0001

Note: Spearman correlation coefficients/Prob > |R| under Hypothesis 0: Rho = 0.

179 days. An exception to this consistent reporting pattern is the situation where 20F/ARK precedes PEA. In this situation, the median reporting lag for 20F/ARK is 119 days and the median reporting lag for PEA is 139 days, indicating unusually late PEA and unusually early 20F/ARK filing.

Table 3 presents summary statistics of firms' reporting lags partitioned according to nationality and stock exchange. To assess if any of these variables are associated with the reporting lags, the present study computed Spearman correlations. The Spearman correlation results indicate that the reporting lags of 20F/ARK and PEA are significantly associated with some country groups. British firms filed 20F/ARK reports to the SEC in a more timely manner (earlier than the statutory filing date). The Scandinavian and Israeli firms filed SEC reports in a less timely fashion (close to the statutory deadline). For PEA, Australian and Japanese firms made timely disclosures, while the Caribbean and Israeli firms made less timely disclosures.

Foreign firms' reporting lags are also associated with stock exchanges. As shown in Table 4, the Spearman correlations between 0/1 stock exchange dummy variables and the 20F/ARK reporting lags are −0.24 with $p = 0.0001$ for NYSE, 0.16 with $p = 0.005$ for AMEX, and 0.14 with $p = 0.01$ for NASDAQ, indicating significant associations of stock exchanges with the 20F/ARK reporting lags. For PEA, only NYSE and NASDAQ are significantly associated with the reporting lags. This result supports the point of view that the foreign firms listed on NYSE/AMEX have more timely disclosures than NASDAQ foreign firms.[10]

Table 5 presents summary statistics of firms' reporting lags partitioned according to size(sales) and industry (SIC) code. The associations of firm size (1992 total sales) with the reporting lags are significant. The Spearman correlations for size, as shown in Table 6, are −0.18 with a p-value of 0.002 for 20F/ARK and −0.28 with a p-value of 0.0001 for PEA. However, the associations of industry groups with the reporting lags are weak. For the 20F/ARK, industrial manufacturing companies (SIC from 3000 to 3999) show a weak correlation of 0.11 with a p-value of 0.07, and consumer products/retail companies (SIC from 5000 to 5999) have a weak correlation of −0.10 with a p-value of 0.08 (see Table 6). For the PEA, agri-

Table 5. Reporting Lags Across Partitions: Sales and Industry

Partition Variables	*Reporting Lag from FYE to PEA* Mean	Std.	Median	*Reporting Lag from FYE to 20F/ARK* Mean	Std.	Median	Number of Observations
Sales (Quartile)							
1st quartile	79.8	29.1	76.0	166.0	35.4	181.0	124
2nd quartile	76.8	27.7	74.0	163.6	38.1	179.0	122
3rd quartile	64.8	24.8	66.0	155.1	35.8	166.0	135
4th quartile	72.3	43.4	59.0	160.0	33.1	178.0	154
Industry by SIC							
1000-1999:	56.1	20.8	59.0	157.7	28.1	175.0	30
2000-2999:	68.9	23.2	62.0	161.6	35.8	178.0	147
3000-3999:	75.0	39.5	68.0	166.1	30.4	179.0	213
4000-4999:	83.4	39.1	75.0	163.9	42.8	179.5	73
5000-5999:	104.6	70.1	85.0	144.6	31.6	138.0	20
6000-6999:	808	6.5	82.0	154.4	36.4	175.5	18
7000- :	69.1	14.2	71.0	149.9	41.4	181.0	34

Key: See Table 2.

Table 6. Association of Reporting Lags With Firm's Reporting Environment Correlation Analysis

Size (Sales		*Industry by*	*1000-1999*	*2000-2999*	*3000-3999*	*4000-4999*	*5000-5999*	*6000-6999*	*7000-7999*
20F/ARK Coefficien	−0.1771	20F/ARK Coefficient	−0.0179	0.0281	0.1064	0.0338	−0.1014	−0.0364	−0.0683
p-value	0.0023	*p*-value	0.7586	0.6304	0.0681	0.5627	0.0819	0.5326	0.2418
PEA Coefficient	−0.2766	PEA Coefficient	−0.1601	0.0528	−0.0895	0.1252	0.0431	0.0901	−0.0282
p-value	0.0001	*p*-value	0.0109	0.4039	0.1536	0.0471	0.4964	0.1536	0.6556

Note: Spearman Correlation Coefficients/Prob > |R| under Ho: Rho = 0.

Table 7. Standardized Squared Prediction Errors around PEA (Conditioned on the Available Disclosure Sequence)

	Daily Prediction Errors			Cumulative Prediction Error		
Disclosure Sequence Obs.	*-1*	*0*	*+1*	*3-day*	*5-day*	*7-day*
PEA precedes 20F/ARK:						
	2.58	1.13	0.92	1.54	1.32	1.26
172						
	(14.53)**	(1.19)	(–1.91)	(5.00)**	(2.97)**	(2.39)*
PEA Only:						
	2.70	1.21	0.86	1.59	1.24	1.15
49						
	(8.36)**	(1.02)	(–0.70)	(2.89)**	(1.19)	(0.73)

Notes: Predictions errors: standardized squared daily and multip;e-day cumulative prediction errors.
Parenthesis: z-statistics; *indicates significance at 0.05 level; **indicates significance at 0.01 level.
PEA: preliminary earnings announcement date on the *Wall Street Journal* 20F/ARK; SEC Form 20F/ARK filing date on the Disclosure Inc.'s microfiche
Obs.: number of observations for each partition.

culture/mining (SIC from 1000 to 1999) companies have a correlation of –0.16 with a *p*-value of 0.01, and transportation/telecommunication companies (SIC from 4000 to 4999) have a correlation of 0.12 with a *p*-value of 0.05.

Prediction Errors Conditioned on Disclosure Sequences

The present study posits that the information content of 20F/ARK and PEA events depends on the relative information arrival sequence. If a firm's PEA event precedes the 20F/ARK report, then the 20F/ARK reports are expected to have no significant information content. Conversely, if a firm's PEA event follows the 20F/ARK event (or the firm's PEA event does not occur), then the 20F/ARK is expected to have significant information content.

Prediction Errors of PEA Conditioned on Disclosure Sequence

Table 7 presents the results of standardized squared prediction errors (SSPE) around the PEA. The table reports the *z*-statistic in parentheses for daily and multiple-day cumulative prediction errors. A significant positive *z*-statistic indicates abnormally large SSPE, while a significant negative *z*-statistic indicates abnormally small SSPE. Abnormally larger or small SSPE would indicate information content of PEA events.

Under the condition where the PEA precedes the 20F/ARK, the *z*-statistic is significant for daily (one-day before) and cumulative (three-day, five-day, and seven-day) SSPEs. The positive *z*-statistics suggest that earnings in the PEA has information content. This result is consistent with previous research findings (Meek 1983, 1991). Similarly, under the condition where only PEA events occur, the result shows that earnings in the PEA has significant impact on stock markets. In the case where 20F/ARK precedes PEA, due to the small number of observations (total of 10), the test result is not reported in Table 7.

Prediction Errors of 20F/ARK Conditioned on Disclosure Sequence

Table 8 presents the results of standardized squared prediction errors (SSPE) around the 20F/ARK events. When PEA events occur before the 20F/ARK events, neither the daily nor the cumulative SSPE of the 20F/ARK reports has a significant *z*-statistic. However, when the 20F events occur without the PEA events, both daily (event day) and cumulative (five-day and seven-day) SSPEs are significant, suggesting that the reported earnings in the 20F/ARK filings have information content. When the 20F/ARK precedes the PEA, both daily and three-day SSPE indicate earnings in the 20F/ARK reports have information content; however, the test result is not shown because of the small number of observations.

The results in Table 9 indicate that information content of a specific event depends on the disclosure sequence and that the first public disclosure of earnings,

Table 8. Standardized Squared Prediction Errors around 20F/ARK (Conditioned on the Available Disclosure Sequence)

	Daily Prediction Errors			Cumulative Prediction Error			
Disclosure Sequence	*-1*	*0*	*+1*	*3-day*	*5-day*	*7-day*	*Obs*
PEA precedes 20F/ARK:							
	1.08	0.94	1.09	1.03	1.03	1.01	177
	(0.72)	(–0.06)	(0.81)	(0.31)	(0.25)	(0.08)	
20F/ARK Only:							
	1.04	1.41	1.06	1.17	1.37	1.37	82
	(0.22)	(2.61)**	(0.38)	(1.07)	(2.36)*	(2.35)*	

Notes: Predictions errors: standardized squared daily and multip;e-day cumulative prediction errors.
Parenthesis: z-statistics; *indicates significance at 0.05 level; **indicates significance at 0.01 level.
PEA: preliminary earnings announcement date on the *Wall Street Journal* 20F/ARK; SEC Form 20F/ARK filing date on the Disclosure Inc.'s microfiche
Obs.: number of observations for each partition.

Table 9. Prediction Errors Across Partition Variables

Partition Variable	*PEA Events* 3-day	5-day	7-day	# of Obs.	*20F/ARK Events* 3-day	5-day	7-day	# of Obs.
Size (quartile)								
1st quartile	1.74	1.40	1.30	56	0.83	1.14	1.07	64
	(3.86)**	(2.12)*	(1.55)		(–0.98)	(0.76)	(0.38)	
2nd quartile	1.81	1.41	1.32	54	1.20	1.17	1.16	66
	(4.19)**	(2.12)*	(1.65)		(1.13)	(0.99)	(0.94)	
3rd quartile	1.78	1.51	1.33	58	0.99	0.98	1.01	64
	(4.14)**	(2.71)**	(1.78)*		(–0.05)	(–0.11)	(0.08)	
4th quartile	0.89	0.93	1.00	57	1.45	1.36	1.31	68
	(–0.57)	(–0.37)	(0.02)		(2.58)**	(2.09)*	(1.78)	
Exchange								
NYSE/AMEX	1.64	1.34	1.30	149	1.02	1.07	1.13	162
	(5.48)**	(2.95)**	(2.54)*		(0.22)	(0.67)	(1.13)	
NASDAQ	1.37	1.24	1.12	76	1.27	1.30	1.16	101
	(2.23)*	(1.52)	(0.73)		(1.88)	(2.13)*	(1.11)	
Share Type								
Common Share	1.49	1.23	1.15	56	0.77	0.90	1.00	57
	(2.57)*	(1.29)	(0.77)		(–1.21)	(–0.54)	(0.00)	
ADR	1.57	1.34	1.27	169	1.21	1.24	1.18	206
	(5.21)**	(3.08)**	(2.44)*		(2.14)*	(2.37)*	(1.78)	
Two-Clusters								
Macro	1.15	1.06	1.00	78	1.27	1.24	1.20	105
	(0.94)	(0.40)	(–0.05)		(1.96)*	(1.71)	(1.47)	
Micro	1.75	1.44	1.36	149	1.01	1.11	1.09	158
	(6.45)**	(3.75)**	(3.10)**		(0.12)	(0.99)	(0.83)	

(continued)

Table 9. (Continued)

Partition Variable	PEA Events 3-day	PEA Events 5-day	PEA Events 7-day	# of Obs.	20F/ARK Events 3-day	20F/ARK Events 5-day	20F/ARK Events 7-day	# of Obs.
Five-Clusters								
Law-based	0.55	0.79	0.74	36	1.56	1.42	1.37	51
	(–1.90)	(–0.90)	(–1.07)		(2.82)**	(2.12)*	(1.82)	
U.S. Influence	1.60	1.32	1.18	31	0.86	0.93	0.93	38
	(2.33)*	(1.25)	(0.72)		(–0.62)	(–0.29)	(–0.30)	
U.K. Influence	1.79	1.47	1.41	118	1.06	1.17	1.15	120
	(6.06)**	(3.57)**	(3.19)**		(0.49)	(1.30)	(1.12)	
Tax-based	1.28	0.95	0.96	19	1.20	1.28	1.32	29
	(0.84)	(–0.16)	(–0.11)		(0.77)	(1.06)	(1.20)	
Government	1.81	1.43	1.30	19	0.83	0.85	0.71	21
(Economics)	(2.49)*	(1.33)	(0.93)		(–0.53)	(–0.47)	(–0.93)	
Country								
Australia	1.21	1.16	1.03	11	0.95	1.33	1.28	21
	(0.48)	(0.37)	(0.07)		(–0.17)	(1.05)	(0.91)	
England	2.10	1.66	1.60	81	1.10	1.09	1.09	74
	(6.97)**	(4.20)**	(3.75)**		(0.60)	(0.57)	(0.54)	
Japan	0.55	0.79	0.74	36	1.56	1.42	1.36	51
	(–1.90)	(–0.90)	(–1.08)		(2.82)**	(2.12)*	(1.82)*	
Netherlands	1.13	1.01	1.05	19	1.17	1.43	1.38	17
	(0.40)	(0.04)	(0.13)		(0.37)	(1.24)	(1.09)	

Notes: Predictions errors: standardized squared daily and multiple-day cumulative prediction errors.
Parenthesis: Z-statistic; *indicates significance at 0.05 level; **indicates significance at 0.01 level.
PEA: preliminary earnings announcement date on the *Wall Street Journal*
20F/ARK: SEC Form 20F/ARK filing date on the Disclosure Inc.'s microfiche
Obs.: number of observations for each partition.

regardless of GAAP, has information content. United States stock markets place more weight on the information which arrives first or occurs in the absence of other events. Previous research findings of no information content regarding 20F events might have been different if the disclosure sequence had been considered.

Prediction Errors of PEA and 20F/ARK Events Partitioned According to Firm Characteristics

Several studies indicate that information content is related to various characteristics or the operating environment of a firm (Meek 1991; Frost and Pownall 1994). Firm characteristics analyzed in this study include firm size, stock exchanges, share type, and nationality. Table 9 presents the summary results of prediction errors partitioned according to firm size, stock exchange, share type, and nationality.

Firm Size

Other studies report that firm size and information content are inversely related (Meek 1991; Frost and Pownall 1994). One plausible explanation for the inverse relation is that the largest firms are Japanese; they are listed on NASDAQ; and their accounting methods are law-based. Consistent with previous studies, the results of the present study on the PEA event indicate that the earnings announcements by large firms have less impact on stock markets than announcements by small firms. The firms are partitioned into four quartiles based on total revenue. Firms in the first three quartiles have significant three-day and five-day prediction errors while firms in the fourth quartile have no significant prediction errors. Table 10 reports the Spearman results for the association of prediction error of PEA with firm's size. The Spearman correlation between three-day prediction errors and total revenue is −0.14 with a p-value of 0.03, providing the inverse relationship.

However, test results on 20F/ARK events indicate that only firms in the fourth quartile have significant three-day and five-day prediction errors. As shown in

Table 10. Association of Prediction Errors of PEA and 20F/ARK with Characteristics Correlation Analysis

Size (Sales)		*Stock Exchange*		
20F/ARK	Sales	20F/ARK	NYSE/AMEX	
Coefficient	0.1585	Coefficient	0.0051	−0.0051
p-value	0.0101	*p*-value	0.9338	0.9338
PEA		PEA	−0.1566	0.1566
Coefficient	−0.1425	Coefficient		
p-value	0.0326	*p*-value	0.0187	0.0187

Note: Spearman Correlation Coefficients/Prob > |R| under Hypothesis 0: Rho = 0.

Table 10, the Spearman correlation is 0.16 with a p-value of 0.01, indicating a positive relationship between size and market reaction to 20F/ARK reports. Consistent with this finding, recent empirical studies report that some specific components of the 20F reports reconciling GAAP differences between U.S. and foreign practices are value-relevant (McQueen 1993; Amir et al. 1993). The present study speculates that the 20F/ARK reports contain firms' financial information which has not been exposed to media, for example, the reporting of consolidated earnings for Japanese firms.

Exchanges and Share Types

For the PEA events, firms listed on NYSE and AMEX have significant z-statistics at level of 0.01 for three-day and five-day standardized squared prediction errors (SSPE) and 0.05 for seven day SSPE. Also, firms listed on NASDAQ have a significant z-statistic at 0.05 level for three-day SSPE. These results indicate that earnings of both NYSE/AMEX and NASDAQ firms have information content. However, like the firm size variable, NASDAQ firms would be expected to have greater information content of PEA events, since some NASDAQ firms (especially those listed before October 1988) are exempt from public disclosure requirements (SEC registration). The Spearman correlation, reported in Table 10, between three-day SSPE and exchange listing variables (NYSE/AMEX versus NASDAQ) is 0.16 with a p-value of 0.02 for NASDAQ firms, indicating a weak positive relationship between SSPE and NASDAQ firms. This positive relationship maybe due in part to the large number of Japanese firms in the sample. For the 20F/ARK events, only NASDAQ firms have a significant z-statistic, at the 0.05 level for five-day SSPE. However, the Spearman correlation shows no significant relation between stock exchange and SSPE.

Nationality (Macro/Micro)

Firms analyzed in the present study are incorporated in foreign countries, and their financial reporting in the United States is influenced by their home country reporting systems. The present study classifies firms into two clusters (macro versus micro) as suggested by Doupnik and Salter (1993). In developing accounting principles, macro countries rely on legislative sources (law-based, e.g., Japan) while micro countries rely on business practices (practitioner-based, e.g., influenced by the United States and United Kingdom). For the PEA events, Table 11 indicates that firms classified as micro cluster have significant z-statistics at 0.01 level for three-day, five-day, and seven-day SSPEs. The Spearman correlation between three-day SSPE and cluster variable (macro versus micro) is 0.22 with a p-value of 0.0005 for the micro cluster, indicating a positive relationship between the market reaction and micro cluster earnings. Therefore, the U.S. markets, whose accounting system is classified as micro cluster, respond to the preliminary

Table 11. Association of Prediction Errors of PEA and 20F/ARK with Firm Characteristics Correlation Analysis

Share Type			*Nationality*		
20F/ARK	Common	ADR	20F/ARK	Macro	Micro
Coefficient	−0.0857	0.0857	Coefficient	0.0283	−0.0283
p-value	0.1658	0.1658	*p*-value	0.6475	0.6475
PEA			PEA		
Coefficient	0.1702	0.1702	Coefficient	−0.2294	0.2294
p-value	0.0105	0.0105	*p*-value	0.0005	0.0005

Note: Spearman Correlation Coefficients/Prob > |R| under Hypothesis 0: Rho = 0.

earnings announcements of familiar micro cluster firms—that is, Canadian and the U.K. However, the U.S. markets do not respond to the preliminary earnings announcements of unfamiliar macro cluster firms—for example, Japanese. For the 20F/ARK filings, firms classified as macro clusters have a significant *z*-statistic (1.96 at 0.05 level) for the three-day SSPE. This supports the viewpoint that the U.S. markets respond to 20F/ARK filings which disclose GAAP differences between the United States and the macro accounting systems.

The firms in the present study fit into five out of nine clusters suggested by Doupnik and Salter (1993). When the firms are classified into five clusters, the present test results are consistent with macro/micro clusters. For the PEA events, firms classified into the U.K.-influenced cluster (England, the Netherlands, Australia, Hong-Kong, and South Africa) have significant *z*-statistics at 0.01 level for three-day, five-day, and seven-day SSPEs. Also, firms from U.S.-influenced (Bermuda, Philippines, and Israel) and government-influenced (Finland and Sweden) countries have a significant *z*-statistic at 0.05 level for three-day SSPEs. The remaining two clusters: (1) law-based cluster (Japan) and (2) tax-based cluster (France, Norway, Denmark, Italy, and Spain) have no significant market reaction to the PEA events.

Under the two-cluster (macro/micro) classification, countries in the U.K.-influence and U.S.-influence clusters are in the micro cluster, and the other three clusters of law-based, tax-based, and government-based are in the macro cluster. As was revealed for the micro cluster, the U.S. markets have a greater reaction to the earnings of familiar U.S.- and U.K.-influenced accounting systems.

Additionally, the present study individually tests the four largest countries represented in the sample to observe country specific effect. For the PEA events, only English firms have significant *z*-statistics at 0.05 level for three-day, five-day, and seven-day SSPE, indicating that the U.S. markets have a greater response to earnings developed using a familiar accounting system. However, Australian and Dutch firms, which are in the U.K. micro cluster, have no significant market reaction to their PEA. This result indicates that the significant market effect of the micro cluster originates mainly from the English firms (81 out of a total 118 micro observations).

The market effect of 20F/ARK events is opposite to the market effect of PEA events. Macro cluster firms have a significant z-statistic for three-day SSPE, and only Japanese firms, which are located in a law-based country under the macro cluster, have a significant z-statistic for three-day SSPE. Hence, for macro country firms, the U.S. stock markets do not have a significant reaction to the earnings in the PEA but do have a significant reaction to the earnings in the 20F/ARK. Considering the fact that the PEA events normally precede the 20F/ARK, this result supports previous research findings that the 20F/ARK reports are value-relevant.

SUMMARY AND CONCLUSIONS

To examine the market effect of foreign financial reports, the present study collected foreign firms' preliminary earnings announcement (PEA) dates and the SEC filing (20F/ARK) dates. These two reporting events were analyzed to observe any systematic reporting pattern across foreign firms. The abnormal returns around the reporting events were calculated and analyzed under different event sequences. Foreign firms in the sample were partitioned according to nationality, size, and industry, to observe the associations of these partition variables with the reporting pattern and abnormal returns.

Null Hypothesis 0-1 of no systematic pattern of foreign financial reports was rejected. Foreign firms file 20F/ARK a few months later than preliminary earnings announcement (PEA). Typically, the 20F/ARK is filed an average of 160.1 days after the fiscal year-end, while the PEA is announced, on average, 73.3 days after the fiscal year-end.

Null Hypothesis 0-2 of no prediction error differences under different disclosure sequences was rejected. If PEA events occur in advance (or in the absence) of 20F/ARK events, they have significant market reactions (prediction errors). Conversely, if 20F/ARK events occur in advance (or in the absence) of PEA events, the 20F/ARK events have a significant market reaction (prediction error). Thus, the findings reinforce the notion that the relative usefulness of PEA and 20F/ARK depends on the information arrival sequence. In other words, the U.S. stock markets place more weight on earnings information which is new to the markets than on earnings information which is already disclosed through other events.

The SEC faces a dilemma of relaxing the U.S. financial reporting requirements for foreign firms while at the same time striving to protect U.S. investments. Maintaining the stringent U.S. rules would shield U.S. investors from unfamiliar foreign reporting practices. Although foreign firms file their 20F/ARK close to the statutory filing date, the 20F/ARK filings are an information relevant event only in the absence of other reporting events such as PEA. It should be noted that the 20F contains financial information adjusting GAAP differences between the United

States and foreign countries. Hence, in the absence of PEA, the filing of 20F/ARK would become an extremely important issue to the SEC as it seeks to protect U.S. investors from unfamiliar foreign reporting practices.

Limitations

The sample firms were based on the availability of data from Disclosure Inc., CRSP, the WSJ, and COMPUSTAT, thus limiting the generalizability of the findings to the firms available in these data bases. Despite the sensitivity analysis covering various return windows, financial reporting event dates can be misspecified. Additionally, there exists a possibility of misspecification in the model. The non-earnings information that may be relevant but excluded in the model is temporal changes in the risk-free rate, changes in the market risk premium, and other changes in value-relevant parameters such as the earnings capitalization rate and growth opportunities in excess of normal return (Griffin 1993). If earnings fluctuations due to foreign GAAP are transitory and the market is efficient, then stock prices at the time of earnings announcement remain invariant to the choice of accounting measurement rules. However, these factors are likely to have little impact on the cross-section model covering a short sample period (five-year) and, thus, have been omitted from the present study. Introduction of these additional variables in the model involves trading-off reduced bias in the coefficients against increased noise in the model (Griffin 1993).

NOTES

1. Foreign firms are required to file interim reports (Form 6K) if they release interim reports in the home country.
2. The present study uses Doupnik and Salter's (1993) micro/macro hierarchical classification.
3. The short-window studies (called event studies) cover from one day to several days, while the long-window studies (called association studies) cover from weeks to years around the reporting events.
4. Compared to Form 10K firms, Form 20F firms have less stringent disclosure requirements for proxies and tender offers, longer filing periods (90 days for 10K but 180 days for 20F after fiscal year-end). Form 20F firms are not required to file an interim report, unless they disclose it in their domicile countries.

20F firms are also exempt from some provisions of the Foreign Corrupt Practices Act (such as insider reporting and short-swing trading profit regulations) but are required to provide information regarding the history of exchange rates between U.S. dollars and their home country currency and names and price data on the securities traded in stock exchanges other than U.S. exchange.

5. These variables are not mutually exclusive. Some studies use the stock exchanges as a proxy for firm size (NYSE and AMEX for large firms and NASDAQ for small firms; Easton and Zmijewski 1993). Other studies use market value of equity instead of total sales.
6. Frost and Pownall (1994) show that the use of a single-country, U.S. index does not produce a difference in the returns generated. Similarly, Meek's (1983) test results using raw returns (domicile currency prices) are identical to the test results obtained using the U.S. market. Meek suggests that a U.S. market index can serve as a proxy for a world index.

7. The ordinary least squares (OLS) beta estimates can be biased for the securities that are traded with trading delays or frequencies different than those of the market index. There are several adjustment techniques mitigating these problems. These adjustment techniques involve a tradeoff between reduced bias in the beta coefficient and increased noise in the estimation. The present study uses the OLS parameters because the focus of the study is on the residuals rather than in the beta estimates.

8. $$S_i = \left[\sum_{i=1}^{T} (R_{it} - R_{it}^{*})^2 / (T-2) \right]^{1/2}$$

where: Si = standard error of the estimate,

Rit* = prediction return for period t within the estimation period.

9. The COMPUSTAT data base and the Fact Books define foreign firms as the firms incorporated outside the United States. However, this number excludes the Canadian firms.

10. These significant correlations are not driven by firm size differences between stock exchanges. Mean 1992 total sales for sample firms listed on NYSE/AMEX and NASDAQ are $10,217.12 million and $11,224.70 million, respectively. Rather, the result is consistent with the foreign exempt firms listing on NASDAQ and having less timely disclosures (Frost and Pownall 1994).

REFERENCES

Amir, E., T.S. Harris, and E.K. Venuti. 1993. A comparison of the value-relevance of U.S. versus Non-U.S. GAAP accounting measures using form 20-F reconciliation. *Journal of Accounting Research* 31(Supplement): 230-264.

Ball, R., and P. Brown. 1968. The empirical evaluation of accounting income numbers. *Journal of Accounting Research* (Autumn): 159-178.

Doupnik, T.S., and S.B. Salter. 1993. An empirical test of a judgmental international classification of financial reporting practices. *Journal of International Business Studies* 24(1): 41-60.

Easton, P.D., and M.E. Zmijewski. 1993. SEC form 10K/10Q reports and annual reports to shareholders: Reporting lags and squared market model prediction errors. *Journal of Accounting Research* 31(Spring): 113-129.

Frost, C.A., and G. Pownall. 1994. A comparison of the stock price response to earnings disclosures in the United States and the United Kingdom. *Contemporary Accounting Research* 11(Summer): 59-86.

Griffin, P.A. 1993. Discussion of noisy accounting earnings signals and earnings response coefficients: The case of foreign currency accounting. *Contemporary Accounting Research* 10(Fall): 167-178.

Hall, C., Y. Hamao, and T.S. Harris. 1994. A comparison of relationships between security market prices, returns and accounting measures in Japan and the United States. *Journal of Financial Management and Accounting* 5(1): 47-73.

McQueen, P.D. 1993. The information content of foreign and US GAAP earnings in SEC form 20-F. Working Paper, CUNY—Baruch College, New York.

Meek, G.K. 1983. U.S. securities market responses to alternative earnings disclosures of non-U.S. multinational corporations. *The Accounting Review* 58(2, (April): 394-402.

Meek, G.K. 1991. Capital market reactions to accounting earnings announcements in an international context. *Journal of International Financial Management and Accounting* 3(2): 93-109.

Peterson, P.P. 1989. Event studies: A review of issues and methodology. *Quarterly Journal of Business and Economics* (Summer): 36-66.

Pope, P., and C.G. Inyangete. 1992. Differential information, the variability of UK stock returns, and earnings announcements. *Journal of Business Finance & Accounting* 19(4): 603-623.

Pope, P., and W.P. Rees. 1992. International differences in GAAP and the pricing of earnings. *Journal of International Financial Management and Accounting* 4(3): 190-219.

REPORTING PRACTICES OF FOREIGN FIRMS LISTED IN THE UNITED STATES

Sylwia Gornik-Tomaszewski and
Heidi Hylton Meier

ABSTRACT

Despite strict registration, reporting and disclosure requirements imposed by the Securities and Exchange Commission (SEC), foreign companies have entered the U.S. capital market in record numbers during the 1990s. Within these SEC requirements, there are various registration and reporting choices available to foreign firms wishing to raise capital in the United States.

A detailed discussion of these choices is presented and followed by a classification scheme developed for this study. The reporting practices for 364 firms for the years 1989 through 1993 are grouped according to this classification and then analyzed. The distributions of each reporting group are examined to determine potential differences and similarities with regard to: (1) the stock exchange on which the foreign firm is listed; (2) total assets, sales, beta, price-earnings (PE) ratio, and total 3-year return; and (3) changes in the reporting practices of these firms within that time

Research in Accounting Regulation, Supplement 1, pages 75-95.

ISBN: 0-7623-0338-7

period. Results of statistical tests show that significant differences exist among these groups.

Current SEC regulation results in diverse reporting practices by foreign issuers of securities listed on U.S. markets. However, the SEC has recently been involved in several initiatives and proposals in order to balance the demands of the growing international market with that of protecting the interests of the public.

INTRODUCTION

As the globalization of capital markets accelerates, multinational firms continue to expand their sources of capital by listing their securities on foreign stock exchanges. Therefore, it is not surprising that in the 1990s foreign companies have entered the U.S. capital market in record numbers. The Securities and Exchange Commission (SEC) is in the position of balancing the need to protect U.S. investors and at the same time provide access to capital markets by foreign firms wishing to raise capital in the United States. To accomplish this, the SEC currently permits several different registration and filing alternatives to foreign firms.

This paper identifies these complex alternatives, discusses the requirements of each reporting option, and presents an original classification scheme, based on accounting measurement, in which to compare these alternatives. Foreign firms listed in the United States are then examined and classified according to their reporting and filing choices. This analysis reveals that foreign firms take full advantage of the flexibility provided by the SEC, raising questions about possible advantages and disadvantages of these various filing options, and potential similarities and differences of those firms. In addition, if those characteristics can be identified and generalized, perhaps valuable insights can be provided to the SEC as they work to streamline current requirements and continue to examine new and additional alternatives.

The only study published to date which deals with the broad spectrum of reporting practices exercised by foreign firms is that by Frost and Kinney (1996). They focus on disclosure levels selected by foreign registrants with securities traded on major U.S. stock exchanges during the calendar year 1990. In contrast, our research concentrates on the measurement aspect—Generally Accepted Accounting Principles (GAAP) regime—of reports filed by foreign firms with the SEC and offers five-year data covering the period between 1989 and 1993.

REGULATORY REQUIREMENTS FOR FOREIGN ISSUERS

In the United States, the securities markets have a dominant influence on accounting regulation. The SEC has legal authority to enforce the securities laws as well as to formulate and enforce accounting standards.[1] Initial issues of securities are regulated by authority of the Securities Act of 1933. Trading of securities on organized exchanges is regulated by the authority of the Securities Exchange Act of 1934.

Generally, the language of the Securities Acts does not distinguish between domestic and foreign registrants. Non-U.S. firms are subject to SEC regulation when the following conditions are present (Choi and Mueller 1992): (1) the firm issues securities for original sale to U.S. investors; (2) the firm wishes to trade its existing outstanding securities on an organized U.S. exchange; and (3) the firm's stock is traded over the counter in the United States and the firm has assets in excess of $1 million and more than 500 shareholders worldwide, of which at least 300 reside in the United States.

Foreign securities are traded in the United States in three forms (Meek 1980): (1) as shares which are issued in the country of the issuer's incorporation; (2) as shares which are issued specifically for trading in the United States; and (3) as American Depository Receipts (ADR). The majority of foreign shares in the United States are traded in the ADR form, which is negotiable certificates held in U.S. banks as American Depository Shares (ADS).

Registration and Periodic Reporting Requirements

Although disclosure requirements for public offerings of registered securities and for periodic reporting are in principle the same for non-U.S. and for domestic issuers, the SEC has adjusted its disclosure requirements for the former. Forms F-1, F-2, F-3, F-4, and F-6 serve as registration statements for non-U.S. issuers making distributions in the United States. The purpose of the forms is (Choi and Mueller 1992):

- F-1: Form used for initial public offering;
- F-2: Form available for issuers previously registered under the Securities Acts; permits incorporation upon delivery of reports filed under the securities Act with the prospectus;
- F-3: Form available only for issuers reporting under the Securities Exchange Act for at least three years and who are considered "world class" issuers or are offering investment grade securities;
- F-4: Form used for business combinations;
- F-6: Form used for the registration of ADSs evidenced by ADRs.

The registration statements of non-U.S. issuers continue to be subject to the disclosure requirements for financial statements as set forth in Regulation S-X. Disclosure requirements for textual material are set forth in Regulation S-K.

Although Regulations S-X and S-K guide both U.S. and non-U.S. firms in their disclosure policy, there are certain exceptions for foreign issuers, which relate to such issues as the set of accounting standards to be used in preparation of financial statements, disclosure of material transactions between the firm and its management, the remuneration of individual directors, and so forth. Non-U.S. companies that have listed their securities on a national securities exchange or the National Market System of the National Association of Securities Dealers Automated Quotation System (NASDAQ), as well as issuers that have made a registered public offering in the United States, must also file periodic reports with the SEC.

Dealing with Cross-Border Accounting Differences

The SEC currently accepts three major approaches to transnational reporting: (1) preparation of financial statements according to foreign GAAP accompanied by reconciliation of significant variations from U.S. GAAP and Regulation S-X; (2) preparation of financial statements according to U.S. GAAP; and (3) limited reciprocal recognition of financial statements prepared according to domestic accounting standards. Recently, the SEC has made an additional accommodation for foreign issuers by recognizing selected International Accounting Standards (IAS).

Reconciliation

Non-U.S. firms presenting their financial statements prepared in accordance with a comprehensive body of accounting principles other than U.S. GAAP have to accompany these statements with a quantitative reconciliation of significant departures from U.S. GAAP. These firms register and file annual reports on Form 20-F, which must be filed within six months of the issuers' fiscal year-end. Non-U.S. issuers filing Form 20-F must also file a semi-annual Form 6-K which incorporates whatever information they disclosed in their countries of domicile, filed with foreign stock exchanges or distributed to their stockholders.

Except in limited circumstances for dollar-based companies, the financial statements must be presented in the issuer's home currency.[2] If the issuer's home country has experienced high inflation (a cumulative three-year inflation rate in excess of 100%), the issuer must quantify the effects of changing prices on its financial condition and results of operations (Beller et al. 1994).

Form 20-F allows two levels of financial statement disclosure, referred to as "Item 17" and "Item 18." If the issuer is trying only to list its securities, financial statement requirements are determined by Item 17 of Form 20-F. Under Item 17, non-U.S. registrants are required to disclose: (1) the accounting principles used to prepare the financial statements; (2) quantified material variations from U.S. GAAP presented in a tabular format, either on the face of the Income Statement or in footnote disclosure; (3) quantified material differences in Earnings per Share (EPS); and (4) quantified material variations in balance sheet line items.[3] Firms utilizing Item 17 for periodic reporting purposes need not provide additional disclosures that would be required under U.S. GAAP and Regulation S-X but are not required under the firms' domestic GAAP.

Item 18 must be used in a public offering of securities and demands full compliance with material financial disclosures required by U.S. GAAP and Regulation S-X. This means that, in addition to the Item 17 requirements, Item 18 calls for other information, such as industry segment information, information about foreign operations and sales, information about major customers, income tax disclosures, and pension disclosures (SEC 1987, 16-35).

The extent of reconciliation depends also upon the nature of the securities offered. Some offerings, such as investment grade debt, securities issued upon the exercise of certain rights or warrants pursuant to a dividend reinvestment plan, or issued upon conversion of outstanding securities, can be accomplished with Item 17. Full reconciliation under Item 18 is required for other offerings (Choi and Mueller 1992).

The advantage of reconciliation of material accounting differences versus full restatement of financial reports is that reconciliation is less time consuming and less costly but still provides U.S. investors with earnings and selected balance sheet numbers that are readily understood and can be used for comparisons. Disadvantages of reconciliation are similar to those of providing secondary financial statements. Corporate managers make business decisions in terms of domestic accounting consequences. Restating accounting results cannot change the underlying managerial decisions (Choi and Mueller 1992). Also, since only summary data are adjusted, some statistical bias is introduced. In addition, because the restatement is only partial, certain financial ratios are meaningless when restated to U.S. GAAP numbers (e.g., earnings) and compared with numbers reflecting foreign GAAP (e.g., assets).

Preparation of Financial Statements According to U.S. GAAP

Non-U.S. issuers may elect to present their financial statements in accordance with U.S. GAAP and file the registration forms used by U.S. firms: S-1, S-7, S-8, and so forth. However, consequently, they must also file the same periodic reporting forms as U.S. firms: 10-K, 10-Q, and 8-K.

Another option available to these firms is to file Form 20-F. Although Form 20-F financial statements need not be prepared in accordance with U.S. GAAP, foreign issuers may elect to do so. Again, they have a choice of the level of disclosure specified by the requirements of Item 17 versus Item 18.

In the case of Japanese companies, the restatement of financial reports according to U.S. GAAP is a common practice. At the time most Japanese companies were originally listed on U.S. markets, the Japanese commercial code required parent-company-only financial reports. Since the companies were required by the SEC to present consolidated financial statements and they had no domestic equivalent, they chose U.S. GAAP and retained this for domestic reporting purposes once the Ministry of Finance (via the Securities and Exchange Law) started to require consolidated financial statements for listed companies (Amir, Harris, and Venuti 1993).

Despite unquestionable advantages of restated financial statements, such as specific recognition of the information requirements of audiences-of-interest in other countries and, consequently, the increased information content of both primary and secondary financial statements, some researchers strongly criticized this transnational reporting mode. Mueller (1965) emphasized a single-domicile notion of reporting by arguing:

> Financial statements are anchored in a single set of underlying accounting data prepared within a framework of quite specific accounting standards, methods and procedures. Restatement of financial statements to a different set of accounting principles produces different relationships between individual account balances and financial ratios. The meaning and implication of these new relationships may convey an entirely different financial substance to statement readers in other countries (p. 4).

Choi (1980) studied the problem empirically by comparing ratio analysis of a Japanese firm's secondary statements and a U.S. firm's primary statements. He concluded that:

> secondary financial statements...fail to recognize that a foreign reader's investment risks and rewards are highly dependent on the socioeconomic environment of the reporting company's country of domicile (pp. 96-97).

Similar research results can be found in Choi et al. (1983), where a sample of Japanese firms was expanded by adding several Korean firms.

McKinnon (1984) expressed an opinion that Anglo-American methods of consolidation failed to reflect adequately the nature of corporate group associations in Japan. Extensive cross-ownership among Japanese companies, with banks' participation in industrial conglomerates, is an important factor impacting accounting in Japan. Choi and Mueller (1992) proposed supplementing secondary financial statements with footnote disclosures that would assist foreign readers in properly interpreting these accounting reports. Several Japanese companies have begun to provide such disclosures in their Form 20-F filings.

Reciprocity

In 1991, the SEC entered into a *Multijurisdictional Disclosure System* (MJDS) with Canada. Canadian issuers are permitted to report under the Exchange Act using Canadian disclosure documents and offering practices (SEC 1991). The system is effective for firms with debt and preferred stock offerings and extends the reciprocal practices to ongoing disclosures and cross-border tender and rights offers.

The MJDS is a first case in the United States of full recognition of foreign financial statements prepared in accordance with home country requirements. Canada was selected as the first country to be subject to reciprocal disclosure for at least two reasons: (1) the similarity between Canadian and U.S. GAAP, and (2) the large number of Canadian companies listed on the exchanges in the United States (McQueen 1992). The MJDS is considered a prototype for similar systems with other countries.

Internationalization

Internationalization means acceptance of the financial statements prepared in accordance with a single common set of international standards. Recently, the SEC has taken an important step toward further accommodation of foreign issuers by selectively accepting standards developed and issued by the International Accounting Standards Committee (IASC). The new SEC rules adopted on April 19, 1994, permit non-U.S. issuers to file a cash flow statement prepared in accordance with IAS No. 7, "Cash Flow Statements," without reconciling to U.S. GAAP.[4]

The Commission also simplified reconciliation requirements for foreign registrants who comply with certain aspects of IAS No. 21, "Accounting for the Effect of Changes in Foreign Exchange Rates," and IAS No. 22, "Accounting for Business Combinations" (SEC 1995).

Some believe that worldwide adoption and acceptance of a common set of international standards will allow sufficient comparability of international financial information and, in this way, remove one of the most important impediments to the flow of international investment (Turner 1983). Many international financial institutions and international capital markets support the use of IASC standards (IAS) as a way to achieve that goal. Although the SEC is far from accepting IAS as a whole, the Commission is committed to the process of piecemeal acceptance of high-quality IASs which produce reliable, relevant, and comparable information.

The Regulatory Dilemma

Global trading of stocks has created a regulatory dilemma for the SEC. The agency wants to protect investors but also encourages multinational stock offerings by loosening requirements for foreign issuers and traders. The SEC has the reputation for toughness and sophistication in protecting the integrity of U.S. markets. Some researchers admit, however, that operations in interconnected international markets may require the SEC to focus on different goals other than enforcement and the prevention of fraud. In particular, it might require greater sensitivity to economic concerns. Khademian (1992) argues that:

> to increase disclosure requirements for multinational corporations or to subject foreign investors to the enforcement powers of the SEC might be to scare away foreign investment in this country. Consequently, if the United States is to be a thriving participant in global markets, a greater understanding of (and sensitivity to) the economic impact of regulation could be regarded as essential (p. 219).

Conflict Between the SEC and the Stock Exchanges in the United States

Although financial reporting requirements for non-U.S. issuers are less extensive than those for U.S. firms, the New York Stock Exchange (NYSE) and American Stock Exchange (AMEX) have lobbied the U.S. Congress and the SEC since 1986 to ease these requirements further. NYSE's representatives have especially argued for elimination of the requirement to reconcile foreign GAAP income statement measurements to U.S. GAAP (Power and Salwen 1991; Bayless et al. 1996). These lobbying activities have generated a debate in the United States, with the arguments of global competition for exchange listings on one side and investor protection on the other.

The NYSE and AMEX and their supporters argue that the winners in global competition will be stock exchanges in countries that allow firms to raise capital at the lowest cost, net of the costs and benefits of the reporting requirements (Saudagaran 1988, 1991). All over the world, national capital markets are increasingly being deregulated and/or restructured. Moreover, capital markets are becoming more and more internationalized, and capital seekers are increasingly looking past national boundaries to satisfy their capital needs. National markets would like to facilitate that movement but are still subject to domestic regulatory authorities.

The European Union (EU) is a good example of a concentrated effort to achieve increased efficiency in international capital raising. To facilitate cross-border offerings, the EU has adopted a number of directives aimed at harmonizing disclosure and listing requirements among member countries.[5] Harmonization will enable an issuer on one member country's stock exchange to use the same disclosure document on all other member countries' exchanges.[6]

Investors are interested in foreign stocks and want to internationally diversify their portfolios. Baumol and Malkiel (1993) argued that SEC disclosure requirements for non-U.S. firms force U.S. investors to purchase stocks in non-U.S. capital markets that have higher transaction costs, higher bid-ask spreads, and less liquidity. In addition, they have to face transaction delays and uncertain foreign currency translations. The NYSE, for example, indicates that the commission for an U.S. investor buying stock on a non-U.S. exchange is eight to 10 times higher than the commission for buying stock on U.S. exchanges (Siconolfi and Salwen 1992).

Another argument used by the stock exchanges is that large and sophisticated institutional investors dominate the market. Also, millions of shares of nonregistered foreign securities are traded every day through the NASDAQ "Pink Sheet" market and electronic bulletin board and the investor protection issue is not raised in this context.

On the other side of the debate, the SEC and its supporters argue that further relaxation of disclosure requirements for foreign firms is inconsistent with its objectives of investor protection and market quality. About half of all equities in the United States are still owned by individual investors, who are also increasing their holdings of equities in absolute numbers. The SEC believes that exchange listings and financial reporting requirements in other countries are less stringent and the accounting standards are pro-management. Regulators' concerns about non-U.S. accounting standards focus on the vulnerability of reported earnings to earnings management, as well as the potential lack of informativeness and timeliness of reported accounting numbers (primarily accounting earnings), undue reliance on tax regulations for financial reporting measurement rules, and the infrequency of disclosure (Alford et al. 1993).

Another major concern of the SEC is the potential disproportion between listing and disclosure requirements for U.S. and non-U.S. firms. Some U.S. firms complain that if the SEC further relaxed its requirements for foreign issuers, the U.S. firms would then be subject to stricter disclosure standards then their foreign competitors. Some critics have even predicted that large U.S. corporations may reincorporate in a foreign country and obtain foreign listing status in the United States to take advantage of allegedly less costly foreign reporting requirements (Siconolfi and Salwen 1992).

Supporters of the SEC position in the conflict provide evidence that since 1990, the number of foreign firms listed on the London, Tokyo, Paris, and Frankfurt exchanges has steadily fallen, while the number of foreign registrants on the NYSE, AMEX, and NASDAQ has risen (Frost and Lang 1996). At the same time, the London Stock Exchange (LSE) has been criticized for not being stringent in monitoring and disciplining market abuses (Dwyer 1995).

As a contra argument to the stock exchanges' position in terms of lower costs, it can be argued that while costs of preparing information may be lower for foreign financial statement preparers, they will be subject to the same legal liability standards as their U.S. counterparts. In addition, the cost of reconciliation does not disappear, it is simply shifted to U.S. investors attempting to compare investment opportunities among foreign and domestic firms.

The SEC's policy towards non-U.S. issuers has resulted in a noticeably diversified approach to reporting. This policy raises some interesting questions about whether all of the options made available to non-U.S. issuers are currently being utilized and whether certain filing options appear to be more or less preferable. Additional questions can be raised about whether firms with similar financial characteristics from the same country of domicile, or those firms listed on certain stock exchanges, use similar reporting modes.

To address these research questions, a thorough search and analysis of non-U.S. issuers was performed. The following section describes the sources of information used, provides a classification for the firms based on filing choices, analyzes certain characteristics of these firms, and presents the research results. The evidence provided by this analysis gives a very complete overview of current filing practices of non-U.S. issuers and gives valuable insight to the SEC for evaluating current policy and directing future decisions regarding filing and reporting procedures.

CLASSIFICATION OF REPORTING PRACTICES EXERCISED BY FOREIGN FIRMS LISTED IN THE UNITED STATES

In order to classify reporting practices exercised by foreign firms, the *Compustat* and *Disclosure* data bases were searched for firms incorporated in countries other than the United States and Canada. Canadian firms are excluded from this study because they are treated differently than other non-U.S. issuers. They are not considered foreign by SEC standards and, therefore, are required to file annual reports on Form 10-K.[7] These firms may use Canadian GAAP to prepare their financial statements but reconciliation of net income to U.S. GAAP is required.[8] The MJDS discussed above allows companies with debt and preferred stock offerings to forego reconciliation (Johnson 1996).

The search yielded 364 firms. Reference to *The SEC Index* and a search through the data base of the Commission's Public Reference Room in Washington, D.C., confirmed that between 1989 and 1993, 316 of these 364 firms filed Form 20-F or Form 10-K reports with the SEC at least once.

The SEC File, the microfiche data base of corporate annual reports and SEC documents, was utilized to:

1. Identify the reporting practice exercised by a given firm in a given year by inspecting the auditors' reports and notes to the financial statements; and
2. Identify the disclosure level by collecting the Item number (17 or 18) under which Form 20-F was filed.

Compustat was also utilized to collect data on variables used to compare firms classified in different groups. These variables are: total assets, sales, beta, price to earnings ratio, and 3-year total return.

Based on the inspection of reports filed by foreign firms with the SEC, the following classification was developed, as shown in Figure 1:

1. Firms filing foreign GAAP financial statements on Form 20-F and reconciling material differences to U.S. GAAP (Group A);
2. Firms filing financial statements on Form 20-F using U.S. GAAP equivalent[9] (Group B);
3. Firms filing U.S. GAAP financial statements on Form 20-F (Group C); and
4. Firms filing U.S. GAAP financial statements on Form 10-K (Group D).

Besides these four major groups and Canadian firms, there is another category of foreign firms not considered in this study. These are firms exempt from the Exchange Act reporting under Rule 12g3-2(a) and firms exempt under Rule 12g3-2(b), who have been "grandfathered" under previous regulations and may continue to list securities without complying with current regulation and reporting requirements.[10] These firms file only their annual reports to stockholders, which

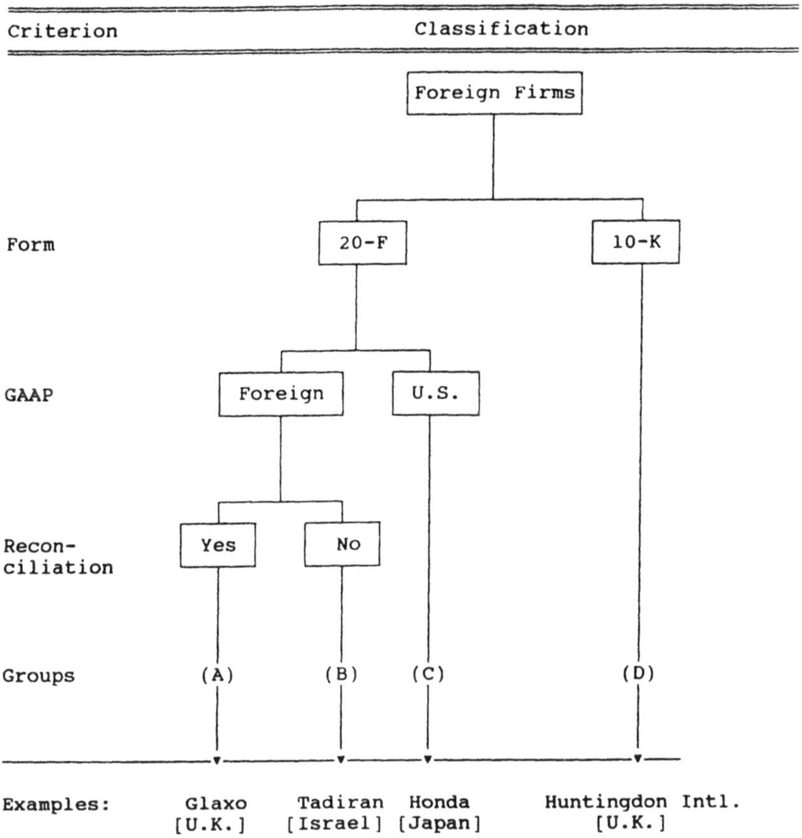

Figure 1. Classification of Reporting Practices by Foreign Firms (except Canadian) Subject to the SEC's Registration and Reporting Requirements

may not be in the English language and may contain financial statements prepared according to foreign GAAP without U.S. GAAP reconciliation.

In summary, the population of firms included in the analysis can be defined as foreign private issuers (as defined by the SEC) who must file under the 1933 and 1934 acts. Figure 1 provides an example of a firm in each category of reporting. Differences in accounting *measurement* are a focus of this classification. Emphasis on *disclosure level* would require further distinction between firms filing Form 20-F under Item 17 and under Item 18.[11]

Table 1 provides distribution data for sample firms classified by their reporting practice in each of the years 1989 through 1993 as well as the summary for the entire five-year period. The classification takes into consideration both the accounting measurement aspect (Group) and the disclosure level (Item).

Table 1. Sample Firms Classified by Reporting Practices (1989-1993)

Group	*A*		*B*		*C*		*Total 20-F*		*Chi-Square*[1]	*D 10-K*	*Total*
Item	*17*	*18*	*17*	*18*	*17*	*18*	*17*	*18*			
1989	17	64	11	11	15	17	43	92	11.07***	20	155
1990	19	69	10	12	15	20	44	101	8.16**	20	165
1991	18	76	12	16	16	20	46	112	11.19***	22	180
1992	23	86	12	20	14	27	49	133	4.79*	24	206
1993	25	108	6	31	13	43	44	182	0.79	28	254
Total	102	403	51	90	73	127	226	620	27.15***	114	960

Notes: ***$p < .01$; **$p < .05$; *$p < .10$;
[1]Chi-square statistics are used to test the null hypothesis of independence between *'Group'* and *'Item'* for firms filing Form 20-F.

Table 2. Classification on Sample Firms by Group and Stock Exchange (1989-1993)

Group	*A*		*B*		*C*		*D*		*Total*		*Chi-Square*[1]
St. Ex.[2]	*1*	*2*	*1*	*2*	*1*	*2*	*1*	*2*	*1*	*2*	
1989	43	38	7	15	15	17	10	10	75	80	3.19
1990	50	38	6	16	18	17	10	10	84	83	7.66*
1991	55	39	6	22	16	20	12	10	89	92	13.27***
1992	69	40	8	24	19	22	13	11	109	98	14.97***
1993	88	45	6	31	28	28	16	12	140	117	29.88***
Total	305	200	33	108	96	104	61	53	495	465	64.09***

Notes: ***$p < .01$; **$p < .05$; *$p < .10$;

[1]Chi-square statistics are used to test the null hypothesis of independence between *'Group'* and *'Stock Exchange'* on which the firm is listed.

[2]1 = firms listed on national stock exchanges (NYSE and AMEX);

2 = all other firms (NASDAQ and OTC).

Data presented in Table 1 indicate that foreign firms are almost evenly distributed between reporting in foreign GAAP (Group A)[12] and reporting in U.S. GAAP or its equivalent (Groups B, C, and D). In terms of form selection, however, the above classification shows a strong preference for Form 20-F (Groups A, B, and C) as compared to the infrequent selection of Form 10-K (Group D).

The most common practice among foreign firms was to file Form 20-F with financial statements prepared according to foreign GAAP and to supplement them with U.S. GAAP reconciliation (Group A). About 52% of all firms, including the majority of European firms, followed this option.

About 21% of firms selected U.S. GAAP as a base for their consolidated financial statements filed on Form 20-F (Group C). All Japanese firms are classified in this group. About 15% of firms claimed that their financial statements were prepared in conformity with accounting principles which were generally accepted both in their country of domicile and in the United States and, therefore, did not provide any reconciliation (Group B). Most Israeli firms fall into this category, although their financial statements are price-level adjusted.

The least popular was Form 10-K (Group D). All foreign firms filing this form used U.S. GAAP and many presented their financial statements in U.S. dollars. These facts may indicate that, although Group D firms are incorporated abroad, at least some of them may be domiciled in the United States since they either have major business operations in the United States, or are listed only on the U.S. stock exchanges, or the majority of their owners is from the United States.

Although the majority of firms filed Form 20-F under the more demanding Item 18 (73%) as compared to Item 17 (27%), the preference for Item 18 was more prevalent among Group A firms (80%) than among either Group B (64%) or Group C (64%) firms. Chi-square statistics were used to test the hypothesized dependence between accounting measurement (Group) and disclosure level (Item). This statistic is significant for the total of firm-year observations as well as for four out of the five years tested individually. Such results can be interpreted as: (1) more firms classified in Group A wish to make public offerings of securities in the United States; or (2) by making more extensive disclosures available to the U.S. public, Group A firms try to compensate for preparing their financial statements according to foreign GAAP; or (3) a combination of the facts presented in (1) and (2).

In Table 2, foreign firms classified by Group are further subdivided between firms listed on the national stock exchanges NYSE and AMEX and firms with securities quoted and traded on the NASDAQ and the Over-the-Counter (OTC) markets.

For the total number of firm-year observations, the distribution between these two types of markets is almost even. However, a group-by-group analysis reveals significant differences. Between the years 1989 and 1993, Group A firms disproportionately tended to favor national markets, while Group B firms show the opposite. Firms in Group C and D are more evenly distributed between the national and

Table 3. Selected Financial Characteristics of Sample Firms Classified by Group (1989-1993)

Characteristics		*A*	*B*	*C*	*D*
Total Assets	($'000)	20,060.27	8,139.08	24,568.40	2,009.06
Sales	($'000)	8,248.48	6,953.66	17,090.10	1,415.69
Beta		0.92	1.05	0.72	1.10
PE		26.27	5.44	43.67	14.47
Total 3-Year Return		10.17	6.55	4.51	−11.04

over-the-counter markets. Chi-square tests confirm these observations, and the null hypothesis of independence between reporting practice exercised by the firm and the stock exchange where the firm is listed can be rejected at the 1% significance level.

Firms classified by their reporting practices with the SEC were also compared on selected financial characteristics. Table 3 presents a comparison of the means of total assets, sales, beta, price-to-earnings (PE) ratio, and total three-year return.

Firms in Group C are the largest in terms of both total assets and sales. Group A firms are a close second. Firms in Groups B, and particularly those in Group D, are much smaller, with more systematic risk, as measured by beta, involved in their operations.

Although PE ratio can be interpreted as representing a variety of attributes of an equity, this study utilizes it to predominantly convey growth potential of the underlying firm. In this context, Group C firms are characterized by a ratio eight times higher than the mean ratio for Group B firms. Group A stock yielded the highest three-year return on investment, over 10%, while in contrast Group D stock yielded a negative 11%.

The null hypothesis of independence between reporting practices and industry membership is also tested. The chi-square statistic could not be used because of the large number of cells with an expected count of less than five for both the three-digit and the two-digit SIC codes. Frequency tables, however, show a strong preference for particular reporting practices among firms from certain industries.

For example, banks and telecommunication firms tend to prepare their financial statements using foreign GAAP. The proportion of observations classified in Group A to observations classified in Groups B, C, and D in these industries is 33:3 for banks and 27:1 for the telecommunications industry. The opposite can be said about water transportation (freight) and the machinery and computer industries, of which the majority of foreign firms report in U.S. GAAP. The proportions of observations for these industries are 26:3 for freight and 28:6 for machinery and computers.

There are also examples of industries where reporting using foreign GAAP and reporting using U.S. GAAP or its equivalent are equally popular. For example, in the electronics industry, the distribution is 22:24 observations.

Table 4. Classification of Changes in Reporting Practices by Sample Firms (1989-1993)

	A-B	*B-A*	*A-C*	*C-A*	*B-C*	*C-B*	*Total*
Switches within Form 20-F	2	7	0	3	2	3	17
	A-B	*B-A*	*A-C*	*C-A*	*B-C*	*C-B*	*Total*
Switches between Forms 20-F and 10-K	1	0	0	0	1	3	5

It is important to emphasize that in terms of reporting practices, foreign issuers are inconsistent not only cross-sectionally but also over time. Between 1989 and 1993, 20 firms changed their annual reporting with the SEC at least once in eight different ways (two firms switched twice). Table 4 summarizes the types of switches among groups present in the data.

Most of the changes are quite neutral and of little consequence. A firm might report a difference between its domestic GAAP and the U.S. GAAP (Group A) and then abandon this report (switch to Group B), or vice versa, simply because its domestic GAAP was very close to U.S. accounting practices and the differences in earnings and stockholders' equity are rarely significant enough to require presentation in the financial statements (most Israeli firms falls into this category). Five changes observed between Groups B and C are even less meaningful, since they represent a formal rather than substantive choice between fully pronounced U.S. GAAP and its equivalent.

The other changes, although rare, are more significant. Three firms chose to abandon the preparation of secondary statements according to U.S. GAAP (Group C) and opted for presentation of primary statements with reconciliation of accounting differences (Group A).[13] There were five instances of more radical changes involving the selection of a different SEC form with all the consequences. Four of these changes, however, did not involve any change in GAAP itself (switches between Groups C and D).[14] The most significant change of all, exercised by ADT Ltd. (Bermuda) in 1991, involved both accounting principles (switch from U.K. GAAP to U.S. GAAP) and form (switch from Form 20-F to Form 10-K).

CONCLUSIONS AND DIRECTIONS FOR THE FUTURE

Contemporary SEC regulation results in diversified reporting practices by foreign issuers of securities listed and traded in the United States. There are cross-sectional differences in forms filed, accounting standards used, and the level of disclosure provided. Reporting choices of foreign issuers are also not stationary over time.

Evidence provided by the data analysis reveals several interesting points. It would appear that some of the choices made by these firms are not completely independent. For example, Group A firms, those choosing reconciliation, are also more likely to choose more detailed disclosure required by Item 18 and are more likely to list on a national stock exchange. On the other hand, Group B firms, those choosing not to provide reconciliation, on average tend to be smaller than firms in Groups A and C and tend to favor listing on the NASDAQ or OTC exchange rather than the larger national exchanges. Questions arise as to whether firms listing on larger national exchanges perceive that higher levels of disclosure and more comparable financial information may be demanded.

Additionally, even though information on firms changing their reporting practices is limited, some interesting issues surface. The majority of changes observed during this time were from Group B to Group A, or to reconciliation, which enhances comparability but at an increased cost to the issuer. Perhaps these firms perceive that by providing a higher level of disclosure, their securities will be more attractive to U.S. investors. It is also noteworthy that these switches occurred during a time period when very costly and controversial financial standards were issued by the FASB (i.e., SFAS 106 and SFAS 109).[15] The implication is that foreign issuers place value on making their statements more comparable despite the increased cost and inconvenience. It is also possible that for some of the firms, compliance with these new standards created new material differences between reported numbers under their domestic GAAP and under U.S. GAAP.

The SEC has reacted to the internationalization of capital markets and changed the disclosure environment in a number of ways. In contrast with its past focus, which was primarily on the United States, the Commission, as a vital member of the International Organization of Securities Commissions (IOSCO),[16] now embraces the worldwide harmonization of regulatory requirements, which includes accounting standards. These efforts are seen as a promising means of increasing comparability and reducing costs.

The major SEC initiatives adopted to further simplify and lower the cost of the registration and periodic reporting processes for non-U.S. companies accessing the U.S. capital market include: (1) in 1990, the SEC introduced Rule 144A, allowing privately placed foreign securities to be resold without any holding period if they are sold to institutional investors with portfolios exceeding $100 million;[17] (2) in 1991, the SEC entered into the MJDS with Canada in order to promote the free flow of capital between Canada and the United States; (3) on April 19, 1994, the SEC extended the short-form F-3 registration to a wider range of non-U.S. issuers, accepted certain IASs as substitutes for U.S. GAAP, required first-time non-U.S. registrants to reconcile financial statements and selected financial data for only the two (previously five) most recently completed fiscal years, adopted amendments to allow Item 17 of Form 20-F for all offerings, and reduced reconciliation requirements for acquired foreign businesses; (4) the SEC adopted a new *safe harbor* rule (Rule 135c) relating to announcements by non-U.S. and

U.S. issuers alike of offerings not registered or required to be registered under the Securities Act of 1933; (5) the SEC proposed amendments to Regulation S-X and Form 20-F to provide non-U.S. issuers with greater flexibility in their selection of a reporting currency for use in SEC filings (Klein 1994); and (6) most recently, the SEC announced that it had engaged Arthur R. Wyatt, former Chairman of the International Accounting Standards Committee, as a senior policy adviser for the Commission's initiatives involving the development of IASs.

At least three major directions for future research emerge from this study. First, it would be important to compare U.S. market perceptions of foreign firms following different modes of reporting allowed under the SEC regulation. Second, an inquiry should be made into the decision process used by foreign issuers as to the reporting practices they adopt when entering the U.S. capital market. A related research question is whether the switch from one approach to another is based on internal or external factors. For example, increased familiarity with U.S. GAAP and U.S. markets may prompt management to consider increased disclosure or reconciliation. Alternatively, new FASB standards could cause material differences requiring reconciliation to U.S. GAAP.

Finally, the third major research avenue would be to study, on the one hand, the degree of compliance by foreign firms with IASs, and on the other, the viability of these standards as U.S. GAAP substitutes to U.S. market participants. The first goal of the IASC is to develop standards which would be accepted by capital markets and the business community all over the world. As the gap between IASs and U.S. GAAP continues to narrow, the SEC may accept more international standards in the future.

ACKNOWLEDGMENT

The authors would like to thank the anonymous reviewers for their constructive and valuable comments.

NOTES

1. The SEC recognizes as authoritative the GAAP embodied in standards issued by the independent Financial Accounting Standards Board (FASB), which was established in 1973 following criticism of the standard setting procedures of the Accounting Principles Board (APB).

2. In December 1994, the SEC changed this requirement to permit a foreign private issuer to state the amounts in its primary financial statements using any currency which it deems appropriate and in which it reports to a majority of its nonaffiliated security holders.

3. No required format is prescribed for this disclosure; firms usually provide a reconciliation of the shareholders' equity section of the balance sheet. However, some also provide restatement of assets and liability accounts (McQueen 1992).

4. The SEC believes that since the amendment of IAS No. 7 in October 1992, most of the differences between cashflow statements prepared under U.S. GAAP and IAS No. 7 are readily apparent and

would not adversely impact the quality of the information available to U.S. investors (Cramer and Stavrakis 1994).

5. It should be clarified that international accounting harmonization implies a more flexible approach compared to standardization, which results ultimately in a state of uniformity. The EU has been involved in international harmonization since the 1960s as a part of the program of company law harmonization. An important part of the company law harmonization process is the public disclosure of comparable and reliable financial information to protect the interests of shareholders, lenders, suppliers, and other interested parties. The harmonization of accounting and reporting in the EU is especially significant because any agreement that takes the form of a Directive has the force of law throughout the Community countries. The Fourth Directive—which regulates disclosure, classification, presentation, and valuation methods—and the Seventh Directive—which regulates consolidation—are fundamental to EU accounting harmonization.

6. An interesting fact is that the London Stock Exchange (LSE), the world's largest equity market for foreign shares, does not require foreign companies to comply with U.K. GAAP. Instead, it encourages listed foreign companies to comply with IAS issued by the IASC (Tondkar, Adhikari, and Coffman 1989).

7. Canadian firms have been allowed in limited circumstances to use the registration and reporting forms for foreign companies (SEC 1987, 16-3). As a result, the majority of Canadian firms have filed Form 10-K. Examples of Canadian firms filing Form 20-F include: American Fiber Corporation, Belmoral Mines, Ltd., Consolidated Nevada Goldfields Corporation, and Unilens Vision Inc.

8. Canadian firms are not required to reconcile their stockholders' equity section of the balance sheet (Johnson 1996).

9. Group B firms do not provide U.S. GAAP reconciliation. Auditors' reports for these firms specifically state that the financial statements are prepared in conformity with accounting principles generally accepted in a given foreign country and the United States and that, as applicable to these financial statements, such accounting principles are in *all material respects identical*. Therefore, this type of GAAP is considered here to be U.S. GAAP equivalent.

10. A Section 12g3-2(b) exemption from the 1934 Exchange Act is usually obtained by firms with a *sponsored level-I* ADRs. These firms cannot list or publicly issue their securities and their shares are traded in the OTC "Pink Sheet" market. Firms with *sponsored level-II* ADRs list their shares on a national stock exchange or the NASDAQ but do not make a public offering in the United States. An ADR is classified as *sponsored level-III* when a firm's listing on a national stock exchange or the NASDAQ is accompanied by a public offering in the United States. In both cases, these firms are subject to SEC registration and filing requirements.

11. The distinction between Items 17 and 18 is based on a classification of the requirements of U.S. GAAP and Regulation S-X into two categories: those specifying the methods of measuring amounts shown on the face of the financial statements (relevant for Item 17 and 18 alike) and those prescribing disclosure which explain, modify, and supplement these measurements (Item 18 only) (SEC 1990).

12. Certain firms use International Accounting Standards (IAS) to prepare their financial statements and announce earnings (e.g., the Italian firms Fiat Spa and Montedison Spa, as well as the Mexican firm Mexican Maritime Transportation). Because these firms also provide a reconciliation to U.S. GAAP, they were classified as Group A.

13. These firms are: Atlas Consolidated Mining & Development Corporation (Philippines), Basic Petroleum International (Bahamas), and Interpharm Laboratories Ltd. (Israel).

14. Challenger International Ltd. (Bermuda) decided to change from Form 20-F to Form 10-K, and three other firms, B&H Bulk Carriers Ltd. (Liberia), Interpharm Laboratories Ltd. (Israel), and Scandinavia Co. Inc. (Caymen Islands) decided to go the opposite way.

15. SFAS No. 106 is titled "Employers' Accounting for Postretirement Benefits Other than Pensions," while SFAS No. 109 is titled "Accounting for Income Taxes."

16. IOSCO is the leading organization for securities regulators, which has as its mission the global coordination of stock exchange rules so as to encourage both multi-listings by corporations and international securities trading. The international standardization of accounting regulations together with sufficiently detailed information disclosures is seen to be an important factor in achieving these objectives (Radebaugh and Gray 1993).

17. Prior to Rule 144A, privately placed foreign securities in the United States had to be held for three years before they could be resold publicly in unlimited quantities without having to be registered under the Securities Act of 1933.

REFERENCES

Alford, A., J. Jones, R. Leftwich, and M. Zmijewski. 1993. The relative informativeness of accounting disclosures in different countries. *Journal of Accounting Research* 31(Supplement): 183-223.

Amir, E., T.S. Harris, and E.K. Venuti. 1993. A comparison of the value-relevance of U.S. versus non-U.S. GAAP accounting measures using form 20-F reconciliations. *Journal of Accounting Research* 31(Supplement): 230-264.

Baumol, W.J., and B.G. Malkiel. 1993. Redundant regulation of foreign security trading and U.S. competitiveness. *Journal of Applied Corporate Finance* (Winter): 19-27.

Bayless, R., J. Cochrane, T. Harris, J. Leisenring, J. McLaughlin, and J.P. Wirtz. 1996. International access to U.S. capital markets—an AAA forum on accounting policy. *Accounting Horizons* 10: 75-94.

Beller, A., E. Marans, R. Davis, C. Austin, and M. Hickman. 1994. Access to the U.S. capital markets. *International Financial Law Review* (Hong Kong/PRC Supplement): 17-24.

Choi, F.D.S. 1980. Primary-secondary reporting: A cross-cultural analysis. *The International Journal of Accounting* (Fall): 84-104.

Choi, F.D.S., K. Min, S.O. Nam, H. Hino, J. Ujiie, and A.I. Stonehill. 1983. Analyzing foreign financial statements: The use and misuse of international ratio analysis. *Journal of International Business Studies* (Spring/Summer): 113-131.

Choi, F.D.S., and G.G. Mueller. 1992. *International Accounting*. Englewood Cliffs, NJ: Prentice-Hall.

Cramer, K., and C. Stavrakis. 1994. SEC further eases registration. *Corporate Finance* 115(June): 43-44.

Dwyer, P. 1995. Not quite cricket in the city. *Business Week* (August 21): 64-66.

Frost, C.A., and W.R. Kinney. 1996. Disclosure choices of foreign registrants in the United States. *Journal of Accounting Research* 34(Spring): 67-84.

Frost, C.A., and M.H. Lang. 1996. Foreign companies and U.S. securities markets: Financial reporting policy issues and suggestions for research. *Accounting Horizons* 10: 95-109.

Johnson, J.D. 1996. *A closer examination of the foreign GAAP reconciliation issue*. Working paper, Middle Tennessee State University.

Khademian, A.M. 1992. *The SEC and capital market regulation*. Pittsburgh, PA: University of Pittsburgh Press.

Klein, A.M. 1994. SEC streamlines rules for non-U.S. issuers. *International Financial Law Review* 13: 41-42.

McKinnon, J.L. 1984. Application of Anglo-American principles of consolidation to corporate financial disclosure in Japan. *Abacus* (June): 16-33.

McQueen, P.D. 1992. The information content of foreign GAAP earnings and shareowners' equity and the U.S. GAAP reconciliation disclosures in SEC Form 20-F. Ph.D. dissertation, New York University. *Dissertation Abstracts International* 54-07: A2643.

Meek, G.K. 1980. Financial reporting in an international setting: Securities price response in the United States to earnings disclosures by non-U.S. multinational corporations. Ph.D. dissertation, University of Washington. *Dissertation Abstracts International* 41-07: A3160.

Mueller, G.G. 1965. The international significance of financial statements. *Illinois CPA* (Spring): 1-10.

Power, W., and X. Salwen. 1991. Big Board's Donaldson says SEC rules could cost exchange its global standing. *Wall Street Journal* (December 12): C1, C18.

Radebaugh, L.H., and S.J. Gray. 1993. *International accounting and multinational enterprises*. New York: John Wiley & Sons.

Saudagaran, S. 1988. An empirical study of selected factors influencing the decision to list on foreign stock exchanges. *Journal of International Business Studies* 19: 101-127.

Saudagaran, S. 1991. The SEC and the globalization of financial markets. In G.J. Previtz, L. Parker, and T.R. Robinson (Eds.), *Research in Accounting Regulation*, Vol. 5, 31-53. Greenwich, CT: JAI Press.

Securities and Exchange Commission. 1987. *SEC Accounting and Reporting Manual*. Washington, DC: SEC.

Securities and Exchange Commission. 1990. *Staff Accounting Bulletin No. 88*. Washington, DC: SEC.

Securities and Exchange Commission. 1991. Multijurisdictional disclosure system. *International Series Release*, No. 291.

Securities and Exchange Commission. 1995. *Foreign Issuers and the U.S. Market*. Washington, DC: SEC, May 22.

Siconolfi, M., and K. Salwen. 1992. Big Board, SEC fight over foreign stocks. *Wall Street Journal* (May 13): C1, C21.

Tondkar, R.H., A. Adhikari, and E.N. Coffman. 1989. The internationalization of equity markets: Motivations for foreign corporate listing and filing and listing requirements of five major stock exchanges. *The International Journal of Accounting* 24: 143-163.

Turner, J.N. 1983. International harmonization: A professional goal. *Journal of Accountancy* (January): 58-59.

AGENCY THEORY, CORPORATE GOVERNANCE, AND THE ACCOUNTING REGULATION OF ISLAMIC BANKS

Simon Archer and Rifaat A.A. Karim

ABSTRACT

Unlike conventional banks, Islamic banks do not take interest-bearing deposits, since *Islamic Shari'a* principles forbid the charging or paying of interest. Instead, Islamic banks offer profit-sharing investment accounts, such that the investors' return depends on the return on the assets financed by the investors' funds. Such investment accounts may be either unrestricted or restricted. In the case of unrestricted investment accounts, the investors' funds are used to finance the bank's general pool of assets, while for restricted investment accounts, the use of investors' funds is restricted to financing a specified type of asset, such as credit sale receivables or leased assets.

Research in Accounting Regulation, Supplement 1, pages 97-114.

ISBN: 0-7623-0338-7

The calculation of the return due to such an investor (investment account holder) for a financial period is thus affected by the accounting policies used by the bank in income recognition, asset valuation, and expense allocation. The choice and application of accounting policies may also affect the allocation of income between investment account holders and shareholders (especially in the case of unrestricted investment accounts holders), or between different classes of investment account holders. As these accounting policies and their application are not known to investment account holders, and the latter have no legal rights to appoint members of the bank's board of directors or auditors, issues arise of asymmetric information, monitoring, and corporate governance. The paper analyzes the problems arising from this situation and discusses how they may be mitigated by accounting and auditing standards promulgated by a self-regulatory organization for Islamic banks.

AGENCY PROBLEMS AND CORPORATE GOVERNANCE

The Relevance of Agency Theory to Accounting Standard-Setting

From the point of view of the economic theory of the firm, the role of accounting standards can be seen in the context of Agency Theory. This body of theory deals with the "agency problem," that is, the type of problem that arises from: (1) the divergence of the economic interests of the *agent* (manager of the firm) from those of the *principal* (investor in the firm) in whose interests the agent is supposed to act; and (2) the existence of *information asymmetry* between the agent and the principal as to what activities the former has undertaken. (This is known as the "internal agency problem," to distinguish it from the "external agency problem" which exists between the firm and *potential* investors.) Accounting and financial reporting are means whereby the principal may be able to mitigate the information asymmetry by *monitoring* the activities of the agent, so as to detect activities which are not in the principal's interest. However, insofar as the accounting and financial reporting systems are themselves controlled by the agent, this reduces their monitoring capabilities. Accounting standards, together with auditing, are ways in which the agent's control over these systems may be curtailed, and their monitoring capabilities reinforced.

Agency theory is relevant to the situation of an Islamic bank[1] in two ways. On the "liabilities" side, the bank is accountable to various categories of investor, including (in addition to shareholders) investment account holders whose returns must be calculated on a profit sharing basis. Islamic investment accounts operate on the basis of the *Mudaraba* contract, according to which the investors receive their share of the profits or bear their share of the losses from the pool of assets in which the funds are invested, while the bank as entrepreneur (*Mudarib*) receives a commission which consists of a share of the profit, being zero in case of a loss or zero profit (Karim 1996). In the case of *restricted* investment accounts, the bank must invest the funds in a designated pool of assets, while funds in *unrestricted* investment accounts are normally comingled with the bank's own funds and invested in the bank's general pool of assets (the *bilateral Mudaraba*).[2] In the latter case (and also in the former case if the bank has invested part of its own funds in the designated pool of assets), profit calculations involve apportioning the profit or loss on the pool of assets between shareholders and holders of investment accounts. The latter are entitled to their proportionate share of profit, less the bank's commission as *Mudarib*; the bank (i.e., the shareholders) receives the proportionate share of profit on any of its own funds which have been invested in the pool, plus its commission. In the case where the return on the pool of assets has been negative, the losses are shared as indicated above, while the amount of the *Mudarib* commission will be zero. These profit and loss calculations are not observable by the investors, and this is a particular instance of information asymmetry (Karim 1994).

While for the ordinary company, it is the relationship between management and shareholders which gives rise to an agency problem (the so-called internal agency problem), a further internal agency problem thus arises in the case of an Islamic bank. This problem is due to the combination of the existence of profit-sharing investors other than shareholders, along with the incentives which the management of the bank may have to favor one category of investors over another. For example, shareholders have the right to vote in general meetings and thus have some control over the Board of Directors and the appointment of independent auditors, but investment account holders do not. Moreover, in some of the largest Islamic banks, the shareholdings are concentrated in a few hands and the separation of ownership and control barely exists.[3] The non-observability of the accounting calculations made to determine the returns due to the various categories of investor thus becomes a crucial agency problem.[4] This indicates that in an Islamic banking context, there is a potential role for accounting standards (and for auditing) *over and above what is the case for the conventional firm*. In this paper, we wish to argue that such non-observability becomes much less of a problem if known rules are being followed and their correct application is being monitored by independent auditors.

This argument also applies to a second way in which Islamic banks may be affected by agency problems, namely, on the "assets" side if they themselves invest funds on a profit-sharing basis, for example, by providing venture capital by means of a *Musharaka* contract. Here, the bank faces the problem that its investee may fail to report its profits correctly, so that the bank is deprived of its rightful share. This agency problem (of asymmetric information and opportunistic behavior) can be overcome only by the use of accounting, financial reporting, and external auditing procedures of a quality such as to provide the bank with adequate assurance that profits are not being misreported. Such procedures are covered by the term "monitoring" in the agency literature.

In this connection, the German experience of banking and auditing may be relevant, for the following reasons: first, German banks are significant equity investors in German industry (Ordelheide and Pfaff 1994, ch.3); and second, the banks played a leading role in developing the German auditing profession at the end of the last century. The Germans are a people known for their rigor, and this extends to their monitoring procedures. Recognition of the importance of auditing led the Financial Accounting Organization for Islamic Banks and Financial Institutions to change its name in 1995 to the Accounting and Auditing Organisation for Islamic Financial Institutions, so as to include a specific reference to auditing. We would suggest, however, that the development of Islamic banking in the field of business finance will be limited by the asset side agency problem so long as potential investees are unable to offer monitoring of the necessary quality. This is because, although the liabilities side of the banks' balance sheet functions predominantly on a profit-sharing basis, in practice the assets side consists mainly of instruments such as *Murabaha* (cost-plus credit sale) and *Ijara* (leasing) on which the return is calculated in advance. What is at issue on the banks' assets side, then, is not so much the accounting and auditing standards applicable to banks but rather the quality of accounting and auditing of their potential investees.[5]

Corporate Governance

The separation of ownership and control of the corporation and the resultant agency problems raise the issues of the accountability of management for its actions in managing the firm and of the powers over the management of the parties affected by its actions—in other words, corporate governance. In the first place, the internal agency problem discussed above concerns the relations between management and shareholders. The problem of the accountability of top management to shareholders has been the focus of recent discussion of corporate governance issues in the United Kingdom, for example, in the Cadbury Report (Cadbury Committee 1992).

But as we have seen in connection with investment account holders in Islamic banks, such issues are not confined to management-shareholder relations. Nor, indeed, need they be restricted to relations between management and investors or suppliers of capital. In the 1970s, questions were raised concerning the accountability of managers, particularly those of very large firms, to other groups in society liable to be affected by their actions as managers. The rights to financial information of such groups as employees and customers were considered and endorsed in the United Kingdom in *The Corporate Report* (Accounting Standards Steering Committee 1975), as well as in the Canadian study *Corporate Reporting: Its Future Evolution* (Stamp 1980). Likewise, in France during the 1970s, there was considerable interest in the *bilan social*, that is, a social report supplementing the corporate annual report and containing information on the activities of the company from the perspective of "corporate good citizenship." In 1977, the management journal *La Revue Française de Gestion* devoted an entire issue to this topic (see Hulot 1977).

During the 1980s, there was a waning of interest in such ideas, dismissed by some as "corporatist" and obsolete, and an increasing focus on the role of markets and competition in offering protection to groups such as customers. The 1990s literature on corporate governance (e.g., Cadbury 1992; Charkham 1994) refocuses on the management-shareholder relationship and the internal agency problem.

Yet for Islamic banks, as for other businesses for which adherence to specific ethical principles is a central part of their mission, this narrower view of the issues of corporate governance hardly seems appropriate. Logically, the managements of such businesses may be held accountable for their adherence to the ethical principles which they have publicly espoused and which constitute an important part of their "customer and investor appeal"; such adherence then becomes an issue of corporate governance. Thus, the managers of Islamic banks are required to follow *Shari'a* principles, including those of *Amana* (trusteeship). Forbidden forms of transaction (e.g., those involving *riba*, or interest) must be avoided, and measures taken to recover delinquent accounts receivable must follow *Shari'a* guidelines (e.g., if the debtor is deemed insolvent and fails to settle the debt, the creditor should defer collection of the debt until the debtor has become solvent (AAOIFI 1996a)). It follows that issues of corporate governance extend to management's managing the bank in accordance with Islamic principles, and this has implications for the monitoring systems and organs of corporate governance used by Islamic banks, such as the *Shari'a* Supervisory Board (Karim 1995). Some implications for monitoring in the interest of investment account holders are discussed further below.

FINANCIAL ACCOUNTING STANDARDS: DEMAND AND SUPPLY

The objectives of accounting standards are concerned with the amount of information disclosed and the formats used to do so (*disclosure* standards), and also with the accounting methods used to calculate the numbers disclosed (*measurement* standards). Measurement issues comprise those of *recognition* (e.g., of income) and *valuation* (e.g., of assets). The objective of financial accounting standards is to ensure that the provision of financial information by reporting entities meets certain minimum standards of informational quantity and quality. Reporting entities in this context include any organizations which have accounts to render to external stakeholders ("accountees"); in the case of commercial entities, the law generally makes the investors the main accountees.

As mentioned above, the demand for accounting standards is related to the agency problem between management and investors. In certain circumstances, accounting standards (coupled with auditing) may be an efficient method of mitigating the Agency Problem, that is, of reducing agency costs. We wish to argue that these circumstances exist in the case of Islamic banks. In general terms, agency costs consist of the reduction in the value of an investment on account of the investor's perception of the agency problem; alternatively, for an investment of a given value, a higher rate of return would be required. From the Islamic bank's point of view, this means that, other things being equal, a higher return must be offered in order to obtain the investment; otherwise, the investor will invest elsewhere.

Accounting standards are a form of *regulation* of the financial reporting process. As such, they may be provided, at least in part, by self-regulation. It will be clear from the above that Islamic banks, for example, may have an incentive to collaborate in the development and promulgation of accounting standards. However, there may also be limits to what can be achieved by self-regulation. The main reason for believing this is the "market failure" argument. Financial accounting information is published in annual reports which are accessible to any interested party at no cost; they are a "free good." Moreover, a company's or bank's management has a monopoly over the production of this information. In these conditions, the economic forces of supply and demand do not operate so as to result in the production of an appropriate quantity and quality of financial accounting information; there is a strong tendency to underproduce. The existence of this tendency can be seen from the history of financial reporting. For example, prior to the passage of the U.K. 1967 Companies Act, U.K. companies did not publish a sales turnover figure. Moreover, in the case of Islamic banks, hardly any information is disclosed about the bases of profit allocation between shareholders and investment account holders, a lack which prompted AAOIFI to issue in February 1996 an exposure draft on the subject (AAOIFI 1996b).

For this reason, while the supply of financial accounting standards may be left partly to self-regulation, this raises the question of the power of enforcement. Self-regulatory accounting standards bodies have little, if any, power to enforce observance of their standards. The acceptance by the regulatees of the rules proposed by the self-regulatory body, and hence the effectiveness of self-regulation, depend on consensus between the self-regulatory body and regulatees, which the latter will withhold if the former is perceived as "too demanding." For the reasons given above, the consensus levels of the quantity and quality of financial accounting information may tend to be unsatisfactorily low. Hence, it is a field in which regulation by governmental or public sector bodies with enforcement powers may play an important part. On the other hand, a wish to avoid governmental regulation is one incentive for self-regulation. Karim (1990) notes that this was a reason for the setting up of the FAOIBFI in 1991.

SOURCES OF ACCOUNTING STANDARDS

National Accounting Standards

As mentioned earlier, regulation by governmental or public sector bodies is generally an important source of accounting standards. The extent of self-regulation varies considerably from country to country. Self-regulation of accounting is prevalent in the English-speaking countries with their tradition of common law and corresponding lack of a comprehensive commercial code, and less prevalent in the countries of Continental Europe where comprehensive commercial codes and "accounting law" are the norm. In the case of the United Kingdom, France, The Netherlands, and the other member states of the European Community (EU), the broad framework of accounting law is governed by the various Accounting Directives of the EU Commission, which are enacted into national law.

International Accounting Standards

The EU Directives are a form of international accounting standard. Their influence extends beyond the EU member states, for example, to some countries (such as Switzerland) currently outside the EU which are possible future members (Alexander and Archer 1995, ch. 19). At the detailed level, however, they are mainly concerned with disclosure; their requirements with regard to measurement are broad and general, so as to accommodate the significant disparities between the national recognition and valuation rules of the EU member states, into whose law they have to be integrated (Alexander and Archer 1995, ch. 1). Standardization of recognition and valuation rules is impeded, notably, by the fact that in many member states the rules used for financial reporting must be the same as those used for tax purposes, or vice versa. On some important matters, such as currency translation in preparing consolidated accounts, the Directives are silent.

A more comprehensive set of international financial accounting standards is provided by the International Accounting Standards Committee (IASC) through its International Accounting Standards (IASs). These are particularly relevant for the purposes of this paper, as in principle they are entirely voluntary (although some countries such as Malaysia and Pakistan have chosen to give them legal backing for the purpose of national accounting standardization). In other words, the IASC provides an interesting example of how an international accounting standard-setting body for Islamic banks, without enforcement powers, might operate.

After its creation in 1973, the IASC proceeded cautiously by issuing flexible standards. It identified for each area of potential standardization the methods which were generally accepted internationally, and where more than one method was generally accepted internationally, the IAS generally allowed a choice between two methods.[6] But in 1989, the IASC felt that its international influence was sufficiently well established for it to publish ED 32, an Exposure Draft setting out its intentions to narrow down the choice in many areas. For example, the completed contract of accounting for construction work-in-progress was to be eliminated.

In general, and especially in its earlier years, the IASC has paid considerable attention to the accounting methods generally accepted in certain countries which are particularly influential in international accounting. However, more recently it has felt able to act more independently. For example, following ED 32, IAS 22 on Business Combinations was amended so as to disallow the treatment of goodwill most used in the United Kingdom (elimination against shareholders' interest) and to require a 20-year maximum amortization period for goodwill, whereas the U.S. standard allows a 40-year maximum period. The IASC's position on goodwill has certainly influenced the discussion of the proposed new U.K. standard which will cover accounting for goodwill; in particular, it is likely that the new U.K. standard will disallow elimination against shareholders' interest and use 20 years as the maximum amortization period (ASB 1996).

We have gone into these matters in some detail because it is likely that the accounting standard-setting body for Islamic banks, AAOIFI, will find it expedient to take note of the IASC's experience as an international standards setting body without enforcement powers.

ACCOUNTING REGULATION OF BANKS

Banking as a Regulated Industry

Because of the key macroeconomic role of banks with regard to the supply of credit, and the importance of this for monetary and exchange rate policies, as well as the issue of public confidence, banking is a regulated industry. Even in the most liberal politico-economic systems, matters such as banks' liquidity and capital adequacy ratios are subject to regulation by a national central bank or monetary agency. In addition, for signatories to the Basle agreements, national capital adequacy requirements are governed by international rules.

Thus, there exist special reasons for the existence of accounting standards for banks. Regulation of liquidity and capital adequacy requires monitoring of banks' financial statements, which in turn calls for the promulgation and application of appropriate accounting disclosure and measurement rules.

Sources of Accounting Regulation for Banks

For the reasons just given, financial accounting standards for banks are normally set by the national regulator, that is, the central bank or monetary agency. In addition, there exist international standards which predate those set by AAOIFI. In early 1991, the IASC promulgated a disclosure standard, IAS 30, "Disclosures in the Financial Statements of Banks and Similar Financial Institutions." The European Union's Directive 86/635 on the Annual Accounts of Banks and Credit Institutions, which was promulgated in December 1986, is also mainly a disclosure standard, though it includes some measurement rules in Articles 35-39. Unlike IAS 30, which has no mandatory force, Directive 86/635 is mandatory for institutions within the EU which fall under its scope.

It is, however, not necessary to study Directive 86/635 and IAS 30 for very long in order to notice that their application to Islamic banks would be problematic, to say the least. With regard to disclosure, many balance sheet and income statement captions are applicable only to the results of interest-based transactions, while captions applicable to Islamic (non-interest-based) transactions are lacking. For example, how are restricted investment accounts and the related assets to be reported: on or off the balance sheet? So far as measurement is concerned, rules applicable to the results of non-interest-based transactions are absent. For example, profit recognition and asset valuation rules for Islamic finance leasing (*Ijara wa-iqtina*) and cost-plus credit sale (*Bai bithaman ajil* and *Murabaha*) contracts are not provided. Moreover, there is no guidance as to the balance sheet status of unrestricted investment accounts, which are neither equity nor debt in the conventional senses (AAOIFI 1993; Karim 1996).

Accounting Regulation for Islamic Banks

Karim (1996) gives some further reasons why accounting standards developed for secular business organizations are of limited applicability to Islamic banks. These include, in particular, the religious-ethical aspect: conceptually, Western accounting standards are secular in nature and have a limited concern with the ethical perspective. The FASB's conceptual framework project, while placing emphasis on such normative properties of financial information as representational faithfulness and freedom from bias which have ethical connotations for professional accountants and auditors, did not succeed (and perhaps did not try) to provide a basis for accounting standards which reflected moral rights and obligations in the provision of financial accounting information. At most, such information was expected to have "decision-usefulness" for investors and creditors according to a stylized and avowedly incomplete view of how they use such information, on the basis of which it was supposed to have usefulness to other categories of user (FASB 1976a, 1976b, 1978; Archer 1993). At bottom, such an approach is linked to a pluralist as well as a secular view of the social environment of accounting, in which a *caveat lector* (let the reader beware) view of users' rights tends to predominate (Archer 1996). According to Islam, on the other hand, rights and obligations in the provision of financial accounting information are matters to be governed by principles of religious duty, the *Shari'a*, including the duty of trusteeship or *Amana*. However, the implications of *Amana* for the corporate governance of Islamic banks are a matter which calls for further research (see, for example, the case of the bilateral *Mudaraba* discussed below).[7]

This, therefore, is the background to the issuance, in October 1993, by the FAO-IBFI of its Financial Accounting Standard No. 1 (FAST 1), "General Presentation and Disclosure in the Financial Statements of Islamic Banks and Financial Institutions," which becomes effective in 1996. As its title indicates, this is a disclosure standard, and it may in part be regarded as a major adaptation of the IAS 30 approach (as well as of other applicable IASC disclosure standards) in order to meet the needs of Islamic banks. One test of the success of this standard is the extent to which it is reflected in the requirements imposed on Islamic banks by national regulators. For example, a number of central banks are considering reflecting it in their disclosure requirements.

Apart from this, however, numerous accounting measurement issues remain to be dealt with, and it is to some of these that we now turn.[8]

Rules for Profit Recognition in Profit-Sharing

In profit-sharing (i.e., *Mudaraba*) contracts, the rules used for profit recognition affect the returns credited, in respect of such a contract, to investment account holders the duration of whose investment differs from the duration of that contract. Consider, for example, a credit sale contract for an item which the bank acquires for £10,000 and sells on to its customer for £12,000 to be paid in 24 monthly instalments of £500. There are at least five different methods of profit recognition which may be applied (methods 1, 2, 3, and 5 are each used, or have been used, by at least one major Islamic bank):

1. The gross profit of £2,000 is recognized when the customer takes delivery of the item;
2. The gross profit of £2,000 is recognized pro rata of the due dates of the monthly payments, that is, one-sixth or £83.33 of each monthly payment when due is recognized as profit;
3. The gross profit of £2,000 is recognized pro rata of the receipt of the monthly payments, that is, one-sixth or £83.33 of each monthly payment when received is recognized as profit;
4. The gross profit is recognized once the capital of £10,000 has been recovered, that is, the final four payments of £500 are treated as profit; and
5. The gross profit is recognized once all the payments have been received (and the transaction is liquidated).

With methods 1, 4, and 5, an investor who placed money in an investment account for 18 months starting (say) two months after the customer took delivery would receive no share of the profit. With methods 4 and 5, an investor who placed money in an investment account for the last four months of the contract would receive a share of the profit proportionate to the time the funds had been invested (i.e., a 1/6th share).

Revenue and Expense Allocation Rules

As noted above, unrestricted investment account holders share in the income earned by the general pool of the bank's assets, together with the shareholders.

The sharing of income is subject to the specific terms of the *Mudaraba* contract between them and the bank.[9] The unrestricted investment account holders' position as regards profit sharing differs from that of the bank's shareholders in various respects, depending on the particular version of the *Mudaraba* contract implemented by the bank.

The *Mudaraba* may be either unilateral or bilateral. In the former case, the bank does not commingle any of its own funds with those of the investment account holders; this is the approach used, for example, by the Faysal Islamic Bank of Bahrain (Karim 1996). However, most Islamic banks use the bilateral *Mudaraba*, acting both as manager (*Mudarib*) and as provider of funds. In this case, certain expenses may be deemed to be chargeable only against the bank's (i.e., shareholders') share of income, while the bank charges a management fee in respect of its role as *Mudarib* (and may make certain other charges) only against the investment account holders' share.[10]

Thus, in the common case of the bilateral *Mudaraba*, the accounting rules used by the bank may affect profit allocation, not just between investment account holders (depending on the timing of profit recognition, as discussed earlier) but also *between unrestricted investment account holders and shareholders*. Given that the Board of Directors is legally subject to the authority of the shareholders in General Meeting, while the investment account holders possess no such power over the Board, the result is a specific agency problem with regard to unrestricted investment accounts.

In fact, the current accounting practices of Islamic banks which use the bilateral *Mudaraba* exhibit diversity in the attribution of revenues and expenses to the *Mudaraba* fund. While a majority tends to restrict the bilateral *Mudaraba*'s revenues and expenses to those which relate to the fund's assets (thus excluding general overheads as well as revenues from other sources), other banks attribute all their revenues and expenses (except directors' and external auditors' remuneration) to the bilateral *Mudaraba*.[11]

The agency problem just mentioned raises a further set of issues regarding the corporate governance of Islamic banks. For example: How are the interests of unrestricted investment account holders to be represented? What is the role of a bank's *Shari'a* Supervisory Board in that regard?

To some extent, such problems may be mitigated by external regulators or self-regulators. Thus, the AAOIFI's FAST 1 addresses the agency problem of asymmetric information by requiring separate disclosure of: (1) those fund items (assets, revenues, expenses, gains, and losses) pertaining to bilateral *Mudarabas*, that is, commingled funds;[12] and (2) those fund items pertaining to investments consisting *only* of the bank's own funds.

There are, however, other revenue and expense allocation issues including the following:

- Do holders of current accounts receive a small share of the income earned on the general pool of assets?

- What pooling arrangements, in respect of provisions for uncollectible receivables and similar losses, exist between different funds held on behalf of different sets of investment account holders?
- What rules apply to the operation of the Qard Hasan (interest-free loan) fund, especially as regards the practice adopted by some Islamic banks of transferring some of their uncollectible receivables to Qard Hassan?

The problems of asymmetric information and of corporate governance already mentioned need to be considered in the context of a lack of standardization both within and also among Islamic banks, which impedes the development of a market for Islamic investments as well-defined and well-understood financial products. While to some extent variations in income-sharing rules may be used as competitive features (such as allowing current account holders a small income share), too much diversity leads to what Cox (1995, p. 8) described as "a series of isolated contracts with individual banks rather than the development of market accessible products." Moreover, as Osama Mohamed Ali (1995, p. 9) noted, "While internal standardisation is necessary and relevant for almost all sorts of legal documentation...global [interbank] standardisation in the area of [relevant] Islamic rulings (fatwas)...appears as an urgent requirement for Islamic banks, as the divergences with respect to certain definitions and the acceptability parameters of certain financial products are likely to impair the progress of Islamic banking by creating confusion and weakening inter-Islamic bank cooperation, as well as cooperation with other institutions or individuals."

Relationship between Product Standardization and Accounting Standardization

When one reflects on the above, it becomes apparent that there is a two-way relationship between the standardization of Islamic financial products and of the accounting rules applicable in determining the profit and loss shares arising from such products. On the one hand, the choice of accounting rules can significantly affect the profit and loss shares. On the other hand, to devise fairly comprehensive accounting standards for nonstandardized contracts would seem to be a daunting task.

Here, the distinction between measurement and disclosure standards is relevant. Accounting measurement standards presuppose a certain level of standardization of the contracts to which they are to be applied. By contrast, in the absence of (or pending) such standardization, comprehensive disclosure standards may help in choosing between products of a nonstandardized nature, and more generally in decisions regarding relationships with Islamic banks.

As Cox (1995) commented, "Lack of common accounting standards does not assist the banks' endeavors to establish reciprocal relationships with others. Islamic financial institutions' accounts must be comprehensible to outside users so that an Islamic bank's performance over a set period of time can be...judged...and consistent [so as] to generate confidence in the banks themselves."

The AAOIFI has developed accounting standards specifically for application to the three common types of Islamic financing contract: the *Mudaraba*, as described above, which is the normal source of non-shareholder funds for an Islamic bank;[13] the *Musharaka*, a form of joint venture;[14] and the *Murabaha*, or credit sale on a cost-plus basis. These standards address measurement as well as disclosure issues (Karim 1996). However, as noted above, the lack of standardization of these contracts impedes the standardization of accounting measurement.

CONCLUDING REMARKS

The major problem with reliance on disclosure standards in the absence of measurement standards is that of "information overload": the reader needs to refer to detailed information in order to know what accounting methods have been used, and then may face a further onerous task of restating (perhaps on an estimated basis) accounting numbers so as to make meaningful comparisons between banks or over time. Thus, there are limits to the extent to which disclosure standards can deal with agency problems linked to asymmetric information, or with a problem of corporate governance such as the lack of representation of unrestricted investment account holders. As regards the latter, it might however be argued that, given adequate information, they could "vote with their feet" by withdrawing their funds in a way not available to ordinary shareholders; this, indeed, is the reason generally advanced to justify their not having any rights of the kind enjoyed by shareholders. For us, this remains an open issue. In any event, from the standpoint of corporate governance, the potential importance of the monitoring role of a bank's *Shari'a* Supervisory Board in the interests of investment account holders is evident.

As regards the avoidance of information overload, however, the situation could be significantly improved if profit recognition and asset valuation rules were made subject to accounting measurement standards applicable across all contracts of the same type.[15] By contrast, unless the use of standardized contracts in which such *allocation* rules are specified becomes the norm (as urged by Cox [1995]), contractual rules for allocation of revenues and expenses between shareholders and investment account holders are likely to remain primarily an area of individual bank policy and competitive decision, in which case they would need to be dealt with by comprehensive disclosure standards. (As mentioned earlier, the AAOIFI's February 1996 Exposure Draft is concerned with the disclosure of such items.)

Finally, but by no means least, there is the matter of auditing and of attestation to compliance with *Shari'a* principles both in the form and in the implementation of the bank's contracts. When religious deontology makes no distinction between religious and secular spheres of life, one can only admire the wisdom of entrusting the elucidation and application of its principles, in the framing of situation-specific deontological prescriptions, to many qualified scholars of jurisprudence and ethics, rather than to a central dogmatic authority.[16] Accordingly, different bank *Shari'a* Supervisory Boards may take different positions on the permissibility of, and also on the accounting rules applicable to, certain forms of contract. Yet, as already noted, in today's global markets there is a strong call for greater standardization, both of contracts and of accounting rules.

In such a context, the role of consensus-building is likely to be crucial. Moreover, a worthwhile level of standardization may be achieved by means of flexible harmonization, rather than rigid uniformization. In this regard, the example of the IASC, although it operates only at the secular level, may nevertheless be instructive for the international accounting standards body for Islamic banks, the AAOIFI.

The characteristic approach of the IASC in setting its first set of standards was, as described above, to promote harmonization by identifying, in each area of accounting method, a subset of (normally two) accounting methods which were "generally accepted internationally." A choice would then be allowed between these identified methods, others being excluded. In this way, the IASC was able to build up its authority while avoiding the risk of trying and failing to exclude methods which had considerable international support. To some extent, this was a political process: "generally accepted internationally" was generally interpreted to mean acceptance by the national accounting standards of the most influential countries and use by leading multinational corporations, especially those based in such countries. In a second phase, with the benefit of established authority, the IASC has sought to promote a further stage of harmonization by eliminating some previously permitted methods and identifying a preferred method and an alternative (less preferred) method among those still permitted.

In the case of the AAOIFI, bearing in mind the foregoing discussion, a similar two-stage process might be envisaged. Moreover, the following criteria might be relevant in drafting its standards:

- Existing accepted practices in key countries and institutions;
- The views of banking regulators in key countries, whose choice to implement a given AAOIFI standard for Islamic banks will be important for its general acceptance;
- Economic consequences for investors (e.g., effects on the calculation of their returns) and for banks (e.g., effects on capital adequacy measures); and
- Implications for audit and for attestation of Shari'a compliance.

Indeed, it is apparent that such considerations have influenced both the structure and composition of the AAOIFI's own organs of governance, and its "due process" (Karim 1995).

This paper has endeavored to indicate the role which a set of international accounting standards for Islamic banks may play in facilitating the corporate governance of Islamic banks as well as promoting the success of the Islamic banking movement, and also the challenges raised by such standard-setting. Given the creation of, and the approach taken by, the AAOIFI there are grounds for hope that this important challenge is being taken up in a manner that will prove fruitful.

ACKNOWLEDGMENT

The views expressed in this paper are those of the authors and do not necessarily represent those of the named institutions or of any other organizations.

NOTES

1. An Islamic Bank is a financial institution which receives funds and invests them on the basis of the principles of Islamic *Shari'a*. These principles require that: (1) the funds be invested in *Halal* (i.e., Islamically acceptable) investments; this excludes, inter alia, businesses concerned with the production or sale of alcohol or pork; and (2) that funds are received and invested only on the basis of contracts which exclude the receipt or payment of interest.

2. An important difference between the situation of an Islamic bank and a non-Islamic financial institution acting as a manager of ethical mutual funds is that the *Mudaraba* (even in the case of restricted investment accounts) is not organized as a legal entity separate from the bank. Instead, a *Mudaraba* consists of the contractual relationship between the bank and those of its clients who have invested under the terms of that *Mudaraba* contract. As such, it has no separate legal existence from the bank and no separate financial statements or audit. Another difference is that, as the manager of a *Mudaraba* fund, the *Murarib* is remunerated by a share of the income of the fund, receiving no remuneration if the income is zero or negative. By contrast, the manager of a conventional investment fund is normally remunerated by a flat-rate management fee (e.g., a percentage of the value of the assets under management). The basis of remuneration of the bank as *Mudarib* raises specific agency issues; for example, the fact that the *Mudarib's* share of the fund income has a lower bound of zero may lead to a conflict of interests, as the *Mudarib* would tend to be less risk-averse than the investors in the *Mudaraba*. There are also the implications for accounting that are discussed in the text.

3. For example, the Al Rajhi Corporation for Banking and Investment and the Albaraka Group.

4. In principle, regulation might give investment account holders the right to request detailed calculations of their shares of profits. But such regulation is absent in those countries (the Middle Eastern countries, Malaysia, Pakistan) of whose regulations we are aware.

5. The existence of this asset-side agency problem for Islamic banks is begining to be recognized in the professional literature. For example:

> Experience has shown that attracting deposits is not the greatest challenge to any new entrant into Islamic banking....Rather, finding good investment opportunities that are acceptable from the Shari'a point of view is the real hurdle for fast growth (Elgari 1996).
>
> Mudaraba and Musharaka financing are not popular with the BIMB (Bank Islam Malaysia Berhad) for the following three main reasons. a. There is a lack of honest and trustworthy entrepreneurs. *BIMB has been cheated by its customers [i.e., investees]* (Al-Harran 1996, emphasis added).

6. For example, IAS 11 allowed a choice between the percentage of completion and the completed contract methods of accounting for construction contract work-in-process (WIP). Likewise, IAS

12 allowed a choice between the full provision and partial provision methods of recognition for deferred tax, and the liability and deferral methods of valuation.

7. As noted in Archer (1997, pp. 235-236):

> It is understandable that [Western] standard-setting organizations continue to feel the need for some body of theory on which to ground their prescriptions. Yet what they come up with is statements of normative accounting theory (NAT), which beg the question as to their own authoritative character. To be sure, statements of accounting standards are essentially normative, in that, as well as being prescriptions, they embody value judgements as to what methods of accounting are desirable. However, a characteristic of NAT has been a failure to spell out adequately the criteria in the light of which the value judgements as to the desirability of accounting methods are to be made....[A]ccounting standards are liable to have economic consequences, and NAT by its nature has treated such consequences as externalities.

On the other hand, with regard to certain aspects of corporate governance and auditing, *compliance with Islamic Shari'a* raises issues that are analogous to compliance issues in the case of ethical investment funds generally: is management complying with the stipulated ethical criteria, and what assurance do investors receive regarding such compliance?

8. The issues of accounting measurement raised by Islamic methods of finance may be considered in the broader context of the great diversity of financial instruments now available, some of which are complex in nature and do not fit easily into traditional accounting categories. The specific problem faced by Islamic banks, however, is that many of the accounting issues raised by Islamic financial instruments are not addressed by standard-setting activities concerned with accounting for non-Islamic financial instruments, such as derivatives or hybrid instruments. For example, a *Mudaraba* is neither a derivative nor (at least in the usual sense) a hybrid instrument; a *Musharaka* differs from a conventional partnership or joint venture (e.g., in respect of rules for profit-and-loss sharing); and a *Murabaha* differs from a conventional credit-sale transaction. Consequently, the accounting issues raised by Islamic methods of financing have motivated the creation of a specialized international accounting standard-setting body for Islamic financial institutions (AAOIFI).

9. This is generally known as a "collective *Mudaraba*," to distinguish it from the single-venture *Mudaraba* with which the contractual form originated in medieval times (Karim 1996). The single-venture *Mudaraba* was the same as the *commenda* used by medieval Italian merchants (see Bryer 1993).

10. According to Islamic *Shari'a*, the *Mudarib's* management fee must be a contractually pre-agreed share of the profit on the invested funds (in case of loss, the fee is zero), but some Islamic banks state in their *Mudaraba* contracts that the bank as *Mudarib* may, at its sole discretion, waive part of its share of profit in favor of the investment account holders.

11. However, it should be noted that in a bilateral *Mudaraba*, the bank as *investor* receives all of the profit (or suffers all of the loss) attributable to its share of the fund, while participating as *Mudarib* in the profit (but not in a loss) attributable to the investment account holders' share (in the case of a loss, the *Mudarib*'s share is zero) (Karim 1994, 1996).

12. As noted above, commingling also occurs in the case of unrestricted investment accounts, since the investment account holders' funds are invested in the same pool of assets as the bank's (shareholders') own funds. There are, thus, two forms or directions of commingling: that which occurs in the case of bilateral *Mudarabas*, and that which takes place in connection with unrestricted investment accounts. Finally, it is worth noting that, even in the case of *Mudarabas* that are in principle restricted and are marketed as such, the bank may reserve the right to invest the funds elsewhere at its discretion.

13. The scope of the existing standard is limited to the relationship between the bank as provider of funds and the client as entrepreneur (*Mudarib*), that is, the assets side of the bank's balance sheet.

14. This form of joint venture has the particularity that profits are shared according to a pre-agreed ratio which may differ from the ratio of equity participation, but losses are shared *pro-rata* to equity participation.

15. As noted above, the AAOIFI has recently issued accounting standards for the three most common types of contract.

16. The practice of a form of *hermeneutics* (interpretive ethical reasoning from revealed religious texts), a form which we might perhaps term *jurisprudential hermeneutics*, has been part of Islam (especially in the Hanafi tradition) since medieval times (see, e.g., Udovitch 1970, ch. III). By contrast, hermeneutics barely affected Christian thinking until the nineteenth century.

REFERENCES

Accounting and Auditing Organisation for Islamic Financial Institutions. 1993. *Financial Accounting Standard No. 1: General Presentation and Disclosure in the Financial Statements of Islamic Banks and Financial Institutions.* Manama, Bahrain: AAOIFI.

Accounting and Auditing Organisation for Islamic Financial Institutions. 1996a. *Financial Accounting Standard No. 2: Murabaha and Murabaha to the Purchase Orderer. Manama, Bahrain: AAOIFI.*

Accounting and Auditing Organisation for Islamic Financial Institutions. 1996b. Financial Accounting Standard No. 5: Disclosure of the Bases for Profit Allocation Between Owners' Equity and Investment Account Holders. Manama, Bahrain: AAOIFI.

Accounting Standards Board. 1996. *Goodwill and Intangible Assets.* FRED 12. London: ASB.

Accounting Standards Steering Committee. 1975. *The Corporate Report.* London: Institute of Chartered Accountants.

Alexander, D., and S. Archer, eds. 1995. *The European Accounting Guide*, 2nd edition. New York: Harcourt Brace & Company.

Al-Harran, S. 1996. Islamic finance needs a new paradigm. *New Horizon* 48(February): 7-9.

Archer, S. 1993. On the methodology of constructing a conceptual framework for financial accounting. In *Philosophical Perspectives on Accounting: Essays in Honour of Edward Stamp*, eds. M.J. Mumford and K.V. Peasnell. London: Routledge. 62-122.

Archer, S. 1996. The ethics of creative accounting. *Science and Engineering Ethics* 2(1), pp. 55-70.

Archer, S. 1977. The ASB's draft statement of principles: A comment. *Accounting and Business Research* 27(107, Summer): 229-241.

Bryer, R.A. 1993. Double-entry bookkeeping and the birth of capitalism: Accounting for the commercial revolution in medieval northern Italy. *Critical Perspectives on Accounting* 4: 113-140.

Cadbury Committee, The. 1992. *The Cadbury Committee Report: Financial Aspects of Corporate Governance.* London: Burgess Science Press.

Charkham, J. 1994. *Keeping Good Company: A Study of Corporate Governance in Five Countries.* Oxford, UK: Clarendon Press.

Cox, S. 1995. Research and development for Islamic banks. *New Horizon*, 42(August): 5-8.

Elgari, M.A. 1996. Islamic banking: Brought to you by Non-Islamic banks! *New Horizon* 48(February): 3.

European Communities. 1986. *Annual Accounts and Consolidated Accounts of Banks and Other Financial Institutions.* Council Directive 86/635.

Financial Accounting Standards Board. 1976a. *Tentative Conclusions on Objectives of Financial Statements of Business Enterprises* Stamford, CT: FASB.

Financial Accounting Standards Board. 1976b. *Scope and Implications of the Conceptual Framework Project.* Stamford, CT: FASB.

Financial Accounting Standards Board. 1978. *Statement of Financial Accounting Concepts No. 1: Objectives of Financial Reporting by Business Enterprises.* Stamford, CT: FASB.

Hulot, J-P. 1977. Au dela du bilan social, un système de gestion: la démarche d'entreprise et progrès et l'expérience de Roussel-Uclaf. (Beyond the social accounting report, a management system: the initiative of 'enterprise and progress' and the experience of Ronssel-McLaf) *La Revue Française de Gestion* (November-December).

International Accounting Standards Board. 1991. *IAS 30:Disclosures in the Financial Statements of Banks and Similar Financial Institutions.* London: IASC.

Karim, R.A.A. 1990. Standard setting for the financial reporting of religious business organisations: The case of Islamic banks. *Accounting and Business Research* 20(80): 299-305.

Karim, R.A.A. 1994. Accounting aspects of profits allocation methods between shareholders and investment account holders in Islamic banks. *Journal of Economic and Administrative Science* 10: 33-44.

Karim, R.A.A. 1995. The nature and rationale of a conceptual framework for financial reporting by Islamic banks. *Accounting and Business Research* 25(100, Autumn): 285-300.

Karim, R.A.A. 1996. Economic consequences of accounting standards and Islamic banks. Working paper.

Ordelheide, D., and D. Pfaff. 1994. *European Financial Reporting: Germany.* London: Routledge.

Osama, M.A. 1995. The Development of Standard Legal Documentation for Islamic Banks. *New Horizon* 41(July): 9-12.

Stamp, E. 1980. *Corporate Reporting: Its Future Evolution.* Toronto: Canadian Institute of Chartered Accountants.

Udovitch, A.L. 1970. *Partnership and Profit in Medieval Islam.* Princeton, NJ: Princeton University Press.

THE ROLE OF THE CODE OF ETHICS FOR THE INTERNAL AUDITING PROFESSION:

AN INTERNATIONAL PERSPECTIVE

Philip H. Siegel, Khursheed Omer, and Khondkar E. Karim

ABSTRACT

The purpose of this study was to compare the impacts of cultural background on the understanding of the Code of Ethics in the internal audit profession in three different regions of the world (United States., Canada, and the Pacific rim countries). Although respondents of all three groups strongly support the Code of Ethics, cultural influences are evident in the responses.

Research in Accounting Regulation, Supplement 1, pages 115-127.

ISBN: 0-7623-0338-7

INTRODUCTION

The purpose of this study is to compare the reaction of internal auditors in different international regions to the Code of Ethics for the internal auditing profession. This study extends the work of earlier research on the Code of Ethics for internal auditors in this area which was restricted to the perceptions of internal auditors from a single country, that is, the United States (Loeb 1984; O'Shaughnessy et al. 1993; Siegel et al. 1995)

Recent international business scandals such as those involving the Bank of Credit and Commerce International (BCCI), Banco di Lavorno, Banco Ambrosiano, Alan Bond, Carrian, and Pan-Electric have brought attention to the need for research on the ethical perceptions of the accounting professionals in different areas of the world (see, e.g., Finn et al. 1988; Poneman 1990, 1992; Arnold and Poneman 1991; Coppage 1992; Cohen et al. 1993a, 1995; Shaub et al. 1993; Poneman and Gabhart 1993; Macintosh 1995). However, this literature does not consider whether differences exist among internal auditors from different world regions.[1]

NATURE OF THE PROBLEM

All types of auditors must have credibility in order to claim objectivity. Credibility is a critical characteristic in establishing importance of the internal auditor's services in an organization. Development of the Internal Auditors' Code of Ethics was an important step toward establishing credibility for internal auditors (Siegel et al. 1995).

Certified Professional Auditors working in corporate environment face enormous pressures. They are responsible for assuring that top management policies are carried out, while at the same time being bound by the ethical standards of their profession. Arnold and Poneman (1991) indicated that there is always a potential for conflict between corporate goals and the internal auditor's professional obligations. Internal auditors often find themselves in situations where they are under pressure to compromise between their ethical standards and the perceived needs of the corporation.

Bollom (1988) suggests two integrated steps in implementing ethical behavior codes in a profession. The first step is to emphasize ethical behavior through a combination of family and formal education. Family education indeed plays an important role in laying down the precursors of adult ethical practice in the early stages of character formation. Formal education is nevertheless necessary for ethical preparation of persons pursuing professional careers (Piper et al. 1993). The second step in implementing ethical behavior codes in a profession is to aggressively seek out and punish unethical behavior.

An important question relating to implementation of ethical codes is the proper strategy to be utilized for ensuring compliance by the members of the profession.

Cohen and Pant (1991) evaluated the relative effectiveness of self-regulatory and externally imposed implementation methods and found the self-regulatory method to be more effective. Siegel et al. (1995), however, found that in the absence of government licensing, self-regulation may not ensure enforcement of the Code of Ethics on the internal auditor.

The globalization of the world economy has created a need for the internal audit profession to understand and integrate general implementation strategies and diverse cultural norms into a unified process for ensuring effective implementation of the Internal Auditors' Code of Ethics internationally. To achieve this goal, it is essential that the relationship between culture and ethical values be clearly understood (Cohen et al. 1993b).

There is little disagreement on broad ethical standards across cultures. However, the cultural differences seem to play an important role in how the ethical standards are implemented and how violations of ethical standards are perceived. In other words, proper strategy for implementing ethical standards is a key to achieving the ethical goals aspired by a profession (Ryan 1992).

LITERATURE REVIEW

Poneman and Gabhart (1993) compared ethical decision making and reasoning of U.S. and Canadian auditors and found that Canadian auditors demonstrated a higher level of ethical reasoning than their American counterparts. Poneman and Gabhart (1993) attributed this difference to divergent socialization processes in these countries. These results were surprising since both Hofstede (1980) and Ronen and Shenkar (1985) had reported that the United States and Canada have similar cultures.

Agacer and Doupnik (1991) reported that there were cultural differences among external auditors from the United States, the Philippines, and Germany in their perceptions of "independence." Karnes et al. (1989) investigated the ethical perceptions of U.S. and Taiwanese external auditors. They identified a perceptual dimension for ethical evaluation of illegal acts and the effect of the action on the individual. They found that the concern of the U.S. auditors about illegal acts and the ensuing effects was driven by high individualism whereas the concern of Taiwanese auditors was driven by collectivist Confucian values.

Schultz et al. (1993) studied the perceptions of accounting professionals from France, Norway, and the United States to determine if there were any cultural differences among the accounting professionals' likelihood of reporting questionable actions of the supervisor. They reported that the likelihood of reporting questionable actions by the supervisor is a function of the professional's national origin.

Lampe and Sutton (1992) examined the effect of cross-cultural forces on the ability of external auditors to achieve quality in performing audits. They found differences based on language (English versus non-English), culture (Western versus Eastern), and stage of economic development (developed versus underdeveloped).

Hofstede (1980) defines culture as the collective view of individuals living in a particular society. Culture both provides the cognitive premises for individuals within a group and sets preconditions for human behavior. Ueno and Wu (1993) indicate that culture consists of numerous elements including beliefs, attitudes, values, and norms. These cultural elements influence the behavior and response of people toward an ethical code or standard.

Siegel et al. (1995) and O'Shaughnessy et al. (1993) focused their attention on internal auditors as they sought to study the internal auditors' perception of the Internal Auditor's Code of ethics. As indicated elsewhere, these studies were restricted to the United States. In order to shed light on possible effects of cultural differences, a questionnaire adapted from Siegel et al. (1995) was sent to 420 certified internal auditors in the United States, Canada, and Hong Kong, Singapore, and Taiwan (herein, the "Pacific Rim group," or PRG) randomly selected from the official directory of the Institute of Internal Auditors (IIA).

THE QUESTIONNAIRE

The questionnaire used in Siegel et al. (1995) was sent to certified internal auditors in the United States, Canada, Hong Kong, Singapore, and Taiwan randomly selected from the official directory of the Institute of Internal Auditors.[2] The questionnaire consisted of nine questions.[3] The objective of the first question was to ascertain the perception of respondents as to the primary purpose of the Code of Ethics and to determine if there were any differences in that perception across regions. One of the most compelling reasons for a code of ethics is to ensure that the profession conducts all of its relationships with government, the public, and its own members in congruence with the ethics which any society must follow to maintain harmony among its constituents (Benson 1989).

It is, therefore, important to know how internal auditors perceive the primary purpose of the Code of Ethics if proper implementation strategies are to be devised to ensure compliance and to have adequate procedures in plans to deal with violations of the Code of Ethics.

A precondition for successful implementation of a code of ethics is that the members of the group covered by the code should consider the code to be useful (Arrow 1973). The concept of usefulness, however, is a value-based concept and is subject to interpretation by individuals or groups depending upon their backgrounds and exposure.[4] The second question was, therefore, aimed at determining the extent to which the responding groups considered the Code of Ethics to be useful.

Webley (1988) developed a manual on behalf of the Institute of Business Ethics in London and found that an important purpose of a code of ethics was to help individuals resolve ethical dilemmas. The purpose of the third question was, therefore, to ascertain the frequency with which internal auditors in each group find it necessary to use the Code of Ethics in the course of performing their responsibilities. It seems logical that internal auditors would refer to the Code of Ethics when they encounter ethical dilemmas.

The fourth question sought to determine what is the perception of the respondents concerning the completeness of the Code of Ethics in terms of coverage and specificity. The perception of completeness is crucial because if the Code is perceived to be incomplete, compliance with the Code would fail to accomplish the intended goal of providing guidance to the internal auditors when they face ethical dilemmas.

Closely related to the perception of completeness is the perception of enforceability. The effectiveness of a code is seriously jeopardized if the individuals who are covered by the code do not believe that the code is enforceable (Ryan 1992). Accordingly, the fifth question asked the respondents to indicate if they thought the Code of Ethics was enforceable.

Questions 6-9 dealt with the issue of effective implementation strategies for the Internal Auditors Code of Ethics. Self-regulation in a profession can mean self-regulation at a collective professional level, thereby excluding the possibility of a government agency regulating the profession. Conversely, self-regulation can be implemented at the individual level where the collective professional body simply establishes general guidelines of a code of ethics and individuals monitor their own conduct (Bollom 1988).

Question 6 queried the respondents as to whether they agreed with the former interpretation of self-regulation giving the authority for disciplining violators to the Institute of Internal Auditors. The seventh question was aimed at determining respondents' opinions about whether or not the Code of Ethics would have more impact if the names of Code violators were published in a national journal. The eighth and ninth questions were designed to determine the attitude of respondents toward the legal and moral responsibility of the internal auditors to report violations of the ethical code. Questions 8 and 9 also concerned the legal responsibility for reporting ethical violations to outsiders such as external auditors, regulatory agencies, or legal authorities.

RESULTS OF THE STUDY

A total of 240 responses were received, yielding a response rate of 57%.[5] Out of the total, 70 respondents were from the United States, 90 from Canada, and 80 from the PRG. Tables 1-9 summarize the responses to the questions asked.

There was agreement among the groups that the primary purpose of the Code was to provide guidance when ethical dilemmas were encountered (Table 1). In the case of Americans, an overwhelming majority (64%) indicated that guidance in ethical dilemmas was the primary purpose of the Code of Ethics. However, 52.5% of the PRG and only 41% of the Canadian respondents indicated guidance in ethical dilemmas as the primary purpose of the Code. The response of the

Table 1. Perceived Purpose of the Internal Auditors' Code of Ethics

Question: Which of the following would you consider the primary reason for the Code of Ethics?
- *a. To serve as guidance in situations requiring ethical judgment*
- *b. To enhance the public's perception of the Certified Internal Auditor*
- *c. To serve as a reminder of what ethical conduct should be to maintain certification*
- *d. None of the above.*

Regions	*Guidance*	*Perception*	*Reminder*	*None*
U.S.A.	45 (64%)	11 (16%)	10 (14%)	4 (6%)*
Canada	37 (41%)	16 (18%)	36 (40%)	1 (1%)*
PRG	42 (52.5%)	28 (35%)	8 (10%)	2 (2.5%)*

Note: *Percentages have been rounded.

Americans was closer to that of members of the PRG than to the Canadians, which shows a difference in the way the three groups perceive the purpose of the Code of Ethics.

An almost equal proportion of American (16%) and Canadian (18%) respondents indicated that the primary purpose of the Code of Ethics was enhancement of the public perception of the certified internal auditors. The percentage of respondents, however, was much higher (35%) among internal auditors in the PRG.

The Canadian respondents had the highest proportion (40%) among those who felt that the primary purpose of the Code was to serve as a reminder of the ethical conduct that needs to be maintained for certification. Only 14% of American and 10% of PRG respondents held that view. An explanation for these responses can be found in Ueno and Wu (1993), who pointed out that individuals in more collective environments would tend to seek public approval more than individuals in more individualistic societies. Although Canada is not a collective society, its political and economic systems are more centrally administered than the United States.

A vast majority of respondents from the three groups found the Code of Ethics to be at least useful (Table 2). Only 9% of the Americans, 14% of Canadians, and 16% of the respondents in PRG thought that the Code was highly useful. A combined 86% of the Americans, 70% of Canadians, and 80% of the PRG consider the Code to be quite useful or useful.

The responses show that the U.S. respondents view the Code to be somewhat less useful than do the other two groups. While 67% of PRG and 49% of Canadians thought that the Code was quite useful, only 37% among the Americans shared that view. However, the situation was reversed in the case of the third quesion, where 49% of the Americans, 21% of the Canadians, and 13% of the PRG indicated that the Code was useful.

These results are consistent with the explanation by Ueno and Wu (1993) and others (such as Schultz et al. 1993; Lampe and Sutton 1992; Poneman and Gabhart

Table 2. Perceived Usefulness of the Internal Auditors' Code of Ethics

Question: How useful have you found the Code of Ethics?

Regions	*Highly Useful*	*Quite Useful*	*Useful*	*Not Very Useful*	*Not at All Useful*
U.S.A.	4 (9%)	17 (37%)	23 (49%)	2 (4%)	1 (1%)*
Canada	10 (14%)	35 (49%)	15 (21%)	10 (14%)	2 (2%)*
PRG	12 (16%)	50 (67%)	10 (13%)	3 (4%)*	0

Note: *Percentages have been rounded.

Table 3. Frequency of Use of the Internal Auditors' Code of Ethics

Question: Has the opportunity arisen to refer to the Code of Ethics?

Regions	*Yes*	*No*
U.S.A.	41 (59%)	29 (41%)*
Canada	38 (42%)	52 (58%)*
PRG	50 (52.5%)	30 (47.5%)*

Note: *Percentages have been rounded.

1993; Wagner and Mock 1986) who have shown that cultural influences play an important role in ethical perceptions. In this case, the results indicate that the more individual-based a culture is, the less likely is the reliance on codes for ethical behavior.

Responses to the third question indicate that 59% of the Americans, 42% of the Canadians, and 52.5% of the PRG respondents had encountered situations where they found it necessary to refer to the Code (Table 3). The American internal auditors differed from the Canadians and the PRG. They had a significantly higher reference rate as compared to their Canadian counterparts. The difference in the reference rate between the Americans and the PRG was, however, not as high.

The difference between the Americans and Canadians was surprisingly large in view of the fact that the two cultures are generally regarded as similar. It should, however, be pointed out that Poneman and Gabhart (1993) reported similar differences between Americans and Canadians in their study of external auditors. They attributed these differences to the variations in the socialization process in these countries.

Countries such as those in the PRG are known to have collective rather than individualistic cultures, which usually grant little autonomy to individuals (Ueno and Wu 1993). The small difference between Americans and the members of PRG, therefore, is also unexpected.

All of the respondents agreed that the Code of Ethics was complete (Table 4). However, there were differences in the degree of agreement among the groups.

Table 4. Perception of Completeness of the Internal Auditors' Code of Ethics

Question: Is the Code of Ethic complete?

Regions	*Yes*	*No*
U.S.A.	61 (92%)	5 (8%)*
Canada	71 (79%)	19 (21%)*
PRG	58 (72.5%)	22 (27.5%)*

Note: *Percentages have been rounded.

Table 5. Perception of Enforceability of the Internal Auditors' Code of Ethics

Question: Is the professional code of ethics enforceable?

Regions	*Yes*	*No*
U.S.A.	43 (65%)	23 (35%)*
Canada	65 (73%)	24 (27%)*
PRG	65 (81%)	15 (19%)*

Note: *Percentages have been rounded.

Table 6. Desirability of Disciplining Violators of the Code of Ethics

Question: Since it is a voluntary organization, in the past the IIA has only disciplined a limited number of members; it has depended instead more upon individual members regulating themselves. In recent years, the IIA has increased its disciplinary action against members. Should the IIA be more active in disciplining members for violating the Code of Ethics when such violations come to their attention?

Regions	*Yes*	*No*
U.S.A.	57 (88%)	8 (12%)*
Canada	80 (81%)	8 (9%)*
PRG	60 (75%)	20 (25%)*

Note: *Percentages have been rounded.

The respondents from United States had a higher agreement rate (92%) than their counterparts in the other two groups (79% for Canadians and 72.5% for PRG). Cultural influence is once again reflected in the pattern of responses. If completeness is interpreted as referring to specificity, then the results indicate that the more individualistic a culture is, the more comfortable they are with less specificity.

Respondents in the three groups overwhelmingly expressed the belief that the Code of Ethics was enforceable (Table 5). These results are consistent with the

Table 7. Desirability of Publishing Names of the Violators of the Code of Ethics

Question: Would the Code of Ethics have more impact if the names of violators were published in a national journal?

Regions	*Yes*	*No*
United States	46 (69%)	21 (31%)*
Canada	72 (80%)	18 (20%)*
PRG	70 (87.5%)	10 (12.5%)*

Note: *Percentages have been rounded.

Table 8. Legal Responsibility for Reporting Violators of the Code of Ethics

Question: Suppose the internal auditor becomes aware of serious ethical violations within their firms, e.g. environmental pollution, and also learns that top management and the board of directors are knowingly not doing anything to correct the situation. Does the internal auditor under these circumstances have the legal responsibility to report such violations to outsiders, e.g., external auditors, regulatory agencies, etc.

Regions	*Yes*	*No*
U.S.A	24 (36%)	42 (64%)*
Canada	35 (39%)	55 (61%)*
PRG	43 (54%)	37 (46%)*

Note: *Percentages have been rounded.

conclusion reached by Cohen et al. (1993a) that members of the accounting profession consider self-regulation to be more effective than externally imposed standards.

Among the three groups, the PRG had the highest percentage of respondents (81%) indicating that the Code was enforceable. These results further reflect the cultural dimension of collectivism, which emphasizes conformity and consensus (Wagner and Mock 1986). The Canadians had a higher percentage of respondents agreeing with the enforceability of the Code (73%) than the American respondents (65%). This difference once again could be the result of disparate socialization process in the two countries.

There was a strong preference among the respondents in all of the groups for the Institute of Internal Auditors to discipline members who violate the Code (Table 6). In this case, the three groups are relatively closer to each other, as 80% of the Americans, 81% of the Canadians, and 75% of the PRG gave a positive response to the question. As noted earlier, this shows that self-regulation is considered an effective way of ensuring the integrity of the profession among all the cultural groups studied.

Table 9. Moral Responsibility for Reporting Violators of the Code of Ethics

Question: Does the internal auditor have the moral responsibility to report such violations to outsiders, e.g. external auditors, regulatory agencies etc.?

Regions	*Yes*	*No*
U.S.A	62 (91%)	6 (9%)*
Canada	72 (80%)	18 (20%)*
PRG	55 (69%)	25 (31%)*

Note: *Percentages have been rounded.

A majority in all groups (69% Americans, 80% Canadians, and 87.5% PRG) indicated that publishing the names of violators will strengthen the impact of the Code of Ethics (Table 7). These results once again show the preference of self-regulation among the three groups. It is, however, somewhat surprising that the Americans have the lowest percentage of respondents agreeing to the proposition of publishing the names of violators in view of the fact that professional self-regulation is a firmly established concept among professional groups.

The response to the question about the legal responsibility of CIAs to report ethical violations to outsiders such as external auditors, regulatory agencies, or legal authorities was subdued (Table 8). A larger percentage of respondents in the PRG (54%) indicated that they had the legal responsibility to report ethical violations as compared to 39% of the Canadian respondents and only 36% of the American respondents. A possible explanation for these results is that individuals in more collective cultures tend to be more concerned with group acceptance and attendant legal responsibility (Kelley et al. 1987).

The pattern of responses to the question about moral responsibility to report ethical violations (Table 9) was the exact opposite of the responses to the earlier question. An overwhelming majority of the Americans (91%) agreed that they had the moral responsibility to report ethical violations. The corresponding percentages for the Canadian and PRG respondents were 80% and 69%, respectively. The results are consistent with the idea that individualistic cultures emphasize the role of individuals and rely more heavily on their personal sense of responsibility for proper functioning of the societal institutions.

SUMMARY AND CONCLUSION

Establishing and enforcing strong codes of ethics is important because they can substantially increase ethical awareness of the members of an organization (Woelfel 1986). Raising ethical awareness encourages individuals to behave in a responsible manner and reduces the need for more external regulations.

Similar to the findings of Siegel et al. (1995), the results of this study indicate that respondents in all three groups support a strong role for the Internal Auditors' Code of Ethics. The influence of cultural background can be discerned from the pattern of responses to different questions. The cultural dimension of informal-traditional societies appeared to be a significant factor in explaining differences in responses to the ethical code.

A sizeable majority of Americans and respondents from the PRG feel that the primary purpose of the Code is to provide guidance when the internal auditor is faced with an ethical dilemma. The Canadians, however, are split equally between guidance in ethical dilemmas and reminder of the conduct needed to maintain certification as the primary purpose of the Code. The results also indicated extensive use of the Code of Ethics. Among the three groups, respondents in the PRG appeared to place greater emphasis on the Code than did those in the other two groups.

A majority of the respondents consider the Code to be enforceable. The PRG in particular believe that the IIA should be more active in implementing the Code. Tidrick (1992) reported that the CIAs in general think that the IIA has significant ability to enforce the Code. In fact, the IIA has taken an active role in the self-regulation efforts of the CIAs in the United States. However, there is a need to incorporate cultural consideration in devising implementation strategies beyond U.S. borders. The response and approach to the ethical code reflects to some degree the culture in which it is operating. Therefore, policymakers, regulators, and managers should be aware of the cultural characterics of each system and prepare for potential differences in response from those within these systems.

NOTES

1. The exception is the work of Cohen et al. (1993a, 1993b, 1995), which emphasized the cross-cultural dimension.
2. Since the number of respondents in Hong Kong, Singapore, and Taiwan was small, respondents from these countries were grouped in one category referred to as FEC (Far Eastern Countries). It should also be noted that the Institute of Internal Auditors in the United States recently extended its Code of Ethics to these countries. Canada was also included based on the research results of Ponemon and Gabhart (1993).
3. Each question asked in the questionnaire is reproduced at the beginning of respective tables.
4. See Chewning (1984) for a discussion of how different backgrounds influence the concept of usefulness in an ethical context.
5. It should be noted that some of the respondents did not answer all of the nine questions asked.

REFERENCES

Agacer, G., and T. Doupnik. 1991. Perceptions of auditor independence: A cross-cultural study. *The International Journal of Accounting 26*: 220-237.

Arnold, D., Sr., and L. Poneman. 1991. Internal auditors' perceptions of whistle blowing and the influence of moral reasoning: An experiment. *Auditing: A Journal of Practice and Theory* (Fall): 1-15.

Arrow, K. 1973. Business codes and economic efficiency. *Public Policy* 21(Summer).

Benson, G. 1989. *Codes of Ethics: Business and Government*. Claremont, CA: The Henry Salvatori Center.

Bollom, W. 1988. Ethics and self-regulation for CPAs in the U.S.A. *Journal of Business Ethics* 7: 55 61.

Chewning, R. 1984. *Business Ethics in A Changing Culture*. Reston, VA.: Reston Publishing.

Cohen, J., and L. Pant. 1991. Beyond bean counting: Establishing high ethical standards in the public accounting profession. *Journal of Business Ethics* 10: 45-56.

Cohen, J., L. Pant, and D. Sharp. 1993a. A validation and extension of a multidimensional ethics scale. *Journal of Business Ethics* 12: 13-26.

Cohen, J., L. Pant, and D. Sharp. 1993b. Culture-based ethical conflicts confronting multinational accounting firms. *Accounting Horizons* 7: 1-13.

Cohen, J., L. Pant, and D. Sharp. 1995. An exploratory examination of international differences in auditors' ethical perceptions. *Behavioral Research in Accounting* 7: 37-64.

Coppage, R. 1992. Supervision: A significant dimension of ethics for management accountants. In *Advances in Management Accounting*, Vol. 1, 231-242. Greenwich, CT: JAI Press.

Finn, D., L. Chonko, and S. Hunt. 1988. Ethical problems in public accounting: A view from the top. *Journal of Business Ethics* 7: 605-615.

Hofstede, G. 1980. *Culture's Consequences: International Differences in Work-Related Values*. Beverly Hills, CA.: Sage.

Karnes, A., J. Sterner, R. Welker, and F. Wu. 1989. A bicultural study of independent auditors' perceptions of unethical business practices. *The International Journal of Accounting* 24: 29-41.

Kelley, I., A. Whatley, and R. Worthley. 1987. Assessing the effects of culture on managerial attitudes: A three-culture test. *Journal of Business Studies* (Summer): 172-231.

Lampe, J., and S. Sutton. 1992. International auditing: Cross-cultural impact on quality. In *Advances in International Accounting*, Vol. 5. Greenwich, CT: JAI Press.

Loeb, S. 1984. Codes of ethics and self-regulation for non-public accountants: A public policy perspective. *Journal of Accounting and Public Policy* 1: 1-8.

Macintosh, N. 1995. The ethics of profit manipulation: A dialectic of control analysis. *Critical Perspectives in Accounting* 6: 289-313.

O'Shaughnessy, J., P. Siegel, J. Rigsby and J. Leavins. 1993. An examination of the professional code of ethics for certified internal auditors. *Management Auditors Journal* 8: 3-9.

Piper, T., M. Gentile, and S. Parks. 1993. *Can Ethics Be Taught?* Boston, MA: Harvard Business School.

Poneman, L. 1990. Ethical judgments in accounting: A cognitive-developmental perspective. *Critical Perspectives in Accounting* 1: 191-215.

Poneman, L. 1992. Auditor under reporting of time and moral reasoning: An experimental lab study. *Contemporary Accounting Research*, pp. 227-251.

Poneman, L., and D. Gabhart. 1993. *Ethical Reasoning in Accounting and Auditing*. Vancouver, Canada: CGA-Canadian Research Foundation.

Ronen, S., and D. Shenkar. 1985. Clustering countries on attitudinal dimensions: A review and synthesis. *Academy of Management Review* 10: 435-454.

Ryan L. 1992. Code of ethics. In *Business Ethics and Common Sense*, ed. R. McGee. Westport, CT.: Quorum Books.

Schultz, J., D. Johnson, D. Morris, and S. Dyrnes. 1993. An investigation of the reporting of questionable acts in an international setting. *Journal of Accounting Research* (Supplement): 75-103.

Shaub, M., D. Finn, and P. Munter. 1993. The effects of auditors' ethical orientation on commitment and ethical sensitivity. *Behavioral Research in Accounting* 5: 145-169.

Siegel, P., J. O'Shaughnessy, and J. Rigsby. 1995. A reexamination of the internal auditors' code of ethics. *Journal of Business Ethics* 14: 949-957.

Tidrick, D. 1992. Ethics and whistle blowing. *Internal Auditing* (Winter): 3-10.

Ueno, S., and F. Wu. 1993. The comparative influence of culture on budget control practices between the U.S. and Japan. *The International Journal of Accounting* 28: 17-39.

Wagner, S., and M. Mock. 1986. Individualism-collectivism: Concept and measure. *Group and Organization Studies: An International Journal* (September): 280-303.

Webley, S. 1988. *Company Philosophies and Codes of Business Ethics: A Guide to Their Drafting and Use*. London: Institute of Business Ethics.

Woelfel, C. 1986. Standards of ethical conduct for management accountants. *Journal of Business Ethics* 5: 365-372.

AN EXAMINATION OF CULTURAL INFLUENCE ON AUDIT ENVIRONMENTS

Michele L. Wingate

ABSTRACT

This study investigates the existence of a relationship between the culture of a country and two aspects of the business environment of that country, the amount of accounting disclosure required, and the level of litigiousness. Hofstede (1980, 1983, 1984) developed measures of the culture of a country which he called cultural value dimensions. His four dimensions—Individualism, Uncertainty Avoidance, Power Distance, and Masculinity—have been used to explain differences and similarities between societies and in the patterns of institutional development in those societies. Gray (1988) hypothesized relationships between Hofstede's measures and a particular institution—accounting. Gray's hypotheses were tested by Salter and Niswander (1995) and found, generally, to be empirically supported.

This study extends the prior research to a particular subinstitution—the audit environment. The audit environment is defined as those country-specific characteristics that influence the demand for and supply of audit services in a particular country. This research tests eight hypothesized relationships between Hofstede's dimensions

Research in Accounting Regulation, Supplement 1, pages 129-148.

ISBN: 0-7623-0338-7

and two aspects of the audit environment—accounting disclosure requirements and the level of litigiousness.

The results of the study support five of the eight hypotheses. In particular, disclosure is positively related to Individualism and negatively related to Uncertainty Avoidance. Litigiousness is negatively related to Uncertainty Avoidance and positively related to Masculinity and Individualism. The existence of a relationship between culture and the business environment—specifically, the audit environment—is partially supported.

The results of this study should be useful to audit firms taking on clients in new markets, to business managers entering new markets, and to regulators who influence and monitor those markets.

INTRODUCTION

Substantial research, both theoretical and empirical, shows that different patterns of accounting exist internationally for both financial measurement and reporting (e.g., Mueller 1967; Zeff 1971; Radebaugh 1975; Choi and Mueller 1984; Nobes 1983; Arpan and Radebaugh 1985; Nobes and Parker 1985; Gray 1988; Bloom and Naciri 1989; Cooke and Wallace 1990; Bavishi 1991; Salter and Doupnik 1992; Doupnik and Salter 1993; Bindon and Gernon 1995; Salter and Niswander 1995). The research generally concludes that the development of national accounting systems varies with environmental factors. However, what the specific environmental factors are and the patterns of development for different systems remains unsettled. This is an important issue, since as business expand across borders, managers need to understand that the accounting environments in which they will operate differ from their home country. Often, these differences are quite significant.

This study expands upon research by Gray (1988) who examines the relationship between cultural factors and the development of various institutional and regulatory processes. Gray (1988) develops four hypotheses based on Hofstede's (1980, 1983) cultural value dimensions—Uncertainty Avoidance, Individualism, Power Distance, and Masculinity. He examines how these cultural dimensions affect the development of accounting systems, in terms of the regulation of the accounting profession and a country's attitude toward financial management and disclosure. Gray's dimensions were Professionalism, Uniformity, Conservatism, and Secrecy. Salter and Niswander (1995) operationalize these hypotheses and find that a significant relationship exists between Professionalism and Uncertainty Avoidance, and among Uniformity and Uncertainty Avoidance and Masculinity. Additionally, they find a positive relationship between Conservatism and Uncertainty Avoidance, and a negative relationship between Conservatism and Masculinity. Finally, they find that Secrecy is positively related to Uncertainty Avoidance and negatively related to Individualism.

This study expands upon this prior research by examining the extent to which the development of *audit environments* can be explained and predicted by Hofstede's (1980, 1983) cultural value dimensions. The *audit environment* is defined as those country-specific (as opposed to client-specific or audit-firm-specific) characteristics that influence the demand for and supply of audit services in a country. These characteristics include the level of development of the capital market, the sophistication of financial information users, the dispersion of equity ownership of companies, the level of litigiousness, and the level of required accounting disclosure.

This study examines the association between culture and two characteristics of the audit environment: (1) the level of litigiousness, and (2) accounting disclosure requirements. These characteristics were chosen for this initial study because they appear to be more directly a result of culture than some of the other characteristics mentioned earlier. Hypotheses of the relationship between cultural dimensions and these two characteristics are developed and tested using both univariate and multivariate regression analysis. The disclosure requirements (for 39 countries) and level of litigiousness (for 49 countries) are the dependent variables, and Hofstede's measures of cultural value dimensions (for individual countries) or groups of countries based on the dimensions are the independent variables.

The results of this study indicate that accounting disclosure requirements are positively related to the level of Individualism in a culture and negatively related to the level of Uncertainty Avoidance. The level of litigiousness is positively related to the levels of Masculinity and Individualism but negatively related to the level of Uncertainty Avoidance. The results suggest that more individualistic cultures and those with less desire for Uncertainty Avoidance, such as the United States and Sweden, will have more disclosure. However, they are also likely to have a higher level of litigiousness than other countries with the opposite characteristics, such as Singapore and Argentina.

This paper should help readers understand how two characteristics of a country's audit environment, (1) the level of required accounting disclosure and (2) the level of litigiousness, are affected by cultural factors. An understanding of this cultural impact is crucial to anyone who is involved in global business. Audit firms entering new global markets can capitalize on their knowledge of cultural differences to more effectively evaluate clients in countries they have not entered before. It is not sufficient to only consider client and industry characteristics in the audit planning process when the "context" of the audit will be different from previous engagements. This study should provide auditors with insights into factors that explain differences across countries, thus allowing them to determine whether a new audit environment is similar to or different from a current environment.

This paper should also help regulators understand the impact of culture on the audit environment and provide them information that can be used in the modification and further development of that environment through legal and standard-setting processes in an attempt to create a level playing field.

The remainder of this paper is organized as follows: The second section describes the theorized relationship between culture and the audit environment. The third section includes the hypotheses of the study. In the fourth section, regression results are reported. The fifth section provides a summary, conclusion, and discussion of future research.

CULTURE AND THE AUDIT ENVIRONMENT

Hofstede (1980, 1983) outlines four constructs or dimensions of common social preference that can be used to measure the base values of individual societies. These constructs may also be used to separate societies from each other and, if correctly drawn, to explain observed institutional structures and behavior at a societal level. Hofstede's societal value dimensions are as follows (1984, 83-84):

> 1. *Strong versus Weak Uncertainty Avoidance.* This dimension concerns how the members of a society deal with uncertainty about the future; that is, whether they try to control the future or to let it happen.
> 2. *Individualism versus Collectivism.* This dimension concerns the degree of interdependence among individual members of a society. It relates to people's self-concepts: "I" or "we".
> 3. *Large versus Small Power Distance.* This dimension concerns how the members of a society handle inequalities among people when they occur.
> 4. *Masculinity versus Femininity.* This dimension is concerned with the way in which the members of a society allocate social (as opposed to biological) roles to the sexes.

Hofstede's (1980) model of the chain of influence flows from external/ecological influences (e.g., trade, investment, forces of nature) to the development of cultural values. The cultural values in turn impact the development of institutional environments, such as the legal system, patterns of corporate ownership, development of capital markets, accounting systems, and, as a subsystem of accounting, the audit environment. If Hofstede's dimensions are descriptive of the cultural aspects of a society and Hofstede's model of the chain of influence is accurate, then his dimensions should be able to explain differences in the audit environment present in various "societies."

Hofstede defines a society as a particular country. That definition has been retained in most studies using Hofstede's dimensions. In this study, however, society (i.e., audit environment) is defined in two ways: (1) as a particular country (e.g., the audit environment in Singapore), and (2) as a "culture area" (e.g., the high Individualism/low Uncertainty Avoidance audit environment). Gray (1988) suggests that the culture area might be the more appropriate unit of examination. Since cultures, and therefore audit environments, may be similar across countries, it is beneficial to determine which definition of society is most appropriate in understanding the culture/audit environment relationship.

Gray suggests that:

> if societal value orientations are related to the development of accounting systems at the sub-cultural level, given that such values permeate a nation's social system, then it may be hypothesized that there should be a close match between culture areas and patterns of accounting systems internationally (1988, 5).

This study extends that connection to audit environments. The audit environment is the system of country/society level characteristics that influence the demand for and supply of audit services in that location; the auditing subculture. This system includes the development of capital markets, the pattern of corporate ownership, the sources/providers of corporate capital, the amount of required accounting disclosure, and the level of litigiousness. Specifically, this study looks at the ability of culture to explain the extent of the last two characteristics: (1) the amount of required accounting disclosure, and (2) the level of litigiousness.

Examining the link between culture and the audit environment in terms of these two characteristics helps to develop a better understanding of the role that culture plays in the development of regulatory environments and institutions. Within one country or society, many aspects of the environment are relatively constant for all clients serviced by a national audit firm (i.e., legal, security market development, economy); however, once the audit firm goes outside a single country/society environment, the environment becomes foreign to the firm and the country-level characteristics vary. Walker and Johnson state:

> differences in...cultural standards are also reflected in the different results of audit market research...These cross-cultural differences and their interrelationships affect the market for audit services, and the Big Six and other large audit firms are not immune to them. Such differences need to be identified in different economies and areas of the world and studied to determine their influences on audit firm behavior (1996, 15).

This paper seeks to add to the understanding of the sources of these differences and to provide information to regulators who create and monitor business environments and audit firms who operate in environments that may be foreign to them.

HYPOTHESES DEVELOPMENT

In this section, the hypothesized relationships between Hofstede's cultural value dimensions and the two characteristics of the audit environment examined in this study, accounting disclosure requirements and the level of litigiousness, are developed.

Strong versus Weak Uncertainty Avoidance

This dimension measures the degree to which members of the society feel uncomfortable with uncertainty and ambiguity. Those societies which exhibit strong Uncertainty Avoidance, such as Argentina, Brazil, and Portugal, strive to avoid conflict and control their worlds. By minimizing the amount of information that is disclosed and to whom it is made available, the use of the information can be controlled. In these societies, only those who need to know—such as government regulators and creditors—are informed. Information disclosure to these two groups is mostly superficial as the recipients are generally highly involved in the operations of the business and have access to any information they want. Since capital in these countries is generally provided by creditors, there is no need for widespread information dissemination.

In contrast, in low Uncertainty Avoidance societies, such as Denmark, Great Britain, and Hong Kong, generally there is less desire to avoid conflict and uncertainty, so financial information is made available to any interested party and the users are left to draw their own conclusions. Since these countries tend to have more sophisticated financial markets, adequate disclosure to inform potential and current investors is necessary. Based on this relationship, the first hypothesis tested is:

Hypothesis 1. A negative relationship exists between the amount of required accounting disclosure and the level of Uncertainty Avoidance.

Strong Uncertainty Avoidance societies are often code law countries, which have laws that are a series of "thou shalts," thus giving permission for acceptable behavior. If permission is not granted, the behavior is not allowed. Deviant behavior is not tolerated publicly, but in reality, underground systems exist where "deviant" behavior is highly acceptable. For example, in some southeast Asian countries, which on average exhibit strong Uncertainty Avoidance, activities such as vandalism and littering can be punishable by caning. However, in these same countries, bribery of government officials is an accepted, and often, expected, behavior—it is the way business gets done. These societies tend not to "let the courts decide", because these underground systems take care of any disputes.

In contrast, in weak Uncertainty Avoidance societies, which are often common law countries, the laws are a series of "thou shalt nots" whereby instruction is given as to which behaviors are not tolerated, but anything not specifically disallowed may be allowed. The judicial systems in these societies are used to determine if a specific behavior is among those disallowed or not. The second hypothesis based on societal uncertainty avoidance is:

Hypothesis 2. A negative relationship exists between the level of litigiousness and the level of Uncertainty Avoidance.

Individualism versus Collectivism

In a society which exhibits Individualism, such as Great Britain and its former colonies, Australia, and the United States, a larger amount of required disclosures would be expected than that required in societies which exhibit Collectivism, such as the countries in Central and South America. A preference for a loosely knit societal framework, in which everyone only looks out for themselves, may lead to the development of regulations that require disclosures that might otherwise not be forthcoming. In a collective society, where the good of the "group" is foremost, it may be assumed that a given level of disclosure is adequate to inform the group members, who are usually directly involved in the operations, and so lesser amounts of required disclosures would be expected. In collective societies, those who need information will have access to the information from other sources.

The development of security exchanges has been put forth as one explanation for increased disclosures of financial information. It is difficult to determine the appropriate cause and effect relationship between securities markets and disclosures. However, it appears that those countries that have high Individualism and low Uncertainty Avoidance also tend to have more developed securities markets in combination with higher disclosure requirements. Based on this relationship, Hypothesis 3 is:

Hypothesis 3. A positive relationship exists between the amount of required accounting disclosure and the level of Individualism.

The desire to "look out for oneself" may also lead to the development of strong judicial processes, whereby the wronged party may seek justice from objective third parties. "Letting the court decide" becomes the preferred method of dealing with differences in individualistic societies. In collective societies, disagreements among individuals would more probably be handled among the members of the group rather than through third party arbitration. Therefore, the level of litigiousness would be higher in societies with higher levels of Individualism. Based on this quality, Hypothesis 4 is:

Hypothesis 4. A positive relationship exists between the level of litigiousness and the level of Individualism.

Large versus Small Power Distance

This dimension measures the degree to which members of the society accept unequal distributions of power in institutions and organizations. It also measures the level of acceptance of hierarchical order without any further justification. Societies with lower Power Distance strive for power equalization and demand justification for power inequalities. The amount of required accounting disclosure would be higher in low Power Distance societies as these societies prefer the level playing field achieved and enhanced by more thorough information dissemination. Disclosure of sufficient information across companies is thought to enhance competition and market development. If competition and the market for goods, services, and capital are healthy, all participants will benefit, despite their places in the hierarchical structure. This is tested in Hypothesis 5:

Hypothesis 5. A negative relationship exists between the amount of required accounting disclosure and the level of Power Distance.

The distaste for power inequality would also lead to the development of processes by which the "Davids" of the society would have recourse against "Goliaths." In large Power Distance societies, the existence of "Goliaths" and their power is generally accepted without question. The "little guy" expects to be trodden upon. Therefore, the level of litigiousness would be higher in low Power Distance societies. Hypothesis 6 is:

Hypothesis 6. A negative relationship exists between the level of litigiousness and the level of Power Distance.

Masculinity versus Femininity

This dimension measures the preference for achievement, heroism, assertiveness, and material success over relationships, modesty, caring for the weak, and the quality of life. Masculine societies have a "performance" orientation, whereas feminine societies emphasize "welfare," that is, caring for all members, even the weakest. In the more Masculine societies, with their emphasis on performance, disclosure of the results of business operations and financial condition allows the reader to evaluate the operating performance of the company. The difference in disclosures between a masculine and feminine society may be evidenced by the *type* of information disclosed, rather than the amount. That is, societies that exhibit Masculinity will place more importance on *performance*-related information (i.e., "bragging") and feminine societies will value *welfare*-related information (e.g., how the company is a "good citizen"). So we would expect to see more accounting (i.e., financial) oriented disclosures required in a masculine society than in a feminine society. The measure of disclosure used in this study looks predominantly at financially related disclosures. Based on this, Hypothesis 7 states:

Hypothesis 7. A positive relationship exists between the amount of required accounting disclosure and the level of Masculinity.

Strongly Masculine societies, which value assertiveness and competition, may encourage challenging an adversary to a "winner takes all" battle which manifests itself as a lawsuit. Therefore, the level of litigiousness is expected to be higher in a masculine society than in a feminine society. Thus, Hypothesis 8 is:

Table 1. Hypotheses

H1:	A negative relationship is hypothesized between the amount of required accounting disclosure and the level of uncertainty avoidance.
H2:	A negative relationship is hypothesized between the level of litigiousness and the level of uncertainty avoidance.
H3:	A positive relationship is hypothesized between the amount of required accounting disclosure and the level of individualism.
H4:	A positive relationship is hypothesized between the level of litigiousness and the level of individualism.
H5:	A negative relationship is hypothesized between the amount of required accounting disclosure and the level of power distance.
H6:	A negative relationship is hypothesized between the level of litigiousness and the level of power distance.
H7:	A positive relationship is hypothesized between the amount of required accounting disclosure and the level of masculinity.
H8:	A positive relationship is hypothesized between the level of litigiousness and the level of masculinity.

Hypothesis 8. A positive relationship exists between the level of litigiousness and the level of Masculinity.

The eight hypotheses are restated in Table 1.

EMPIRICAL ANALYSIS

This study examines the relationship between Hofstede's four cultural value dimensions and each of two aspects of the audit environment—accounting disclosure requirements and the level of litigiousness—for 39 and 49 countries, respectively. The countries included and their respective values for the cultural dimension measures, measures of the amount of accounting disclosure required, and levels of litigiousness are presented in Table 2.

The cultural value dimension measures for each country represent index scores based on local employees' value data collected by the multinational corporation who participated in Hofstede's original studies. The original survey process included more than 100,000 employees. The scores used in this study are from Hofstede (1984) in which he measures cultural values for 50 countries. The measures are relative scores in which the lowest country is situated around zero and the highest around 100. Recently, there have been some concerns as to the validity of Hofstede's dimension measurements, but as he states in his paper:

> Although the four dimensions were originally derived from data on the values scored by multinational corporation employees, subsequent research has shown that the same or closely similar dimensions can be found in other research data, collected from different researchers

Table 2. Cultural Value Dimensions and Measures of Audit Environment By Country

Country	*Uncertainty Avoidance*	*Individualism*	*Power Distance*	*Masculinity*	*LITIGATE*	*DISCLOSE*
Argentina	86	46	49	56	3.61	45
Australia	51	90	36	61	10.00	75
Austria	70	55	11	79	3.61	54
Belgium	94	75	65	54	4.82	61
Brazil	76	38	69	49	4.82	54
Canada	48	80	39	52	8.07	74
Chile	86	23	63	28	2.42	52
Colombia	80	13	67	64	2.42	50
Costa Rica	86	15	35	21	3.61	*
Denmark	23	74	18	16	4.82	62
Ecuador	67	8	78	63	2.42	*
Finland	59	63	33	26	3.61	77
France	86	71	68	43	6.22	69
Germany	65	67	35	66	6.22	62
Great Britain	35	89	35	66	10.00	78
Greece	112	35	60	57	3.61	55
Guatamala	101	6	95	37	2.42	*
Hong Kong	29	25	68	57	10.00	69
India	40	48	77	56	2.42	57
Indonesia	48	14	78	46	3.61	*
Iran	59	41	58	43	1.00	*
Ireland	35	70	28	68	6.22	*
Israel	81	54	13	47	*	64
Italy	75	76	50	70	6.22	62
Jamaica	13	39	45	68	3.61	*
Japan	92	46	54	95	4.82	65
Korea (South)	85	18	60	39	3.61	62
Malaysia	36	26	104	50	3.61	76
Mexico	82	30	81	69	4.82	60
Netherlands	53	80	38	14	6.22	64
New Zealand	49	79	22	58	10.00	70
Norway	50	69	31	8	6.22	74
Pakistan	70	14	55	50	1.00	*
Panama	86	11	95	44	3.61	*
Peru	87	16	64	42	2.42	38
Philippines	44	32	94	64	3.61	65
Portugal	104	27	63	31	3.61	36

(continued)

Table 2. (Continued)

Country	Uncertainty Avoidance	Individualism	Power Distance	Masculinity	*LITIGATE*	*DISCLOSE*
Salvadore	94	19	66	40	1.00	*
Singapore	8	20	74	48	4.82	78
South Africa	49	65	49	63	4.82	70
Spain	86	51	57	42	4.82	64
Sweden	29	71	31	5	4.82	83
Switzerland	58	68	34	70	6.22	68
Taiwan	69	17	58	45	3.61	65
Thailand	64	20	64	34	3.61	64
Turkey	85	37	66	45	2.42	51
Uruguay	100	36	61	38	1.65	31
USA	46	91	40	62	15.00	71
Venezuela	76	12	81	73	3.61	40
Yugoslavia	88	27	76	21	1.65	*

Note: *data not available

with different methods from different sources: from groups of students, from random samples of entire national populations, from statistics compiled by international bodies like the World Health Organization. Thus, there is solid evidence that the four dimensions are, indeed, universal (1984, 84).

The accounting disclosure requirement measure (*DISCLOSE*) is a disclosure index developed by the Center for International Financial Analysis and Research (CIFAR) (Bavishi 1991). CIFAR examined and rated the annual reports for 1,000 companies from 44 countries, of which 39 are included in Hofstede's study. The reports were rated on the inclusion or omission of 90 suggested items of information. This is an objective, quantifiable measure of the amount of information presented by large companies in these countries. The index can take on values ranging from zero to 90, representing the average number of items that appear in the companies' annual reports for that country. The index, however, does not directly measure *required* information but instead measures *actual* information. The index is adjusted if an item on the list of suggested information is not required in a particular country, so if in Country A, only 84 of the items are required, the highest score a company in that country could achieve is 84. In that sense, the accounting disclosure requirements of the country are indirectly reflected in the index. However, if these large companies, on average, disclose more than is required in their country, the score will be biased upwards, making it appear that the disclosure required in that country is higher than it actually is.

The level of litigiousness (*LITIGATE*) is a risk rating developed by an international insurance underwriter for one of the Big 6 audit firms. The rating may take

Table 3.

Descriptive Statistics

Variable	*Mean*	*Median*	*Std. Dev.*	*Min.*	*Max.*
UA[1]	65.90	69.50	24.91	8.00	112.00
IND[2]	43.94	38.50	25.85	6.00	91.00
PD[3]	55.82	59.00	21.99	11.00	104.00
MAS[4]	48.86	49.50	18.83	5.00	95.00
LITIGATE	4.64	3.61	2.74	1.00	15.00
DISCLOSE	61.92	64.00	12.33	31.00	83.00

Correlation Matrix

Variable	*UA*	*IND*	*PD*	*MAS*	*LITG*
UA					
IND	–0.350				
PD	0.245	–0.680			
MAS	–0.032	0.071	0.059		
LITIGATE	–0.416	0.693	–0.429	0.229	
DISCLOSE	–0.689	0.515	–0.263	–0.084	0.546

Notes: [1]Uncertainty Avoidance
[2]Individualism
[3]Power Distance
[4]Masculinity

on values from one to 10 and represents the "risk of doing business as an auditor" in a particular country. It is based on all international audit firms' claims experience, other professional firms' (i.e., lawyers, engineers, etc.) claims experience, legal and regulatory environments, political and economic environments, and the professional accounting environment in the country. The rating increases with the risk and cost of performing audit services in a particular country. The audit firm requested a rating for each of 169 countries, of which 49 were included in Hofstede's study. The United States was not one of the original countries rated. However, in speaking with the partner-in-charge of the international audit practice for the firm that requested the rating, he suggested that the U.S. rating would be at least 15.[1] One deficit of this measure is that it is created using publicly available claims and cost information—so if a large portion of the settlements of disputes between audit firms (or other professionals) and their clients takes place "under the table," the measure for that country will be biased downwards.

Descriptive statistics of the variables are presented in Table 3.

"Society/Audit Environment" Defined as a Particular Country

The hypotheses outlined above were tested using an individual country as the definition of society/audit environment, using univariate and multivariate least

Table 4. Results of Regression Analysis - Univariate (Audit environment = single country)

Model: DISCLOSE = $b_0 + b_1 X + e$; *where X = UA, IND, PD, or MAS, respectively*

	UA	*IND*	*PD*	*MAS*
Est. Coeff	−0.3485	0.25562	−0.15094	−0.0532
Std. Dev.	0.05974	0.06995	0.09093	0.1031
t-ratio	−5.79	3.65	−1.66	−0.52
p-value	0.000	0.001	0.105	0.609
n	39	39	39	39
F-value	33.51	13.36	2.76	0.27
p-value (overall)	0.000	0.001	0.105	0.609
R^2 (adj)	46.1%	24.5%	4.4%	0.00%

Model: LITIGATE = $b_0 + b_1 X + e$; *where X = UA, IND, PD, or MAS, respectively*

	UA	*IND*	*PD*	*MAS*
Est. Coeff	−0.04547	0.07272	−0.05512	0.03296
Std. Dev.	0.01448	0.01105	0.01692	0.02043
t-ratio	−3.14	6.58	−3.26	1.61
p-value	0.003	0.000	0.002	0.113
n	49	49	49	49
F-value	9.86	43.33	10.62	2.60
p-value (overall)	0.003	0.000	0.002	0.113
R^2 (adj)	15.6%	46.9%	16.7%	3.2%

squares regression.[2] The audit environment factors for each country are the dependent variables in separate estimation models, and the four cultural value dimensions are the independent variables. The univariate and multivariate results are shown in Tables 4 and 5, respectively. The results support some of the hypotheses in a statistically significant manner. It appears that accounting disclosure requirements (*DISCLOSE*) are negatively related to the level of Uncertainty Avoidance, supporting Hypothesis 1, and positively related to the level of Individualism, supporting Hypothesis 3. Likewise, the level of litigiousness (*LITIGATE*) is negatively related to the level of Uncertainty Avoidance, supporting Hypothesis 2, and positively related to the levels of Individualism and Masculinity, in support of Hypotheses 4 and 8.

So higher levels of disclosure are expected to be required in countries which exhibit high Individualism and low Uncertainty Avoidance, such as the United States, New Zealand, and Sweden. Higher levels of litigiousness are expected in countries that exhibit high Masculinity and Individualism and low Uncertainty Avoidance, such as the United States and Great Britain. Knowledge of the cultural dimensions present in the country will, according to the results of this study, allow

Table 5. Results of Regression Analysis - Multivariate (Audit environment = single country)

Model: $DISCLOSE = b_0 + b_1\,UA + b_2\,IND + b_3\,PD + b_4\,MAS + e$

Variable	*Est. Coeff.*	*std. dev.*	*t-ratio*	*p-value*
Intercept	68.626	9.376	7.32	0.000
UA(-)	−0.29184	0.05946	−4.91	0.000
IND(+)	0.19555	0.07769	2.52	0.017
PD(-)	0.04925	0.08722	0.56	0.576
MAS(?)	0.00085	0.07207	0.01	0.991
$n = 39$				
F-value = 11.80				
p-value = 0.000				
R^2 (adj) = 53.2%				

Model: $LITIGATE = b_0 + b_1\,UA + b_2\,IND + b_3\,PD + b_4\,MAS + e$

Variable	*Est. Coeff.*	*std. dev.*	*t-ratio*	*p-value*
Intercept	1.251	1.860	0.67	0.505
UA(-)	−0.02143	0.01187	−1.81	0.078
IND(+)	0.06956	0.01535	4.53	0.000
PD(-)	0.00965	0.01829	0.53	0.600
MAS(+)	0.02466	0.01480	1.67	0.103
$n = 49$				
F-value = 13.31				
p-value = 0.000				
R^2 (adj) = 50.6%				

an audit firm to more fully understand the environment it might be entering, particularly as far as expectations about disclosure requirements and the level of litigiousness. Additionally, this knowledge allows the audit firm to decide whether a new market is similar to or different from other markets in which it operates, thus giving it the ability to capitalize on information it has already obtained.

The level of Power Distance is insignificant in explaining variation in either of the dependent variables when examined in concert with the other independent variables. However, Hypotheses 5 and 6 are supported when examined using univariate analysis (Disclosure: *t*-statistic = −1.66, *p*-value = .105; Litigiousness: *t*-statistic = −3.26, *p*-value = .002). The negative correlation between Power Distance and Individualism may be confounding the multivariate results (see Table 3).[3]

The hypothesized positive relationship between Masculinity and disclosure is not supported by the data using either a univariate or a multivariate model. A more appropriate relationship to examine may be between Masculinity and the *type* of disclosures required rather than the *amount* of disclosure. A more masculine soci-

Table 6. Culture Areas

(1) More Developed Latin	*(5) Near Eastern*	*(9) Nordic*
Belgium	Greece	Denmark
France	Pakistan	Finland
Argentina	Turkey	Netherlands
Brazil	Yugoslavia	Norway
Spain	Sweden	
Italy		
(2) Less Developed Latin	*(6) Asian-Colonial*	
Colombia	Hong Kong	
Ecuador	Singapore	
Mexico		
Venezuela		
Costa Rica	*(7) Germanic*	
Chile	Austria	
Guatemala	Germany	
Panama	Israel	
Peru	Switzerland	
Portugal		
Salvador		
Uruguay	*(8) Anglo*	
	Australia	
(3) More Developed Asian	Canada	
Japan	Ireland	
	Jamaica	
(4) Less Developed Asian	New Zealand	
Indonesia	United Kingdom	
Pakistan	United States	
Taiwan	South Africa	
Thailand		
India		
Malaysia		
Philippines		
South Korea		

ety may promote the disclosure of performance-related information whereas in a more feminine society, the disclosures may concern environmental and social items. Unfortunately, it is not possible to determine which particular disclosures are represented by the CIFAR index for a specific country.

"Society/Audit Environment" Defined as a Culture Area

In a second set of tests the audit environment characteristics are again the dependent variables, but the independent variables are "culture areas" as defined by Hof-

Table 7. Results of Regression Analysis
(Audit environment = culture area - See Table 6)

Model: DISCLOSE = $b_0 + b_1$ *Group 1* + b_2 *Group 2* + b_3 *Group 3* + b_4 *Group 4* + b_5 *Group 5* + b_6 *Group 6* + b_7 *Group 7* + b_8 *Group 8*

Variable	*Est. Coeff.*	*std. dev.*	*t-ratio*	*p-value*
Intercept	72.00	3.379	21.31	0.000
Group 1	−12.833	4.576	−2.80	0.009
Group 2	−28.143	4.425	−6.36	0.000
Group 3	-7.000	8.278	−0.85	0.404
Group 4	−7.167	4.576	−1.57	0.128
Group 5	−19.000	6.322	−3.01	0.005
Group 6	1.500	6.322	0.24	0.814
Group 7	−10.000	5.069	−1.97	0.058
Group 8	1.000	4.576	0.22	0.828

$n = 39$
F-value = 8.89
p-value = 0.000
R^2 (adj) = 62.4%

Model: LITIGATE = $b_0 + b_1$ *Group 1* + b_2 *Group 2* + b_3 *Group 3* + b_4 *Group 4* + b_5 *Group 5* + b_6 *Group 6* + b_7 *Group 7* + b_8 *Group 8*

Variable	*Est. Coeff.*	*std. dev.*	*t-ratio*	*p-value*
Intercept	5.0717	0.7734	6.56	0.000
Group 1	0.013	1.081	0.01	0.990
Group 2	−2.2375	0.9398	−2.38	0.022
Group 3	-0.252	2.005	−0.13	0.901
Group 4	−1.5843	0.9593	−1.65	0.106
Group 5	−2.819	1.051	−2.68	0.011
Group 6	2.338	1.519	1.54	0.132
Group 7	0.278	1.318	0.21	0.834
Group 8	3.392	1.013	3.35	0.002

$n = 49$
F-value = 8.15
p-value = 0.000
R^2 (adj) = 54.4%

stede. These groupings were developed based on the member countries' scores on the four culture dimensions, using cluster analysis and allowing for geographical and historical factors. The groupings are shown in Table 6. The groups represent countries with similar cultures and as such may exhibit similar patterns of institutional and regulatory development.

The independent variables are dummy variables indicating whether a country is a member of a particular group, of which there are nine choices. The results of the second set of tests, using only a multivariate model, are shown in Table 7. The results show that being a member of the *More Developed Latin* (1), *Germanic* (7), *Less Developed Latin* (2), and the *Near Eastern* (5) groups is negatively related to disclosure requirements. Additionally, being a member of the *Less Developed Asian, Less Developed Latin* (2), and the *Near Eastern* (5) groups is negatively related to litigiousness. However, being a member of the *Anglo* (8) group is positively related to the level of litigiousness. None of the groups are positively related to the amount of accounting disclosure at any acceptable level of significance.

Overall, the culture areas have more explanatory power than the four cultural value dimensions (adjusted R^2 = 62.4% for Disclosure, and 54.4% for Litigiousness). This result supports the idea that the group to which a country belongs will be more helpful in evaluating certain aspects of that country's audit environment than looking at the country in isolation. This would allow an audit firm to draw on information that it may already have obtained about other members of a group when considering entrance into a new country that is also a member of that group. Membership in a particular group gives information about the member countries without the audit firm having to collect supplemental data; for example, members of the *More Developed Latin* (1) group tend to exhibit high Uncertainty Avoidance, high Power Distance, and lower Masculinity. So, given the relationships between the individual dimensions and the audit environment characteristics established in the first set of tests, the members of the *More Developed Latin* group can be expected to have a smaller amount of required disclosures and lower levels of litigiousness.

SUMMARY AND CONCLUSIONS

This study has examined the relationship between Hofstede's four cultural value dimensions—Uncertainty Avoidance, Individualism, Power Distance, and Masculinity—and two characteristics of the audit environment present in a particular country. The aspects of the audit environment studied are: (1) the level of litigiousness, and (2) the amount of required accounting disclosure. The results of the study add further support to the theory that cultural values influence the creation and operation of institutions, which in turn impact the development of accounting systems (Gray 1988), of which the "audit environment" is an outcome.

The hypothesized relationships were supported for five of the eight hypotheses. Both Individualism and Uncertainty Avoidance were strongly significant in the hypothesized directions for both characteristics of audit environment. Individualistic societies will require more disclosure to maintain a level playing field. Similarly, in those societies which exhibit low levels of Uncertainty Avoidance, fuller information dissemination promotes competition and offers opportunities for conflict. This may lead to an understanding of the connection between these two dimensions and litigiousness—an openness to conflict and challenge is also present in high Individualism/low Uncertainty Avoidance societies. Masculinity was helpful in explaining the variation in the level of litigiousness but not in the amount of accounting disclosures required. Power Distance was effective in explaining both of the audit environment characteristics when used in isolation, but lost its power when placed in the multivariate model.

Membership in a particular culture area is also effective in explaining variation in these aspects of the audit environment. Membership in the *Less Developed Latin* or the *Near Eastern* groups is negatively related to the amount of accounting disclosure required and the level of litigiousness present in a country. Membership in the *More Developed Latin* or the *Germanic* groups is negatively related to the amount of accounting disclosure but not significantly related to the level of litigiousness. Finally, being part of the *Anglo* group is positively related to the level of litigiousness. None of the other groups were significant in explaining the audit environment characteristics. Overall, culture areas are more significantly related to the dependent variables than the individual country cultural dimensions.

The results of this study add to the understanding of the connection between culture and business, in particular, the audit environment present in a particular country. This understanding is critical to managers and audit firms entering a country as a new market and to the regulators that create and monitor that country's business environment. An understanding of the differences between the new and current environments allows managers and audit firms to compensate or control for the differences in their planning and operations. The knowledge is also useful to domestic regulators as they create environments to attract or repel business from other countries.

Further work in this area should develop measures to look at other aspects of the audit environment—for example, the development of security markets, corporate ownership structure, and licensing and regulation of auditors. Additionally, it may be useful in determinng whether these different audit environments create different costs to be faced by the audit firms operating in them. This would allow the audit firms to quantify the effects of differences in audit environments as part of their decision process for entering a new market. The ability to place a price tag on the differences in accounting and auditing systems that exist between countries would further our understanding of the impact of these differences. It would also provide information to regulators as to how their institutional framework, and the outcomes thereof, impact the cost of doing business in that country.

With the strong interest in harmonization of various aspects of the accounting process, it is worthwhile to generate data that aids that discussion. The results of this study establish yet another link between culture and the business environment.

ACKNOWLEDGMENT

The author would like to thank her dissertation committee at the University of Oregon—Helen Gernon, Craig Lefanowicz, Steve Haynes, and Alyce Campbell. Additional thanks are due to Gary Colbert, Dennis Murray, L. Ann Martin, and participants in workshops at the University of Oregon and the University of Colorado at Denver.

NOTE

1. A variety of measurement values for the level of litigiousness in the United States were used. Using a value higher than 15 caused the United States to exert undue influence on the results of the regression estimation. The partner-in-charge of the firm that uses the rating, as well as an international professional liability underwriter, both stated that the United States was "substantially more" litigious than any other country in the world during the year under examination (1987).

2. Appropriate diagnostics were performed examining the presence of influential observations, multicollinearity, and heteroscedasticity. While there were some seemingly influential observations, according to variance inflation factor scores and other diagnostics, their removal did not change the results in a significant fashion. Heteroscedasticity does not appear to be a concern and the impact of the collinearity is discussed in note 3.

3. Running both models without individualism improved the significance of power distance. For the LITIGATE model, the significance increased from a p-value of .6 to .007. For the DISCLOSE model, the significance increased from a p-value of .576 to .172. However, individualism is a strong predictor, according to partial F-tests, so it was retained. Power distance is not a strong predictor unless individualism is excluded.

REFERENCES

Arpan, J.S., and L.H. Radebaugh. 1985. *International Accounting and Multinational Enterprises*. New York: Wiley.

Bavishi, V.. 1991. *International Accounting and Auditing Trends*. Princeton, NJ: Center for International Financial Analysis and Research.

Bindon, K., and H. Gernon. 1995. The European Union: Regulation moves financial reporting toward comparability. In *Research in Accounting Regulation*, Vol. 9, 23-48. Greenwich, CT: JAI Press.

Bloom, R., and M. Naciri. 1989. Accounting standard setting and culture: A comparative analysis of the United States, Canada, England, West Germany, Australia, New Zealand, Sweden, Japan, and Switzerland. *International Journal of Accounting Education and Research* 24(1): 70-97.

Choi, F.D.S., and G.G. Mueller. 1984. *International Accounting*. Englewood Cliffs, NJ: Prentice-Hall.

Cooke, T.D., and R.S.O. Wallace. 1990. Financial disclosure regulation and its environment: Review and further analysis. *Journal of Accounting and Public Policy* (Summer): 79-110.

Doupnik, T.S., and S.B. Salter. 1993. An empirical test of a judgmental international classification of financial reporting practices. *Journal of International Business Studies* 24(1): 41-60.

Gray, S.J. 1988. Towards a theory of cultural influence on the development of accounting systems internationally. *ABACUS* 24(March): 1-15.

Hofstede, G. 1980. *Culture's Consequences*. Beverly Hills, CA: Sage.

Hofstede, G. 1983. Dimensions of national cultures in fifty countries and three regions. In *Expiscations in Cross Cultural Psychology*, eds. J.B. Deregowski, S. Dziurawiec, and R. Annis. Swets and Zeitlinger.

Hofstede, G. 1984b. Cultural dimensions in management and planning. *Asia Pacific Journal of Management* (January): 81-99.

Mueller, G.G.. 1967. *International Accounting*. London: Macmillan.

Nobes, C.W.. 1983. A judgmental classification of financial reporting practices. *Journal of Business Finance and Accounting* (Spring).

Nobes, C.W., and R.H. Parker. 1985. *Comparative International Accounting*. Philip Allan.

Radebaugh, L.H.. 1975. Environmental factors influencing the development of accounting objectives, standards, and practices in Peru. *International Journal of Accounting Education and Research* (Fall).

Salter, S.B., and Doupnik, T. 1992. The relationship between legal and accounting systems: A classification exercise. In *Advances in International Accounting*, Vol. 5, ed., 3-22. Greenwich, CT: JAI Press

Salter, S.B., and F. Niswander. 1995. Cultural influence on the development of accounting systems internationally: A test of Gray's (1988) theory. *Journal of International Business* 26(2): 379-397.

Walker, K.B., and E. Johnson. 1996. A review and synthesis of research on supplier concentration, quality, and fee structure in non-U.S. markets for auditor services. *The International Journal of Accounting* 31(1): 1-18.

Zeff, S.A. 1971. *Forging Accounting Principles in Five Countries: A History and Analysis of Trends.* Stipes.

AN EXAMINATION OF BRITISH, IRISH, AND U.S. PARTNERS' RESPONSES TO ETHICAL DILEMMAS

Donald F. Arnold, Sr., and Richard A. Bernardi

ABSTRACT

The research seeks to explain the differences in extent and specificity of accounting and auditing standards between countries by examining the relationship between moral development and auditing ethical dilemmas. The sample includes 102 partners from the United Kingdom, the Republic of Ireland, and the United States. The research found that partners from the United Kingdom and Ireland were more likely to do additional audit work and that higher-moral-development partners had lower estimates of underreporting. The data did not support the anticipated difference in moral development between partners from the British Isles and the United States. However, about 41% of the partners from the British Isles did not have a college education, which has been shown to increase moral development.

Research in Accounting Regulation, Supplement 1, pages 149-172.

ISBN: 0-7623-0338-7

INTRODUCTION

This research examines whether or not differences in accounting standards and the level of moral development (Kohlberg 1969) could influence the level of detail examined in an audit, as well as concerns about retaining a higher proportion of lower-moral-development auditors (Bernardi and Arnold 1997; Ponemon 1992). Although one might expect that countries with similar cultures (Hofstede 1988, 1991) and close ties would produce similar standards, standard-setting is a product of social-choice systems (Gorelik 1994). While the governing body for setting accounting standards in the United Kingdom was recently restructured, is the legacy of the past still a major factor? Gorelik (1994, 119) notes that "The standards that the FASB produces tend to be much more detailed than the standards in...the United Kingdom." Gorelik also notes that the standard-setting process in the United Kingdom is an "incremental [one that relies on the] use of due process [and] reliance on individual judgments of Committee members" whereas the process in the United States is still "incremental but [is] increasingly supported by substantive research, conceptual framework and extensive use of due process" (1994, 114). To date, research has only addressed differences in countries with widely differing cultures (Cohen, Pant, and Sharp 1995). As suggested by Schilder (1996), this research examines whether or not differences in standards of similar cultures influence auditors' willingness to do additional audit work if risk increases.

The last few decades have seen an ever-increasing number of required audit guidelines, procedures, and standards that are aimed at enhancing the technical aspect of the audit. However, one is struck by the differences in the explicit versus implicit dimensions of those standards among the United Kingdom, the Republic of Ireland, and the United States when examining the historical development of auditing and accounting standards.[1] In the United States, auditing and accounting standards have followed the path of intricate pronouncements that specify both how to account for various economic events and how to audit them. In contrast, the United Kingdom and Ireland traditionally have fewer and more general guidelines for the practice of accounting and auditing (Gorelik 1994). The Ryan Commission's report is a major factor in the similarity between U.K. and Irish standards (McHugh and Stamp 1992, 429):

> The report's main recommendation is in keeping with the stated desire of the Irish Government—that the Irish accounting profession should realign itself formally with the UK standard setting process as soon as possible.

Prior attempts to explain the differences in accounting standards in the United States and the British Isles have focused on the legal and structural nature of their business environments. For example, Benston (1975) provides a conceptual framework consisting of four factors that explain why differences in the specificity of accounting and auditing rules were very natural developments. First, while the state governments have considerable authority for the licensing procedures for accountants in the United States, professional bodies are more influential in the United Kingdom and Ireland. Second, economically, there is a greater dispersion of individuals in the United States who use financial statement information for investment decisions than in either the United Kingdom or Ireland. Third, while the Securities and Exchange Commission is active in the regulatory environment and has specific responsibilities in the United States, the Department of Trade and Industry does not promulgate rules and regulations in the United Kingdom. The legal environments are dramatically different; U.S. accountants are more vulnerable to suits claiming negligence and misrepresentation.

However, Ijiri (1983) notes that until the early 1980s, there was a basic difference in the objectives of financial accounting and reporting. Since financial information should report information that is useful to investors, creditors, and others, this information must be designed to meet each of these user groups' needs. Ijiri (1983) suggests that two differing contexts have evolved in developing and meeting the information needs: the accountability context and the decision usefulness context. Gorelik (1994) notes that, while the first type had been emphasized in the United Kingdom, the second type was most prevalent in the United States.

Prior behavioral research that included multiple-country data found country effects in the perception of conservatism (Belkaoui and Picur 1991). Other research has reported an association between ethical sensitivity in auditor judgments (Cohen et al. 1995; Ponemon and Gabhart 1990). Using Hofstede's constructs, discussed below, as a measuring tool, Cohen et al. (1995) evaluate the ethical decision making of auditors from three countries. Cohen et al. report differences in ethical judgments between U.S. auditors, who are individualistic and low power distance, and auditors from Japan and Latin America, who are collective and high power distance:

> [T]he values associated with respect for and acceptance of authority (high power distance), coupled with concern for one's place in a social group (collectivism), are more conductive to high ethical standards (1995, 57).

Cohen et al. based their analysis on three national areas (Japan, Latin America, and the United States) that "exhibit strong cultural differences" for Hofstede's (1991, 1980) constructs. These authors did not examine whether or not differences in decision making occur among countries or groups of countries that are not at opposite ends of Hofstede's scale. This research uses a sample of 102 partners from Ireland, the United Kingdom, and the United States (i.e., countries that exhibit a smaller degree of dispersion in Hofstede's constructs) to examine the influence of moral reasoning when resolving ethical conflicts in an auditing environment with the analysis focusing on between-country differences.

The remainder of the research is divided into four sections. After reviewing the six stage levels in Kohlberg's theory of moral development, the theory section develops research hypotheses on: differences in moral development, auditor responses to ethical dilemmas, and potential country differences in these responses. The subjects and materials section explains the sample selection process and the development and pilot testing of the research instrument. The research hypotheses are then tested and the results of the research are discussed.

THEORY DEVELOPMENT

Inkeles and Levinson (1969) and Hofstede (1991, 1980) suggest that cultural differences could explain differences in responses to similar problems. Inkeles and Levinson note that national culture may affect how individuals in various societies deal with common problems. Hofstede (1991 pp. 13-14), expanding on Inkeles and Levinson, indicates that cultural differences may also affect the way that organizations function in various societies and the differences in solutions among countries to common problems:

1. Social inequality, including the relationship with authority;
2. The relationship between the individual and the group;
3. Concepts of masculinity and femininity: the social implications of having been born as a boy or a girl; and
4. Ways of dealing with uncertainty, relating to the control of aggression and the expression of emotions.

Research shows that the cognitive process of moral reasoning also relates to the "rule-oriented" nature of some individuals. Bernardi (1994), Pincus (1990), Waller and Felix (1984), Lewis, Shields, and Young (1983), and Sanders (1980) examined the behavior of auditors and their decision-making process. Bernardi (1994), Bernardi and Arnold (1994), Arnold and Ponemon (1991), Ponemon (1992), and Ponemon and Gabhart (1990) all find that moral reasoning (using Rest's (1979a) Defining Issues Test) affects a wide array of auditing decisions. This behavioral research might help to explain the different approaches to standard setting among countries.

Moral Reasoning

Factors influencing an auditor's performance cannot be limited to generally accepted auditing procedures that require auditors to have adequate technical training and proficiency. Kohlberg's (1969, 1976) research on moral judgment led to the development of a model that defines the thought process an individual uses to reason in ethical situations. The model does not attempt to predict or provide guidance in terms of the application of a moral code of right and wrong. Instead, the model describes the frame of reference that an individual might use in reaching a conclusion in an ethical dilemma.[2]

In Kohlberg's model, individual moral judgment develops through a series of six stages, which each have their own perspectives for ethical behavior. Stage 1 norms are perceived as concrete rules of behavior; right is guided by strict obedience to what the person with power expects. In Stage 2, an individual guides his or her behavior by his or her interests; decisions are based on the "cost-and-benefit-to-oneself" criteria. By Stage 3, an individual's moral perspective is grounded on relationships with others in the immediate social environment. Stage 3 norms expect "good" persons to be cooperative and to consider the costs versus benefits to their group. Stage 4 individuals are very rule oriented; these rules are those of the more global society not just of those in their immediate environment. Stage 4 individuals believe that everyone is obligated to follow the rules to ensure the society's proper functioning. At Stage 5, the focus is on the "fairness" of the law or rule as determined by the fairness of the process by which the rules were developed. Maximizing and protecting all individuals' rights and welfare defines Stage 5's conception of norms. In Stage 6, the individual separates the conventions and laws of the society from more general moral principles. These general principles now take precedence, and the society's rules are followed when they are rational and impartial.

While Kohlberg's model consists of six discrete stages, a variation of his theory developed by Rest maintains that an individual possesses some percentage of each stage, with a certain stage or stages being dominant. Rest's theory holds that a person's moral cognition forms a distribution centered around one stage level, with cognitive development being a shift in the distribution. Rest developed the Defining Issues Test (1979a) to measure moral development based on the distribution of an individual's moral cognitions at Stages 5 and 6. The Defining Issues Test (DIT) presents subjects with a series of dilemmas and a choice of standard responses distributed among Kohlberg's highest five stages (Stage 1 considerations are not included in the DIT). Each of Rest's responses represents the style of moral reasoning at one of the highest five stages of moral development (Rest 1986a). An individual's score on the DIT represents "the relative importance a subject gives to principled moral considerations in making a decision about moral dilemmas" (Rest 1979b, 5). While responses corresponding to Stages 2-6 are considered on the Defining Issues Test, an individual's P score measures the percentage of responses the subject makes at either Stage 5 or Stage 6 (Rest 1986b).

Auditor Moral Judgment

The relevance of Kohlberg's model to the research questions lies in the comparison of differences in the responses of Stage 3 and 4 auditors with those of Stages 5 and 6 auditors.[3] For instance, while a Stage 3 auditor's responses to dilemmas would be based on considerations such as making sure his or her fellow auditors are not hurt, a Stage 4 auditor's responses would be governed by following the auditing standards (i.e., rules of the society). Stage 5 and 6 auditors would be concerned with the broader "what should be" notions that are associated with Kohlberg's two highest stages. These auditors would also follow the auditing standards but would be more sensitive to ethical problems, which may indicate a need to increase the scope of the audit. However, Bernardi and Arnold (1997) and Ponemon (1992) report that the profession has been retaining and promoting a higher proportion of lower-moral-development auditors, which could result in a lower level of sensitivity to ethical issues.

Rest (1986b) and Armstrong (1993) argue that liberal arts courses in the humanities, social studies, literature, contemporary issues, and ethics increase one's sensitivity to ethical issues and moral development. Ponemon and Glazer (1990) found that accounting students and CPAs from the liberal arts college have higher average P scores than similar groups from a large university with a conventional (AACSB) accounting program. While the current level of education for accountants in the British Isles is quite diverse, the current trend is to hire individuals with

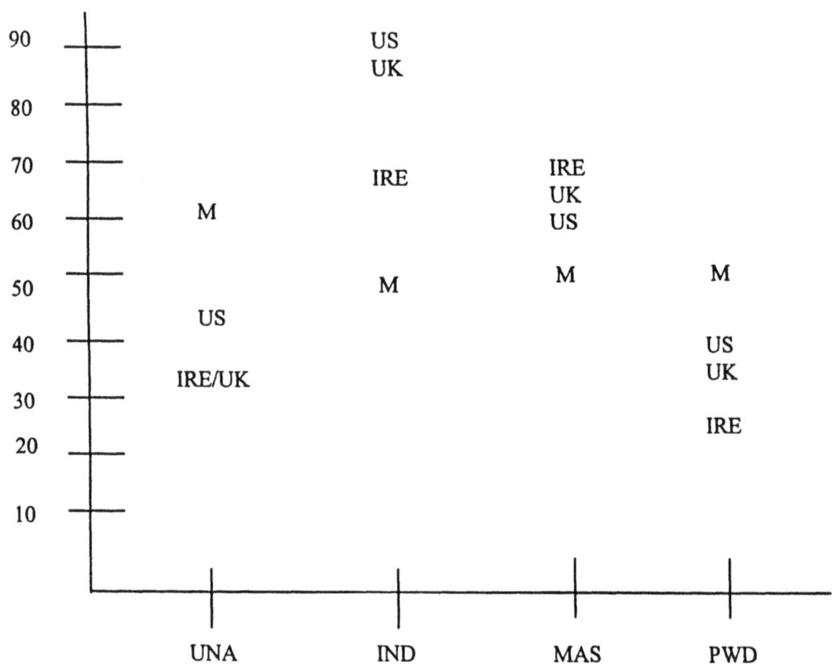

Notes: Hofstede's Index scores along vertical axis
Where: UNA Uncertainty Avoidance; IND Individualism; MAS Masculinity; PWD Power Distance; M Mean of 39 countries sampled; UK United Kingdom; US United States; IR Ireland

Figure 1. Hofstede's Four Country Indexes

an undergraduate education. Up until recently, schools in the British Isles had not granted undergraduate degrees in accounting, so audit partners from the British Isles with three-year honors degrees should have a stronger background in liberal arts at the undergraduate level.[4] However, while the United States and the United Kingdom require college prior to entering practical training for accounting, Ireland has a provision that allows 17-year-olds to enter practical training (Schilder 1996, 105). Since moral development increases throughout one's life and education plays a substantial role in this development (Rest 1986b), Irish auditors' average moral development could be affected by this provision.

Hofstede (1991) notes that cultural aspects may cause differences in decisions in similar circumstances among managers in various countries. In his research, Hofstede uses four measures: uncertainty avoidance, individualism, masculinity, and power distance. Individualism and power distance could affect a person's perceptions of an ethical situation (Cohen et al. 1995) and, thus, that person's responses on the Defining Issues Test (Rest 1979a). As shown in Figure 1, all three countries have scores which are in the same general range; however, there are some notable differences. While the United States tends more toward uncertainty avoidance, Ireland scores lower on the individualism and power distance areas.

Given the difference in individualism between Ireland and the other two countries, one might expect that auditors from the United States and the United Kingdom would score lower on the Defining Issues Test than auditors from Ireland (Cohen et al. 1995). Although Hofstede provides an expectation for cultural differences, the accounting profession may depart from the norms of the general population in particular countries. For instance, while Rest notes that there is only a small difference between the scores of males and females on the Defining Issues Test, most recent accounting research indicates that female accountants score higher than male accountants on this test (Bernardi and Arnold 1997; Bernardi 1995; Etherington and Schulting 1995; Sweeney 1995; Shaub 1994; Lampe and Finn 1992).

A major factor in many cultures is religion. Using the Catholic/Protestant ratio [(%Catholic – %Protestant)/(%Catholic + %Protestant)], Taylor and Hudson (1972, Table 4.16) report ratios of: –0.75 for the United Kingdom (i.e., predominantly Protestant), 0.75 for Ireland (i.e., predominantly Catholic), and –.09 for the United States (i.e., essentially neutral). Bernardi (1995) found that students from a predominantly Catholic college were 50% less likely to have attended both public elementary and public high schools than students attending a large public university and a public college. He also found that the average level of moral development (as measured by Rest's Defining Issues Test) varied by college type. While the average P score on the Defining Issues test was 51.2 for accounting majors at the Catholic college, it was 45.1 (36.5) for the accounting majors at the large public university (public college). Hofstede's (1980) data indicate that, for individualism and power distance considerations which are associated with ethical sensitivity (Cohen et al. 1995), the United Kingdom and United States were nearly equal with Ireland outside the cluster group (Hofstede 1980, 223).

Given the data from Armstrong (1993), Ponemon and Glazer (1990), and Rest (1986b) that exposure to a strong liberal arts education increases moral development, one would expect accountants from the British Isles to be at a higher level of moral development than accountants from the United States. However, if all auditors have not experienced the same level of formal education, other differences could influence their level of moral development. Therefore, in view of results in Bernardi (1995), Cohen et al. (1995), and Hofstede (1980), one might anticipate that Irish partners whould score higher than auditors from the United Kingdom and the United States, and Hypothesis 1 can be stated (all research hypotheses are stated in their alternate form):

Hypothesis 1. The average level of moral judgment for auditors from Ireland will be higher than average level of moral judgment for auditors from the United States and the United Kingdom.

Auditor Actions

Recently, research has examined the cognitive processes involving personally held beliefs or opinions that auditors draw upon when resolving a conflict. Empirical studies report that the level of one's moral reasoning is correlated with actions taken in specific situations (Bernardi 1994; Bernardi and Arnold 1994; Shaub, Finn, and Munter 1993; Arnold and Ponemon 1991; Ponemon and Gabhart 1990). Shaub et al. found that ethical orientation was associated with an increased sensitivity to ethical issues. Ponemon and Gabhart reported that low-moral-development auditors were sensitive to factors relating to personal penalties. However, Arnold and Ponemon found that high-moral-development auditors were more conscious of harming others.

Arnold and Ponemon (1991) also found that moral development was associated with an individual's propensity to whistle-blow in ethical situations. These authors reported that low-moral-development internal auditors were less likely to predict whistle-blowing as a way of reporting wrongdoing if there was a high probability of the whistle-blower facing retaliation and/or job termination. Ponemon and Gabhart (1990) concluded that an auditor's moral development can affect the strategy and effectiveness of an audit. Bernardi and Arnold (1994) found that moral development influenced managers' estimates of materiality. Bernardi (1994) reported that, except for high-moral-development managers, fraud detection was not influenced by client-integrity and competence ratings. Therefore, it appears that one would conclude that high-moral-development individuals should be more sensitive to the ethical cues and implications of a scenario.

Auditors continuously face issues requiring judgment that involve conflicts between the client's management (who hires them), the client's present and potential stockholders/creditors (who rely on their audit attestation), and the auditing firm who employs them. These conflicts include decisions concerning the amount of audit work required, which can involve under-auditing (Bernardi and Arnold 1996; Raghunathan 1992; Kelley and Margheim 1990; Pany, Pourciau, and Margheim 1989; Cook and Kelley 1988; Margheim and Pany 1986; Alderman and Dietrick 1982). Another problem is not having sufficient time in the budget, which can lead to underreporting (Bernardi and Arnold 1996; Ponemon 1992; Kelley and Margheim 1990; Pany et al. 1989; Cook and Kelley 1988; Margheim and Pany 1986).

The association between an auditor's moral development and sensitivity to ethical issues suggests the use of audit scenarios that imply some degree of conflict of interest. The scenarios (described below), which were developed for this research, dealt with the potential for premature sign-off (under-auditing) or underreporting the number of hours actually worked (i.e., eating time). Underreporting and under-auditing issues were chosen since they posses the requirements of a "moral dilemma" (Colby and Kohlberg 1987, 10):

> [T]hey deal with personally-held values and not tangible facts; are based upon some issue involving oneself and others; and are framed around an issue of "ought" instead of personal likings or preferences.

Bernardi (1994), Arnold and Ponemon (1991), and Ponemon and Gabhart (1990) found that increased moral development intensifies one's sensitivity to the ethical implications in conflict-resolution situations. Given this increased sensitivity to the implications of ethical cues, one would anticipate that higher-moral-development auditors would increase the scope of the audit as perceived risk increases, which leads to the second hypothesis:

Hypothesis 2. An auditor's estimate of the probability of doing the additional audit work required to complete the task will increase as that auditor's level of moral judgment increases.

Country Differences

Cohen et al. (1995), Otley and Pierce (1996), Agacer and Doupnik (1991), Belkaoui and Picur (1991), Ponemon and Gabhart (1990), and Karnes et al. (1989) examined auditor behavior using international samples. While Cohen et al. (1995) and Ponemon and Gabhart (1990) addressed the question of cross-country effects on ethical dilemmas in auditing, only Ponemon and Gabhart's study included measuring auditors moral development. Ponemon and Gabhart found an association between moral development and auditor judgments that differs between U.S. and Canadian auditors. Canadian auditors were less likely to perceive premature sign-off or shifting time as solutions to time-budget problems. Otley and Pierce (1996) and Kelley and Margheim (1990) found that Irish (U.S.) auditors perceived

Table 1. Comparing the United States and United Kingdom's Generally Accepted Accounting Principles

Accounting Principles	U.S. GAAP Proun		U.S. GAAP Para	U.K. GAAP Proun		U.K. GAAP Para	Ratio US:UK
Specific Examples							
Earnings per Share	APB	15	70	SSAP	3	40	1.75:1
Acquisitions and Mergers	APB	16	96	FRS	6	30	3.20:1
Contingencies	FASB	5	54	SSAP	18	24	2.25:1
Pensions	FASB	87	260	SSAP	24	105	2.48:1
Issued between 1970 and 1990:							
Accounting Principles		121			34		3.56:1
Technical Bulletins and Interpretations		97			65		1.49:1

Notes: Note: The data for Ireland is not provided because, while "There are some differences between legal requirements relating to financial statements in the Republic of Ireland and the United Kingdom, [the] generally accepted accounting principles are common to both countries" (Price Waterhouse 1993, 90).

Proun The specific pronouncement or number of pronouncements in that country's GAAP.

Para The number of paragraphs in the pronouncements in that country's GAAP including special adaptations for Ireland and Scotland. However, it does not include illustrations or "Basis of Conclusions" paragraphs.

budget tightness; however, Otley and Pierce found that the extent of auditor responses to budget tightness varied between the two studies. Hofstede (1980) would not have predicted these differences in responses since the United States, Canada, and Ireland are all nearly identical on his four dimensions.

Hofstede (1991) notes that cultural aspects may cause differences in decisions on similar circumstances among managers in various countries. Hofstede (1991, 187) notes that one of the consequences of low uncertainty avoidance would be "few and general laws and rules." Since all three countries in this study would be considered low for uncertainty avoidance, one would anticipate that their professional standards would all be short. However, this premise seems to be violated by the U.S. accounting profession because there are differences in the number and length of pronouncements in the generally accepted accounting principles among countries. As shown in Table 1, the average length of the U.S. versions of four selected pronouncements is over twice those of the British Isles' versions.

Further evidence of this is shown in the AICPA's Code of Professional Conduct, Section on Independence, Integrity and Objectivity, which has 16 paragraphs of interpretation in addition to 98 specific rulings. These case rulings cover specific topics such as (Delaney 1995, 591):

1. A university faculty member cannot be independent to a student senate fund if the student senate is part of the university which is the member's employer;

2. If a client financial institute merely services a loan, independence is not impaired; or
3. If a member's spouse, as an employee, performs only bookkeeping services for a client, independence is not impaired.

Specific examples such as these are not found in the Institute of Chartered Accountants in England and Wales' (ICAEW) (1996) code, which cautions:

> The threat to objectivity will depend upon the closeness of the relationship and associations, the strength of an associate's interest in the firm's retaining a client, and the extent to which the introduction of business by an outside source is able to affect the firm's fee income.

Economic and legal factors have also played an important role in the historical development of the observed differences in specificity and volume between the accounting and auditing standards of the United States and the British Isles (Gorelik 1994). However, such explanations do not address the human dimension of the profession and correspondingly the official bodies that created the pronouncements. An equally important element in the auditing process is the auditor's professional judgment. Developmental differences in the professional standards could also be caused by differences in both the social and psychological characteristics of those individuals who choose careers in public accounting in each country (Hofstede 1980, 1991).

While some theories hold that the organization's environment affects individuals' behavior, Schneider (1987) maintains the reverse is more prevalent. His data suggest that the personal characteristics of the participants affect the environment and the organization's functioning within that environment. Differences in the pronouncement-generating cycle, noted above, might be attributable to selected characteristics of the individuals in the organizations (i.e., such as those identified by Hofstede) as well as the legal and structural nature of the accounting and business environments. Cohen et al.'s (1995, 57) data support this premise; they conclude that the "U.S. group [of auditors] was more tolerant of actions that would either maintain or expand their client base". Hampden-Turner and Trompenaars (1995) find that 75% (55%) of U.S. (U.K.) managers believe that "a company is a set of tasks and functions." The other 25% (45%) of U.S. (U.K.) managers believe that a company is a group of people who have a social relationship with the organization and other employees. Schilder (1996, 100) posits that "Such differences may have material consequences for auditing methodologies" especially as they concern top-down communications, group responsibilities, and the decision-making process. Schilder (1996, 101) observes that "the issue of cultural differences adds a specific dimension to questions about the effectiveness of audit methodologies in different European countries."

Given these differences, one would expect that the estimates of auditors from countries with similar values for Hofstede's constructs would vary and that the estimates of U.S. auditors would be lower than those of auditors from the British Isles (Hypothesis 3).

Hypothesis 3. Estimates of the probability of doing more audit work will be lower for auditors from the United States than for auditors from the British Isles.

SUBJECTS AND MATERIALS

Subjects

The subjects used in the sample were randomly selected from the membership books of the Institute of Chartered Accountants in England and Wales, the Institute of Chartered Accountants in Ireland, and the American Institute of Certified Public Accountants. The U.K. group (England and Wales) included one Institute member per Big Six office and names selected from a listing of regional firms with five or more partners. The Irish partners were randomly selected from members currently working in the Republic of Ireland. Mailings in the United States included all partners of two Big Six accounting firms located in one city. The U.S. sample also included partners from regional CPA firms throughout the Northeast region of the United States.[5] Each subject received a questionnaire that consisted of three audit-

Table 2. Demographic Characteristics of the Sample

		Ireland	*United Kingdom*	*United States*
Experience	(yr)	23.1	27.6	27.6
P score	(DIT)	27.8	22.7	23.9
Sample	(n)	20	31	51
Gender				
Male	(%)	100.0	90.3	74.5
Female	(%)	0.0	9.7	25.5
Education[1]				
One	(%)	35.0	45.2	5.9
Two	(%)	0.0	3.2	0.0
Three	(%)	30.0	48.4	74.5
Four	(%)	35.0	3.2	19.6
Firm size[2]				
One	(%)	35.0	9.7	74.5
Two	(%)	25.0	25.8	0.0
Three	(%)	10.0	6.5	3.9
Four	(%)	30.0	58.0	21.6

Notes:

1. Education:	Highest Level	2. Firm Size:	Professionals
One	High School	One	1 to 10
Two	Two year	Two	11 to 50
Three	Bachelors'	Three	51 to 100
Four	Graduate	Four	100+

ing scenarios, the Defining Issues Test, and a background data sheet.[6] Table 2 presents the demographic characteristics of the sample.

The most notable differences in Table 2 are for gender and firm size. The entry of a significant number of females into the partner ranks is a recent phenomena in the United States (Hooks and Cheramy 1994). Dalton, Hill, and Ramsay (forthcoming) report that males are more likely to remain in public accounting after leaving their original firms than females. If females remain in public accounting, they normally chose smaller firms (Hooks and Cheramy 1994).

The overall response rate was approximately 27.6% (138 of 500), which is considered a satisfactory response rate for this type of survey (Emory 1985). Although the mailings were intended to survey only audit partners, 36 of the responses came from individuals who were not at the partner level. While most of these auditors were managers, their experience varied widely and they were not included in the sample. The final sample of partners all had between 12 and 48 years of audit experience; this experience range did not differ between the Big Six and regional firms.

Audit Scenarios

The first part of the questionnaire consisted of a set of instructions (Appendix A) and three audit scenarios involving dilemmas that were worded so that only one of two actions could be taken (e.g., "Do More" or "Do Not Do More" audit work prior to signing off on the audit). After reading the background for each scenario, the subjects were asked to predict the probabilities that the auditor described in the scenario would actually follow each of the two alternatives (probabilities totaled 100% for each case).[7] Each scenario had to have a dilemma that did not provide an obvious right-or-wrong decision. While one might argue that there is a "textbook" correct answer (e.g., Do enough audit work and report all time), other considerations can influence an auditor's thought process and create a dilemma (Appendix B). Scenario 1's dilemma is potentially making a client unhappy and possibly losing this client in the future. Scenario 2 raises the question of doing work when there is only a limited chance of being paid by the client. Scenario 3 creates the dilemma of violating company policy.

The three auditing scenarios were developed from discussions with partners and senior managers in public accounting in the United States. An original list of eight cases was developed and pilot-tested to determine the reasonableness of each scenario and dispersion of results. Twenty-eight partners and senior managers from regional and national accounting firms took part in the pilot testing.[8] The auditors participating in the pilot test came from a random sample from firms in the Northeast region of the United States. The mix of auditors asked to participate in the pilot-testing phase reflected the anticipated mix of auditors from large and regional firms for the actual sample.

Defining Issues Test

The second part of the questionnaire was the three-scenario version of the Defining Issues Test (Rest 1979a). The DIT presents subjects with a series of dilemmas and a choice of standard responses distributed among Kohlberg's highest five stages. Each of Rest's responses represents the style of moral reasoning at one of the highest five stages of moral development. An individual's score on the DIT represents "the relative importance a subject gives to principled moral considerations in making a decision about moral dilemmas" (Rest 1979b, 5). While responses corresponding to Stages 2-6 are considered on the Defining Issues Test, an individual's P score measures the percentage of responses the subject makes at either Stage 5 or Stage 6 (Rest 1986b).

Rest (1986b, 101) notes that the DIT has been widely tested and shows a high degree of validity and internal consistency even in cross-cultural studies. In a review of international studies using subjects from Australia, Hong Kong, Iceland, Korea, Taiwan, and the United States, P scores consistently increased from approximately 25 at age 14 to 40 at age 20 (Rest 1986b, 108). The range of P scores at age 20 was within four points for the subjects from Australia, Iceland, and the United States. Kohlberg's (1969) model has been applied to a wide variety of social and ethical problems or conflicts arising out of individual self-interest versus the interests of the society (i.e., conflict situations or moral dilemmas). The three scenarios used in this research possess the requirements of a "moral dilemma" (Colby and Kohlberg 1987).

ANALYSIS

Since the sum of the two responses to each scenario had to equal 100%, the analysis was based on the response for the first option only (e.g., "Do more audit work"). The data were analyzed three ways: (1) a comparison of DIT P scores among partners from the British Isles and United States, (2) a comparison of DIT P scores to scenario responses, and (3) a comparison of the responses of partners from the British Isles and the United States. Since a Kolmogorov-Smirnov test for normality indicated the data were not normally distributed, all research hypotheses were tested using the conservative Dunn multiple comparison test (Hollander and Wolfe 1974, 125-126).

Research Hypotheses

As shown in Table 3, Hypothesis 1, that the average level of moral development for partners from Ireland would be higher than for partners from the United States and the United Kingdom, was not supported by the data. While Irish partners scored higher than partners from both the United States and the United Kingdom,

Table 3. P Scores, Experience, and Scenario Responses by Country

	DIT P Score	Education Level	Scenario Responses S1	S2	S3
Ireland	27.8	2.65	43.9	65.3	47.0
United Kingdom	22.7	2.10	31.1	59.9	49.0
United States	23.9	3.08	32.8	56.2	42.9

Note: Education level from Table 2

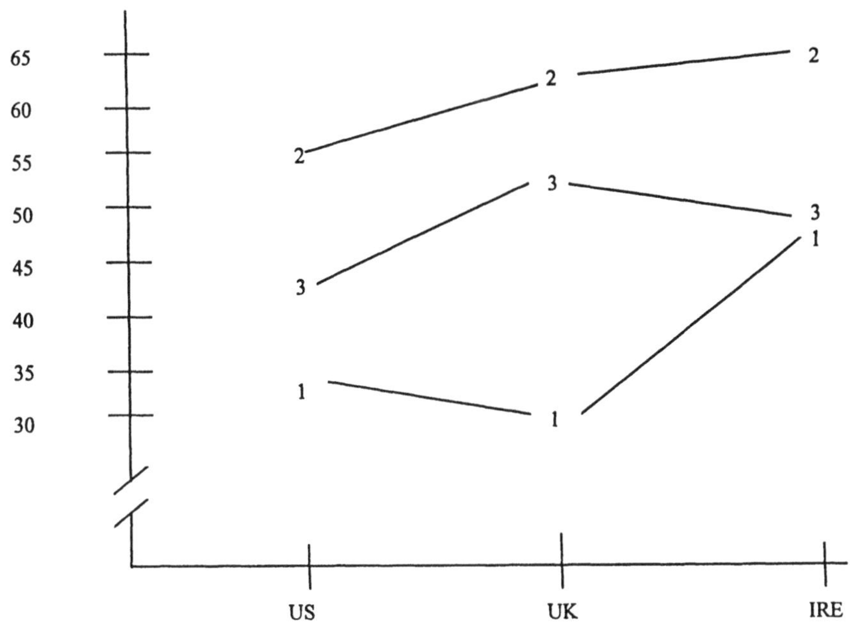

Notes: Scenario Response on Vertical Axis.
Numbers within the figure represent the means for the three scenarios.

Figure 2. Mean Estimate by Scenario and Country

the difference was not significant ($p = .123$). However, 35% of the Irish auditors and 48.4% of the U.K. audit partners only have a high school or two-year college education (Table 2), which is important since prior research has shown that education and moral development are correlated. One might hypothesize that, as the older partners in the British Isles retire (i.e., those with only high school or two-year college degrees), the average level of moral development should increase for partners in the British Isles.

The effect of auditor moral judgment on the probability estimates of "doing more audit work" (Hypothesis 2) compared those individuals who scored above

26.7 (i.e., in the top third of the sample) on the DIT with those who scored below 26.7. This procedure has been used in prior research (Bernardi 1995; Ponemon and Gabhart 1993; Pincus 1990). Hypothesis 2, that there would be a difference for higher moral development auditors, can only be rejected (p = .063) for Scenario 3 (underreporting). The data indicate that high-moral-development partners (i.e., those who scored in the upper third on the DIT) estimated the probability of underreporting lower than did the other partners in the sample. If one aligns the countries as hypothesized for scores on the DIT, four of the six scenario comparisons (see Figure 2) follow the anticipated direction with respect to moral development (i.e., United States to United Kingdom to Ireland).

Hypothesis 3, which evaluated country differences for each scenario independent of DIT scores, was partially supported by the data (Table 3). In response to Scenario 1, Irish partners estimated the probability of doing more audit work, even if it meant delaying the audit opinion, higher than partners from both the U.K. ($p < .10$) and the United States ($p < .10$). For Scenario 2, Irish partners estimated the probability of doing more audit work even in the face of client disapproval higher than did partners from the United States ($p < .10$) but not higher than partners from the United Kingdom. There were no differences in responses to Scenario 3.

The data for the three scenarios were combined into one set composed of 306 (102 auditors × 3 scenarios) data points to evaluate the overall probability of "doing more audit work." This provided a way to evaluate the probability of "doing more audit work" for each country compared to the responses given by auditors of the other two countries. Using this methodology, Irish auditors were more likely to do the additional required audit work than were auditors from the United States (52.1% versus 44.0%, $p < .10$), but not than auditors from the United Kingdom (52.1% versus 46.7%).

Supplementary Analysis

Since age is normally a surrogate for education in professional organizations, it was anticipated that partners would essentially be at the same education level, with only minor differences for the British Isles; however, the actual sample did not support this assumption. One possible explanation for this lack of association may be that the level of moral development was lower than the levels of moral development found in other research, which may have influenced the research. For example, Bernardi (1994) found that auditors who have P scores of 40 or higher (lower than 40) were (not) sensitive to cues on client integrity and competence. A second possible cause is that, while the education systems in Ireland and the United Kingdom are similar, the United Kingdom is a more culturally diverse country than Ireland. So, although GAAP for these two countries are similar, the individuals who implement these rules could be significantly different.

A final explanation is that the education levels between auditors from the United States and the British Isles are dramatically different (Table 3). While it is still technically possible to enter public accounting without a four-year degree in the British Isles, in practice firms rarely hire individuals with only these credentials. The difference in the average education levels between the British Isles and the United States (2.31 versus 3.08) is significant ($p < .02$).

DISCUSSION

Ponemon (1992) observed a decrease in average DIT score at upper staff levels and advanced the notion that this decrease may have been caused by the organization's selection-socialization processes. Thus, by virtue of an "up or out philosophy," individuals at a high level of ethical reasoning appear to leave public accounting. In this study, the similarity among the partners from Ireland, the United Kingdom, and the United States suggests that the selection-socialization process may be as pervasive in Ireland and the United Kingdom as it is in the United States. The only mitigating fact is that, as the education level for auditors in the future increases beyond the high school and two-year college levels, the average level of moral development should also increase for auditors in the British Isles.

With respect to the socialization process and quality auditing, the results of this research are disturbing. In the absence of the more specific guidance provided in the U.S. standards and codes, auditors from the United Kingdom and Ireland indicated they were more prone to do the additional audit work required. Hofstede (1980, 1991) would attribute this difference to the fact that both Ireland and the United Kingdom rank below the United States in uncertainty avoidance; however, as shown, U.S. standards are more lengthy than are those of the British Isles. The evidence in this research suggests that, in the course of moving toward more specific standards, the British Isles could nurture the belief of U.S. managers that "a company is a set of tasks and functions" (Hampden-Turner and Trompenaars 1995). This could affect the level of top-down communications, group responsibilities, and the decision-making process (Schilder 1996). Another explanation for this could be that U.S. standards spell out what should be avoided, in essence making audit judgments forced-choice questions (i.e., yes, it's O.K., or no, it's against the standard). Since standards in the British Isles are not as specific as those in the United States, they equate the determination of the level of audit work to an open-ended question, which is harder to answer. Given the movement toward harmonization in Europe, the trend in these countries recently has been to become more specific in their standards and codes (i.e., more like U.S. standards and codes). If there is a relationship between the concept of "do what is necessary to assure a quality audit" and more general standards, which appears to prevail in Ireland and the United Kingdom, the relationship may be lost when auditors have to comply with very intricate standards and codes (i.e., the United States).

A final concern is that the level of moral development for Irish partners may not increase with time should the provision for non-college graduates entering the profession continue. Most proposals for implementing the 150-hour requirement in the United States include a number of courses that have been shown to increase ethical sensitivity (Armstrong 1993; Rest 1986b). Since Armstrong and Rest report that moral development is related to educational attainment, policy-setting bodies in the British Isles should consider the negative impact on ethical sensitivity of not having a college education as a qualification for the profession.

The nonsignificant results in ethics measurement and cross-national determination of sufficient auditing have practice and research implications. While the level of moral development for auditors from the British Isles is only slightly higher than that of auditors from the United States, the scenario responses and DIT scores follow the hypothesized relationship that higher average DIT scores result in higher average scenario responses. Since education and age explain 52% of the variation in DIT scores (Rest and Thoma 1985), the transition to a minimum education level of a bachelors degree for essentially all auditors from the British Isles should result in the average DIT score increasing by about 10 points (Rest 1986b). Given prior research on the increased sensitivity to ethical implications for high-moral-development auditors (Bernardi 1994; Bernardi and Arnold 1994; Arnold and Ponemon 1991; Ponemon and Gabhart 1990), an increase in moral development should be accompanied by an increase in scenario estimates.[9] Finally, the lack of significance for the first two scenarios and the proximity of U.K. and U.S. auditors' responses (Figure 2) provide evidence that "differences may have material consequences for auditing methodologies" (Schilder 1996, 100). Irish auditors were more willing to do the additional audit work in all three scenarios (Figure 2). This suggests that Cohen et al.'s (1995, 57) finding that the "U.S. group [of auditors] was more tolerant of actions that would either maintain or expand their client base" may also apply to auditors from the United Kingdom.

This study has at least four limitations. First, while a strength of this research is its use of partners rather than staff, this also creates the research's most notable limitation. The sample size is only 102; however, part of the justification for the study was to determine what the impact on the audit was when the profession retains and promotes lower-moral-development auditors. Second, although the U.S. sample came from offices located in the Northeast, most research has similar geographic limitations.[10] Third, differences in education level in the sample were considerable (Table 2); however, the proportion of partners in the British Isles with only a high school education (41.2%) was not anticipated prior to gathering the data. Fourth, most behavioral studies are hampered by time constraints that influence the amount of information that can be reasonably elicited from any subject. This study was no exception; the short form of the Defining Issues Test and three audit scenarios were used because of time constraints.

Before one can correctly assert the presence (or lack of) a relationship between moral judgment and responses to specific auditor actions, additional testing is needed. However, the findings of this study indicate that investigating the effects of intercountry behavioral differences among auditors should be a continuing area for future research. Research could use similar scenarios for a group of auditors from countries within the European Union; this could assist regulatory bodies in addressing policy issues.

APPENDIX A: INSTRUCTIONS IN LETTER

The three case scenarios contained in Questionnaire #1 are based on actual situations and were selected at random from a group of 50 similar cases all involving an employee or partner with a public accounting firm. In exactly 50% of these 50 cases, the employee or partner took the first of the two actions identified on the response sheet. In the remaining 25 cases, the second action was taken.

Your job is to read three randomly selected case scenarios and from the information provided try to predict for each case which action the employee or partner took. Using your professional judgment, please assign up to 100 points to each of the following two categories:

(A) The first alternative provided . . . . ________
(B)The second alternative provided . . . . ________
Total Points: 100

Unless you are absolutely sure of your prediction, do not allocate all 100 points to a single response. For example, if you believe that the employee or partner did in fact take the action described in the first of the two alternative choices provided but you are only 80% certain of your prediction, you should assign 80 points to choice (A) and 20 points to choice (B).

The sequence of the cases is important. So please complete each case before starting the next one. Please place your responses on the sheet provided.

APPENDIX B

Scenario 1: The February 28th "Sign-Off" Problem

Company "X" is a long-standing, significantly large audit client that has given some indication of displeasure with the amount of time it has taken the auditing firm to complete the audit each year and has even mentioned the possibility of seeking a different auditing firm. The company has called a press conference for February 28 to announce the audited earnings figure. The audit partner noted that while it would take a major effort, there should be no problem in completing the audit by that date. Throughout February, the client has been assured that all is going well.

On February 27, in the very final stages of the audit, a staff auditor discovers something which probably should be investigated a little further. The audit manager and partner agree that further investigation would normally be warranted and that they will only be sure by conducting additional work prior to signing off. However, they also believe that such an investigation will probably NOT produce anything significant. The problem is that it will take at least TWO DAYS to complete such an investigation, thus prohibiting the client from releasing "audited" figures on February 28.

Scenario 2:
Statistical Sampling versus More Audit Work

A chartered accounting firm uses a statistical sampling procedure when auditing a client. The results of the statistical tests fall within the allowable limits, indicating that no further audit work is needed. It is quite reasonable to assume that such a conclusion based on the test results would adequately hold up in any legal action. However, the audit senior has a "gut feeling" that the test results, while statistically sound, indicate a certain pattern of client activity which should be further investigated. The audit manager and partner agree with the senior and present the case to the client. The client's response is, "Do the work if you want. But don't expect us to pay for the extra work. The statistical sampling results are good enough for us and should be good enough for you."

The audit manager and partner realize that the job is already over budget and do not what to have to absorb the extra time. Assume that the amount of extra time needed would be material.

Scenario 3:
Reporting of Time to Complete the Audit Task

A staff accountant with about one-and-one-half years of experience is in the midst of completing the substantive test. The scope of the audit and the statistical sampling plan call for sampling, testing, and tracing 50 transactions through the entire accounting record system. After having traced 28 of these 50 transaction and having noticed a number of errors, he realizes that he will never be able to complete this task with in the allocated time. While this is the first area in which he has fallen behind the time-budget on this audit, he knows that he has been receiving relatively low evaluations on prior jobs due to time-budget problems.

To complicate matters, the senior has been having problems with other staff accountants on this job and it appears that the entire job will not be completed within the time-budget. When this staff accountant notifies the senior about this newly developed time problem, the senior replies: "This is all we need. We cannot reduce the sample size at this point, so I guess we will have to finish all 50 transactions. However, I expect that a good portion of any time over the budget will go unreported. The last thing you need, with your record, is to go over budget. And don't give me that look about 'eating-time' being against firm policy. Everyone does it once in a while including those partners who preach against it. Furthermore, we both realize that no one is going to catch you doing it."

NOTES

1. The Republic of Ireland will be referred to as Ireland for the remainder of this research. When Ireland and the United Kingdom are referred to jointly, the term British Isles will be used.
2. For an extensive review of moral development theory, see Kohlberg (1969) and Rest (198b6).
3. The discussion is limited to the Stages 3-6 range since Bernardi and Arnold (1997) found that 97.4% (i.e., 49.8% at Stages 3 and 4 and 47.6% at Stages 5 and 6) of a group of 494 auditors' scores on the Defining Issues Test were in this stage range.
4. This implicitly assumes that a three-year honors degree is equivalent to a four-year bachelors degree.
5. This sample included accountants attending the New England Graduate Accounting Studies Conference (NEGASC), who received the survey questionnaires as part of their conference materials.
6. In order to ensure anonymity, subjects were asked not to include their name on any of the returned materials; therefore, follow-up questionnaires could not be distributed to nonrespondents.
7. Prior research (Ponemon and Gabhart 1990; Rest 1986) indicates that when discussing ethical issues, subjects often provide more representative answers (i.e., closer to their own actions) when asked to predict what others might do. In part, this is based on research findings on the "False Consensus Effect" (Marks and Miller 1997; Ross, Greene, and House 1977) and "Social Desirability Bias" (McDonald and Ho 1996) phenomena.
8. Partners and senior managers who helped to develop the scenarios were not used in the pilot-testing phase. Information and offices used in the pilot-testing phase were not included in the final study. The decision to use only three scenarios was based on time constraints given the other material used in the research. In the final sample, many of the partners from the regional firms indicated that they had worked for Big Six firms in the past.
9. There are, of course, other possibilities that may explain the lack of a relationship between moral development and scenario responses.
10. At the partner level, this limitation may not be as severe given the socialization and promotion processes. Additionally, many partners in larger firms are mobile; this may be caused by opportunities for promotion to office managing partner, client movements, or the rule that audit partners must change after seven years.

REFERENCES

Agacer, G.M., and T.S. Doupnik. 1991. Perceptions of auditor independence: A cross-cultural study. *The International Journal of Accounting* 26: 220-237.

Alderman, C.W., and J.W. Dietrick. 1982. Auditors' perceptions of time budget pressures and premature audit signoffs: A replication and extension. *Auditing: A Journal of Practice & Theory* (Winter): 54-68.

Armstrong, M. 1993. Ethics and professionalism in accounting education: A sample course. *Journal of Accounting Education* 11: 77-92.

Arnold, D.F., and L.A. Ponemon. 1991. Internal auditors' perceptions of whistle-blowing and the influence of moral reasoning: An experiment. *Auditing: A Journal of Practice & Theory* 10(Fall): 1-15.

Belkaoui, A., and R.D. Picur. 1991. Cultural determinism and the perception of accounting concepts. *The International Journal of Accounting* 26: 118-130.

Benston, G. 1975. Accounting standards in the United States and the United Kingdom: Their nature, causes and consequences. *Vanderbilt Law Review* 28: 235-268.

Bernardi, R.A. 1994. Fraud detection: The effect of client integrity and competence and auditor cognitive style. *Auditing: A Journal of Practice and Theory* 13 (Supplement): 68-84.

Bernardi, R.A. 1995. Ethics research in accounting: A note on using the defining issues test. *Accounting Educators' Journal* 7(Fall): 1-16.

Bernardi, R.A., and D.F. Arnold. 1994. The influence of client integrity and competence and auditor characteristics on materiality estimates. *The Irish Accounting Review* 1: 1-23.

Bernardi, R.A., and D.F. Arnold. 1996. Auditor underreporting and premature sign-off: A behavioural study. *The Irish Accounting Review* 3(Fall): 1-22.

Bernardi, R.A., and D.F. Arnold. 1997. An examination of moral development within public accounting by gender, staff level, and firm. *Contemporary Accounting Research* 14(4).

Cohen, J.R., L.W. Pant, and D.J. Sharp. 1995. An exploratory examination of international differences in auditors' ethical perceptions. *Behavioral Research in Accounting* 7: 37-64.

Colby, A., and L. Kohlberg. 1987. *The Measurement of Moral Judgement*, New York: Cambridge University Press.

Cook, E., and T. Kelley. 1988. Auditor stress and time budgets. *CPA Journal* 58(7): 83-86.

Dalton, D.R., J.W. Hill, and R.R. Ramsay. Forthcoming. Women as managers and partners: Context specific predictors of turnover in public accounting, *Auditing: A Journal of Practice & Theory.*

Delaney, P.R. 1995. *Wiley CPA Examination Review* 21 ed., Vol. 1. New York: J. Wiley & Sons.

Emory, C.W. 1985. *Business Research Methods*, 3rd edition. Homewood, IL: Richard D. Irwin.

Etherington, L.D., and L. Shulting. 1995. Ethical development of accountants. In *Research on Accounting Ethics*, Vol. 1, ed. L.A. Ponemon, 235-251. Greenwich, CT: JAI Press.

Gorelik, G. 1994. The setting of accounting standards: Canada, the United Kingdom, and the United States. *International Journal of Accounting* 29: 95-122.

Hampden-Turner, C., and F. Trompenaars. 1995. *The seven cultures of capitalism: Value systems for creating wealth in the United States, Britian, Japan, Germany, France, Sweden and the Netherlands.* London: Judy Piatkus Ltd.

Hofstede, G. 1980. *Culture's Consequences*. Beverly Hills, CA: Sage.

Hofstede, G. 1991. *Cultures and Organizations: Software of the Mind*. New York: McGraw Hill.

Hollander, M., and D.A. Wolfe. 1973. *Nonparametric Statical Methods*, New York: John Wiley.

Hooks, K.L., and S.J. Cheramy. 1994. Facts and myths about women CPAs. *Journal of Accountancy* (October): 79-86.

Ijiri, Y. 1983. On the Accountability-Based Conceptual Framework of Accounting. *Journal of Accounting and Public Policy* 2: 75-81.

Inkeles, A., and D.J. Levinson. 1969. National character: The study of modal personality and sociocultural systems. In *The Handbook of Social Psychology*, Vol. 4, eds. G. Lindsay and E. Aronson, 418-506. Reading, MA: Addison-Wesley.

Institute of Chartered Accountants in England and Wales. 1996. *Members' Handbook*, Guide to Professional Ethics Section: Integrity, Objectivity, and Independence, Par. 4.15, p. 194.

Karnes, A., J. Sterner, R. Welker, and F. Wu. 1989. A bicultural study of independent auditors' perceptions of unethical business practices. *The International Journal of Accounting* 24: 29-41.

Kelley, T., and L. Margheim. 1990. The impact of time budget pressure, personality, and leadership variables on dysfunctional auditor behavior. *Auditing: A Journal of Practice & Theory* (Spring): 21-42.

Kohlberg, L. 1969. Stages and sequences: The cognitive developmental approach to socialization. In *Handbook of Socialization Theory and Research*, ed. by D. Goslin, 347-480. Chicago, IL: Rand McNally.

Kohlberg, L. 1976. Moral stages and moralization. In *Moral Development and Behavior*, ed. T. Likona, 31-53. New York: Holt, Rinehart, and Winston.

Lampe, J.C., and D.W. Finn. 1992. Reply. *Auditing: A Journal of Practice and Theory* (Supplement): 68-73.

Lewis, B., M.D. Shields, and S.M. Young. 1983. Evaluating human judgements and decisions aids. *Journal of Accounting Research* 21(Spring): 271-285.

Margheim, L., and K. Pany. 1986. Quality control, premature signoff, and underreporting of time: Some empirical findings. *Auditing: A Journal of Practice & Theory* (Spring): 50-63.

Marks, G., and N. Miller. 1977. Ten years of research on the false-consensus effect: An empirical and theoretical review. *Psychological Bulletin* 102: 72-90.

McDonald, R., and K. Ho. 1996. Questioning techniques and social desirability response bias in ethical scenarios. Paper presented at the National Meeting of the American Accounting Association, Chicago, IL.

McHugh, G., and B. Stamp. 1992. Financial reporting in Ireland: Meeting the expectations of users. *European Accounting Review* 1: 427-436.

Otley, D.T., and B.J. Pierce. 1996. Auditor time budget pressure: Consequences and antecedents. *Accounting, Auditing, and Accountability Journal* 9(1): 31-58.

Pany, K., S. Pourciau, and L. Margheim. 1989. Controlling audit staff underreporting of time and premature signoffs: Some preliminary findings, In *Advances in Accounting*, Supp. 1, ed. B.N. Schwartz, 181-194. Greenwich, CT: JAI Press.

Pincus, K.V. 1990. Auditor individual differences and fairness of presentation judgments. *Auditing: A Journal of Practice & Theory* 9(Fall): 150-166.

Ponemon, L.A. 1992. Auditor underreporting of time and moral reasoning: An experimental lab study. *Contemporary Accounting Research* (Fall): 171-189.

Ponemon, L., and D.L. Gabhart. 1990. Auditor independence judgments: A cognitive-developmental model and experimental evidence. *Contemporary Accounting Research* 7(Fall): 227-251.

Ponemon, L., and D.L. Gabhart. 1993. *Ethical Reasoning in Accounting and Auditing*. Research Monograph No. 21. Vancouver, BC: CGA-Canada Research Foundation.

Ponemon, L.A., and A. Glazer. 1990. Accounting education and development: Influence of liberal learning on students and alumni in accounting practice. *Issues in Accounting Education* 5: 195-208.

Raghunathan, B. 1991. Premature signing-off of audit procedures: An analysis. *Accounting Horizons* (June): 71-79.

Rest, J. 1979a. *Defining Issues Test*. Minneapolis, MN: Center for the Study of Ethical Development/ University of Minnesota Press.

Rest, J. 1979b. *Development in Judging Moral Issues*. Minneapolis, MN: University of Minnesota Press.

Rest, J. 1986. *Moral Development: Advances in Research and Theory*. New York: Praeger.

Rest, J. 1986a. DIT Manual. Minneapolis: University of Minnesota Press.

Rest, J., and S.J. Thoma. 1985. Relation of moral judgment development to formal education. *Developmental Psychology* 21: 709-714.

Ross, L., D. Greene, and P. House. 1977. The "false consensus effect": An egocentric bias in social perception and attribution process. *Journal of Experimental Social Psychology* 13: 279-301.

Sanders, D.R. 1980. Psychological perspectives in management fraud. In *Management Fraud: Detection and Deterrence*, eds. R.K. Elliott and J.J. Willingham. 107-115. New York: Petrocelli.

Schilder, A. 1996. Research opportunities in auditing in the European Union. *Accounting Horizons* 10(4): 98-108.

Schneider, B. 1987. The people make the place. *Personnel Psychology* 40: 437-453.

Shaub, M. 1994. An analysis of the association of traditional demographic variables with moral reasoning of auditing students and auditors. *Journal of Accounting Education* 1: 1-26.

Shaub, M.K., D.W. Finn, and P. Munter. 1993. The effects of auditor's ethical orientation on commitment and ethical sensitivity. *Behavioral Research in Accounting* 5: 143-169.

Sweeney, J. 1995. The moral expertise of auditors: An exploratory analysis. In *Research on Accounting Ethics*, Vol. 1, ed. L.A. Ponemon, 213-234. Greenwich, CT: JAI Press.

Taylor, R.N., and M.C. Hudson. 1972. *World Handbook of Polidtical and Social Indicators*. New Haven, CT: Yale University Press.

Waller, W.S., and W.L. Felix. 1984. The effects of incomplete feedback on auditor's self-perception on judgement ability. *The Accounting Review* 59(October): 637-646.3

U.K. ACCOUNTING:
RECENT DEVELOPMENTS WITH AN INTERNATIONAL PERSPECTIVE

Marilynn Collins and Robert Bloom

ABSTRACT

To introduce recent developments in U.K. accounting, U.K. standard-setting is described and compared to and contrasted with U.S. standard-setting. Also, the elements and organization of typical financial statements are reviewed. The standards selected for discussion are those that illustrate the conflict between economic substance and legal form, namely, business combinations and the related areas of consolidated financial statements, goodwill, long-term investments, foreign currency translation, segmented reporting, and off-balance-sheet reporting. These standards evidence changes in the role of accounting and financial statements in the United Kingdom.

Research in Accounting Regulation, Supplement 1, pages 173-197.

ISBN: 0-7623-0338-7

INTRODUCTION

This paper describes recent developments in U.K. standard-setting and standards, including: (1) the Accounting Standards Board (ASB) as the principal standard-setter, (2) income and cash flow statements, and (3) selected accounting standards issued by ASB. The impact of European Union (EU) directives and International Accounting Standards Committee (IASC) standards on U.K. accounting is also considered. The principal research method used in this paper was a review of U.K. accounting standards and exposure drafts as well as U.K. accounting periodicals.

Accounting is a function of the historical traditions, legal framework, economic conditions, and social customs of a country.[1] In view of such factors, accounting standard-setting mechanisms and standards differ from country to country.

The United Kingdom includes England, Wales, Scotland, and Northern Ireland. Financial reporting in the United Kingdom reflects what can be called the Anglo-Saxon model. This model is also reflected in such other countries as the United States, Canada, Australia, and New Zealand. The model emphasizes fairly sophisticated investors and creditors, in that order, as the principal users of financial reports. Emphasis is placed on the application of financial reports to decision making. The reports, therefore, generally provide significant disclosures.

Established in 1957, the European Union seeks to eliminate trade restrictions among member countries by harmonizing laws and promoting development of a unified capital market. In addition, EU issues directives to harmonize accounting standards—pertaining, in particular, to the format of financial reports, valuation bases, disclosure provisions, the concept of a "true and fair view," and consolidated financial statements. The United Kingdom incorporates EU directives into its laws.

The EU consists of 15 member countries,[2] some of whose accounting systems reflect the Anglo-Saxon, and some the Continental, models.[3] As a result, significant differences in accounting systems exist among these countries, creating major challenges with respect to harmonization.

The IASC is interested in more than harmonizing accounting standards. It plans to produce a set of global standards by March 1998. According to Arthur Levitt, chairman of the U.S. Securities and Exchange Commission (SEC), the International Organisation of Securities Commissions, of which the SEC is a member, has worked with the IASC toward developing these accounting standards for cross-border offerings. If the IASC's plan is successful, the SEC has agreed to consider allowing foreign issuers to use IASC standards in offering their securities in the United States (Levitt 1997, 67). The challenge of harmonization and the compatibility of IASC standards with those of any country can be demonstrated by the fact that 255 variations exist between U.S. GAAP and IASC standards (Cairns 1997, 60). According to Levitt (1997, 67), 856 foreign companies are registered in U.S. capital markets; thus, cooperation among standard-setters throughout the world is critical to reconciling different interests. Many concerns have been raised about the IASC's plan. One is that international accounting standards are not suitable for all styles of management control and may lead to inappropriate if not harmful changes in management style (Hatherly 1997, 66). Another concern, voiced by FASB chairman Dennis Beresford, is the quality of IASC standards, particularly as compared to FASB standards. Though IASC standards enhance the accounting standards in many countries, they are broadly written with little detail, and the FASB fears dilution of its more thoroughly written standards ("IASC Culture Clash" 1996, 7).

The adoption by different countries of different financial reporting models or of different accounting systems is a function of different cultures, and an understanding of these cultures may be useful to regulators in the attempt to harmonize accounting standards. Marilyn Zarzeski sampled 256 enterprises to identify the culture/accounting relationship that determines relative amounts of disclosure among seven countries. For countries that use an Anglo-Saxon model, her results explain the reasons for greater disclosures in that model. Enterprises disclosing more investor-oriented information are those that are dependent on and competing for resources (customers, material, labor, and capital), have more foreign sales, have lower debt ratios, are larger in size, and are in countries that are less secretive, more individualistic, and more masculine and have less uncertainty due to more open business and financial relationships (Zarzeski 1996, 72).

AN OVERVIEW OF U.K. STANDARD-SETTING AND BASIC STANDARDS

While the United States has many accounting standards tightly written in a legal style, the traditional approach in the United Kingdom has been to have far fewer written standards,[4] and these by and large are guidelines rather than rules. Traditionally, the accent has been on professional judgment and professional regulation in U.K. accounting standards in order to allow accountants to apply the standards themselves. In the United Kingdom, no attempt has been made as in the United States to cover every subissue in each standard. Also, Britain is not a litigious society. No tradition of contingent fee arrangements or class action suits exists in the United Kingdom, in marked contrast to the United States where "injured" investors and other users of financial reports institute legal proceedings. Thus, demand has not existed in the United Kingdom for numerous, detailed accounting standards—for example, to use in court to justify the actions of accountants and auditors.[5]

It was not until 1970 that accounting standards became required in the United Kingdom, with the establishment of the Accounting Standards Committee (ASC).[6] The standards were, however, formulated earlier. There was much dissatisfaction with ASC in view of the slowness it displayed in developing accounting standards. Accounting Standards Committee standards were eligible for issuance based on a two-thirds vote of its 21 members. However, the ASC had to obtain the approval of six consultative bodies before a standard could be issued. The ASC was also criticized for failure to use a conceptual framework and for the lack of compliance by many companies with its standards. However, the ASC had no ability to enforce its standards.

The Accounting Standards Board (ASB) was established in the United Kingdom in 1990, replacing the ASC. An independent Financial Reporting Council oversees the ASB and the Review Panel (RP). Compared to the ASC, the ASB has better funding and greater resources at its disposal, and the ASB itself is authorized to issue its own standards rather than consult with other bodies. The ASB is the main standard-setting body in a four-part structure, modeled after the U.S. Financial Accounting Standards Board (FASB). Independent of the other organizations, the ASB consists of a full-time chair, a full-time technical director, and seven part-time members. In contrast to the FASB, the ASB has nine members versus seven. Whereas the FASB can issue standards based on a 5:2 vote, the ASB can do so only based on a 6:3 vote. Also, the seven FASB members serve full-time, so they may be considered independent in appearance and fact. That ASB members are mostly part-time, and thus hold other positions, is not an issue in the United Kingdom. What is suitable for such a body in one country may be unsuitable in another country.

In addition to the ASB, an Urgent Issues Task Force (UITF) was created, modeled after the Emerging Issues Task Force (EITF) in the United States. The main role of the UITF is to provide timely guidance on issues calling for rapid resolution. Whereas the EITF in the United States deals primarily with narrow, industry-specific issues, that does not seem to be the case with its U.K. counterpart, which thus far has been concerned with particular aspects of issues on which the ASB or the Task Force has deliberated.

While the ASB can be viewed as a hybrid of the FASB and the U.S. Governmental Accounting Standards Board, the ASB bears a resemblance as well to the defunct U.S. Accounting Principles Board (APB), the main standard-setting body in the United States from 1959 to 1973. Both the APB and ASB have had part-time members—21 on the APB, seven 7 on the ASB—most likely independent in fact, but not in appearance since they were employed by accounting firms, corporations, and other organizations while serving on these boards. APB members had a full-time job in standard-setting, but in view of their part-time status, among other factors, were slow to take action.

In one of its first actions, the ASB put together a conceptual framework of objectives, qualitative traits, and elements. The ASB's predecessor, the ASC, like the APB, lacked such a framework. The ASC was replaced because of its ineffectiveness in producing and issuing new standards. APB was terminated for its inability to deal with pressures from constituents, its part-time nature, and the fact that it was strictly an accounting body of the U.S. Institute of Certified Public Accountants (AICPA). Accounting standards produced by the ASB are complex and detailed, a break with tradition in U.K. standard-setting.

The new enforcement body, the Financial Reporting Review Panel (RP), was created to be essentially independent of the other related bodies and charged with the responsibility to examine departures by major companies from standards issued by the ASB. Concerned with ensuring fairness in financial reporting, the RP consists of 15 members, assigned in groups to individual cases. Voluntary compliance is expected by companies with RP decisions. If such compliance is not forthcoming, then the RP, not to mention the U.K. Department of Trade and Industry, has the option of applying to court for disciplinary action. As financial markets are self-regulatory, the United Kingdom lacks a Securities and Exchange Commission.

A Financial Reporting Council (FRC) was also established to finance the overall operations of the ASB, UITF, and RP. Providing guidance on matters of basic policy, not on the specifics of any accounting standard, the FRC consists of 25 members, including preparers, auditors, and users of financial reports. Thus, the FRC can be viewed as an amalgam of the Financial Accounting Foundation and the Financial Accounting Standards Advisory Council at the FASB.

The ASB develops accounting standards while the RP deals with compliance. Emphasis is placed in standard-setting on conveying "a true and fair view," on economic substance rather than legal form. The standard setting process in the United Kingdom, as in the United States, is influenced by a conceptual framework and economic consequences. Furthermore, U.K. standard-setting is characterized by openness, as is its U.S. counterpart, in terms of holding public hearings, issuing exposure drafts and standards, and providing the rationale for its standards.

The U.K. Companies Acts constitute the basic legal framework and a source of "standards" in the broad sense of the term. The Companies Acts incorporate EU directives on the scope and quality of financial reports, though emphasis in the United Kingdom traditionally has been on common law. Besides the Companies Acts, court decisions pertaining to compliance with accounting standards also represent standards for all intents and purposes. In addition to the Companies Acts and the standards, "best practice" and court decisions are other sources of U.K. GAAP.

In the conceptual framework recently set forth in the United Kingdom, the principal objectives of U.K. financial reports parallel those in the FASB's and IASC's frameworks. However, the U.K. user group goes beyond investors and creditors—encompassing employees, customers, and the government. Additionally, the FASB's objectives of providing information to assist users in decision making, to assist in forecasting cash flows to the firm and users to enhance shareholders' value, and to provide stewardship and accountability information are also reflected in the U.K. conceptual framework. Furthermore, the U.K. conceptual framework, called a "Statement of Principles," unlike its U.S. counterpart, is sympathetic to current values.

The United Kingdom, as do so many other countries, lends to, and borrows from, other standard-setting bodies' accounting standards, standard-setting processes, and conceptual frameworks. Moreover, the ASB considers IASC standards in formulating new standards.

U.K. FINANCIAL STATEMENTS

In the typical U.K. balance sheet, fixed assets precede current assets, and debt is subtracted from assets to arrive at net assets. In the United Kingdom, traditional emphasis has been on the stockholder rather than the creditor—hence, the importance of net assets in this balance sheet.

The typical U.K. income statement appears in one of two formats. Similar to the U.S. multistep income statement, the first format shows gross profit. The second format reflects revenues first, followed by expenses, analogous to the U.S. single-step income statement. Based on the ASB's Financial Reporting Standard (FRS) No. 3, "Reporting Financial Performance" (1992), in the new U.K. income statement, discontinued operations are shown separate and apart from continuing operations and acquisitions with respect to sales (i.e., turnover) and operating profit or loss. Also gains and losses on disposal of discontinued operations are shown separately. Thus, discontinued operations are no longer considered part of extraordinary items in U.K. financial reporting. The category for extraordinary gains and losses has essentially been eliminated. Furthermore, earnings per share is now based on the net income figure (i.e., after extraordinary items, if any).

Prior period adjustments, appearing in the statement of total recognized gains and losses, represent a much broader category than their U.S. counterpart, including not only material errors from prior periods but also settlements of lawsuits from prior periods and the income impact of changes in accounting principles. Revaluations of inventory and property, plant, and equipment are permitted in the United Kingdom, showing the surplus in stockholders' equity, but such revaluations have to be reconciled with the corresponding historical cost figures. That is done in the note of historical cost profits and losses, below the income statement, as well as in the statement of total recognized gains and losses. Moreover, U.K. companies are allowed to use current replacement cost in the primary financial statements.

FRS 1, "Cash Flow Statements," (1996) calls for a statement of cash flows, replacing the U.K. funds statement on a working capital basis. Whereas its U.S. counterpart consists of three parts—operating, investing, and financing—the U.K. cash flow statement has eight parts:

- Operating activities;
- Returns on investments and servicing of finance;
- Taxation;

- Capital expenditure and financial investment;
- Acquisitions and disposals;
- Equity dividends paid;
- Management of liquid resources; and
- Financing

The revised statement is based on cash, excluding cash equivalents. Also called for in the revised standard are reconciliations between: (1) operating profit and net cash flow from operating activities, and (2) movement in cash and the movement in net debt during the period.

SELECTED RECENT U.K. STANDARDS

The United Kingdom has had a long history of creative accounting in business combinations and related areas, as reviewed by Edwards (1989). The topics of business combinations, consolidated financial statements, goodwill, long-term investments, foreign currency translation, segmented reporting, and off-balance-sheet reporting have been selected for analysis because their U.K. standards have been addressed in recent years and because they illustrate the conflict between economic substance and legal form. Emphasis on reflecting the economic substance of transactions rather than their form should be the principal U.K. qualitative characteristic of financial reporting (Arnold et al. 1991). The U.K. accounting standards for these selected topics are evidence of changes in the role of accounting and financial statements in the U.K.

BUSINESS COMBINATIONS

The ASB has given considerable attention to accounting problems stemming from business combinations, as indicated by its recently issued financial reporting standards. Napier and Noke (1992) analyze the history of business combinations, explaining how they were regulated and revealing tensions between law and accountancy, stemming from the need of the accounting profession to appeal to law to enforce its views on business. Business combinations, emerging at the end of the nineteenth century, were exploited in the early twentieth century as a means of maintaining secrecy through subsidiaries that were not required to publish accounts. Historically, controversy evolved over the sources of capital—namely, reserves and share premium available for dividends (Napier and Noke 1992, 42-43). As a result, merger accounting became more popular in the 1960s because a concept of pre-acquisition earnings is meaningless in the context of merger, and subsidiaries' earnings prior to combination are therefore available for dividends, not frozen as in acquisition accounting (Napier and Noke 1992, 44-45).

The United Kingdom is the only EU country where merger accounting ("pooling of interests") has been important. Therefore, a striking difference between U.K. and international accounting standards lies in the detail prescribed for merger accounting. According to the EU Seventh Directive and IAS 22, "Accounting for Business Combinations" (IASC 1993b), merger accounting is appropriate for a unity of interests effected by an exchange of voting equity shares with only minor cash payments allowed and with continuing participation by management. Carrying amounts existing at the date of combination are used for assets, liabilities, and minority interests. Profits and losses are included from the beginning of the reporting period.

Acquisition, or purchase accounting, is used in the United Kingdom to record transfers of ownership. Under the EU Seventh Directive, the purchase method is the main approach to account for business combinations, and in IAS 22 (IASC 1993b), the purchase method is used for combinations not requiring conditions for a uniting of interests. In both the United Kingdom and international accounting standards, fair value is the basis for the separable assets and liabilities, and thus goodwill can result. In the United Kingdom, the minority interest is based on fair values with no imputation of goodwill, while in international accounting standards, the minority interest may or may not be based on fair value.

The ASB, like the FASB, presently finds itself in the position of having to respond to creative uses of accounting standards surrounding business combinations that keep liabilities off the balance sheet—that is, "netting off" techniques, as they are commonly called, that artificially inflate earnings. With an alternative to use a "merger" in accounting for business combinations, opportunities arise: (1) to immediately inflate the earnings of the parent company through inclusion of the subsidiary's earnings for the entire fiscal period regardless of combination date, and (2) to artificially inflate the future earnings of the group through retention of the book values at the combination date for the subsidiary's net assets and through nonrecognition of goodwill. To the extent that the liabilities of the subsidiary have a current value higher than book value, merger accounting can be an off-balance-sheet technique.

In September 1994, the ASB issued FRS 6, "Acquisitions and Mergers," which substantially restricts the circumstances for using merger accounting that had been permitted under *Statement of Standard Accounting Practice 23*, "Accounting for Acquisitions and Mergers" (SSAP 23) (ASC 1985). This new standard was issued because the criteria in SSAP 23 for using merger accounting were too easily circumvented. The need to clarify when merger accounting should be used stems from actual cases of applying this method inappropriately and of using both merger and acquisition (purchase) accounting together in a series of related combinations to inflate earnings while avoiding recognition of subsidiary losses (see, e.g., Irvine 1993, 21). Almost a quarter of a century earlier in the United States, the APB issued Opinion No. 16, "Business Combinations" (1970), to limit pooling of interests accounting for the same reasons. While abusive applications of pooling of interests accounting, historically developed for public utilities, were prevalent in the United States during the business combinations of the 1960s, the United Kingdom did not have a similar history.

In the twentieth century, the focus of financial reporting was on separate legal entities. Smoothing of income through concealment of financial information from shareholders began to be accomplished by the formation of holding companies that created subsidiaries for some of their business activities. Since the subsidiaries were accounted for on a cash basis, profits were reported only on the basis of dividends (Edwards 1989, 226). During the 1920s, the financial press provoked controversy over such policies, but the climate for financial reporting was one of professional conservatism and complacency with existing standards (Edwards 1989, 227). Some group accounts were produced, and during the 1920s the equity method gained support and efforts to legislate group reporting were thwarted (Edwards 1989, 228-229). Accountants in the United Kingdom had little expertise in the preparation of consolidated accounts, U.K. professional examinations neglected the area, and British management was reluctant to publish group information. (Edwards 1989, 230). Reasons suggested by Edwards (1989, 231) for this slow response include prejudice against change, perceived or real legal barriers due to the implication that statutory balance sheets were confined to the legal entity, the British accountants' view that strong initiative is unprofessional, and the view that the problem was unimportant. Business combinations, occurring on a large scale after World War II and during the 1960s and 1970s, were often accounted for under the advantageous merger accounting method or merger relief, using merger for parent company's accounts but choosing acquisition for group accounts so that a reserve could be created to absorb reorganization costs and writedowns of current assets and thereby improve reported results following the merger (Edwards 1989, 232-238). Merger accounting was used before the issuance of the Companies Act of 1981, which retroactively legalized former practice. Merger accounting had been prevented under the Companies Act of 1948. However, restrictions on merger accounting in SSAP 23 and the Companies Act pertain to the form of the transactions, not to an underlying concept of circumstances for which merger accounting is appropriate. This situation leads to possibilities of purposeful structuring of transactions to meet the form. With FRS 6, the ASB (1994a) seeks to restrict the use of merger accounting with the expectation that merger accounting will be rarely applicable, by using the following five criteria:

1. The way the roles of each party to the combination are portrayed;
2. The involvement of each party to the combination in the selection of the management of the combined entity;
3. The relative sizes of the parties to the combination;
4. Whether shareholders of the combining entities receive any consideration other than equity shares in the combined entity; and

5. Whether shareholders of the combining entities retain an interest in the performance of only part of the combined entity.

Merger accounting is intended to emphasize economic substance over legal form—specifically, to reflect a unity of interests for mutual sharing of risks and benefits. This standard, in particular, limits such accounting to a unity of interests, a situation in which neither company controls the other, thus emphasizing substance over form.

CONSOLIDATED STATEMENTS

Business combinations effected through stock acquisitions raise questions regarding consolidation of group accounts. When a subsidiary is not consolidated, the equity method of accounting, essentially a one-line consolidation, is used in group accounts. In consolidated balance sheets, since subsidiaries' liabilities as well as assets are reflected, companies explore ways to avoid recognition of those liabilities. One such means is leaving subsidiaries unconsolidated, so that they are reported only as an asset under the equity method, with the advantage of allowing the parent to include in income its share of the earnings of the subsidiary. Another means is structuring combinations so that subsidiaries are not created. The ASB is responding to both possibilities.

According to Buckley (1991, 34), the Companies Act of 1989 uses two sets of terms for parents and subsidiaries. "Holding company" and "subsidiary" are the general terms appearing in certain disclosure requirements, while the terms "parent undertaking" and "subsidiary undertaking" are used in accounting standards. As Buckley explains (1991, 34):

> The definition of subsidiary undertaking applies for determining which entities are consolidated....[A]n undertaking is a parent undertaking in relation to another undertaking, a subsidiary undertaking, if it has a participating interest in the undertaking and either actually exercises a dominant influence over it, or if it and the subsidiary undertaking are managed on a unified basis.

Buchan, Peasnell, and Yaansah (1992, 207-208) discuss the U.K. experience with off-balance-sheet approaches, which the ASB addresses in FRS 2, "Accounting for Subsidiary Undertakings" (1992), and FRS 5, "Reporting the Substance of Transactions" (1994). These approaches primarily involve finance subsidiaries accounted for with the equity basis. Liabilities have been netted against assets with the desirable effect of reducing "gearing" or financial leverage. In the United States, the FASB has also addressed off-balance-sheet reporting of subsidiaries, again primarily finance subsidiaries, in SFAS 94, "Consolidation of All Majority-Owned Subsidiaries" (1987).

Consolidated statements in the United Kingdom are prepared according to FRS 2, "Accounting for Subsidiary Undertakings" (1992), which was issued partly to implement the EU Seventh Directive and to comply with IAS 27, "Consolidated Financial Statements and Accounting for Investments in Subsidiaries" (1990), apart from one exclusion—accounting for different activities. Both U.K. and international accounting standards exempt from consolidation small or medium-sized groups and wholly owned parent undertakings, and in some cases, majority-owned subsidiaries of other EU members. The Seventh Directive excludes financial holding companies from consolidation. To determine when consolidation is required, the international standards begin the definition of control with majority ownership of voting shares and include rights to appoint or remove directors, dominant influences, and unified management as guidelines. The essence of control is the ability to direct the financial and operating policies of another entity to gain economic benefits.

FRS 2 likewise uses those concepts, though for accounting purposes it defines a parent undertaking not directly in terms of its percentage ownership but indirectly through defining a subsidiary undertaking. The term "undertaking" is used because consolidation is not confined to limited liability companies but can, as examples, include partnerships and unincorporated associates carrying on trade with or without a view to profit. Dominant influence is exercized over the operating and financial policies of the subsidiary. The concept of an undertaking managed on a unified basis refers not merely to a sharing of managers but to an undertaking integrated and managed as a single unit.

In order to restrict off-balance-sheet schemes, the United Kingdom is becoming innovative in standard-setting and now includes a "quasi-subsidiary"—a subsidiary in substance, but not form—in consolidated statements. These formerly were known as consolidated nonsubsidiaries. FRS 5, "Reporting the Substance of Transactions" (1994), is concerned with accounting for the substance of transactions rather than their legal form. Taking this broad approach, the ASB considers several accounting areas of interest in which emphasis on legal form leads to off-balance-sheet reporting. These areas include, as examples, non-recourse finance arrangements, options, and ceasing the recognition of assets. In the latter area, the ASB addresses the concept of control, which in turn determines whether an entity is a quasi-subsidiary. By emphasizing substance and thereby recognizing quasi-subsidiaries, the ASB tackles the problem of off-balance-sheet reporting of subsidiaries based on legal form. A quasi-subsidiary is defined as follows (ASB 1994b, ¶1):

> Sometimes assets and liabilities are placed in an entity (a "vehicle") that is in effect controlled by the reporting entity but does not meet the legal definition of a subsidiary. Where the commercial effect for the reporting entity is no different from that which would result were the vehicle a subsidiary, the vehicle will be a "quasi-subsidiary."

Quasi-subsidiaries are companies controlled by the reporting company, though not subsidiaries in fact. They are included in group accounts analogous to subsidiaries under FRS 2. Moreover, where an undertaking has a quasi-subsidiary but no subsidiary and therefore does not prepare group accounts, it must consolidate its financial statements. International accounting standards do not address the subject of quasi-subsidiaries.

Subsidiaries may be excluded from consolidation in U.K. and international accounting standards based on severe long-term restrictions that hinder control, an interest never before consolidated that is held exclusively for resale, and different activities that would hinder a true and fair view if combined. FRS 5 allows exclusion of quasi-subsidiaries from consolidation only where both the interest in the quasi-subsidiary is held for resale and the quasi-subsidiary has not previously been included in the consolidated accounts of the reporting entity. A linked presentation, which is an offset specified by FRS 5 rather than an off-balance-sheet approach for non-recourse finance arrangements, is used where the quasi-subsidiary holds a single portfolio of similar items and the financing arrangements meet the conditions for such presentation (ASB 1994b, ¶26ff). The latter exclusion appears in the EU Seventh Directive, though not in IAS 27.

The exclusion based on different activities stands in marked contrast to U.S. accounting standards, which no longer allow nonhomogeneity of activities as a basis for exclusion in consolidated financial statements. Equity accounting, the one-line consolidation for unconsolidated subsidiaries, illustrates off-balance-sheet reporting with an aim of improving debt ratios. Prior to SFAS 94, "Consolidation of All Majority-Owned Subsidiaries," in conjunction with the exclusion of dissimilar activities, the equity method was abused in U.S. financial reporting. Obviously, if information about the subsidiary is unobtainable or immaterial, the subsidiary can be excluded, which is expressly stated in the EU Seventh Directive and would by implication be appropriate for U.K. reporting.

Both U.K. and international accounting standards require separate balance sheet and income statement presentations for the minority interest. In the United Kingdom, a separate presentation of capital and reserves attributable to the minority interest is called for.

The United Kingdom's FRS 4, "Capital Instruments" (ASB 1994a) proposes that an analysis be presented of amounts attributable to equity and non-equity shares. In its definition of capital instruments in consolidated statements, FRS 4 includes those capital instruments issued by subsidiaries apart from such instruments held by other members of the group included in the consolidation. Except for joint ventures, full consolidation is called for in the U.K. and international accounting standards. In both standards, uniform evaluation criteria and the same dates are recommended for all entities in the group.

In 1995, the ASB released FRS 8, "Related Party Disclosures," expanding the disclosure of information on related party transactions to all material related party transactions rather than only those outside normal operations (Wild and Creighton 1996, 66). The standard defines the term "related parties." While relevant to group accounts, FRS 8 disclosures are not required for transactions eliminated in the course of preparing consolidated financial statements. Nor are disclosures required in financial statements for transactions with related entities by subsidiaries at least 90% of whose voting rights are controlled by a group provided that the consolidated statements that include the subsidiary are publicly available. As noted by Matthew Curtis of Ernst & Young, the objective of the exemption was to prevent lengthy disclosures of information that is eliminated in consolidation or disclosed in group accounts (Curtis 1996, 76). Curtis criticizes the exemption as written because it permits nondisclosure through manipulative construction of transactions. He gives an example to demonstrate the ease with which circumvention of disclosure can be accomplished through use of the exemption.

GOODWILL

Goodwill arising from business combinations accounted for as acquisitions—that is, using the purchase method—basically is the difference between the exchange price and the fair value of the identifiable net assets of the acquired entity. Only purchased, not internally generated, goodwill can be recognized. Specific examples of such items that cannot be considered liabilities of an acquired business nor capitalized include relocation and rebranding of vehicles, stationery, and the like of an acquired business as well as changes in pension and other post-retirement benefits (Holgate and Nailor 1996, 68).

The United Kingdom, however, also has had unique features in accounting for goodwill that are not part of international accounting standards nor, for that matter, the standards of other countries. As to measurement of goodwill, U.K. standards had allowed the inclusion of future losses and costs of reorganization costs. The ASB eliminated this practice in FRS 7, "Fair Values in Acquisition Accounting" (ASB 1994d). Under FRS 7, the ASB clearly disallows provisions for future losses, calling for all post-acquisition events to be recognized in the periods in which they occur. The main objective of this standard is to ensure that all assets and liabilities in acquisitions are reflected at the date of such acquisition using fair values. All subsequent changes in the acquired assets and liabilities should be reported when incurred. According to Nailor, a member of ASB, user groups supported the proposed treatment while preparers objected (1994, 82). The ASB was not persuaded by arguments that: (1) the acquirer views post-acquisition reorganization as part of the combination transaction, (2) the acquirer's intentions about the future use of assets are relevant in determining their cost, and (3) that harmonization, notably with U.S. GAAP, would allow for future provisions (Nailor 1994, 82).

In U.K. accounting practice, acquired intangibles, including brands, usually have not been separated from goodwill. However, brands are increasingly reflected as assets on the balance sheet to improve gearing (debt to assets). The recognition of brands as assets is a practical response for those companies that write off goodwill to reserves immediately rather than capitalize and amortize it subsequently, because immediate write-off depletes or eliminates equity. Immediate write-off was the preferred treatment in SSAP 22, "Accounting for Goodwill" (ASC 1984, revised 1987), and in U.K. practice. Such treatment is allowed in the EU Seventh Directive but eliminated in the Revised IAS 22, "Accounting for Business Combinations" (IASC 1993b), which specifies capitalization with amortization over a five-year period. U.K. practice permitted immediate write-off, so that purchased goodwill was accounted for on a consistent basis with internally generated goodwill, which is charged to income as incurred, not capitalized. That practice gave U.K. companies an edge over U.S. companies inasmuch as it produced higher income figures.

Negative goodwill in the United Kingdom similarly has been credited immediately to a separate capital reserve. International accounting standards follow more closely the U.S. treatment of allocating negative goodwill to nonmonetary assets or treating it as deferred income with systematic amortization to income.

The ASB was accused by some of failing to address important issues such as goodwill (Singleton-Green 1993, 26). Mullen of Coopers & Lybrand in the United Kingdom describes the importance of intangibles in an article discussing various valuations that might be used (1993, 92-94). Intangibles have long played a major role in building competitive advantage, especially as industry has shifted toward technology-intensive industries and toward creating added value through product differentiation (1993, 92). According to Mullen, the market recognizes the importance of intangibles, but the accounting profession, though pressured for years to reach a decision on intangibles, had been reluctant to deal with this issue due to the subjectivity of the measures.

In FRS 7, the ASB decided that the difference between the acquisition cost and the fair values of net assets acquired represents goodwill. However, the Board has not reached an agreement on which of the approaches to accounting for goodwill is acceptable (Kennedy 1994, 90-91). Acher (1994, 91) of KPMG Peat Marwick in the United Kingdom praised the ASB for facing considerable controversy in maintaining its position that reorganization costs or trading losses cannot be apportioned to the assets or liabilities of the undertaking. He observed (p. 91) that if the ASB were to retract its views, its authority would weaken. Acher also asserted that mandatory amortization of goodwill conforms to international practice (p. 92).

In June of 1996, the ASB issued FRED 12, "Goodwill and Intangible Assets" (1996b), addressing the nature of and accounting for goodwill. Maintaining that goodwill is not in itself an asset but a part of the investment, it requires that purchased goodwill be capitalized as if it were an asset and amortized over no more than 20 years. The 20-year amortization period can be rebutted. Negative goodwill is recognized on the balance sheet and amortized. A unique feature of FRED 12 is the requirement for impairment reviews. In impairment reviews, the recoverable amount, that is, current value, of goodwill is evaluated, and this recoverable amount includes internally generated goodwill at the date of combination. FRED 12 has received majority support, especially from the corporate sector which would enioy greater flexibility in deciding the timing and amount of the goodwill amortization impact on earnings (Phipps 1996, 69). FRED 12 is consistent with the Revised IAS 22 (IASC 1993b) on capitalizing goodwill but diverges from its treatment of negative goodwill (Keegan and King 1996, 64-65). The 20-year amortization period differs from the EU Seventh Directive.

Given the increasing importance of intangible assets (other than goodwill), FRED 12 addresses their recognition. Intangible assets are initially recognized when purchased or, in the case of internally created intangibles, when they have a readily ascertainable market value. Intangibles are presumed to have a maximum 20-year life unless rebutted and may be revalued by referring to market value.

LONG-TERM EQUITY INVESTMENTS

In the United Kingom, the cost method applies in individual accounts. The equity method, as required by SSAP l, "Accounting for Associated Companies" (ASC 1971), applies only in consolidated accounts with respect to the following:

1. Associated undertakings, entities in which the group has a participating interest and significant influence (presumed to exist with 20% or more of the voting rights);
2. Subsidiaries excluded from consolidation on the basis of long-term, severe restrictions if the parent has significant influence; and
3. Subsidiaries excluded from consolidation on the basis of dissimilar activities.

The U.K. standard is more specific than IAS 27 and the EU Seventh Directive, both of which mandate the equity method in consolidated accounts for associated undertakings unless the parent loses or lacks significant influence or if the investment is held exclusively for resale. The U.K. standard differs in that IAS 27 and the EU Seventh Directive allow the use of the equity method in the investor's separate statements. Compared to U.S. GAAP, SSAP 1 is similar in defining significant influence at the 20% level of voting rights but dissimilar in allowing an exclusion from consolidation of subsidiaries on the basis of dissimilar activities. SSAP 1 is unique in its requirement that any goodwill in the valuation of the investment be disclosed separately from the fair value of net assets.

In the United Kingdom, the equity method is of concern for several reasons. One is that the equity method is, or can be inappropriately used as, a netting off technique. Equity accounted subsidiaries can and are used purposely to net off selected activities. On the other hand, recognition is given to the fact that the equity method can lead to fuller disclosure because separate financial statements are required for subsidiaries excluded from consolidation and reflected on the equity basis. The concern over abusive uses of the equity method to effect netting off, especially of finance subsidiaries, was addressed in the United States in 1987 by SFAS 94, which reacted with the requirement that all majority-owned subsidiaries be consolidated and which disallows exclusion from consolidation based on dissimilar activities.

Another and very different concern in the United Kingdom regarding the equity method is that, in practical application, SSAP 1 is solely interpreted as requiring the equity method at the 20% level of ownership. SSAP 1 is not in practice interpreted, as was its intent, to require an assessment of whether the investor exercises significant influence. This concern is addressed in FRED 11, "Associated and Joint Ventures" (ASB 1996a, 99-109). FRED 11 also addresses the topic of joint ventures, a topic not covered comprehensively in SSAP 1.

In FRED 11, as in SSAP 1, the equity method is applied only in consolidated accounts, the cost method being applicable in individual accounts. FRED 11 retains the 20% threshold but subordinates its role to that of the relationship in substance between the investor and investee. It accomplishes this through rebutting the presumption that 20% ownership results in significant influence if the investor does not meet two conditions for significant influence by the investor. These are the investor's active and influential participation in the investee's policy decisions, strategic issues and dividend payments, and over time, implementation of policies by the investee consistent with and not contrary to the investor's strategy.

Another significant change from SSAP 1 is that the investor's share of investee earnings is included in operating profit as opposed to inclusion at the level of profits before tax. Additional disclosures also are proposed, including turnover, debt of equity accounted entities, and assets and liabilities analyzed by major balance sheet headings.

FRED 11 distinguishes joint ventures on the basis of whether the investors share benefits, risks, and obligations in common or whether they have separate—that is, undivided—interests in the benefits, risks, and obligations of the venture. SSAP 1 did not so distinguish joint ventures. Where the benefits, risks, and obligations are shared, the equity method should be applied following the same principles as for associates. Where the interests are undivided—that is, separate—proportional consolidation is applied with separate disclosure for goodwill.

International accounting standards allow the cost or equity method for long-term investments held exclusively for resale. U.K. standards prescribe the lower of cost and net realizable value.

FOREIGN CURRENCY TRANSLATION

The EU has not succeeded in harmonizing methods of translation, merely requiring disclosure of the basis of translation. The United Kingdom's SSAP 20, "Foreign Exchange Translation" (1983) and IAS 21 are essentially similar to SFAS 52, "Foreign Currency Translation" (FASB 1981), in the United States, apart from specific requirements for hyperinflationary conditions. For foreign entities operating as separate entities, that is, not integral to the operation of the parent, the current rate method is used. In the United Kingdom, all assets and liabilities are translated at the current rate on the balance sheet date, and income statement accounts are translated at current rates on the date of the transactions generating them or, for practical reasons, an appropriate average rate for the year. Translation adjustments arising from applying a different rate to the opening balances of assets and liabilities are usually reflected in stockholders' equity.

The United Kingdom adopts the temporal method for foreign entities representing direct extensions of the investor's trade. The translation adjustments from remeasurement of the opening net monetary position are reflected in profit and loss. SFAS 52 uses the temporal method for remeasurement of the foreign entity's financial statements when its operations are integral to those of the parent. Assets and liabilities are remeasured by current or historical rates, respectively, for monetary and nonmonetary accounts with those rates then applying to allocations in the income statement.

SEGMENTED REPORTING

The United Kingdom leads EU countries in developing a standard for segmental reporting—SSAP 25, "Segmental Reporting" (1990). While segment disclosure is discretionary under IAS 14, "Reporting Financial Information by Segments" (1981), and the EU Seventh Directive with no tests of significance given to determine reportable segments, in the United Kingdom, segmented reporting is required for all companies and encouraged for all entities. SSAP 25 addresses line-of-business segments and geographical area segments. Like the U.S. standard, SSAP 25 calls for a 10% threshold of significance. A segment is reportable if its third-party sales (turnover), segment profit or loss, or net assets is equal to or greater than 10% of the respective totals. In the case of profit or loss, the greater of the combined result for the profit or loss is used. The reference to net assets means that in the United Kingdom, liabilities as well as assets directly traceable to a segment are determined. In the United Kingdom, sales, profit or loss, and operating assets are required to be reported by line of business and geographic area. The United Kingdom also requires disclosure of sales by origin and destination as well as separate presentation of intersegment sales and transfers. Financing amounts, interest costs, interest-bearing operating assets, and interest-bearing liabilities are not disclosed by segment. Geographic areas generally are the United Kingdom, the United States, Europe, and the rest of the world.

The IASC is proposing a revision to IAS 14 that, like SSAP 25, encompasses the presentation of both lines of business and geographical areas and that requires significantly more disclosures, most notably of segment liabilities (Dove 1996, 65-67). U.S. and Canadian standards also are being revised. According to Robert

Dove of Price Waterhouse, the proposed revision to IAS 14 stresses form over substance in defining business and geographical segments, in his view creating the risk that artificial segment data will be produced (Dove 1996, 67).

OFF-BALANCE-SHEET REPORTING

The United Kingdom appears to be innovative in addressing the problems of "netting-off." FRS 5, "Reporting the Substance of Transactions" (ASB 1994b), has no international basis of comparison. This standard stresses the concept that assets and liabilities should not be offset unless a right to do so exists. That concept is a logical extension of the separate entity assumption applied not to the reporting entity but to its debtors and creditors. In addition to the earlier discussed equity method, FRS 5 addresses the following items: consignment stock, sale and repurchase agreements, factoring of debts, securitised assets, and loan transfers. To ensure that the substance of such transactions is reported in financial statements, FRS 5 calls for a linked presentation of the assets and related liabilities as opposed to netting the amounts. According to this standard (¶26), for non-recourse financing to be repaid only from the item it finances, a linked presentation reflects the finance deducted from the amount of the item on the balance sheet. This presentation indicates the underlying gross resources of the business and emphasizes that the business has limited risk exposure. The specific circumstances for using a linked presentation are restricted. The linked presentation recognizes the right of offset of assets and liabilities but provides greater disclosure than a single figure. The circumstances for linked presentation are as follows (ASB 1994b, ¶27):

1. The finance relates to a specific item and is secured on that item but not on any other assets of the entity;
2. The provider of the finance has no recourse to the other assets of the entity for losses;
3. The entity is not obliged to support any losses, nor does it intend to do so;
4. The provider of the finance has agreed that it will not seek recourse in other forms;
5. If the funds generated by the item are insufficient to pay off the debt, that does not constitute default by the entity; and
6. There is no provision for the entity to repurchase the item financed.

CONCLUDING COMMENTS

Various features can be identified with U.K. accounting standards. U.K. GAAP traditionally have been loosely written guidelines, allowing accountants and auditors latitude to exercise professional judgment in their application. The low number of U.K. codified accounting principles attests to the need to develop standards that allow accountants and auditors to exercise considerable professional judgment in their application. In the United Kingdom, standards have traditionally been guidelines rather than rules to follow.

However, the loose nature of U.K. GAAP may well have ended with the creation of ASB. To date, the standards issued by ASB have been more or less complex and detailed. ASC standards used to be so general and flexible that they were readily circumvented. Additional detailed standards could prove to be more difficult to circumvent.

A conceptual framework has been put together in the United Kingdom, so ASB members can pass judgment on standards based not only on their own experience and knowledge of accounting but also on the conceptual framework. The United Kingdom considers "economic consequences" a key factor in the formulation of accounting standards.

ACKNOWLEDGMENTS

This manuscript has benefited considerably from the specific comments made by three anonymous reviewers and the editor. The authors are grateful to each of them for the time and effort they devoted to evaluating the manuscript.

NOTE

1. Hofstede (1980) derived five cultural values from a survey of employee attitudes in 50 countries. Below, those cultural values are applied to the United Kingdom:

Hofstede's Cultural Values	*Application to the United Kingdom*
Individualism—a preference for individual responsibility, emphasizing the individual rather than the group.	The United Kingdom is a high individualism, as opposed to a collectivist society.
Power distance—the extent to which people accept unequal distributions of power (i.e., hierarchies) in institutions and organizations.	A low power distance exists in the U.K. mind-set.
Uncertainty avoidance—the extent to which people feel uncomfortable about uncertainty and ambiguity.	U.K. people, while risk-averse, have a high threshold for uncertainty and ambiguity. They are fundamentally flexible.
Masculinity and femininity—a tradeoff between self-assertiveness, the need to achieve, if not be a hero, versus a concern for quality of life, caring relationships, and sympathy for the unfortunate.	The United Kingdom demonstrates both traits—masculinity when necessary, as in the Falklands War, yet femininity as a country in its never-ending desire to become involved in the settlement of international disputes.
Short-term versus long-term orientation.	The United Kingdom accents the short-term while not ignoring long term.

Gray derived the following framework of accounting attributes from studying Hofstede and his wide array of research publications. These attributes are applied to the United Kingdom below:

Gray's Accounting Attributes	*Application to the United Kingdom*
Professionalism—a preference for exercise of individual professional judgment and professional self-regulation in contrast to adherence to legal requirements and statutes.	The United Kingdom has a high degree of professionalism and professional self-regulation as opposed to statutory control.
Uniformity—a preference for standardized accounting practices among companies and organizations as opposed to flexibility based on different accounting circumstances.	The United Kingdom places more emphasis on flexibility than uniformity.
Conservatism—a tendency in accounting when alternatives exist to reflect the least favorable immediate effect on net income. Conservatism represents a pessimistic, yet prudent, approach to accounting measurement.	The United Kingdom, while conservative in accounting, is not overly so.
Secrecy—a desire for confidentiality in financial reporting, so as not to divulge information to the public.	People in the United Kingdom are "open" by nature and, therefore, favor public disclosure over secrecy. Their standard-setting process is anything but secretive—with public hearings and other opportunities for public input.

2. The 15 member countries are: Austria, Belgium, Denmark, Finland, France, Germany, Greece, Ireland, Italy, Luxembourg, The Netherlands, the United Kingdom, Spain, Sweden, and Portugal.

3. The principal users of financial statements in the Continental model are bankers and governments. Emphasis is placed on conveying stewardship information for credit purposes and for adherence to national economic policies. Accounting standards in this model have a legal orientation. The government is usually the principal standard setter. Accordingly, the accounting standards and tax regulations are similar, if not the same.

4. Of the 25 standards issued between 1970 and 1990, those on accounting for changes in the purchasing power of money, the statement of source and application of funds, and current cost accounting are not currently in effect. The standards on extraordinary items, group accounts, income tax, and acquisitions and mergers have been revised.

5. However, such circumstances may well be changing in the United Kingdom. In fact, as Freedman and Power (1992, 9) observed:

> Pressures for change in financial regulation arise in part from attempts to satisfy expectations of corporate control in a world of global markets, multinational groups not easily susceptible to regulation by national agencies acting alone, and seemingly limitless levels of creativity amongst highly trained and well remunerated professionals. Such pressures are particularly acute in the wake of visible regulatory "failure." In an important sense, scandal has been the moving force in the professionalisation of regulation, setting in motion waves of codification and institutionalisation.

6. According to Napier and Noke (1992, 48-49), the war years changed the pre-1940 attitude of accountancy bodies toward making authoritative pronouncements on accounting issues, and in 1942 the Institute of Chartered Accountants in England and Wales began issuing Accounting Recommendations. Napier and Noke observe a change toward issuing standards (1992, 61):

By 1970, the accountancy profession was ready to attempt a new approach to regulation of financial statements, through the issue of accounting standards. Where standards appeared to conflict with law, however, they were not regarded as sustainable: accountants still had to acknowledge the supremacy of law in the regulatory domain of financial reporting.

REFERENCES

Accounting Principles Board. 1970. *Opinion No. 16: Business Combinations.* American Institute of Certified Public Accountants.

Accounting Standards Board. 1991a. *Financial Reporting Standard No. 1: Cash Flow Statements.* London: Accounting Standards Board.

Accounting Standards Board. 1991b. *Interim Statement*: "Consolidated Accounts." *Accountancy* (February): 121-128.

Accounting Standards Board. 1992a. Financial reporting standard no. 2: Accounting for subsidiary undertakings. *Accountancy* (July): 124-135.

Accounting Standards Board. 1992b. *Financial Reporting Standard No. 3*: "Reporting Financial Performance." *Accountancy* (December).

Accounting Standards Board. 1992c. *Urgent Issues Task Force Abstract 3*: "Treatment of Goodwill on Disposal of a Business." (December 19, 1991). *Accountancy* (February): 112-116.

Accounting Standards Board. 1994a. *Financial ReportingStandard No. 4*: "Capital Instruments." *Accountancy* (January): 100-112.

Accounting Standards Board. 1994b. *Financial Reporting Standard No. 5: Reporting the Substance of Transactions.* London: Accounting Standards Board.

Accounting Standards Board. 1994c. *Financial Reporting Standard No. 6: Acquisitions and Mergers.* London: Accounting Standards Board.

Accounting Standards Board. 1994d. *Financial Reporting Standard No. 7: Fair Values in Acquisition Accounting.* London: Accounting Standards Board.

Accounting Standards Board. 1995a. *Financial Reporting Standard No. 8: Related Parties Disclosures.* London: Accounting Standards Board.

Accounting Standards Board. 1995b. *Revision of FRS 1: Cash Flow Statements.* London: Accounting Standards Board.

Accounting Standards Board. 1996a. *Financial Reporting Exposure Draft No. 11*: "Associates and Joint Ventures." *Accountancy* (April): 99-109.

Accounting Standards Board. 1996b. *Financial Reporting Exposure Draft No. 12*: "Goodwill and intangible Assets." *Accountancy* (July): 96-109.

Accounting Standards Committee. 1971. *Statement of Standard Accounting Practice No. 1: Accounting for Associated Companies.* London: Accounting Standards Board.

Accounting Standards Committee. 1978. *Statement of Standard Accounting Practice No. 14: Group Accounts.* London: Accounting Standards Board.

Accounting Standards Committee. 1979. Setting Accounting Standards. *Accountancy* (June): 72-76

Accounting Standards Committee. 1983. *Statement of Standard Accounting Practice No. 20: Foreign Currency Translation.* London: Accounting Standards Board.

Accounting Standards Committee. 1985. *Statement of Standard Accounting Practice No. 23: Accounting for Acquisitions and Mergers.* London: Accounting Standards Board.

Accounting Standards Committee. 1989. *Statement of Standard Accounting Practice No. 22: Accounting for Goodwill* (1984, revised 1989). London: Accounting Standards Board.

Accounting Standards Committee. 1990. *Statement of Standard Accounting Practice No. 25: Segmental Reporting.* London: Accounting Standards Board.

Acher, G. 1994. One step forward, one step back. *Accountancy* (February): 91-92.

Ainsworth, P. 1993. TAC spells transparency in action. *Accountancy* (February): 106-107.

Alexander, D., and S. Archer. 1991. *The European Accounting Guide*. San Diego, CA: Harcourt Brace Jovanovich.

Alexander, D., and S. Archer. 1992. *The European Accounting Guide*. London: Academic Press.

Al Hashim, D. 1980. Regulation of financial accounting: An international perspective. *International World of Accounting* (Fall): 47-62.

Arnold, J. 1992. Goodwill: A problem that will not go away. *Accountancy* (June): 35.

Arthur Andersen & Co., 1991. *Survey of International Accounting Practice*.

Benson, H. 1981. Establishing standards through a voluntary professional process across national boundaries. In Arthur Young Professors' Roundtable: *The International World of Accounting*, Reston, VA: 27-48.

Benston, G.J. 1975. Accounting standards in the United States and the United Kingdom: Their nature, causes and consequences. *Vanderbilt Law Review* (January): 235-268.

Birch, A.H. 1970. Small-town politics. In *The Sociology of Modern Britain*, eds. E. Butterworth and D. Weir. London, U.K./William Collins Sons & Co. Ltd. (originally published 1959): 92-95.

Blake, J. 1992. A classification system for economic consequences issues in accounting regulation. *Accounting and Business Research* 22(88): 305-321.

Brunovs, R., and R. Kirsch. 1991. Goodwill accounting in selected countries and the harmonization of international accounting standards. *Abacus* 27(2): 135-161.

Buchan, M.G., K.V. Peasnell, and R.A. Yaansah. 1992. Netting off assets and liabilities. *Accounting and Business Research* (Summer): 207-217.

Buckley, E. 1991. The practical problems of consolidation. *Accountancy* (November): 34.

Butterworth, E., and D. Weir, eds. 1970. *The Sociology of Modern Britain*. London. U.K. William Collins Sons & Co. Ltd., 1970.

Cairns, D. 1997. Are IASs and US GAAP compatible? *Accountancy* (February): 60-61.

Chandler, R., and I. Davies. 1993. Accounting for an attractive option. *Accountancy* (July): 81.

Choi, F., and G. Mueller. 1984. *International Accounting*. Englewood Cliffs, NJ: Prentice Hall.

Choi, F.D.S., and G.G. Mueller. 1992. *International Accounting*, 2nd edition. Englewood Cliffs, NJ: Prentice Hall.

Citron, D.B. 1992. Financial ratio convenants in UK bank loan contracts and accounting policy choice. *Accounting and Business Research* 22(88): 322-335.

Cook, A. 1989. International business: A channel for change in United Kingdom accounting. In *The International Pressures for Accounting Change*, ed. G. Hopwood, 33-70. Englewood Cliffs, NJ: Prentice-Hall.

Cooke, R. 1992. Influence in the community. *Accountancy* (July): 86-87.

Coopers and Lybrand International. 1991. *International Accounting Summaries: A Guide for Interpretation and Comparison*. New York: John Wiley.

Crichton, J. 1991. Consolidated accounts: Interpreting the act. *Accountancy* (March): 30.

Curtis, M. 1996. Shadydeals, smokescreen and other related parties. *Accountancy* (March): 76.

Dezalay, Y. 1992. Territorial battles and tribal disputes. In *Law and Accountancy*, eds. J. Freedman and M. Power, 24-41. London: The Modern Law Review Limited.

Dove, R. 1996. A two-tier slice for segments. *Accountancy* (April): 65-67.

Edwards, J.R. 1989. *A History of Financial Accounting*. London: Routledge.

Emenyonu, E., and S.J. Gray. 1992. EU accounting harmonization: An empirical study of measurement practices in France, Germany, and the U.K. *Accounting and Business Research* 23(89): 49-58.

Financial Accounting Standards Board. 1981. *Statement of Financial Accounting Standards No. 52: Foreign Currency Translation*. Stamford, CT: FASB.

Financial Accounting Standards Board. 1987. *Statement of Financial Accounting Standards No. 94: Consolidation of All Majority-Owned Subsidiaries*. Stamford, CT: FASB.

Financial Accounting Standards Board. 1990. Facts about FASB. *Accountancy* (June): 86-87.

Flower, J. 1991. Foreign currency translation. In *Comparative International Accounting*, 3rd edition, eds. C. Nobes and R.H. Parker. New York: Prentice-Hall: 306-341.

Treadgold. S. "The force and financial reporting." 1991. *Accountancy* (June): 27.

Freedman, J., and M. Power. 1992. Law and accounting: Transition and transformation. In *Law and Accountancy*, eds. J. Freedman and M. Power, 1-23. London: The Modern Law Review Limited.

Ghosh, J. 1993. Conflicts resolutions and enforcement. *Accountancy* (April): 90-91.

Gibbons, C., and J. Freedman. 1991. ED 49: The importance of being legal. *Accountancy* (March): 29.

Gray, S. 1988. Towards a theory of cultural influence on the development of accounting systems internationally. *Abacus* (March): 1-15.

Hagerty, B. 1993. Firms retain trainers to teach expatriates about foreign ways. *Wall Street Journal* (June 14): B1, B6.

Hanks, J. 1992. Accounting for capital instruments. *Accountancy* (February): 32-33.

Hastie, S., and R. Rhodes. 1990. Goodwill: Are we really making progress? *Accountancy* (October): 28.

Hatherly, D. 1997. Global or local accounting: The debate in context. *Accountancy* (February): 66.

Hegarty, J. 1993. Accounting integration in Europe: Still on track? *Journal of Accountancy* (May): 92-95.

Hofstede, G. 1980. *Culture's Consequences*. Sage: 65-251.

Holgate, P., and B. Johnson. 1991. Financial instruments: An international issue. *Accountancy* (December): 32.

Holgate, P., and H. Nailor. 1996. Acquisition costs. *Accountancy* (December): 68.

IASC culture clash is cause for concern. 1996. *Accountancy* (September): 7.

International Accounting Standards Committee. 1981. *International Accounting Standard 14: Reporting Financial Information by Segments*. London: IASC.

International Accounting Standards Committee. 1989. *Statement No. 32: Comparability of Financial Statements*. London: IASC.

International Accounting Standards Committee. 1990. *Statement No. 27: Consolidated Financial Statements and Accounting for Investments in Subsidiaries*. London: IASC.

International Accounting Standards Committee. 1993a. *Statement No. 21: Accounting for the Effects of Changes in Foreign Exchange Rates* (Revised). London: IASC.

International Accounting Standards Committee. 1993b. *International Accounting Standard 22: Accounting for Business Combinations* (Revised). London: IASC.

Irvine, J. 1993. A classic of creative accounting. *Accountancy* (August): 21.

Keegan, M., and H. King. 1996. Together but different. *Accountancy* (October): 64-65.

Kennedy, C. 1981. Setting accounting standards. *World Accounting Report* (July): v-viii.

Kennedy, S. 1994. Goodwill: There is no obvious solution. *Accountancy* (February): 90-91.

Kirkman, P. 1991. Inflation accounting. In *Comparative International Accounting*, 3rd edition, eds. C. Nobes and R.H. Parker. Hartfordshire, U.K.: Prentice-Hall International (U.K.): 363-389.

Kroeber, A.L. 1944. *Configuation of Culture Growth*. Berkeley, CA: University of California Press.

Kroeber, A.L. 1953. The delineation of civilizations. *Journal of the History of Ideas* 14: 264-275.

Freedman, J., and M. Power, eds. 1992. *Law and Accountancy*. London: The Modern Law Review Limited.

Lee, T.A. 1975a. Accounting standards and effective financial reporting—I. *The Accountants Magazine* (January): 25-30.

Lee, T.A. 1975b. Accounting standards and effective financial reporting—II. *The Accountants Magazine* (February): 73-81.

Matters raised by the DTI arising from accounts and reports filed with the registrar of companies. 1991. *Accountancy* (November): 141-142.

McBarnet, D., and C. Whelan. 1992. The elusive spirit of the law: Formalism and the struggle for legal control. In *Law and Accountancy*, eds. J. Freedman and M. Power, 80-105. London: The Modern Law Review Limited.

McGee, A. 1992. The "true and fair view" debate: A study in the legal regulation of accounting. In *Law and Accountancy*, eds. J. Freedman and M. Power, 106-120. London: The Modern Law Review Limited.

McLeay, S. 1991. International financial analysis. In *Comparative International Accounting*, 3rd edition, eds. C. Nobes and R.H. Parker. Hartfordshire, U.K.: Prentice-Hall International (U.K.: 391-426.

McMillan, J. 1992. Accounting for capital instruments. *Accountancy* (April): 34.

Mead, M. 1953. National character. In *Anthropology Today*, ed. A.L. Kroeber. Chicago, IL: University of Chicago Press.

Mueller, G., H. Gernon, and G. Meek. 1991. *Accounting: An International Perspective*, 2nd edition. Homewoord, IL: Irwin: 78-85.

Mullen, M. 1993. How to value intangibles. *Accountancy* (November): 92-94.

Nailor, H. 1994. Towards fairness in acquisition accounting. *Accountancy* (January): 82.

Napier, C., and C. Noke. 1992. Premiums and pre-acquisition profits: The legal and accountancy professions and business combinations. In *Law and Accountancy*, eds. J. Freedman and M. Power, 42-61. London: The Modern Law Review Limited.

Nobes, C.W., and R.H. Parker. 1985. *Comparative International Accounting*, 2nd edition. Oxford, UK: Phillip Allan.

Nobes, C.W. 1991a. Conservation and accruals. In *Comparative International Accounting*, 3rd edition, eds. C. Nobes and R.H. Parker. Hartfordshire, U.K.: Prentice-Hall International (U.K.): 24-26.

Nobes, C.W. 1991b. Harmonization of financial reporting. In *Comparative International Accounting*, 3rd edition, eds. C. Nobes and R.H. Parker. Hartfordshire, U.K.: Prentice-Hall International (U.K.): 70-90.

Nobes, C.W. 1991c. International classification of financial reporting. In *Comparative International Accounting*, 3rd edition, eds. C. Nobes and R.H. Parker. Hartfordshire, U.K.: Prentice-Hall International (U.K.): 38-51.

Nobes, C.W., and R. Parker. 1991. Introduction, and causes of differences. In *Comparative International Accounting*, 3rd edition, eds. C. Nobes and R.H. Parker. Hartfordshire, U.K.: Prentice-Hall International (U.K.): 3-21.

Opler, M.E. 1945. Themes as dynamic forces in culture. *American Journal of Sociology* 51: 198-206.

Orsini, L., J.P. McAllister, and R.N. Parikh, 1989. *World Accounting*, contributing editor. Ernst & Whinney, Vol. 2. New York: Matthews Bender: UK-6-UK-75.

Parker, R., and C. Nobes. 1991. Consolidation. In *Comparative International Accounting*, 3rd edition, eds. C. Nobes and R.H. Parker. Hartfordshire, U.K.: Prentice-Hall International (U.K.): 283-305.

Parker, R. 1991a. Financial reporting in the United Kingdom and Australia. In *Comparative International Accounting*, 3rd edition, eds. C. Nobes and R.H. Parker. Hartfordshire, U.K.: Prentice-Hall International (U.K.): 122-157.

Parker, R. 1991b. Regulating financial reporting in the United Kingdom, the United States, Australia and Canada. In *Comparative International Accounting*, 3rd edition, eds. C. Nobes and R.H. Parker. Hartfordshire, U.K.: Prentice-Hall International (U.K.): 52-69.

Patient, M., and R. Elwell. 1993. A question of scope and timing. *Accountancy* (February): 107-108.

Peerless, S. 1993. No more flattery in acquisitions and mergers. *Accountancy* (July): 95.

Perera, M.H., and M.R. Mathews. 1990. The cultural relativity of accounting and international patterns of social accounting. In *Advances in International Accounting*, ed. Kenneth Most Vol. 3. Greenwich, CT: JAI Press: 215-251.

Phipps, E. 1996. Peace and goodwill to all accountants? *Accountancy* (November): 69.

Pope, P.F., and A.G. Puxty. 1992. What is equity? New financial instruments in the interstices between the law, accounting and economics. In *Law and Accountancy*, eds. J. Freedman and M. Power, 121-143. London: The Modern Law Review Limited.

Price Waterhouse. 1991. *Doing Business in the United Kingdom*. London, U.K.: Price Waterhouse World Firm Services BV, Inc.: 129-138.

Rennie, E.D., and C.R. Emmanuel. 1992. Segmental disclosure practice: Thirteen years on. *Accounting and Business Research Research* 22(86): 151-159.

"Review of the Standard Setting Process: A Report by the Accounting Standards Committee." 1983. *Accountancy* (July): 115-120.

Singleton-Green, B. 1993. The ASB: Critics that won't be pacified. *Accountancy* (November): 26.

Stamp, E. 1979a. Does the English institute have a death wish? In *Annual Accounting Review*, Vol. 1, eds. S. Weinstein and M. Walker. Chur, Switzerland: Harwood Academic Publishers.

Stamp, E. 1979b. *The Future of Accounting and Auditing Standards*. Occasional paper No. 18. Lancaster, UK: International Centre for Research in Accounting, University of Lancaster.

Terpestra, V., and K. David. 1985. *The Cultural Environment of International Business*. Cincinnati, OH: South-Western Publishing.

Tonkin, D., and B. Robertson. 1991. Brand names in a conceptual framework. *Accountancy* (March): 28.

Tweedie, D.P. 1993. The accounting profession and financial reporting: Why should anyone believe us? *Research in Accounting Regulation*, Vol. 7. Greenwich, CT: JAI Press: 161-182.

Van Der Tas, L.G. 1992. Measuring international harmonization and standardization: A comment. *Abacus* 28(2): 211-223.

Violet, W.J. 1983. The development of international accounting standards: An anthropological perspective. *International Journal of Accounting* (Spring): 1-12.

Walker, D. 1991. Foreign exchange risk management.In *Comparative International Accounting*, 3rd edition, eds. C. Nobes and R.H. Parker. Hartfordshire, U.K.: Prentice-Hall International (U.K.): 454-475..

Walton, P. 1992. Harmonization of accounting in France and Britain: Some evidence. *Abacus* 28(2): 186-199.

Watts, T. 1984. The role of the Accounting Standards Committee. In *Contemporary Issues in Accounting*. Deloitte Haskins & Sells Distinguished Lectures series. London: Pitman.

Webb, S. 1993. The off balance sheet finance solution. *Accountancy* (March): 83-84.

Wild, K., and B. Creighton. 1966. Implementing FRS8: Some practical aspects. *Accountancy* (October): 66-67.

Willmott, H.C.,A.G. Puxty, K. Robson, D.J. Cooper. 1992. Regulation of accountancy and accountants: A comparative analysis for research and development in four advanced capitalist countries. *Accounting Auditing & Accountability Journal* 5(2): 32-56.

Zarzeski, M.T. 1996. Culture clash? *Accountancy* (March): 70-72.

THE RELATIONSHIP BETWEEN CULTURE AND ACCOUNTING REGULATION:
QUESTIONING CONVENTIONAL ANALYSIS WITH THE CASE STUDY OF INDONESIA

Sudarwan and Timothy J. Fogarty

ABSTRACT

A substantial literature has indicated the role of culture in the development of accounting regulation. However, the conclusions drawn from this work have depended on cross-sectional empirical analyses of many nations. Whether the underlying ideas can stand the scrutiny of more in-depth case studies of particular countries, with particular attention to longitudinal dimensions, is uncertain. This paper considers theoretical ideas about cultural values developed by Hofstede and accounting values developed by Gray as they apply to Indonesia, a nation whose size and importance in the world economy belies its neglect in the accounting literature. The case approach allows us to question the meaningfulness of the research designs and measures currently employed in the literature. The analysis also suggests that "culture" and "accounting" may be more dynamic than sus-

Research in Accounting Regulation, Supplement 1, pages 199-219.

ISBN: 0-7623-0338-7

pected. Further nation-specific work on empirical and theoretical issues is suggested in order to more precisely specify the link between cultural differences and accounting regulation.

INTRODUCTION

This study concerns the relationships between culture and accounting regulation. The general consensus of the literature is that culture is associated with the form of accounting regulation (e.g., Belkaoui 1989; Pourjalali and Meek 1995; Gray and Vint 1995). We suggest that the association is much more problematic and complex than currently thought. What we believe we know about this relationship may be a product of the methodology of this research. Supplementing this work with alternative research designs might shed light on this possibility. For these purposes, we analyze the nature of Indonesian culture, Indonesian firms' financial reporting practices, and Indonesian accounting standards. The purpose of this analysis is not as much to identify the important aspects of Indonesian culture and their association with the development of Indonesian accounting practice as to clarify the role of culture in the development of accounting practice in a general way. We argue that in order to understand these basic theoretical relationships, a much higher quality of specific information is needed.

Clarifying the relationship between culture and accounting regulation is important for several purposes. Cultural differences may underlie the possibilities for accounting regulatory development within nations. To the extent that this would enhance global business practice, a predictable course of accounting development, especially in emerging markets, is important. The chances that ongoing harmonization efforts will be successful would also seem to depend upon the impact of cultural factors. The role of culture may also be valuable as we attempt to gain self-insight about accounting practices.

The first section of this paper reviews the literature on cultural values, the values that are believed to underlie accounting practice and regulation, and the relationship between the two. This section focuses upon a particular model of culture and one of accounting development that have begun to dominate the literature. This analysis argues that conventional research has many shortcomings, some of which can be mollified by alternative approaches such as case studies. The second section provides a case study of Indonesia. It begins by summarizing relevant information about recent Indonesian political, economic, and social history. It also summarizes recently completed longitudinal work pertaining to Indonesia that contrasts with what would be expected from cross-sectional research designs. The final section identifies the major problems with the application of the theory, as illustrated by the Indonesian case, in an effort to direct future research toward more specific case studies of international accounting regulation.

CULTURE AND ACCOUNTING

The Nature of Culture

The role of culture in human activities is pervasive. Culture influences societal behavior in dealing with economic, political, and social affairs. Varying concepts of culture have originated in the field of anthropology. Smircich (1983, 342) has summarized the differing perspectives of culture, citing the consideration of culture as need-fulfilling instrument, regulatory mechanism, system of shared cognition, and a universal unconscious infrastructure. In more applied work, some writers stress the role of culture in the business decisions made and the negotiations undertaken by managers of different nationalities (e.g., Graham 1985; Oikawa 1992; Bedi 1993; Hoffman 1987). Others (e.g., Hofstede 1980; Schreuder 1987) have observed that cultures function to bind people to organizations and nations. Therefore, cultural influence permeates a large set of interpersonal and societal relationships.

Hofstede (1991, 5) defines culture as the "collective programming of the mind which distinguishes the members of one group or category of people from another." He argues that culture develops through shared value systems in a society (see also Turner and Trompenaars 1993). Values are defined as "broad tendencies to prefer certain states of affairs over others" (Hofstede, 1991, 8). Once certain values are adopted by a society, these values become the societal norms to which societal behavior is expected to conform. The adherence of behavior to societal norms results in a pattern of consequences for individuals, organizations, and society.

General Approaches to the Interaction of Culture and Accounting

A common topic found in studies of the interactions between culture and accounting is the association between control, culture, organizational order, and accounting systems (e.g., Dermer 1988; Birnberg and Snodgrass 1988). Most of these studies deal primarily with issues related to changes in the practice of management accounting (e.g., Boland and Pondy 1983; Nahapiet 1988; Bhimani 1993; Preston 1992).

The relationship between culture and financial accounting also has received attention. This literature has been reviewed by Wallace and Gernon (1991) and Gernon and Wallace (1995). Some previous studies have examined the relationship between culture and accounting practices across nations. However, these studies focus on the accounting standard-setting process, omitting the process of changes in the disclosure of financial reports (e.g., Bindon and Gernon 1995; Bloom and Naciri 1989; Harrison and McKinnon 1986). The studies that have considered financial reporting practices, such as Nair and Frank (1980), Burchell et al. (1985), and Zeff et al. (1992), have not considered more than a singular accounting issue each.

In sum, a considerable curiosity exists in the literature about how accounting is influenced by cultural variations. A limitation of the development of the literature has been its tendency to be highly variable in what it meant by culture and highly selective in what accounting phenomenon it considered.

Toward a General Theory of Culture

The theory of cultural dimensions developed by Hofstede (1980, 1991) has been widely studied in the fields of sociology, organizational theory, and more recently, accounting. An analysis of the Social Citation Index reveals that over the period 1981-1992, the theory has been cited in 583 studies in many different fields. This suggests a substantial consensus among researchers on the theory of culture. Hofstede emphasizes the dimensions of culture by which cultural values across nations can be distinguished. The following description of the five dimensions of cultural values is based on Hofstede's studies of culture in 53 countries:

Power Distance

Power Distance is a measure of the interpersonal power or influence between superiors and subordinates as perceived by the least powerful of the two. It shows the extent to which the less powerful members of institutions acknowledge that power is distributed unequally. Low Power Distance implies that there is limited dependence of subordinates on superiors, where the two groups bound in an interdependence relationship. Communications between subordinates and superiors reflect a consultative mode in which subordinates feel free to approach and contradict their superiors. High Power Distance, on the other hand, indicates a considerable dependence of subordinates on superiors. The relationship between superiors and subordinates is more autocratic or paternalistic, with subordinates unlikely to approach or contradict their superiors.

Uncertainty Avoidance

Uncertainty Avoidance measures anxiety levels of the members of a society or an institution about uncertain or unknown situations in the future. To cope with anxiety, people turn to technology, rules, and rituals. Technology reduces some forms of uncertainty caused by nature. Rules, meanwhile, provide defense against uncertainties in the behavior of others. Finally, rituals help people peacefully accept uncertainties against which they cannot defend themselves. Uncertainty Avoidance suggests a desire to achieve a reduction of ambiguity. People in high Uncertainty Avoidance cultures look for structure in their organizations, institutions, and relationships that makes events clearly interpretable and predictable.

Individualism versus Collectivism

Individualism is a measure of relationships between individuals and the collectivity. Individualism pertains to societies in which the ties between individuals are loose wherein responsibility extends in a very confined scope. Collectivism, on the contrary, describes societies in which people from birth onwards are integrated into strong and cohesive ingroups, which offer protection in exchange for unquestioning loyalty.

Masculinity versus Femininity

Masculinity is a measure of the desirability of assertive behavior as opposed to the desirability of modest behaviors. Masculinity and femininity reflect gender roles in societies in which the former are more concerned with achievements outside the home and the latter are more concerned with taking care of homes, children, and people in general. A masculine culture prioritizes achievements that require assertiveness and competition.

Long-term Orientation versus Short-term Orientation

Long-term and short-term orientations reflect the extent to which societies rely on their synthesizing and analyzing capacities. Long-term oriented societies synthesize different parts into the whole in a persistent and flexible way. They tolerate a slow construction process that may require diverse ways to build the whole. Short-term oriented societies, on the other hand, tend to decompose the whole and analyze it in parts. Short-term oriented societies favor certain consistent ways of doing things. They expect quick results as a consequence of their confidence in their approach.

Toward the Identification of Accounting Values

Gray (1988) and Perera (1989) initiated the building of a theoretical model of the nature of accounting regulation. They propose that certain accounting values, which represent a subset of societal values, underlie accounting practices. The model describes cultural-based accounting values in four dimensions.

Professionalism versus Statutory Control

Professionalism measures a preference for the exercise of individual professional judgment and the maintenance of professional self-regulation as opposed to compliance with prescriptive legal requirements and statutory control.

Uniformity versus Flexibility

Uniformity is a preference for the enforcement of distinct and certain accounting practices between companies and for the consistent use of such practices over time. This opposes flexibility in accordance with the perceived circumstances of individual companies.

Conservatism versus Optimism

Conservatism is preference for a cautious approach to measurement so as to cope with the uncertainty of future events. A more optimistic, laissez-faire, risk-taking approach would more equally balance the changes for overstatement of assets, understatement of liabilities, acceleration of revenues, and deceleration of expenses.

Secrecy versus Transparency

Secrecy is a preference for confidentiality and the restriction of disclosure of information about the business only to those who are closely involved with its management and financing. This is opposed to a more transparent, open, and publicly accountable approach toward business information.

With these dimensions, we have a general means to grapple with the variability of accounting regulation and practice. Together, these four oppositions inform us about who is in charge of the process, systematic choices that will be followed, and how accounting is conceived as a public or private good.

Theoretical Relationships between Cultural Values and Accounting

Gray (1988) and others have suggested that the relationship between culture and accounting regulation, although complicated, should be relatively straightforward. Since Hofstede's dimensions of culture are suggested to be less alterable than the general accounting values, the former should provide exogenous (independent) variables that can influence the latter, which would operate as endogenous (dependent) variables. In this way, the two sets of value orientations should provide empirical evidence that culture affects accounting regulation and practice.

Used in this manner, neither theory anticipates the prospect and importance of change. As such, individual studies do not benefit from the insights of other work that has suggested that accounting change is important (e.g., Gilling 1976; Solomons 1991). In this regard, it is possible that relationships between accounting and culture that are true at one moment in time will not be true at other temporal points.

All theories attempt to simplify and abstract in order to generalize. Many of the particular circumstances are lost in the process. Although this is typically accepted without great concern, a reality check is needed to ensure that theory has not substantively departed from that which it purports to describe. The great ambition of Hofstede's rendition of culture, and to a lesser extent, Gray's accounting values, creates this concern. The intimate details of a particular national history become much more relevant when one considers the shortcomings of analyses limited to singular points in time.

In sum, our understanding of culture, accounting, and the relationship between them has been greatly enhanced by the development of theories broad enough to facilitate meaningful progress to be made in the literature. However, these advantages may create some costs in terms of our reluctance to look at these constructs in other ways. For these purposes, a closer examination of particular countries is needed in order to see if basic relationships hold over time and are connected to socioeconomic conditions of importance.

THE INDONESIAN CASE STUDY

Indonesia contains an interesting juxtaposition of forces relevant to accounting change. Slightly more than a half century into its existence, Indonesia reflects its origins and its attempt to orient itself to modern political and economic conditions. This section provides background detail in the first three subsections. It then summarizes previous empirical work that has applied the theoretical ideas of Hofstede and Gray.

Political History

In 1945, after 350 years of Dutch and Japanese colonial government, Indonesia became a sovereign country. From 1945 to 1965, the Indonesian government was occupied with maintaining and consolidating its rule over the Indonesian archipelago. The Dutch colonial leader surrendered its authority with great reluctance. Many internal struggles to establish the ideological, political, economic, and social hegemony of the nation peppered the transition period. During this time, the government faced a communist rebellion, parliamentary gridlock and frequent leadership turnover, rebellion in the outer islands, and persistent confrontation with Malaysia. The government was also confounded by economic difficulties that created budget deficits and runaway inflation. Most notable among the causes of these problems were the lack of management skills in key state-run enterprises and inadequate monetary controls.

A major turning point occurred in the mid-1960s, when the Indonesian government was rocked by a failed communistic coup. This led to a power transition to the military and the emergence of Major General Suharto as the primary political power in the nation. This regime has been solidified over the last 30 years by near unanimous election victories.

The basic concepts of property, individual, and contractual rights were formulated in the text of the 1945 Constitution. Pompe (1992) summarizes the three most notable concepts as the unity of the state with the people, the process of decision making by consensus, and the organization of society based on collectives of individual citizens. The concept of unity between people and the state offered no clear guidelines about the proper course of conduct in cases where a conflict arises. Tension, however, is not expected since every citizen is deemed a member of the larger state family. The interests of each citizen are assumed to be taken into account by the state family and accommodated in any decision the state takes. Furthermore, the concept of "collectivity" emphasizes the duties owed by individuals to the state. Individual rights are assumed to be an product of the full discharge of individual duties. The concept of "collectivity" has constructed a theoretical foundation for the idea that the ownership of national territory and natural resources reside with Indonesian nationals. In the case of natural resources deemed "strategic," (such as land or water), the government can preempt all individual ownership.

Recent Economic Developments

When President Suharto took office in 1966, economic deprivation was widespread. Annual income per capita amounted to only $50, the lowest among southern Asian countries (Bresnan 1993; Robinson 1991). In the pursuit of both stability and growth, the government let the process of capital accumulation and investment concentrate in a small group of large state and private enterprises. In 1980, 55 Indonesian conglomerates accounted for 75% of capital accumulation in the private sector, and 180 state enterprises generated revenues equal to 15% of the nation's Gross Domestic Product (World Bank 1993). At the same time, the government subsidized prices of certain vital commodities such as fuel, rice, and sugar and provided massive credit and contracting subsidies to small enterprises.

This economic policy became unviable following decreases in the prices of oil and natural gas in the mid-1980s. This led to the realization that insufficient capital was available to enact governmental economic programs. To keep the economy growing, the government turned to the private sector by lessening economic restrictions, offering economic incentives for private investments, and reducing subsidies. Since this time, Indonesia has enjoyed an average annual Gross Domestic Product growth of 7% and an average annual increase in per capita income of 6%. The component of the total population in absolute poverty declined from 60% in 1970 to 15% in 1990.

In 1977, the government reopened the Jakarta Stock Exchange, which had been closed since 1968. To facilitate the operation of the Exchange, the government created two agencies to supervise the operation of the Exchange and periodically intervene in the trading of the securities. Initially, the number of companies listed on the Exchange was low and the total value of stocks and bonds issued through the Exchange was modest, especially relative to total bank credit outstanding

(Data Consult 1992). This reflects restrictions placed on valuation, trading, and ownership, which were imposed to further widespread public ownership. However, since 1989, the abandonment of many of these restrictions, plus the opening of the Exchange to foreign investors, has led to dramatic increases in values, participation, and activity (Data Consult 1992).

The economic policy of deregulation followed by the government opened the way for a more competitive market-oriented economy. This has been marked by the transformation of manufacturing from labor-intensive to capital-intensive technology. This industrialization has resulted in the emergence of new industries that employ more capital and encounter higher risks in their operations.

The Accounting Profession and Accounting Regulatory Developments

The accounting profession, accounting education, and accounting practice in Indonesia continue to be greatly influenced by government policies. This began with the enactment of the 1954 Accountant Act, which prescribes comprehensive occupational regulation and preconditioned licensure on the completion of an appropriate accounting education and the passage of a series of examinations.

Early education for accountants was initiated by the Ministry of Finance in the 1950s (Tjitrosidojo 1982). The Ministry of Finance opened an inhouse training program for adjunct accountants requiring a three-year course of study. Shortly thereafter, the Ministry of Finance established the Higher School for Public Finance to train its prospective employees. The school required a five-year course of study and offered four fields of study: taxation, accountancy, customs, and treasury. In the 1970s, this program became more autonomous when it was reorganized as the School for Government Accountants. This transition led to the incorporation of the principles of Anglo-American accounting and the abandonment of the Dutch system. Graduates now hold positions in government agencies, accounting firms, state enterprises, and private companies. Accounting education in universities started in 1954 when the University of Indonesia extended its School of Economics to include Accountancy. It also gradually transitioned, with the help of visiting faculty, to an Anglo-American style of accounting education.

The 1954 Act was a great impetus for the establishment of the Association of Indonesian Accountants. At its inception, the Association had 11 members, the total of all qualified Indonesian accountants. The formation of the Association had the effect of providing a national identity for the practice of accountancy in Indonesia. The influence of the government in the Association remains significant. Leadership of the Association is vested in a prominent governmental official. In addition, accountants working in government agencies and state enterprises constitute the majority of Association members.

The influence of the government on accounting and audit standards also has been significant. The Government Accountant Office released an accounting guide for state enterprises before the Association of Indonesian Accountants promulgated its 1974 Indonesian accounting principles. The latter is largely based on the former. Likewise, the 1974 auditing standards promulgated by the Association were largely derived from the audit standards previously set by the Government Accountant Office.

The Relationship between Culture and Accounting in Indonesia

The previous subsections attest to the significant changes that have occurred in government policies, the economic structure, and the business environment in Indonesia. These changes have occurred in tandem with the emergence of an accounting profession and the development of an accounting infrastructure. In order to more systematically appreciate this interface, Sudarwan (1995) empirically analyzed the relationships between culture and accounting regulation in Indonesia using measures recommended by Hofstede and Gray and data from 1982 to 1991. In addition to restricting his attention to this single country, and along with considering change over time, his contribution was to hypothesize that the *change* in cultural values would be associated with the *change* in accounting values. This provides an excellent opportunity to consider some fundamental questions that are often made obscure by the literature.

What are the dimensions of culture in a particular nation?

With the confirmatory factor analysis capabilities of LISREL, Sudarwan investigated the construct validity of Gray's accounting values and Hofetede's culture constructs. He found support for the independence of all four of the accounting values, but only four of five of Hofstede'cultural dimensions. The inability to conclude that time dimension was a necessary element of Indonesian culture represents an important finding. It suggests that the conceptual apparatus that we have brought to the question of culture itself may need refining for specific national contexts.

The reasons why time horizon does not prove to be a meaningful dimension of Indonesian culture might pertain to the religious grounding of Hofstede's measure of this variable. Hofstede (1991) suggests a link between time horizon and the *Confucian dynamism*. Countries familiar with the teaching of Confucius (e.g., China, Taiwan, Japan) score higher on the long-term orientation index. Countries with populations primarily from the Malay race and of the Moslem faith (e.g., the Philippines, Pakistan) score much lower in Hofestede's original work. Indonesia, with racial and religious characteristics much more in common with the latter group, therefore encounters the time horizon concept as a rather alien construct. This creates the suspicion that Hofstede's five-dimensional description of culture will be an imperfect fit for any particular country over any particular period.

When all of the cultural values are not independent, it is necessary to pursue explanations for the unexpected interactions that are then created. In Sudarwan's results, time horizon merged with Individualism. Because Individualism is measured in terms of the accumulation of material resources, the particular religious and economic meanings of wealth may be examined. According to Hofstede (1991), Confucianism urges people to have few desires and to be sparing with resources. A society with this attitude tends to set aside a high proportion of income for savings. Savings would be the primary source of financing for the investments that these societies make. Western societies, meanwhile, tend to satisfy their consumption needs first, before saving. Here, the primary driving factor for savings is not an attitude of being sparing with resources but the availability of excess income over the demand for consumption. In this sense, savings is not a substitute for present consumption but a vehicle to maintain the financial steadiness and stability of individuals. Thus, investment serves the interests of individuals in accordance with Hofstede's principle of Individualism.

An analysis of the Indonesian Gross Domestic Product reveals that the steady increase in Gross Fixed Investment is not the result of a reduction in consumption spending. Gross Fixed Investment increased from 24.3% of Gross Domestic Product in 1980 to 35% in 1991. Meanwhile, during the same period, consumption also increased, from 62.8% to 64% of Gross Domestic Product (Data Consult 1992). This suggests that the investment motives of Indonesian society mirror those of Western societies more closely than those of Confucian-influenced societies.

This suggests that not only must the measure of culture be overlaid against the history of the nation but its treatment must cut across individual facets of culture. Each nation is likely to present a unique set of interactions that have idiosyncratic meaning.

Are all the cultural dimensions related to all the accounting values?

Sudarwan's general results are summarized in Table 1. For these purposes, the deletion of time horizon left 16 possible effects (four cultural variables × four accounting

Table 1. Empirical Evidence on the Relationship between Culture and Accounting in Indonesia

	Culture			
Accounting Value	*Power Distance*	*Uncertainty Avoidance*	*Individualism*	*Masculinity*
Conservatism	S	S	S	NS
Professionalism	NS	US	S	NS
Secrecy	NS	US	S	NS
Uniformity	S	S	US	NS

Notes: NS = Not Significant.
S = Significant at the $p < .01$ level in the expected direction.
US = Significant at the $p < .01$ level in the unexpected direction.

values). Ten were found significant at $p < .01$. Of these, however, only seven (or less than 50% of all effects) were consistent with the hypothesized direction.

It is clear from Table 1 that the relationship between culture and accounting regulation is rather problematic in Indonesia. In general, nonsignificant results suggest that the cultural variable may not be salient for purposes of accounting regulation. Perhaps more importantly, the significant effects that ran contrary to their expected direction suggest a fundamentally flawed understanding of the underlying relationships.

What factors underlie the specific patterns wherein culture and accounting are related?

Our consideration of Indonesian history and traditions allows us to interpret the Sudarwan findings for Indonesia in a way that will amplify what is meant by culture for purposes of its relevancy to accounting regulation.

Governmental Presence

Much of the conventional wisdom in the relationship between accounting regulation and culture is predicated on the relative roles of the public and private sectors. The dominance of the former is supposed to, for example, maintain a high Power Distance in social relationships. Since the private sector is thought to be the engine of wealth production, its expansion should signal the emergence of a different culture (e.g., one marked by low Power Distance and higher Individualism). However, such generalities do not seem to control developments in Indonesia.

An analysis of Indonesian economic development indicates that the creation of national wealth depends heavily on government initiatives. In this situation, the process of national wealth creation does not reduce the importance of government authority. Thus, the increase in national wealth may not necessarily result in a reduction in Power Distance or an increase in professionalism. The success of both state and private enterprises, to some degree, has been the result of a great reliance on government policies and access to government authority. Professionalism in conducting business, vital as it may be in private-sector economies, may have become secondary.

The preparation of firms' financial reports also reflects this pattern of doing business. The government has played, and will continue to play, a larger than expected role in the development of the accounting profession in Indonesia. Since the accounting profession needs to cautiously avoid any conflict in setting professional standards, the environment is not conducive to the emergence of self-regulation. Accordingly, professionalism may not be a key factor in the process of financial reporting. In Indonesia, the demand for accounting and auditing services closely parallels governmental decree. In 1979, the Ministry of Finance issued decree No. 108, which stated that its tax agency would accept firms' audited financial statements as the basis for the computation of income tax due from the firms. As a result, demands for audit service increased significantly. When the decree was repealed in 1982, demand for audit services decreased sharply (Frederick and Worden 1993). Accounting practice does not seem driven by an autonomous value basis. Furthermore, changes in the economic and social environment may not have any clear impact on Indonesian accounting practice.

Another part of the government's role in the culture-accounting regulation nexus pertains to the interaction of professionalism and individualism. According to conventional reasoning, as Individualism increases, competition among firms becomes stronger. In a competitive environment, managers of firms are under constant pressure to incorporate more professionalism. Accordingly, the preparation of firms' financial reports and the development of accounting standards will be marked by professional standards of behavior. However, access to government authority can circumvent the need for professionalism, even in an increasingly competitive environment. Government can alter the returns to professionalism, and thereby mitigate its production. This is especially possible in nations where the self-governance structure of the professional community is relatively immature and the independence of the accounting discipline from the government is historically weak

Gender Stereotypes

Hofstede's treatment of the gender roles that are imprinted on cultures also seems particularly problematic for general purposes. The theory suggests that the adoption of a societal preference for traits more typically associated with masculinity or femininity can be inferred from such measures as the ratio of male to female students in higher education and secondary school. This tends to automatically confer certain psychological expectations upon the biological genders. The extent to which men and women would have the same attitudes toward assertiveness, concern for others, and other traits, once one controlled for factors like education and occupation, is uncertain. Both have high loading on Masculinity. Sudarwan's contradictory results on this value suggest that Indonesian women tend to maintain and champion a uniquely feminine value. More skilled and educated women are in a position to play a leading role in this effort. They do so because of their commitment to a unique femininity value rather than through a tendency toward masculinity. Historical analysis of the woman's movement in Indonesia supports this interpretation. The prominent pioneers of women's rights, such as Kartini and Dewi Sartika, did not associate with radical ideas for women (Soeroto 1979; Wiriaatmadja 1977). Instead, they came from families with traditional gender values. While they advocated improvement in education and more active roles for women in society, they did not urge women to abandon their traditional roles. This suggests that a middle position that is neither classically masculine or feminine is a distinct possibility.

The involvement of women in the Indonesian accounting community thus far has been so minimal that it has not had any impact on the development of accounting practice in Indonesia. However, since it is the classic male and female stereotype that should matter in this regard, much depends upon how these stereotypes are reproduced in an empirical sense in any given nation.

The Absolute Level of Accounting's Autonomous Development

Although Sudarwan's results suggest that it is meaningful to analyze the four hypothesized dimensions of accounting values (professionalism, conservatism, secrecy, and uniformity), the relatively simple and general nature of Indonesian accounting standards needs to be considered. These standards often do not provide Indonesian firms with the specific guidelines necessary for determining specific accounting treatments. A provision in the Indonesian accounting standards also allows Indonesian firms to apply any accounting methods in matters not sufficiently explained in the Indonesian accounting standards as long as minimal consistency with "sound business practice" is attained. This permeation of non-Indonesian accounting regulation causes us to question the sufficiency of the phenomenon under study.

Sudarwan (1995) shows a rejection of the expected negative relationship between Individualism and the conservatism of accounting practice. As part of Indonesian development, increasing competition motivates firms to favor risk-taking behavior and to select less conservative accounting methods. The extent to which this can be done will depend upon the rigor of existing accounting standards. This attribute will depend upon the cumulative effort that has gone into the restriction of accounting choices in particular reporting circumstances.

It is also difficult to project expectations about the role of the conservatism of accounting practice without assumptions pertaining to the means whereby firms compete for capital. In the Indonesian case, there is a lack of competition among firms to attract funds from capital markets. Accordingly, firms are not as subject to the levels of public scrutiny that those accustomed to developed economies might assume. Information about firms' operating results and asset positions can be limited to a few well-connected groups. Firms do not need to be overly concerned about providing information regarding their success to outside investors and other parties. Although at some point an expanded need for financing might enhance the salience of capital markets, many nations quite simply have not reached the point where there are automatic implications for accounting values.

The reliance of the business community on government authority may also negate the effects of the increase in national wealth on the process of lessening the secrecy of accounting practice. As many share the "trickle down" effects of successful access to government authorities, increases in national wealth may not be followed by a reduction in Power Distance or in the secrecy of accounting practice. Access is predicated on restricted privilege and very limited communication.

Although at some point the wealth creation process required to support large-scale enterprises may necessitate that firms develop capital sources from potential investors and, consequently, attain incentives to reduce the secrecy of accounting practice, it is not clear that this has occurred in any great degree in Indonesia or other West Pacific Rim developing nations (Cooke and Parker 1994).

Problems with Economic Data

Hofstede suggests that income per capita can be a measure of Individualism. Examinations of this data indicate that the Individualism of Indonesian society may have decreased over the 1980s. Income per capita data show that although it increased from U.S.$591 in 1981 to U.S.$650 in 1992, it had a decreasing trend through most of the period from 1981 to 1990. Likewise, the Gross Fixed Investment ratio had a decreasing trend from 1981 to 1986 before it began climbing in 1987. Therefore, for most of the 1980s, the data reveal a rather ambiguous conclusion pertaining to individualism.

The current movement toward deregulation of the Indonesian economy may eventually wean the Indonesian accounting community away from the certainty currently provided by its guidance. However, instead of boosting confidence, deregulation may increase anxiety among firms and the accounting profession. This may result in a more secretive accounting regulation and contradict the expected relationship with Uncertainty Avoidance. These two possibilities should introduce "noise" into the statistical relationships. Moreover, the impact of large-scale changes in governmental approaches will introduce difficult-to-interpret discontinuities into the economic data. Second, there is likely to be a lag effect that reflects the institutinal difficulies in a state-managed economy of producing the accounting needed for a recently deregulated business community.

In the wealth creation process, business firms may experience increased complexity in their financial reporting. This parallels increases in substantive complexity in firms' operation and transactions. It will probably prove difficult to unravel these two sources of change in ways that will make the culture-accounting relationships non-tautological. That firms are mature enough and have enough confidence to accept the risk of reporting under different accounting methods suggests that less uniform accounting practices will result. However, the true causal linkage is obscure. For example, the lack of uniformity could also result from a situation where firms cannot find uniform guidelines for the preparation of their financial reports. Uncertainty about the proper guidelines may cause companies to select different approaches to the preparation of their financial reports. Thus, accounting results may have little to do with either the competitive environment or cultural Individualism.

The presence of managerial discretion complicates the appreciation of cultural influence on accounting. Managerial discretion emerges from a firm's specific situation, which may or may not represent the general environment that influences the culture of society at large. Specific situations may lead to certain organizational cultures that may differ from one firm to another. State enterprises, privately held companies, and publicly held corporations, for instance, may operate in different organizational cultures through which the management decision process is shaped, including managerial discretion over accounting choice. Other factors, such as firm-specific leadership or market situation, may also influence this relationship. This further demonstrates that the relationship between culture and accounting is complicated and difficult to generalize.

DISCUSSION

We believe that these results suggest a need to explore three issues pertaining to work on the cultural underpinnings of accounting regulation. First, we need to explore the implications of longitudinal work. Cross-sectional work tends to provide a very static analysis that tends to suggest that change is either immaterial or unsystematic. Second, we need to closely examine our measures, especially those that purport to capture "culture". It is quite possible that we are simultaneously measuring too little and too much about a nation. When we use as inherently vague a construct as culture, we may also be measuring something different in each country when we have not carefully scrutinized our operationalizations. This overlaps with the third issue, data analysis. Throughout, the idiosyncratic aspects of each nation's development cannot be ignored. There may be important qualitative aspects of the social relations that underlie accounting regulation that are ignored when researchers attempt to assess a few bits of standard information about a large number of countries.

Longitudinal versus Cross-Sectional Designs

The brief history of Indonesia outlined earlier argues for the fact that large-scale and widely experienced social change has occurred in a rather short number of years. Accounting, as it is known in that nation, has been built from the ground up in a relatively short time period. These conditions suggest that what is truly of interest is the trajectory of the relationship between these factors over time. How these constructs change *in relation to each other* provides much more information than a one-time measure of each does.

Indonesia is not necessarily typical in the magnitude of its social and accounting change. Other nations, such as the United States, have encountered much less turbulence over the same time frame. This suggests that the extent of change is a variable and one well-worth explicit consideration in international accounting studies.

In the case of many nations with emerging economies, the course of development is not random. The measures employed to describe culture in the Hofstede model tend to reflect the direction of classic modernization and industrialization changes. Therefore, to measure these indicators at a single point in time ignores the fact that they are continuously evolving. In a similar vein, accounting values are systematically influenced by the progressive expansion of the accounting profession. Structures for professional organization adopted in developed nations sometimes are exported for the consideration of less developed nations (Briston et al. 1995). The values consistent with those structures also are subject to revision over time. Therefore, the failure to specify longitudinal models ignores not only transition but potentially parallel or opposite movement in the culture and accounting regulation.

Measurement

Culture, as a concept, has been used in many different ways in the social sciences. That which distinguishes one group from another can use many alternative perspectives. The capture of the culture measure by one discipline or worldview could deny, or make less viable, other sences of the root construct. To a large degree, Hofstede's measures are economic in nature. The few that are not are either demographic (i.e., gender of students) or reflective of governmental policy (i.e., number of deregulation packages proposed). It could be argued that the noneconomic measures are indirect reflections of the economic state. Thus, it is possible that the construct called "culture" by Hofstede, and used rather indiscriminately as such by many others, is more directly an index of economic development.

The conventional approach to culture is to delimit the construct by nation states. This classification originates from a premise that shared values are the basis for a nation to exist. This assumption makes it possible to use economic data, since economic data is typically reported on a national level. In Indonesia, great flows of people have migrated due to economic and political instability uncoupled from the pursuit of more homogenous values. The Indonesian population comprises different ethnic groups with different languages, religions, and customs. Ethnic and race criteria may be more valid lines to use to draw conclusions about cultural diffusion. The focus on national culture borrowed from the literature may overlook the impact of these ethnic groups on Indonesian accounting practice. This may limit the validity of the culture-accounting literature to situations where a "pure" national culture exists.

Measurement error refers to the discrepancy between the theoretical constructs and the operational measures. Even when data analysis carefully controls for this possibility, statistical procedures do not allow for the possibility that the constructs themselves may be fundamentally misconstrued and labeled as something which they are not. Most authors do not consider this possibility of reductionism when they impose economic measures as if they were identical to the entirety of constructs firmly ground in social experience.

Methods of Data Analysis

Above, we argued that in order to consider the problematic application of the theories of Hofstede and Gray to any particular country, it is necessary to unravel the measurements that these authors endorse. Care was recommended in the selection of proxies, especially in the attempt to operationalize constructs, such as culture, that defy simple and unequivocal transformation to measurable form. Beyond this, however, is the related question of how these measures will be associated with others.

Hofstede and Gray contemplate the need to approach complex constructs with more than a single measure. This is an attempt to capture the multidimensionality of the construct. However, neither author provides a means to combine the measured variables in a way that does justice to the constructs that they represent. Previous authors have either selected singular measures (and implicitly asserted that these constitute an unproblematic representation of the construct) or algebraically combined (usually summing) scores on different measures. The advantages of either of these approaches is that they enable the researcher to use ANOVA or regression methods to analyze the data. However, such an approach fails to acknowledge that constructs are imperfectly measured.

The various forms of Latent Variable Structural Equation methods (e.g., EQS, LISREL) provide a means whereby measurement error can become part of the analysis. This may become increasingly important as longitudinal designs are employed. As individual measurements change, we should expect that their association with other measures used to measure the same construct will also vary. Put simply, the commonality that exists between multiple measures of cultural or accounting values must become an essential part of the analysis.

Hofstede's theory of culture also does not address the interaction effects among each dimension of culture. For example, his theory predicts that when people become better educated, contributing to the development of a strongly middle-class society, Power Distance in that society will decrease. It is possible, however, that the decrease in Power Distance may also be followed by a decrease in Uncertainty Avoidance. Better education may also enable people to feel confident about themselves and less anxious about uncertainty. If this is the case, it may be more difficult to attribute changes in accounting regulation to changes in any particular dimension of culture.

CONCLUSIONS

This study has conceptually examined the applicability of the theories of cultural dimensions (Hofstede 1980, 1991) and accounting dimensions (Gray 1988). Through the use of the Indonesian case, the precariousness of culture as a factor associated with accounting has been shown. This paper also attempted to focus researchers on research design, measurement, and national history. As such, it serves as a sharp contrast to previous studies that used index scores of cultural values across nations to assert cross-sectional associations.

The research issues raised above express the notion that the complexity of the relationships between culture and accounting practice exceed the capabilities of our traditional research designs and measures. Great care should be taken when interpreting results of the line of study that continues to employ singular points in time, purely economic measures, and ahistorical perspectives. A rich panoply of evidence and multifaceted considerations of any society need to be explored before reaching distinct conclusions.

Detailed case studies may enable us to have an understanding about cultural differences and similarities among nations which would be of value in the continuing effort to harmonize accounting standards for external financial reporting. These insights may also protect the study of culture from the limitations of Hofstede's conceptions. Importantly, a tendency to blur the economic and the social may lead to an unwise proclivity to equate economic development with cultural progress. Getting beyond Hofstede may also better equip researchers to cope with the complexities about human differences that should not be suppressed.

This paper has attempted to make a contribution to our understanding of the relationships between cultural and accounting values in Indonesia. Although this was a secondary objective, many interesting refinements were observed. Particularly noteworthy is the fact that market competition and the reliance of the business community on access to government authority are factors which appear to both confirm and distort the relationships between cultural values and the dimensions of accounting practice. The reliance of the business community on government authority may have caused the relationships between cultural values and Indonesian accounting practice to sometimes contradict the conventional assumptions. Particular degrees of market competition, on the other hand, sometimes stimulate the realization of the expected relationships. The further study of Indonesia should include more a detailed observation of how nascent market competition and governmental-authority traditions struggle for influence on Indonesian accounting.

REFERENCES

Bedi, H. 1993. In my view: Sensitivity and success. *Asian Business* 29: 4.

Belkaoui, A. 1989. Cultural determinism and professional self-regulation in accounting: A comparative ranking. In *Research In Accounting Regulation*, Vol. 3, 93-102. Greenwich, CT: JAI Press.

Bhimani, A. 1993. Indeterminacy and the specifity of accounting change: Renault 1898-1938. *Accounting Organizations and Society* 18: 1-39.

Bindon, K., and H. Gernon. 1995. The European Union: Regulation moves financial reporting toward comparability. In *Research in Accounting Regulation*,eds. G. Previts and L. Parker. Vol. 9, 23-49. Greenwich, CT: JAI Press.

Birnberg, J.G., and C. Snodgrass. 1988. Culture and control: A field study. *Accounting, Organizations and Society* 13(5): 447-464.

Bloom, R., and M.A. Naciri. 1989. Accounting standard setting and culture: A comparative analysis of the United States, Canada, England, West Germany, Australia, New Zealand, Sweden, Japan, and Switzerland. *The International Journal of Accounting Research and Education* 24: 70-97.

Boland, R., and L. Pondy. 1983. Accounting in organizations: A union of natural and rational perspectives. *Accounting, Organizations and Society* 8: 223-234.

Bresnan, J. 1993. *Managing Indonesia: The Modern Political Economy*. New York: Columbia University Press.

Briston, R., D. Alexander, and H. Yunus. 1995. Financial reporting in the West Pacific rim: An extension and update. In *Research in Accounting in Emerging Economies*, eds. R. Wallace, J. Samuels, J. Briston and S. Saudajan. Vol. 3, 299-317. Greenwich, CT: JAI Press.

Burchell, S., C. Clubb, and A.G. Hopwood. 1985. Accounting in its social contexts: Towards a history of value added in the United Kingdom. *Accounting, Organizations and Society* 10: 381-414.

Cooke, T., and R. Parker. 1994. *Financial Reporting in the West Pacific Rim*. London: Routledge.

Data Consult, Inc. 1992. *Indonesian Economic Trends 1992: Anticipating Globalization Era of 1990s*. Jakarta: Data Consult, Inc.

Dermer, J.D. 1988. Control and organizational order. *Accounting, Organizations and Society* 13: 25-36.

Frederick, W. and Worden 1993. *Indonesia: A Country Study*. Washington, DC: Library of Congress Federal Research Division.

Gernon, H., and R. Wallace. 1995. *International accounting research: A review of its ecology, contending theories and methodologies. Journal of Accounting Literature* 14: 54-106.

Gilling, D. 1976. Accounting and social change. *International Journal of Accounting Education and Research* 11: 59-71.

Graham, J.L. 1985. The influence of culture on the process of business negotiations: An exploratory study. *Journal of International Business Studies* 126: 81-96.

Gray, S.J. 1988. Towards a theory of cultural influence on the development of accounting systems internationally. *Abacus* 24: 1-15.

Gray, S.J. and H. Vint. 1995. The impact of culture on accounting disclosures. *Asia-Pacific Journal of Accounting* 2: 33-44.

Harrison, G.L., and J.L. McKinnon. 1986. Culture and accounting change: A new perspective on corporate regulation and accounting policy formulation. *Accounting, Organizations and Society* 11: 233-252.

Hoffman, R.C. 1987. Political versus rational sources of decision power among country clusters." *Journal of International Business Studies* 18: 1-14.

Hofstede, G. 1980. *Culture's Consequences: International Differences in Work Related Values*. Beverly-HillsCA: Sage.

Hofstede, G. 1991. *Cultures and Organizations: Software of the Mind*. New York: McGraw-Hill.

Nahapiet, J. 1988. The rhetoric and reality of an accounting change: A study of resource allocation. *Accounting, Organizations and Society* 13: 333-58.

Nair, R.D., and W.G. Frank. 1980. The impact of disclosure and measurement practices on international accounting classifications. *The Accounting Review* 55: 426-450.

Oikawa, N. 1992. The influence of Japanese culture on business relationships and negotiations. *Journal of Service Marketing* 6: 67-74.

Perera, M.H.B. 1989. Towards a framework to analyze the impact of culture on accounting. *The International Journal Of Accounting Research and Education* 24: 42-56.

Pompe, S. 1992. *Indonesian Law, 1949-1989*. Boston, MA: Martinus Nijhoff.

Pourjalali, H., and G. Meek. 1995. Accounting and culture: The case of Iran." In *Research in Accounting in Emerging Economies*, eds. R. Wallace, J. Samuels, J. Briston and S. Saudajan. Vol. 3, 3-18. Greenwich, CT: JAI Press.

Preston, A.M. 1992. The birth of clinical accounting: A study of the emergence and transformation of discourses on costs and practices of accounting in U.S. hospitals. *Accounting, Organizations and Society* 17: 63-100.

Robinson, R. 1991. *Power And Economy in Suharto's Indonesia*. Wollongong, Australia: Journal of Contemporary Asia Publishers.

Schreuder, H. 1987. Accounting esearch, practice and culture: A European perspective. In *Accounting And Culture*, ed. B.E. Cushning, 12-22. Sarasota, FL: American Accounting Association.

Smircich, L. 1983. Concepts of culture and organizational analysis. *Administrative Science Quarterly* 28: 339-358.

Soeroto, S. 1979. *Kartina: A Biography*. Jakarta: Gunung Agung.

Solomons, D. 1991. Accounting and social change: A neutralist view. *Accounting, Organizations and Society* 16: 287-293.

Sudarwan. 1995. The dynamic relationship between culture and accounting: An empirical examination of the Indonesian setting. Unpublished Ph.D. disseration, Case Western Reserve University.

Tjitrosidojo, S. 1982. Sekelumit perkembangan Ikatan Akuntan Indonesia. In *Tahun Ikatan Akuntan Indonesia*, Vol. 25, ed. Ikatan Akuntan Indonesia, 75-110. Jakarta: IAI.

Turner, C.H., and A. Trompenaars. 1993. *The Seven Cultures Of Capitalism*. New York: Currency-Doubleday.

Wallace, R., and H. Gernon. 1991. Frameworks for international comparative financial accounting. *Journal of Accounting Literature* 10: 209-264.

Wiriaatmadja, R. 1977. *Dewi Sartika: Pahlawan Nasional*. Jakarta: Departemen Pendidikan dan Kebudayaan.

World Bank. 1993. *Indonesia Sustaining Development*. Washington, DC: World Bank.

Zeff, S.A., F. van der Wel, and K. Camfferman. 1992. *Company Financial Reporting: A Historical And Comparative Study Of The Dutch Regulatory Process*. New York: North-Holland.

ETHOS ABANDONED:
ACCOUNTING AS AN INSTRUMENT OF CORPORATE REGULATION

Graeme W. Dean and Frank L. Clarke

ABSTRACT

Professional attention to reforming accounting has for many years been directed to important, but mainly peripheral, issues. Official standard-setting bodies have been established and modified over time. Due process for forging accounting standards has been devised and revised, but the quality of the end products has not improved. Arguably, it has deteriorated. A miscellany of often inconsistent processing and valuation rules continues to form the basis of the compulsory conventional accounting procedures and policies. Diversity in accounting practice persists. There is retention by the profession of its long-stated position that the balance sheet is not a statement of net worth and that all that is required is that the public be educated as to the limitation of accounts. When there is an inquiry into accounting's (and auditing's) effectiveness, invariably the public is fed the notion that the financial data are misleading and creative, by virtue of practitioners deviating from, or deliberately misinterpreting, the prescribed accounting standards.

Research in Accounting Regulation, Supplement 1, pages 221-243.

ISBN: 0-7623-0338-7

This paper considers the dilemma facing accountants, directors, and auditors in Australia's mixed professional and legislative-based regulatory regime, with its overriding emphasis on statutory authority. In this regime, mandatory compliance with promulgated and approved accounting standards is taken to be prima facie evidence that the accounts show a "true and fair view" of an entity's financial state of affairs and performance. That assumed outcome is highly contestable. It is argued here that compliance is being mandated, even when it contravenes financial common sense.

Implications of downgrading the true and fair override in the Australian corporate disclosure regulatory regime are examined and we put forward a case for it regaining its primary override position. It is argued that accounting information as a serviceable product and accountancy as a professional endeavor are undeniably at the cross roads! Without change, users will continue to lament as another writer suggests that "corporate accounting does not do violence to the truth occasionally, and trivially, but comprehensively, systematically, and universally, annually and perennially." (Chambers 1991, p. 17).

INTRODUCTION

> *We should speak...of the immorality of accounting; for it has been the quirks of accounting that have provided many of the opportunities for misdemeanors of...corporate officers.*
>
> —Chambers (1991, 16-17)

Ever since the specification of accounting provisions in the 1844 United Kingdom Companies Act, the explicit legislative theme in many countries has been that published financial information in the form of a company balance sheet and, subsequently, the income statement were to be *full and fair* ("truthful") representations of the company's financial state of affairs and changes therein. Truthful accounts were deemed a quid pro quo of general incorporation. Unquestionably, the ethos of corporate accounting was that those interested in a company's financial affairs were to be accurately informed through the annual financial statements made public. Beyond question, that was the explicit charge emerging from the Gladstone Committee of Enquiry which preceded the 1844 U.K. Act and followed a series of major joint stock company collapses. Accounting reports have been an instrument of corporate regulation in the *British* commercial system ever since incorporation became effective upon mere registration under the 1844 United Kingdom Companies Act. As such, balance sheets and income statements were properly to fill their role as modes of instrumentation, providing indicators of the wealth and progress of corporations in general and, in particular, data which were to be serviceable for the assessment of companies' critical financial characteristics. To that end, the accounting reports were to present a "full and fair view," a "truthful depiction" of a company's financial position.

Accounting, like all instrumentation, in this manner was to provide information which those who were monitoring companies' affairs could not observe by immediate observation. It was implicit that the data which emerged from the accounts and were presented to the national corporate regulatory body, the U.K. Board of Trade, and the shareholders, demanded by bankers and creditors, and generally disseminated, gave truthful readings of the financial phenomena to which they referred. That was the unequivocal ethos of accounting, uniquely enshrined in legislation.

One-hundred-and-fifty years later in Australia, that unique ethical peg appears to have been lost in the wake of ill-founded regulatory responses to spates of corporate failure and the litigation embroiling directors and auditors over their alleged actions or inactions. One such response has been to blame declining ethics. Indeed, talking ethics has become a growth industry in the 1990s. Regulators of corporate activity, the financial press, and politicians have been quick to jump on the ethics bandwagon. Immediate post-1980s headlines in the Australian financial press are representative of the ethics *push*: "Ethics Becoming the Buzzword of the 90s" (Fox 1990), "Call for Higher Business Ethics" (Boyd 1990), "Ethics Rise in the West" (1990), "Corporate Ethics Come Under the Microscope" (Hurst 1990), "Accounting Education in 'Chronic Neglect'" (Lewis 1990), and "Big Business Elders Crusade for Higher Ethics" (Stephens 1990), as are subsequent accounts: "Declining Ethics...Bad Company" (Collins 1990), "Profession Begins to Get Serious about Its Ethics" (Lyons 1992), "Society Needs Dose of Ethics to Purge Its 'Moral Chaos'" (Forester 1991), "Phillips Bows Out with Call for Code of Ethics" (Kaye 1992), "Another Counselling Centre for Ethically Troubled Accountants" (Lawson 1992), "Ethics Is a Tricky Business" (Mackay 1993), "The Selling of Ethics" (Niemarck 1995; see also Gaa 1993), and "Where Does the Buck Stop?" (Edwards 1993).

Against that background, one could imagine that the issue of the corporate and professional ethics of accountants might have been a relatively simple matter to grasp, notwithstanding that many have perceived "ethics" as being a dynamic concept. In the context of accountants' professional endeavors, Roslender has noted, their quest for professional recognition should have pointed them immediately toward the social orientation—a primary duty to the public—which is universally accepted to be a primary and determining characteristic of the professional (Roslender 1992). Confronting the issue should have been assisted by having the "full and fair" ethos already enshrined in legislation.

Over time, in most Anglophile countries, the "full and fair" phrase has undergone minor changes—for example, "full and correct, true and correct" in the 1936 NSW Companies Act, "true and fair" in the 1948 U.K. Companies Act and in the 1961 Uniform Companies Acts, and similar phrases used elsewhere. But there has never been a compelling argument that the original ethos was no longer the pervading essence, despite lengthy debate in the literature as to precisely what the phrases mean—whether, for example, the words should be read separately or as one. That debate continues and gains momentum in Europe with the need to harmonize regulatory mechanisms, under some form of either "truthful" or "prudence-based" corporate disclosure regime.[1] Accordingly—notwithstanding countless changes in recommended accounting practices in Australia since the 1960s, then promulgation of prescribed accounting standards, then changes in the standard-setting mechanism (Clarke and Craig 1993), and successive revisions of Australian company laws up to 1992—the overriding requirement has been that a company's published accounting data is to show a true and fair view of its state of affairs at a stipulated date and its financial performance in the period prior to that date. This specification follows the British *tradition,* in which those words have generally been taken to have a stronger implication that the accounts are truthful than the U.S. counterpart "agree with generally accepted accounting principles" wording (McEnroe and Martens 1996). That true and fair has been rated in that manner enhances its ethical significance for practicing accountants.

ETHICS PUSH

In the Western world, embracing the tenets of market-driven commercial activity, it is less than clear what *is* ethical commercial behavior and what is not. And, given its dynamic nature it is clearly difficult to define unambiguously. With a set of secular laws in place and voluntary compliance with the principles of the underlying Judeo-Christian framework, staying within the law and being constrained financially by the market are the final determinants of the manner in which Western commerce proceeds. An exemplar is David Fischel's attack on "greed bashing" and the "greed is good" stance implicitly forming the basis of his support for the actions of the embattled Michael Milken, the 1980s "junk bond king" (Fischel 1995).

Motherhood statements have characterized the ethics push in Australia. Talk of corporate responsibility to protect the environment, responsibility to warn customers of limits on the serviceability of products, obligations to provide community services, contributions to charities, and the like are rather empty platitudes, without legal force or the force (sometimes) of common sense. First, it is interesting to note how the personification of corporate activity sheets home the blame for what is considered a dubious corporate activity to the legal entity itself, not to its human agents—its directors, managers, employees, accountants, and auditors.[2] Yet, only the human agents can conceive, implement, and follow through the actions complained of—only they make the choices between alternative proposals, only they direct the manner in which the corporate vehicle interacts with other corporations and real individuals within the community. Second, there can be considerable doubt whether corporate managers are acting in the best interest of the corporation if its resources are diverted from the market-driven financial objectives.

It needs to be noted that Australia's regulatory framework conforms to some degree with parts of the U.K. and U.S. regulatory regimes. Regarding accounting standard-setting, there is a cooperative arrangement between the national regulatory authority, the Australian Securities and Commission, and the private sector accounting standard-setting bodies, the Australian Accounting Standards Board and the Public Sector Accounting Standards Board. Since the early 1990s, accounting standards have been given legal backing, but the quid pro quo has been the possible government intervention in the standard-setting process through the establishment of the Accounting Standards Review Board (subsequently renamed the Australian Accounting Standards Board). This body has the authority to approve accounting standards (Miller 1994; Clarke, Dean, Wells and Lowry 1997; Epstein and Mirza 1997). Briefly, the main features of this system are that, while in the United Kingdom and the United States, accounting standards are set primarily in the private sector, in Australia there is legislative backing for the standards generally originating from the private sector. Australia, like the United States, has a Securities Commission which monitors and enforces the application of accounting standards. Relative to the United States, in Britain and Australia, there is a less open mechanism for the inclusion of the views of interested parties outside the accounting profession in the formal standard-setting process.

Returning to the consideration of ethics, corporate collapse, and accounting, cause and effect have been preoccupations in the regulators' analyses of Australian corporate crises. Although cause and effect is a hotly disputed relationship in the discipline of history (see Oakeshott 1933; Block 1954; Carr 1964),[3] the contemporary and sometimes superficial histories accorded many corporate collapses embrace a rather strong willingness by observers to jump to simplistic explanations (Keats 1964; Daughen and Binzen 1971; Dirks and Goss 1974; in the United Kingdom, Gray 1971; Raw 1976; Bower 1991; in Australia, Ross 1988; Janetzki 1989; Maher 1990; Barry 1990). Corporate regulators in Australia—that is, the National Companies and Securities Commission and its successor the Australian Securities Commission—the accounting profession, and say, the Cadbury Committee in the United Kingdom have all been quick to attribute many of commerce's problems to declining ethical behavior by managers and financiers (e.g., Bosch 1990, 24-39.) Of course, accountants who have allegedly departed from the prescribed accounting standards have been targeted as deviants, as engaging in creative accounting. We have provided evidence elsewhere (Clarke, Dean, and Oliver 1997) in support of the view that some may have been precisely the opposite—that creative accounting as likely arose from complying with Australian accounting standards as from deviating from them.

In any event, whether the moral behavior of businessmen has declined is contestable.[4] In the past, as now, the practices of leading Australian businessmen and accountants have been the subject of criminal and civil cases and professional disciplinary cases.[5]

Distinguishing business ethics as a class of behavior of its own is a curious fad of the commentators on corporate failure. Business activity is really only one of many facets of human endeavor. No good reason exists why business ought to be different from other human relations in respect to how it proceeds regarding the relations of one participant to another. A delineation of business ethics from other human behavior has skewed the debate from the real issue deserving attention—the features of the general commercial and financial framework in which corporate fraud and unexpected failure have occurred. Concentrating on the financial shenanigans of a few individuals who have either set out to deceive or by dint of unfortunate temporary financial circumstances were forced to do so, has little to commend it. This has been a fertile ground, producing many 1990s reports (and codes) including, in Australia, several editions of Henry Bosch's *Corporate Procedures and Conduct*; in the United Kingdom, Lord Cadbury's *Code of Corporate Governance*; and in the United States, the American Law Institute's *Principles of Corporate Governance: Analysis and Recommendations*. Missing has been an exhaustive discussion of the framework within which, and the processes by which, a commercial society may proceed about its business in a reasonably well-informed manner, fairly and equitably. Of course, "fairly and equitably" are open to definition and virtually every definition will attract complaints and dispute. At the other end of the scale, nobody could claim that the publication of unserviceable financial data *is* informing fairly and equitably.

There can be no doubt that the behavior of some Australian entrepreneurs in many of the enterprises which failed in the 1980s constituted less than a fulfilment of their fiduciary responsibilities. Descriptions of the collapses, including those contained in reports of government-appointed investigators, those revealed at several public enquiries initiated by court-appointed liquidators, and the observations of the judiciary (for example, regarding Bond Corporation, Estate Mortgage, Spedley, and Hooker) and the laying of charges by the Australian Securities Commission (at Qintex, Rothwells, Interwest, Linter, Duke, Westmex, Budget, and Independent Resources) pointed to the action and inaction of managers, directors, accountants, and auditors which was questionable at least morally, and often legally, insofar as it affected the fortunes of investors (for details of cases see Clark, Dean and Oliver 1997, Table 11.1).

Managers and directors whose behavior is now under the microscope might well be said to have been buoyed along on the encouragement of the investors (including bankers and financiers) who "stumped up" their ventures, and who were happy to hunt with the pack in the pursuit of expected high returns. Investors generally were quite content with the modus operandi. It is instructive to note that initially, few were publicly vocal in questioning the entrepreneurial push. Just the opposite: this push was almost universally applauded,[6] as were those who were driving it. They were feted nationally and internationally, seemingly never short of friends and admirers, many in high places.

The behavior of many 1980s Australian entrepreneurs was in many respects no worse than that of their counterparts in the previous two decades. The history of corporate failure is replete with allegations of con men, cheats, swindlers, and crooks, who set out from day one to deceive investors deliberately regarding the financial state of their companies, and deliberately manipulated accounting records and reports. The 1990s has exposed its own allegations of high-rollers on the world scene, for example, Leeson (Baring's derivatives trader), Iguchi (Daiwa's bond trader), Benson (Metallgesellscahft's oil futures trader), and Hamanaka (Sumitomo's copper trader) (Bloomberg 1996).

It might well be argued, in mitigation of the questionable deeds of Australia's 1980s entrepreneurs, that they were spurred on by an investing public and even governments, who were right behind them, supportive of and applauding their ventures—and, we might presume, applauding their tactics, too. A contentious view is that it would not have mattered too much what the entrepreneurs' intentions were, for even if they had complied with many of the official accounting standards, their financial reports were bound to be creative and potentially misleading. Deceit and evil intent mattered little insofar as investors were fed misleading financial signals about the financial wealth and progress of public entities. It was going to happen anyway. That is important, for it begs the question as to who or what ultimately should have ended up in the dock on trial. Our contention is that it is the system that should be on trial.

Accordingly, the personal ethics of the main public players in Australia's 1980s corporate collapses ought not to be on trial, or at least on trial as much as they are, and in particular not so insofar as accounting is an issue. In the Australian financial press, McKay (1993, p. 15) succinctly noted a theme pursued here, that "the exploitation of morality is one of the most corrosive of contradictions." Media attention on the individuals—the "cult of the individual"—has turned public attention away from the whales and toward the minnows to capture the human interest angle (Edwards 1993). Such attention is short-lived. Those individuals will leave the scene anyway, to be replaced by others—inevitably, unless the circumstances in which they operated are changed to prevent it.

What ought to be under close scrutiny are the principles and practices in the loose framework in which commerce and industry proceeds and is supposed to be accountable. This is particularly so insofar as accounting data are held out as indicative of the wealth and progress of companies to an unsuspecting public, by accountants who (in their professional literature) admit that the data are not. For that framework will endure unless deliberate action is taken to alter it. Attention ought to be on the relationship of accounting to commerce, industry, and society as a whole, not on the personal strengths and weaknesses of individual members of it.

TRUE AND FAIR: FARE-THEE-WELL

Neither accountants nor corporate managers should have had any doubts as to their overriding ethos. The true and fair override is consistent with a commonly held view embodied in this dictum: "To be effective as a stimulus to ethical thought and behavior, a code of ethics should set out principles, ideals, virtues and values. What it should not do is prescribe behavior through a set of rules and regulations" (Mackay 1993, p. 15). Under the true and fair ethos, ethical behavior by accountants necessitates that they assist directors as the preparers of financial statements in producing financial information that is indicative of the financial characteristics that such information is held out to show. Few professional groups have as explicit an ethical charge presented to them as that, and few have had it embodied consistently (over 150 years) in legislation as widely used as the British-based company laws. One might have expected accountants and corporate managers to have jealously guarded that edict.

Just the opposite has occurred in Australia. Effectively, this ethic has been abandoned, having been described by one regulator as an "accounting anachronism." Some have claimed that it has been replaced by industry and professionally developed codes and rules (standards) of practice. Already, an accounting textbook has referred to it as being carried forward in legislation "as something of a museum piece" (Jubb and Haswell 1993, 65). Without vehement objection by the accounting profession to its most explicit ethical peg being at best demoted, the current Australian Corporations Law arguably has relegated the true and fair override clause in respect of financial statements to a second-order imperative, preferring to enforce stricter compliance with the profession's accounting standards. This is interesting, given the IASC's avowed preference to provide a conceptual framework as a guide rather than producing an ever-increasing cookbook of standards. In Australia, the position in the late 1990s is that if directors or auditors are of the view that the published data are not true and fair, they are to report to that effect, not in the Accounts proper, but in the Notes to the Accounts. Not surprisingly, some maverick practitioners and corporate managers have reacted quickly and strongly. Several examples to date include the tactics of the directors of Westfield Holdings, the QBE and NRMA Insurance Groups, and the Orbital Engine Company. The latter was refused permission to account for intangibles by writing off $236 million against the Share Premium Reserve Account (it should be noted that it had been allowed to do this in the United States under U.S. reporting requirements). Australia's regulatory watchdog, the ASC, determined that Orbital was required to follow the Australian standard (AAS 1010) and charge the write-off to the Profit and Loss account.[7] Directors at QBE, after being refused court exemption from compliance with the standard covering Accounting for General Insurance Business (AASB 1023), reported its 1992 results under two heads—as per the accounting standards, and according to the directors' preferred method of accounting (QBE 1992). The directors at Westfield exercised their judgement to satisfy their true and fair Corporations Law obligations when they "derecognized" management agreements as an asset—a sensible move, we would claim. However, their action did not accord with Australian accounting standards. But to complicate matters even further, it *was* in accord with international accounting standards. They eventually followed Australia's AASB 1023 prescribed approach in the accounts and "noted" the results of using the other approach. Further evidence of the effects of complying with the profession's cookbook of rules is provided in *Corporate Collapse* (Clarke, Dean and Oliver 1997).

It is surprising that the accounting profession in Australia generally has traded such a unique ethical benchmark, the true and fair criterion, for the misguided safe harbor afforded by compliance with its standards. However, the trade fits neatly into concurrent attempts by accountants to legislatively limit the liability arising from their professional work (Walker 1993, 107). That drive, however, is likely at best to provide a short-run fix for any professional.

LIMITING LIABILITY: IF THE *CAP FITS, WEAR IT!*

Faced with increasing litigation, Australian auditors have lobbied government (both state and federal) to limit their exposure to damages for negligence. Consistent with the international phenomenon, the level of professional indemnity insurance that corporate directors and auditors take out is the primary factor limiting the extent to which damages for negligence might be extracted through litigation. Those individuals' "residual" personal wealths are unlikely to amount to relatively much. Divesting of property ownership is expected to mitigate exposure to personal loss. In the wake of past litigation and with the prospect of more to come, it is to be expected that insurance cover will be increased and premiums will continue to rise.[8] Accountants in general and auditors in particular are finding the insurance slug unpalatable. Their responses, while predictable, are somewhat questionable, and certainly short-sighted. As professionals, accountants claim sizeable fees for their services, but a cynic could be excused for thinking that they appear unwilling to accept the relationship between the level of fees and the risk for which it compensates.[9] While it might be claimed that fees have increased to meet the high insurance premiums, it is far from clear that fees were correspondingly lower before the spate of litigation or the surge in indemnity premiums. The same is true of company directors and valuers; insurance premiums are high, but then so are directors' and valuers' fees (Este 1995). Many seem to want to have their cake and eat it too.

To that end, following similar moves overseas (e.g., Public Oversight Board 1993; Big Six 1992), accountants in Australia have pursued having financial liability for the consequences of their professional services limited by statute. A statutory cap on their liability arising through actions under the Corporations Law has been sought.[10] Such a proposal has an approximately 70-odd year history (Napier

1996). The matter remains under Australian parliamentary review—perhaps even given new life by the change of federal government in early 1996. A separate document prepared in June 1993 (updated in March 1996) by the Working Party of the Ministerial Council for Corporations canvassed the professional bodies' alternative mechanisms to statutory capping, inter alia: combining self-regulation and auditor rotation, placing a limit on the useful life of financial accounts, permitting accountants to incorporate with consequential limited liability, and permitting companies to pay directors' indemnity premiums so as to split the claims on auditors by having directors well insured too.[11] While the 1990s New South Wales and Western Australian state legislation supposedly restricts liability, accounting firms are not satisfied as the Federal Trade Practices Legislation (equivalent to U.S. Restrictive Trade Practices legislation) is perceived still—as shown by several large negligence claims against auditors (and out-of-court settlements) during the mid-1990s—to provide users of accounts with the opportunity to seek damages of an *unlimited* amount.

Most of that brouhaha appears to be clutching at phantoms. It is questionable whether financial statements prepared in compliance with the professions' accounting standards ever had a useful life to limit. In the final analysis, that is the root cause of many grounds for the litigation. Incorporation by a professional runs counter to the exercise of individual judgement, the very hallmark of professional behavior—that which distinguishes the professional from the artisan. Nonetheless, it looms as the most likely outcome. Incorporation, in part, damages accountants' claims to professional status. Proposals for proportionate liability ensuring directors with sufficient insurance cover would share the damages with accountants are reasonable, provided the objective is to increase the recovery of financial losses by the aggrieved. But they are less than honorable and defensible if undertaken as an alternative to rectifying a primary cause for the actions in the first place. It is difficult to imagine how accountants, directors, or valuers can gain public respect by solely liability limiting.

It is even more difficult to understand how such actions can remedy unethical behavior. Public opinion is more likely to view them as adding to it. Directors and valuers cannot expect to collect sizeable fees and not fulfil their fiduciary obligations in return. Accountants and auditors cannot expect to collect large fees and not deliver quality products, with impunity. It has been suggested, perhaps unkindly, by a leading accounting academic that those who are finding it too hot in the kitchen ought to get out.[12]

TECHNICAL SUBSERVIENCE: PROFESSIONALISM LOST?

Attacks on the professionalism of auditors and accountants following corporate collapses are now commonplace worldwide. Whereas Australians are said not to be litigious by nature, they have found it in their water in recent times to launch

Table 1. Selected Negligence Claims, Notifications Lodged with Insurers, and Reported Settlements

Plaintiffs (Clients and Clients' Liquidators)	*Defendants*	*Damages Claims/ (Result) (in $ millions)*
Duke Group	Ernst & Young, KPMG Peat Marwick & Ors, settled out of court, reportedly for $35 million	$175 ($35)
Farrow Finance Company	Civil action against ANZ Executors Trustee Co. and the auditors, Day Neilsen Jenkins	$50
Rothwells	KMG Hungerford	$40
National Safety Council	Horwath and Horwath	$263
Estate Mortgage unit-holders	Priestley and Morris and Ors	$650 (31)
Estate Mortgage Financial Services	Tyshing Price and Co.	$25
Deposit and Investment Group	KPMG Peat Marwick	$73
Battery Group	Deloitte Ross Tohmatsu, settled out of court reportedly for $12 million	$132 ($12)
AWA	The initial judgment against Deloitte Ross Tohmatsu of $23.9 million was appealed and settled out of court, reportedly for $12 million	$50 ($12)
Titan Hills	Coopers and Lybrand & Ors, settled out of court, reportedly for $17 million	$17
State Bank of Victoria	Day Neilsen Jenkins, Ian Johns & Ors	$900
Spedley Securities	Priestley and Morris & Ors, settled out of court, reportedly for $22 million	$320 ($22)
Tricontinental	KPMG Peat Marwick, settled out of court, reportedly paying the Victorian Government $136 million	$1,094 ($136)
Independent Resources	Deloitte Ross Tohmatsu	$44.5

(continued)

Table 1. (Continued)

Plaintiffs (Clients and Clients' Liquidators)	*Defendants*	*Damages Claims/ (Result) (in $ millions)*
Adelaide Steamship	Deloitte Ross Tohmatsu and former directors; appeal of auditors against validity of ASC action was successful in April 1996 but the ASC successfully overturned the decision on appeal	$340
Bond Corporation Holdings	Arthur Andersen	$276.1
Colombia Tea and Coffee	Nelson Parkhill	Nominal damages
Keydata	Coopers & Lybrand & Westgarth Baldick	$17 ($17)
Linter Group	Price Waterhouse, concerns deals worth $320 million	$300
State Bank of South Australia	KPMG Peat Marwick	$3,100
Beneficial Finance	Price Waterhouse	$1,100 ($120)
Westmex	Thomson Douglas	$60

Note: Figures in this table are as of October 1996.

Source: "Clients-and liquidators" (1991); see also Ries (1992), Gill and Pheasant (1992), Falvey (1992), "ASC seeks $20m. damages" (1993), Pheasant (1993a, 1993b), Hogan (1994, esp. Table 1)

numerous negligence suits against members of the accounting profession. Avowed litigants (presumably by nature) in the United States no doubt have shown the way, been good teachers. But the locals have been willing students. Claims in the United States have generally dwarfed those in Australia and the United Kingdom in the past. In the United States, for example, in 1991 the seventh largest accounting firm, Laventhol & Howarth, was placed in bankruptcy due to the settlement of litigation claims. The number of substantial claims in Australia against auditors are catalogued in Table 1. Indeed, it is no wonder that Australia recently ranked number two in the world after the United States in the litigation-against-auditors stakes (Lawson 1993).

A common theme implied in the reports of those claims is that auditors have either acted unprofessionally, been negligent in carrying out their audits, and/or that their ethics have declined. In certain cases, this may have been so. However, explanations of what auditors generally were expected to do that they did not, how they were expected to have behaved differently, are curious omissions in most of that reportage. Actually, there are no good explanations within the framework of accounting and auditing rules with which accountants have to comply and in which they work. Exposure to litigation is inherent in the former and risk to their professional status in the latter. That is a tragic outcome for a professional group. They are on a hiding to nothing from the start—a "mission impossible".

Auditors are in a no-win situation. The inherent creativity of conventional accounting data assures that even where fraud is absent, auditors must provide unqualified reports when published income statements and balance sheets have been prepared in conformity with the prescribed accounting standards and to qualify when they do not, even though to do the opposite in many cases might be the more prudent in ensuring serviceable data were produced. Curiously, no action alleging that the accounts were misleading because they were the product of compliance with accounting standards has arisen in the litigation surrounding corporate collapse, though such an action may well eventuate within that setting when the impact of compliance on the published financial data of some failed companies becomes more apparent.

If that were to happen, argument as to whether compliance with professional rules is a strong defence against negligence claims will be riveting stuff—déjà vu of the events surrounding the 1931 U.K. *Royal Mail* case, but with the benefit of over 65 years of case studies to draw upon. This could damage accountants' professional status considerably. It might also evoke a hasty about face by the legislators regarding compulsory compliance with the prescribed standards. Facing those prospects, auditors may well be as diligent as possible within the framework in which they are forced to work but nonetheless incur uncontrollable exposure to litigation; damned for certain if they do not comply and likely to be damned some day if they do.

Some of the blame for that situation must be borne by auditors themselves. Again, consistent with international experience—for example, the 1930s *Royal Mail* case in the United Kingdom and the 1960s *United States v. Carl J. Simon et al. (Continental Vending)* case—many Australian auditors have embraced specification of the professionally accepted practices within which they are to work as a kind of safe harbor against litigation (Moonitz 1974). In this regard, some auditors have been willing travellers with the regulators, who find sets of rules convenient benchmarks against which to test corporate reporting performance. Neither can have it both ways. If auditors and accountants are to have any defence against claims that their compliance with the "cookbook" accounting standards was itself negligent, they need to distance themselves from the standards as quickly as possible. We are not alone in holding this view, as shown by David Tweedie's comments in "True and Fair versus the Rule Book" (1988). Such a concern applies equally to the regulatory watchdogs. It is not beyond the realm of possibility that regulatory enforcement of compliance with the accounting and auditing standards currently in force could, some time in the future, be viewed as negligence on part of regulators. If those watchdogs do not protect the community at large as they are expected to, then it is not beyond reason that they might be replaced.

So, too, may the quasi-regulators, the accounting standard-setters be replaced, or even perhaps challenged in court. For when it is realized how inadequate the standards are for producing serviceable accounting data, the work of those who devised them may well attract more attention from the financial victims of corporate failures than that of the directors, managers, accountants, or auditors. In this respect, it is sobering to note how, in U.S. product liability cases, manufacturers are being sued for poor quality products. For example, it is the manufacturers of breast implants who are being sued rather than the surgeons!

In Australia, both the Crown and the professional accountancy bodies, legal draftsmen and standard-setters, may be sitting on a timebomb ready to explode!

Like most maturing professions, accountancy wants to get there fast. In this respect, the professional accountancy bodies in Australia, as elsewhere before them, have spent considerable time and fortune over the past two decades trying to create a public image of their not-to-be-denied professional status. It probably has changed the image, though likely not for long. Unfortunately, the professional bodies appear to believe their own propaganda, and the product that so needs an overhaul remains virtually unchanged. Professional Centres of Excellence are emerging under Australian Society of Certified Practising Accountants' patronage—in financial accounting, management accounting, public sector accounting, and treasury, not in recognition of excellence but to seek it. It is credentialism at its extreme. They do not appear to have spent nearly as much on either the education of entrants to the profession, by way of untied grants and the like, or on funding pure research.

One strategy of the Australian profession's research body, the Australian Accounting Research Foundation, has been to commission monographs, either to give existing practices the appearance of having the underpinning force of a body of theory or to pave the way for "official" solutions to accounting problems. Both have further entrenched the accounting and reporting status quo, which has been shown in Australia (and overseas) over many decades in official enquiries into corporate failures and reportage in the financial press to fall far short of the true and fair ethos. This deficiency prevails notwithstanding a long recognition of its existence.

Sociologist Bernard Barber identified the features of an emerging or maturing profession—middle-ranking in respect of generalized knowledge and community orientation, heterogeneous membership, struggling to enforce its own rules of conduct and ethics (Barber 1963). Accountancy would seem to fit those characteristics well. Conformity to that pattern sends an important message to the commercial world regarding the efficacy of accounting products to be used for the assessment and evaluation of the financial health, wealth, and progress, of companies—the products are technically very crude.

Few groups act with as much faith in the power of their own rhetoric. Attempts to talk away the supposed *gap* between what accountants and auditors do and what they are expected by the public at large to be doing is apposite. We are told that what accountants do and how they do it is not questionable, that everybody other than members of the profession and regulators has unreasonable, misguided, expectations—there is an *expectation gap* (see International Federation of Accountants 1990 and Clarke, Dean and Oliver 1997)—that is, a gap—between what consumers reasonably expect from accounting and auditing and what they actually get. While the expectations gap might remain were the current batch of accounting standards and the true and fair view override to coexist, removing the true and fair override—that quality benchmark—can only exacerbate the potential for that expectation gap to widen.

One would think a better way of fixing the image would be to improve the product, to improve what consumers get, or at least to argue it is not a hazard—as the tobacco industry lobby (albeit, with less and less success) is doing worldwide. What is inexplicable is the promotion of the idea that the way to repair the damaged image of accounting and auditing is to have consumers understand that accounting data are not serviceable, that published financial statements are *limited* in their function and do not disclose the wealth and progress of companies, and whereas they are to be declared true and fair, they are no such thing. That is, to explain that there is not so much an expectation gap as what amounts to a *performance gap*. That is tantamount to the tobacco industry lobby agreeing that smoking is dangerous and that smokers merely have false expectations—set them right and the danger will be gone. Possibly, there is a message from the anti-smoking movement—perhaps the way forward for accounting reform is to have income statements and balance sheets labeled *financial hazards*.

ACCOUNTING AT THE PROFESSIONAL CROSSROADS

Corporate accounting is "in crisis" (Pheasant 1993, 6). It *is* in a chaotic state, as we (and others, including partners of Big Six firms) have demonstrated elsewhere.[13]

Further testimony to this state is the settlements of claims against audit firms. In Australia, settlements include one of over $135 million (Tricontinental). There are litigation claims pending against auditors, including one of $3.1 billion (State Bank of South Australia), a $276.1 million damages claim by the liquidators against the auditors of Bond Corporation alleging breach of duties and failure to warn the company of its impending demise, and even the recent *smaller* $60 million claim by Bankers Trust and several Westmex shareholders against Westmex's 1987-88 auditor and partners, seeking damages for negligence and misleading and deceptive conduct. Some of these actions were brought under Australia's Trade Practices legislation pertaining to negligence. However, that legislation potentially has a wider ambit. It is reasonable to suggest that many of the data which appear in balance sheets and income statements prepared in compliance with the accounting standards do not meet the criteria contained in §52(1) of the Australian Trade Practices Act, which says, "A corporation shall not, in trade or commerce, engage in conduct that is misleading or deceptive or is likely to mislead or deceive." Publishing financial statements containing misleading data of the kind we have described would appear to be apposite. Intent to mislead is not necessary (*Hornsby Building Information Centre Pty Ltd v Sydney Building Information Centre Pty Ltd* (1978) 140 CLR 126 at 223 per Stephen J.); and that meshes with many of the outcomes of diligent compliance with the accounting standards without any intention to deceive. The focus of the Act is the class of consumers likely to be affected by the conduct (*Parkdale Custom Built Furniture Pty Ltd v. Puxu Pty Ltd* (1982) 149 CLR 191 at 199). It is not unreasonable to place the consumers of accounting data in that setting. It has been held (*Taco Co of Australia v. Taco Bell Pty Ltd* (1982) 42 ALR 177) that those who might be considered misled extend to "the public, including the astute and the gullible, and the intelligent and the not so intelligent, the well educated and the poorly educated." This clearly includes reasonable recourse to companies' published financial statements by those without any technical understanding of the machinations of accounting in general or the accounting standards in particular. It would appear that recourse to Australia's Trade Practices Act by the consumers of companies' published financial data is a time bomb waiting to be detonated.

From published financial statements containing an amalgam of cost values, market values, and fictions, it remains impossible to assess the wealth and progress of a company, virtually impossible to calculate reliable indicators of solvency, rate of return, asset backing, gearing, and the like. Published financial statements contain data which are mere artifacts of the processing and valuation rules primarily aimed at achieving a matching of expenses with revenues. They are imposed upon accountants through the compulsory imposition of accounting standards, some of which lead to balance-sheet data being pure fiction. The latter are not merely unrepresentative of what they describe—they have nothing to describe and they have no referent in the real world. In the Australian setting, this is particularly true of the data emerging from the application of tax effect accounting, expenditure carried-forward practices, depreciation and amortization procedures, and the application of conventional consolidation accounting procedures. For example, future income tax benefits ("deferred tax debits") and provisions for deferred income tax ("deferred tax credits") are neither legally recoverable from or by the Australian Taxation Office, respectively, being neither assets nor liability; capitalized expenses are not necessarily recoverable; depreciation calculations and amortization charges under the Australian standards do not have any identifiable relationship to declines in the worth of the related *asset*; and consolidation practices in Australia give rise to arbitrarily adjusted asset and liability data by virtue of the compulsory application of the "elimination" rule to intragroup transactions (Dean and Clarke 1993).

Notwithstanding the best of intentions and the highest integrity, compliance with many accounting standards will almost certainly lead to creative (untruthful) accounting; deliberate deviation from historical-cost-based, fiction-laden standards is necessary to produce serviceable (truthful) financial information. All of which begs further questions: Whither regulation, whither quality, whither professionalism?

Evidence has not been produced by the professional bodies or the corporate regulators to support the idea that the serviceability of reported accounting data for informing decision makers can be guaranteed through compelling compliance with the current prescribed practices. And even the avowed goal of comparability is suspect given the permissible optional treatments in the current standards. It is reasonable to presume that the regulation is intended to protect users of the data in company accounts from, rather than expose them to, financial peril. It is inexplicable why the regulators' push for more of the same, in the face of irrefutable evidence from the events relating to recent Australian corporate failures (see cases described in Clarke, Dean and Oliver 1997 and, over 20 years earlier, in Chambers 1973) that the accounting data emerging from the existing regulated process fail to inform and, hence, protect. Similar evidence appears in Berloff (1972, 1976, 1981).

In a reasonably well-ordered society, one would expect, indeed demand, regulation to be directed to achieving quality, reliability, fitness for use—serviceability of the product rather than mere standardization of the "rule book." That standardization is a virtue per se is a contestable proposition at the best of times. Yet, the accounting profession appears to have led the field in the pursuit of standardization as a means to achieve comparability—but, incongruously, divorced from the pursuit of serviceability. The latest seemingly successful moves by the international accounting standard-setting body to have the IASC standards adopted worldwide indicates that the malaise is universal.

Internationally, prescribed data that are aimed at achieving comparability first and serviceability second seem to be doomed to repeat the errors that have befallen national standard-setters for several decades. Consider the recent moves to have a balance sheet approach adopted in respect of accounting for income taxes. There is no apparent desire on the part of the international standard-setters to rethink whether deferred tax debits and credits (future income tax benefits and provisions for deferred income tax), which possess no real world referent in respect of an individual entity, are serviceable for assessing solvency, calculating meaningful rates of return and asset backing, or, for example, the relationship of debt and equity. A similar line of argument applies in respect of the implementation of internationally accepted "control" definitions for consolidation, and to standards aimed at booking, then writing off, goodwill. The aim is always to seek comparability of method. Comparability of method (of the comparable standard accounting procedures) does not ensure comparability of output (the resulting financial data). Compliance with the comparable "lower-of-cost-or-market" inventory valuation rule, depreciation and amortization rules, historical-cost asset valuation rules, or tax effect (deferred tax) accounting rules, can in each instance produce myriad conflicting *outcomes* by entities accounting for essentially similar transactions. Consideration of how the data which result from applying such standards will improve accounting as a form of instrumentation does not emerge as a priority.

Perhaps accountants would do much better to adopt the current commercial vogue, to have mission statements and the like directed toward producing serviceable data. As it is, they have "mission impossible" forced upon them by an obligation to follow prescribed rules (now more often than not internationally prescribed by the IASC) notwithstanding that common sense might dictate their rejection.

Clearly, the above suggests that compliance with prescribed processes and idiosyncratic valuation rules (under the accounting standards) is assumed by many in the accounting profession and other regulators to be an effective regulatory mechanism. Missing, however, is the demonstrated link between the prescribed practices and the serviceability of the end product for acknowledged commercial uses. So, whereas there is regulation to ensure compliance with the rules, the quality of the end product is not assured. Not one of Australia's accounting standards nor its Statement of Accounting Concepts (Dobbie 1993)[14] specifies a commercial *serviceability* or *quality* characteristic that the emerging data are to possess, singly or in combination. There is no demonstrated link within any national or international "framework" document showing how the data produced by complying with professional standards meshes with the data required for informed commercial decisions. This point was made strongly by Chambers (1996).

Also, the current "crisis" provides justification for questioning whether compulsory compliance with prescribed processing standards is compatible with the notion of a profession. Professional activity is differentiated from that of the artisan. Since the emergence of the gilds, artisans have plied their craft according to hands-on experience, using regular and proven technology known to all in the craft without necessarily understanding why it is used. Methods have been handed down from artisan to artisan. Their knowledge and skill, though considerable, is a common matter, rarely idiosyncratic. By contrast, the distinguishing feature of a professional is the exercise of accumulated skill and wisdom, the out-of-the-ordinary, extraordinary expertise applied equally to both the ordinary and out-of-the-ordinary, extraordinary, circumstances. Professionals and their professions are distinguished from others by the exercise of the *differentia specifica* of their practices which set them apart from the rest of the community. That entails recognition of a social obligation to apply one's skill and wisdom for the general benefit—requiring independent judgement as to how best to proceed.

Specifying compulsory rules (standards) for processing accounting data, without also specifying necessary end qualities or characteristics to be achieved, poses a serious threat to accountants' claims to professional status. So does the pursuit of limited liability for the consequences for their actions. That leads to other propositions: compulsory compliance with accounting standards which concentrate on processes not outcomes is not necessarily conducive to producing serviceable financial data; in any event, compulsory compliance with the prescribed processing standards is incompatible with professional activity.

We referred above to the accumulated evidence over many decades that conventional accounting practices complying with the prescribed standards have masked impending failure, exacerbated losses to creditors and shareholders, and provided regulators with a recurring dilemma.

Regulators of corporate activity have not heeded the lessons of history—the wailing, gnashing of teeth, and rhetoric of indignation at the sequential episodes of corporate failure have been recurrent but ineffective responses. Possibly, the current litigation against corporate officers, accountants, and auditors is only the first phase of inevitable outcomes for those whose actions further entrench the status quo in respect of corporate financial reporting.

It is not difficult to imagine that somewhere, somehow, some day, an alert judge will question the serviceability of conventional accounting data. In Australia, a 1996 New South Wales' Supreme Court judgement by McLelland CJ suggests it is nigh—he described the untangling of one standard prescription on goodwill as "almost a metaphysical problem" (Bice 1996). Against financial commonsense, the financial nonsense promoted in some accounting standards will be nigh impossible to defend.

Accounting information as a serviceable product and accountancy as a professional endeavor are undeniably at the crossroads! Without change, users will continue to lament that "corporate accounting does not do violence to the truth occasionally, and trivially, but comprehensively, systematically, and universally, annually and perennially" (Chambers 1991, 17).

NOTES

1. Two articles by Chambers and Wolnizer (1990, 1991) provide detailed references to many recent articles contained in an anthology by Parker, Wolnizer, and Nobes (1996). The anthology includes articles by Alexander and Ordelheide discussing true and fair in the European context.

2. Graphically illustrating this was the 1950s mercury poisoning at Minamata by the Japanese chemical company, Chisso. For decades, victims seeking compensation were fighting an amorphous corporate giant. It was *as if* humans had played no role in the poisoning of the sea around Minamata (see Smith and Smith 1975). In Australia, this issue was considered by senior federal and state law officers, resulting in a proposed new legal code that avoids the need to prove criminal intent, in order to "jail dirty incorporates" (Spiers 1992). Legal commentators Fisse and Braithwaite (1993, esp. chaps. 2 and 3) summarize the individualism versus corporate criminality perspectives discussed in legal and cognate disciplines.

3. The issue is discussed in an accounting context by Clarke (1980).

4. A similar view was recently expressed by Tomasic and Bottomley (1993). Consider also the headline covering the recent arrest of a leading 1970s U.S. corporate cowboy, "Robert Vesco...A Man Who Makes Christopher Skase Look Like Mother Theresa" (cited in Casey 1995)

5. Consider "Poseidon Chief Faces Charges" (1993), just after that business chief had been voted 1993 *Australian Business Monthly* Businessman of the Year; and in the same issue, "$66 Million Theft: Elliot Charged" and, referring to former W.A. Premier, "Burke on $124,585 Charge," as well as the headlines referred to earlier regarding the Budget Corporation case.

6. Notable exceptions included Australian financial consultants such as Mark Burrows and Ashley Donnelly, and regulators like Henry Bosch and certain financial journalists.

7. This event is described in Dunn (1997).

8. It has been reported that in 1993 and 1994, premiums rose by 15% each year, following a 20% rise in 1992 (Clafton 1996).

9. This view is implicit in an interview by S. Harrison of ASC Chairman, Alan Cameron (Harrison 1993).

10. The cap in the NSW Act may be set at an amount or at a multiple of fees. Professional bodies must seek permission for the cap by applying to Professional Standards Council. In the United Kingdom, the Department of Trade and Iindustry has proposed a limit on auditors' libility through changes to the companies laws. It has suggested that regulations will be made under §310(4) of the Companies Act 1985 ("DTI Acts on Auditors' Liability" 1993).

11. These and other proposals are listed in Working Party of the Ministerial Council for Corporations (1993, esp. 10-35).

12. This comment was reportedly made by M.C. Wells during the proceedings of the "Crime and the Professions: The Accountancy Profession" Institute of Criminology Seminar, September 18.

13. This crisis has been long recognized (see Chambers 1973; Briloff (1972, 1976, 1981). This label was used in the December 1993 AICPA/ASCPA monograph, *A Research Study on Financial Reporting and Auditing: Bridging the Expectations Gap*, and in a 1994 Ernst and Young Foundation monograph, *Measurement Research in Financial Accounting*, reporting the proceedings of a 1993 workshop that discussed the "crisis in accounting research" claimed in an unpublished pamphlet by six leading U.S. academic researchers (for further details, see Mattessich 1995; Big Six 1992).

14. SAC 4, which was put on hold in 1994 after vehement opposition from practitioners and their clients, was intended to prescribe the concepts to underpin accounting practices. It was rereleased in 1995 but this time its application was voluntary.

REFERENCES

ASPCA/ICAA. 1993. *A Research Study on Financial Reporting and Auditing: Bridging the Expectations Gap.* December. Sydney, Australia: ASPCA/ICAA

"ASC Seeks $20m. Damages in Farrow Case." 1992. *Australian Financial Review* (March 24): 3.

Barber, B. 1963. Some problems in the sociology of the professions. *Daedalus* (Fall): 669-688.

Barry, P. 1990. *The Rise and Fall of Alan Bond.* Sydney, Australia: Bantam.

Bice, K. 1996. Judgement reserved on the Acacia Part A. *The Australian Financial Review* (March 27): 92-93.

Big Six (Coopers & Lybrand, Deloitte & Touche, E&Y, KPMS-Peat Marwik, PW). 1992. *Statement of Position: The Liability Crisis in the United States: Impact on the Accounting Profession.* August 6.

Block, M. 1954. *The Historian's Craft*, trans. P. Putman. Manchester, UK: Manchester University Press.

Bloomberg. 1996. From high-roller to has-been. *Australian Financial Review.*

Bosch, H. *The Workings of a Watchdog.* Melbourne, Australia: William Heineman Australia.

Bower, T. 1991. *Maxwell: The Outsider.* London: Mandarin Paperbacks.

Boyd, A. 1990. Call for higher business ethics. *The Australian Financial Review* (May 24): 4.

Briloff, A.J. 1970. *More Debits than Credits: The Burnt Investors Guide to Financial Statements.* New York: Harper & Row.

Briloff, A.J. 1976. *Truth about Accounting.* New York: Harper & Row.

Briloff, A.J. 1981. *Unaccountable Accounting.*

"Burke on $124,585 Charge." *The Sydney Morning Herald.*

Carr, E.H. 1964. *What Is History*? UK: Penguin.

Casey, M. 1995. Wall street swindler's pals finally desert him. *Sunday Telegraph* (June 18): 131.

Chambers, R.J. 1973. *Securities and Obscurities.* Melbourne, Australia: Gower Press.

Chambers, R.J. 1991. Accounting and corporate morality: The ethical cringe. The Australian Journal of Corporate Law 1(1): 9-21.

Chambers, R. 1996. *Ends, Ways, Means and Conceptual Frameworks. Abacus* (September).

Chambers, R.J. 1991. Accounting and corporate morality: The ethical cringe. *Australian Journal of Corporate Law* 1(1): 9-21.

Chambers, R., and P. Wolnizer. 1990. A true and fair view of financial position. *Company and Securities Law Journal* (December): 353-368.

Chambers, R., and P. Wolnizer. 1991. A true and fair view of financial proposals and results: The historical background. *Accounting, Business and Financial History* (March): 197-213.

Clafton, S. 1996. Professional bodies review call for liability limits. *Business Review Weekly*: (April 1): 68-69.

Clarke, F.L. 1980. Inflation accounting and the accidents of history. *Abacus* 16(2): 78-99.

Clarke, F.L., and R. Craig. 1993. Phases in Australian accounting standards. *Australian Journal of Corporate Law* 3(1): 50-66.

Clarke, F.L., G.W. Dean, and K.G. Oliver. 1997. *Corporate Collapse: Regulatory, Accounting and Ethical Failure.* Cambridge, UK: Cambridge University Press.

Clarke, F.L., G.W. Dean, M.C. Wells and J.F. Lowry. 1997. Financial and management accounting in Australia. In *Accounting in the Asia Pacific Region*, eds. N. Baydhoun, R. Willett, and A. Nishimura. Singapore: John Wiley.

"Clients—and Liquidators of Clients—Sue Firms for Damages Totalling $2 Billion Plus." 1991. *Chartac* (September).

Collins, J. 1990. Declining ethics . . . bad company. *The Australian* (July 10): 13.

Daughen, J.R., and P. Binzen. 1971. *The Wreck of the Penn Central.* New York: Mentor.

Dean, G.W., and F.L. Clarke. 1993. Law and accounting: The separate legal entity principle and consolidation accounting. *Australian Business Law Review* (August): 249-270.

Dirks, R.L., and L. Goss. 1974. *The Great Wall Street Scandal.* New York: McGraw Hill.

Dobbie, M. 1993. ASB wants SACs to be mandatory. *Financial Forum* (August): 1.

"DTI Acts on Auditors' Liability." 1993 *Accountancy* (April): 13.

Dunn, J. 1997. ASC forces engine company out of orbit in conflict over write downs. *Business Review Weekly* (April 7): 76-77.

Edwards, K. 1993. Where does the buck stop? *Time* (April 19): 24-29.

Epstein, B.J., and A. Ali Mirza. 1997. *IAS 97*: Interpretation and Application of International Accounting Standards. Wiley.

Ernst and Young Foundation. 1994. *Measurement Research in Financial Accounting.*
Este, J. 1995. Interchase claim worsens valuers' indemnity problem. *The Australian* (July 2): 3.
"Ethics Rise in the West." 1990. *The Bulletin* (June 5): 22.
Falvey, J. 1992. Spedley claim may be $750 million. *Daily Telegraph Mirror* (June 10): 36.
Fischel, D. 1995. *Payback: The Conspiracy to Destroy Michael Milken.* New York: Harper Business.
Fisse, B., and J. Braithwaite. 1993. *Corporations, Crime and Accountability.* Cambridge, UK: Cambridge University Press.
Forester, T. 1991. Society needs dose of ethics to purge its "moral chaos." *The Australian* (May 14): 46.
Fox, C. 1990. Ethics becoming the buzzword of the 90s. *The Australian Financial Review* (June 12): 44.
Gaa, J.A. 1993. *The Ethical Foundations of Public Accounting* Vancouver, BC, Canada: Canadian Certified General Accountants Research Foundation.
Gill, M., and B. Pheasant. 1992. Record claim against KPMG. *Australian Financial Review* (June 2).
Gray, R. 1971. *Rolls on the Rocks.* Salisbury, UK: Compton.
Harrison, S. 1993. Civil or criminal remedies and the ASC. *Charter* April: 10-12.
Hogan, W. 1994. Accounting introspection. *Australian Accounting Review* (November): 54-64.
Hurst, J. 1990. Corporate ethics come under the microscope. *The Australian Financial Review* (January 29): 3.
International Federation of Accountants. 1990. *Understanding Financial Statement Audits.* Melbourne, Australia: AARF.
Janetzki, D. 1989. *The Gollin Years.* Brisbane, Australia: Don Janetzki.
Jubb, P., and S. Haswell. 1993. *Company Accounting.* Melbourne, Australia: Nelson.
Kaye, T. 1992. Phillips bows out with call for code of ethics. *The Australian Financial Review* (April 3): 61.
Keats, C.B. 1964. *Magnificent Masquerade.* New York: Funk and Wagnalls.
Lawson, M. 1992. Another counselling centre for ethically troubled accountants. *The Australian Financial Review* (March 27): 3.
Lawson, M. 1993. Accountants "top for claims." *The Australian Financial Review* (August 2): 3.
Lewis, S. 1990. Accounting education in "chronic neglect." *The Australian Financial Review* (July 5): 10.
Lyons, M. 1992. Profession begins to get serious about its ethics. *Business Review Weekly* (February 21): 73, 75.
Mackay, H. 1993. Ethics is a tricky business. *Financial Review* (March 23): 15.
Maher, M. 1990. *Bond.* Melbourne, Australia: William Heinemann.
Mattessich, R. 1995. *Critique of Accounting.* Westport CT: Quorum Books.
McEnroe, J., and P. Martens. 1996. International differences in audit report phraseology: Present fairly versus true and fair view. Paper presented at the Critical Perspectives in Accounting Conference, New York, April.
Miller, M. 1994. Australia. In *Financial Reporting in the West Pacific Rim,* eds. T.E. Cooke and R.H. Parker pp. 333-382 London: Routledge.
Moonitz, M. 1974. *SAR No. 8: Obtaining Agreement on Standards in the Accounting Profession.* Sarasota FL: American Accounting Association.
Napier, C. 1996. The antecedents of unlimited liability in the United Kingdom: A study of corporate governance. Paper presented at the 19th EAA Congress, Bergen, May.
Niemarck, M. 1995. The selling of ethics. *Accounting, Auditing and Accountability* (Special issue on ethics, politics and academic accounting) 8(3): 81-96.
Oakeshott, M.J. 1933. *Experience and Its Modes.* Cambridge, UK: Cambridge University Press.
Parker, R.H., P. Wolnizer, and C. Nobes. 1996. *Readings in True and Fair.* New York: Garland.
Pheasant, B. 1993a. Auditors in danger from $2.5bn claims. *Australian Financial Review* (June 30): 1, 6.
Pheasant, B. 1993b. Auditors want to stop the damage. *Australian Financial Review* (August 30): 14.

"Poseidon Chief Faces Charges." 1993. *The Sydney Morning Herald* (December 24): 11.

Public Oversight Board. 1993. "Issues Confronting the Accounting Profession," Report by Public Oversight Board. Stamford CT: AICPA.

QBE Insurance Group. 1992. *Annual Report.*

Raw, C. 1976. *Slater Walker.* London: Andre Deutsch.

Ries, I. 1992. Auditors find themselves in the hottest seat of all. *Australian Financial Review* (January 10): 44.

Roslender, R. 1992. *Sociological Perspectives on Modern Accountancy.* London: Routledge.

Ross, B. 1988. *The Ariadne Story.* Victoria, Australia: Greenhouse.

"$66 Million Theft: Elliot Charged." 1993. *The Sydney Morning Herald* (December 24).

Smith, W.E., and A.M. Smith. 1975. *Minamata.* New York: Holt, Rinehart & Winston.

Spiers, B. 1992. New law to jail dirty corporates. *The Australian Financial Review* (September 16): 3).

Stephens, T. 1990. Big business elders crusade for higher ethics. *Sydney Morning Herald* (May 26): 6.

Tomasic, R., and S. Bottomley. 1993. *Directing the Top 500: Corporate Governance and Accountability in Australian Companies.* Sydney, Australia: Allen and Unwin.

Tweedie, D.J. 1988. True and fair v. the rule book: Which is the answer to the creative accounting? *Pacific Accounting Review* (December): 1-21.

Walker, R.G. 1993. A feeling of deja vu: Controversies in accounting and auditing regulation in Australia. *Critical Perspectives in Accounting* 4: 97-109.

Working Party of the Ministerial Council for Corporations. 1993. *Professional Liability in Relation to Corporations Law Matters*, June. Canberra: Government Printer.

RESEARCH REPORT

VARIATION IN AND CONSEQUENCES OF AUDITOR SELECTION AND AUDIT REPORTS IN SCANDINAVIA:

A REGULATORY FRAMEWORK WITH MULTIPLE AUDITORS

Wanda A. Wallace

ABSTRACT

An examination of annual reports of three Scandinavian countries—Denmark, Sweden, and Norway—provides insights that larger entities seem to often use Big Six CPA firms, whereas smaller entities use two to three auditors. The issuance of other than a boilerplate report is associated with higher interest cost. Specifically, clean audit reports are associated with lower costs of borrowing, quantified as a 2.38% differential. Interestingly, clean audit reports are more likely to be issued in two-auditor settings. Some greater return is suggested for the presence of two auditors, but may be size related or a proxy effect of the differential auditors' reporting observed, and no similar effect is discernible for three auditors. Tentative insights are provided that

Research in Accounting Regulation, Supplement 1, pages 247-274.

ISBN: 0-7623-0338-7

use of two to three auditors, often observed in Scandinavia, may be a means of "substitution" for the use of Big Six auditors by larger entities. Implications for regulators are discussed.

INTRODUCTION

The auditing function, as well as attendant regulation, facilitates markets in the presence of incentive problems (Akerlof 1970; Spence 1973; Ross 1977, 1979; Wallace 1980; Antle 1982, 1984; Baiman et al. 1987). An interesting phenomenon is the presence of multiple auditors in Scandinavia; rather than a single auditing relationship, some entities contract with two and even three audit firms. This research answers the following questions: (1) what is the incidence of multiple versus single auditor selection in Denmark, Sweden, and Norway; (2) what are the characteristics of the firms selecting multiple auditors; (3) how does variation in such selections interact, if at all, with the choice of an association with a Big Six firm; and (4) what are the observed consequences of the choices made in terms of (a) the type of auditor's report issued and (b) the cost of capital incurred by the entity.

As Healy and Lys argue (1986, 254), "investors' information costs of assessing audit quality are lower for a Big Eight[1] firm than for a non-Big Eight firm, since the Big Eight firm has a higher potential reputation loss from failing to supply this level of quality....Big Eight reputations are likely to be particularly valuable to clients that anticipate raising debt or equity in national or international financial markets, since the Big Eight reputation lowers the information costs of potential investors." These researchers report findings "consistent with the hypothesis that clients that issue new debt securities remain with the Big Eight firm to take advantage of its reputation and thereby lower investors' information costs in assessing audit quality" (p. 263). Investments in reputation represent a bond by auditing firms to assure clients that they will receive the contracted-for audit quality (Klein and Leffler 1981). Conditions that can affect such quality through a reduction in independence are described in Magee and Tseng (1990) and interrelate with the nature of accounting standards. Such evidence creates an expectation that Big Six selection may differ from other auditors in some systematic manner due to this perceived trademark effect. Evidence of such a valued effect domestically is quantified by Craswell, Francis, and Taylor (1995): a Big Six brand-name premium over non-Big Six auditors averages around 30%.

Beyond accounting and auditing choices, financing choices can affect firms' cost of capital (Myers and Majluf 1984) by offering a form of signaling as to choices between public and private forms of financing, varying degrees of concentration of ownership, block holdings in corporate governance, and other means of mitigating information gaps between managers and owners (Healy and Palepu 1993). Healy and Palepu (1993, 8) call for research on "How does voluntary disclosure affect a firm's cost of capital?" Since part of voluntary signaling is the selection of the auditor and, in many cases, actions that influence the type of auditor's report received, this inquiry is responsive to their question. The international regulatory context in which audit reports are observed from one, two, and even three auditors, permits assessment of signaling involving multiple auditor choices and the consequences of such choices in terms of both report type and the entity's cost of capital.

EVIDENCE FROM EXISTING LITERATURE

Elliott and Jacobson (1994), in their paper titled "Costs and Benefits of Disclosing Information," describe why an entity benefits by disclosure through its effect of lowering that entity's cost of capital. Specifically, the information risk premium is reduced as a component of such a cost when the informativeness of disclosure improves. They cite both the work of Dhaliwal (1978) and Conover and Wallace (1995) as findings consistent with the lower cost of capital thesis. The analysis proceeds to recognize that with more informative disclosure, the information risk premium and litigation cost are expected to decrease, while information cost and net competitive cost would increase. The quality of information can be expected to be improved through the audit process, based on conceptual (Wallace 1980) and empirical (Kinney and Martin 1994)[2] analyses. Information signals that can be expected to relate to cost of capital include: which auditor does an entity select and what type of audit report is issued?

Despite very disparate accounting practices, histories of standard setting, and cultural influence on reporting characteristics (Choi and Levich 1991; Purvis et al, 1991), the global markets (Biddle and Saudagaran 1991) have included a choice of auditors from various world firms that have a demonstrable "trademark and reputation effect" on markets (see DeAngelo 1981; Palmrose 1986; Francis and Simon 1987; Francis and Wilson 1988; Eichenseher, Hagigi, and Shields 1989).[3] Such an effect has been documented in past research in the market for initial public offerings (Simunic and Stein 1987; Balvers et al. 1988; Beatty 1989; Menon and Williams 1991; Jang and Lin 1993, focusing on trading volume),[4] in the presence of auditor litigation (Palmrose 1988)[5] and bankruptcy (Menon and Williams 1994),[6] in various bond market settings (Wallace 1981; Wilson and Howard 1984), and in the market for audit services (Raman and Wilson 1992; Ettredge and Greenberg 1990).[7] Part of the demand for audits has been attributed to the notion that a form of insurance is provided through the audit process, and such potential loss recovery would be expected to have value in the determination of the cost of capital (Wallace 1980, 1987; Chow et al. 1988; Schwartz and Menon 1985; Melumad and Thoman, 1990). This past research has focused largely on domestic practices, and three traits of the United States constrain inquiry: first, most public companies are audited by the Big Six CPA firms; second, most public companies receive clean

Table 1. Professional Requirements in Scandinavia

Training for the Profession	*Denmark*	*Norway*	*Sweden*
Professional Title Used	Statsautoriseret revisor	Statsautoriseret revisor	Auktoriserad revisor
Title Protected By Law/ Membership in professional body compulsory to use title	Yes/No	Yes/No	Yes/No
All must pass professional exam and	Be Authorized by the appropriate government Ministry	Be Authorized by the appropriate government Ministry	-.-
Educational background	University degree in auditing	High school for the lower degree "auditors' exam" and University (i.e., NHH—The Norwegian School of Economics and Business) for the higher degree "higher auditors' exam"	University degree (Professional Institutes also administer required courses)
Practical Experience Required: mandatory time period	The candidate will work for a Statsautoriseret revisor's office and will take part in any job related to the profession: 3 years minimum, but usually 4 years or more	Work under supervision of a registered auditor (lower degree) and Statsautoriseret revisor (higher degree): 2 years. Average about 4 or 5 years.	Work in auditing field for an Auktoriserad revisor; a imited period of time may be spent in another qualified economic work such as the accounting department of a large industry, bank, etc.: 5 years.
Professional indemnity insurance compulsory for auditors	Yes	Yes	No

Source: Adapted from Föreningen Auktoriserade Revisorer Far, "Training for the Profession: A Comparative Study 1988," *The FAR International Omnibus 1990*, pp. 654-673.

auditors' reports; and third, the litigation environment is not varied as is possible when studying multiple countries. Moreover, multiple auditors is a phenomenon observed outside of the domestic market. Hence, this research contributes to past literature by examining a regulatory context with multiple auditors and more variety observed in both type of auditor and type of auditor's report.

Prior research on the opinion formulation process has posited, as one example, that a going concern opinion for bankrupt companies is a function of financial stress, hidden fraud, client size, and audit delay (McKeown et al. 1991). Such work demonstrates the underlying complexity of cross-sectional variations. Yet, behavioral and decision-making experiments involving creditors and investors consistently find that unqualified opinions are considered to be more influential than other types of opinions in encouraging investment and lending decisions and in their influence on higher prices paid or lower interest charged (Wallace 1995). Firth (1978), Ball et al. (1979), and Chow and Rice (1982) conclude that qualified opinions contain information; Banks and Kinney (1982), Elliott (1982), Dodd et al. (1984), and Dopuch et al. (1986) all provide evidence of a market association with information in qualified reports, acknowledging—as does Bailey (1982)—that the audit opinion is concurrently reported with the financial statements, making it difficult to isolate market reactions to the audit opinion. This latter issue is explored further by Hopwood et al. (1989) through use of a log-linear modeling approach, producing results consistent with an incremental information value to opinions qualified for consistency and uncertainty when used in predicting financial failure. Dopuch, Holthausen, and Leftwich (1987) and Bell and Tabor (1991) provide statistics on report types that can be compared and contrasted with this Scandinavian analysis.

Past international research has described the characteristics of the training, certification, liability indemnity, and experience requirements of various countries. Table 1 summarizes the traits associated with the Scandinavian countries. The presence of two levels of auditor in Norway may be one of the institutional explanations for multiple auditors. However, this phenomenon of multiple auditors exists in other countries with single certifications to a sufficient degree that a specific pronouncement was issued by the International Federation of Accountants (September 1983) titled "Statement of Guidance on Conditions for Acceptance of an Appointment When Another Accountant in Public Practice is Already Carrying Out Work for the Same Client." The content of that statement recognizes that "it is impracticable for any one accountant to acquire special expertise or experience in all fields of accountancy" (¶6), leading to some entities' contracting with multiple accountants. This research provides evidence regarding descriptive traits of entities making choices and leaves inquiry into "why" selections are made to future research. It may be that exploration of retention and continuity patterns, as well as nonauditing services, could provide related insights as to needs by a particular entity that might encourage a "portfolio of auditors" strategy over time. Unfortu-

Table 2. Economic Profiles of Scandinavian Countries and Trade Relationships

COUNTRY/ MAJOR SOURCES OF IMPORTS: Value [in mil] (%)	*Sweden GDP: $230.55 bil (1990) PER CAPITA INCOME: $27,041 (1990) POPULATION 8.53 mil (1990) TOTAL IMPORTS: $48.20 bil. (1989) TRADE BALANCE: $3.4 bil (1990)*	*Denmark GDP: $125.16 bil (1989) PER CAPITA INCOME: $24,389 (1989) POPULATION: 5.1 mil (1990) TOTAL IMPORTS: $26.616 bil. (1989) TRADE BALANCE not available*	*Norway GDP: $106.85 bil (1990) PER CAPITA INCOME:$25,192 (1990) POPULATION 4.2 mil (1990) TOTAL IMPORTS: $23.254 bil. (1989) TRADE BALANCE: $7.2 bil (1990)*
West Germany(FRG) [now Germany]	9,665 (20%)	5,917 (22%)	2,880 (12%)
United States	3,952 (8%)	1,831 (6%)	1,684 (7%)
France	2,574 (5%)		
United Kingdom	3,903 (8%)	1,849 (6%)	1,758 (7%)
Netherlands		1,507 (5%)	
Norway	3,347 (6%)		
Sweden		3,212 (12%)	3,596 (15%)
Denmark			1,573 (6%)

Source: "World Trader" a GateWaze, Inc. information base, 1990 Edition.

nately, such information was not accessible in the archival data base assembled for the study.

SAMPLE COMPOSITION

Denmark, Sweden, and Norway are the focus of this study. To understand the economic nature of these countries and their interrelationships with other countries, Table 2 provides some macroeconomic statistics: the GDP, per capita income statistics, population, total imports, and trade balance information (when available) are reported for each of the countries. A description of trading partners—the five major sources of imports as of 1989/1990, based on "World Trader" a GateWaze, Inc. information base, 1990 edition—demonstrates the close trading interrelationships among the Scandinavian countries which is one dimension of homogeneity and comparability of entities within the data set. Another advantage of this mix of countries is that they are homogeneous within the accounting system clusters defined by Nobes and Parker (1985), permitting assessment of auditing effects holding this attribute constant. Nobes (1992) describes a classification framework for financial reporting and measurement practices which classifies Sweden, Denmark, and Norway within the "Government, Economics" macro-based system (see Nobes 1992, Appendix V, category 5).

Cost of capital analyses in the extant literature suggest numerous dimensions of financial measures that could be expected to influence the measurement of both equity and debt costs. A thorough review of the finance literature from the 1950s to date provided the basis for assimilating the determinants of cost of capital as delineated in Table 3 (wherein exemplary citations are provided). These factors provided the framework within which the database reflected in Appendix 1 was structured. The broad set of financial and market-based characteristics reflected were those available from annual reports of Scandinavian companies and were evaluated to describe more completely the profile of entities under study, to permit comparisons of samples studied in future inquiry, and to explore their interaction with auditor selection and report type. Insights into the variability of disclosure practices (including some desired metrics about which no information was reported by the sample companies) also provide the context for interpreting the information signals associated with auditor selection and auditors' reports.

Specifically, letters were written to 58 Norwegian, 59 Danish, and 150 Swedish companies, for a total of 267 requests. The responses were 17, 24, and 62, respectively, which were in English except for two, one, and six foreign annual reports. Note that while many of the companies provided foreign reports along with English language reports, nine companies did not transmit an English version. Scandinavian dictionaries were obtained for each language in order to permit consideration of these nine reports. The overall 38% response was considered sufficient for analysis. Since great diversity exists as to what measures are pro-

Table 3. Determinants of Cost of Capital

Concept	*Empirical Measure*
Risk Class of Security	Variability of earnings streams; beta
Business Risk Measure	Variability of earnings before interest and taxes
Tax Effects	Marginal Tax Rate, Average Tax Rate, Effective Tax Rate, Presence of large tax loss carryforwards
Growth Rates	Rate of Growth in Assets, Dividends, Earnings, and Sales
Industry Averages	5-Year Weighted Average Earnings Before Interest and Taxes divided by Total Invested Capital (i.e., net fixed assets plus working capital)
	Variability of earnings to capital ratios
	Growth Rate of Industry
	10-Year log linear growth rate of industry sales
	Long-term Debt in Industry/Invested Capital
	5-Year Weighted Average Earnings Before Interest and Taxes/ Fixed Charges
Uncertainty	Variance Rate of Firm's Assets
	Volatility in Earnings Before Interest, Depreciation, and Taxes
Return	Expected Rate of Return on the Firm's Stock (a function of the firm's business risk *and* debt ratio);
	Accounting rate of return on assets in place after allowing for economic depreciation
	Rate of return on new and existing assets
	Liquid assets' rate of return
Individual Debt Offerings	Year, Bond Rating (Investment/Noninvestment Grade), Term to Maturity, Coupon Interest Rate, Coupon Interest Payment Date, Size of Issue, Age of Issue in Years,
	Yield to Maturity, Sinking Fund, Seniority, Conversion Costs, Call Schedule, Redemption Terms
	By matching on coupon interest rate, avoids duration and bond yield effects and by matching on coupon interest payment dates, avoids accrued interest adjustment
Type of Debt Placements	Private Placement, Negotiated Transactions, Bankers, Competitive Bidding, Bank Term Loans, Shelf Registration
Cost of Issuance	Underwriting spreads
Indenture Data	Boundary Conditions
	Payout Terms
Complications	<$10 million public prices are cited as less accurate
	Packages of common stock and warrants with convertible debt
	Merger financing
Internal Financing	Net profit retained after dividend distributions
	Retained net profit plus depreciation and depletion accruals
	Dividend level
	Retention rate
	Rate of disinvestment (selling of assets)
	Rate of cash flow available for distribution
	Rate of cash distributions to stockholders and bondholders

(continued)

Table 3. Determinants of Cost of Capital

Concept	*Empirical Measure*
Leverage	Ratio of book value of debt to book value of equity Rate of growth in earnings available to common stockholders' equity (i.e., elasticity or rate of proportional change)/(rate of growth of earnings before interest and taxes) Long-term measure, for example, 20 years: Mean value of long-term debt (book value)/Mean value of long-term debt + value of equity over same time period Affected by entry into market, i.e., level of competition Operating leverage is the ratio of Percentage Change in Earnings to Percentage Change in Sales
Refunding Transactions	Call premium on refunded bonds Duplicate interest payments Issue expenses on the refunding of bonds Any discount on the refunding of bonds, less premium, less any tax saving Discount rate Term through maturity of refunded bonds Quality Rating
Capital Mix	Proportion of new stock issues to total new issues, Cost of equity capital, Convertible Bonds, Preferred Stock, Stock Repurchase Plans, Capital Expenditures, Current market price of shares, Rights Offering, Conversion Price, Expected Growth Rate of Shares, Bonds' Redemption Value at Maturity, Rate of growth of debt, Short-Term Notes Payable as a proportion of total capital
Other Features of Operations Affecting Capital Structure	Presence of Captive Finance Subsidiaries Leases: pre-tax lease payment, depreciation deduction, amount of debt displaced, marginal tax rate, pre-tax interest rate on similar duration and class of debt, termination date of lease Pensions: unfunded liabilities and unfunded past service costs Industry type: industry/utility/financial Loan Commitment Contracts: commitment size, risk premiums, commitment fees, contract length, collateral requirements, restrictive covenants Rate of Capital Expenditures (e.g., relative to sales) Asset Composition: % intangibles and % tangibles Intensity of research and development and advertising Supplier and Customer Terms Litigious Exposure Type of Products and Processes in Use Timing Auditor/CPA Firm Relationship

(continued)

Table 3. Determinants of Cost of Capital

Concept	*Empirical Measure*
	Potential Substitutes or complements to the audit, including consideration of complementary governance controls
	Operating Characteristics to control for risk factors potentially influencing cost of capital: industry type, regulated industry status, size, market share, capital intensity, changes in management, unionization, centralization, international operations, credit rating, merger prospects, management compensation considerations to evaluate risk tied to incentive effects—existence of bonuses, stock appreciation rights, and stock options

Source: Alberts and Hite (1983), Alexander et al. (1979), Ang (1975), Antia and Meyer (1984), Arditti (1973 and 1975), Barton (1975), Ben-Shahar (1970), Bloomfield and Ma (1975), Blume and Keim (1987), Boness and Frankfurter (1977), Bowlin (1966), Bradley et al (1984), Brennan and Schwartz (1984), Brigham (1966), Brown and Dybvig (1986), Bublitz and Ettredge (1989), Buse (1975), Caks (1977), Carleton and Silberman (1977), Carleton and Lakonishok (1985), Cohan (1960), Courtadon (1982), Davenport (1970), Dobrovoksly (1958), Estep (1987), Fisher (1988), Friend and Tokutsu (1987), Fung and Rudd (1986), Ghandi (1966), Gordon and Halpern (1977), Haugen and Pappas (1970), Huberman (1984), Jones et al (1984), Kane et al (1984), Kim et al (1977), Kwong et al (1995), Lee and Gupta (1977), Lerner and Carleton (1966), Lewellen and Emery (1980 and 1986), Lindberg and Ross (1981), Litzenberger and Jones (1970), McCauley and Zimmer (1989), McConnell and Sandberg (1975), McConnell and Servaes (Working Paper), Mendelson (1970), Myers (1984), Nantell and Carlson (1975), Peterson and Benesh (1983), Pettit (1975), Salamon (1988), Scott (1977), Smith and Warner (1979), Sougiannis (1994), Tajika and Yuji (1988), Tobin (1969), Vickers (1970), Wallace (1984), Weston and Lee (1977), Whittington (1988), Wild (1992), and Yagil (1982).

vided in annual reports, particularly in the sometimes reduced English versions, the analysis is limited by the information set derivable directly from the reports (with a final sample size of 89 entities containing sufficient information for evaluation).[8]

DATA BASE AND RESULTS

Annual reports from Denmark, Sweden, and Norway were analyzed and the database described in Appendix 1 resulted. Note that reason exists to expect these countries to be comparable based on homogeneous cultural (e.g., see Lynn, Zinkhan, and Harris 1993; Monsen and Wallace 1995) and historical linkages, trading activities, and joint initiatives in the accounting standard-setting arena. As is evident from the descriptive statistics, the number of countries reporting various information items varied rather widely, from zero to 89 potential data points. One-way analysis was performed for Big Eight (Big Six), other than a Boilerplate Auditor's Report, the presence of two auditors, and the presence of two auditors along with an appointed auditor, that is, three auditors. Those associations found to be statistically significant at a .05 level are reported in Table 4.

Table 4. Statistically Significant Results From Oneway Analysis

Variable	*BIG 6: mean value (n=number of observations)*	*NOT BIG 6: mean value (n=number of observations)*	*F-Ratio (probability)*
Two Auditors	.20 (n=10)	.86 (n=43)	26.69 (.0000)
Three Auditors	.20 (n=10)	.85 (n=40)	24.21 (.0000)
Operating Income	9,071,885,814 (n=7)	3,895,401 (n=33)	6.05 (.0185)
Interest Expense	856,344,649 (n=5)	1,753 (n=26)	14.39 (.0007)
Profit After Financial Income and Expenses	2,254,135,500 (n=4)	22,391,664 (n=38)	15.04 (.0004)
Profit Before Appropriations and Taxes	1,999,333,267 (n=6)	3,117,781 (n=30)	9.93 (.0034)
Net Income	173,322,300 (n=7)	4,973 (n=30)	30.85 (.0000)
Price Per Earnings Ratio	10,000 (n=1)	15.47 (n=12)	12476 (.0000)
Return on Capital Employed	.22 (n=1)	24 (n=5)	11.35 (.0281)
	BOILERPLATE	*NON BOILERPLATE*	
Involves Two Auditors	.88 (n=26)	.17 (n=23)	48.63 (.0000)
Market Share	.25 (n=5)	4.46 (n=20)	6.15 (.0209)
Interest	.10 (n=9)	218 (n=12)	18.72 (.0004)
Marginal Tax Rate	.24 (n=2)	.11 (n=8)	7.68 (.0242)
Interest Rate	.10 (n=7)	.12 (n=2)	6.19 (.0417)
Dividends Per Share	5 (n=10)	12.3 (n=6)	8.03 (.0133)

(continued)

Table 4. (Continued)

	TWO AUDITORS	*NOT TWO AUDITORS*	
Big 6 Auditor	.10 (n=40)	1.47 (n=38)	103.22 (.0000)
Three Auditors	.97 (n=38)	.6 (n=40)	19.56 (.0000)
Non Boilerplate Report	.15 (n=27)	1.26 (n=27)	35.24 (.0000)
Market Share	.22 (n=7)	3.92 (n=24)	7.18 (.0120)
Age of Company	210 (n=13)	1271 (n=17)	4.74 (.0380)
Interest	.11 (n=10)	213 (n=13)	21.48 (.0001)
Marginal Tax Rate	.24 (n=2)	.11 (n=9)	8.51 (.0171)
Dividends Paid	1393 (n=25)	9826 (n=5)	5.43 (.0272)
Interest Expense	1841 (n=23)	475747389 (n=9)	5.61 (.0245)
Net Income	5419 (n=27)	93327633 (n=13)	9.998 (.0031)
Capital Expenditures in Equipment	141772515 (n=9)	8408186 (n=13)	7.18 (.0144)
Return on Adjusted Stockholders' Equity	56960760 (n=4)	9.33 (n=19)	5.78 (.0255)
	THREE AUDITORS	*NOT THREE AUDITORS*	
Two Auditors	.61 (n=61)	.06 (n=17)	19.56 (.0000)
Operating Income	5449083 (n=48)	5800603602 (n=11)	5.38 (.0240)
Advertising Expense	6964934 (n=21)	145910325 (n=3)	18.55 (.0003)
Interest Expense	1737 (n=22)	535215811 (n=8)	6.21 (.0189)
Profit After Financial Income and Expenses	22036299 (n=52)	872980947 (n=10)	6.01 (.0172)
Profit Before Appropriations and Taxes	3463845 (n=27)	1332889369 (n=9)	5.32 (.0272)
Net Income	5341 (n=27)	121325897 (n=10)	14.66 (.0005)
Equity Capital I, Percent	8.87 (n=3)	42 (n=1)	27.43 (.0346)
Return on Equity Before Tax	11.09 (n=3)	127000000 (n=1)	1.75E+14 (.0000)

Big Six Auditor

The results indicate that when a Big Six auditor is involved, the presence of two or three auditors is far less likely. Moreover, Big Six auditors are associated with larger companies with greater dollar profits. Since only a single company in the Big Six category had information regarding the price per earnings ratio and return on capital before tax results, the observed differences should not be generalized.

Auditors' Reports

Turning to the presence of other than a boilerplate auditor's report, these are less likely to involve two auditors. They represent a larger market share, higher dollar interest, lower marginal tax rate, higher interest rate (by .0238—that is, .12 versus .0962), and higher dividends per share.

Two Auditors

The analysis of two auditors suggests these are, again, less likely to be Big Six audited entities, are more likely to also have an appointed auditor, are less likely to have a non boilerplate report, are likely to have less market share, are likely to be younger in age, have fewer dollars of interest expense, have a higher marginal tax rate, have fewer dividends paid in dollars, have fewer interest expenses, have lower net income, have larger capital expenditures on equipment, and have greater return on adjusted stockholders' equity.

Three Auditors

As the presence of three auditors is analyzed, the presence of two auditors, of course, is far more likely, the operating income is lower, the advertising expenses are lower, the interest expenses are lower, and profitability by three different metrics is lower. While the return ratios are lower, these findings only have one entity in one group and, therefore, provide few insights.

CONCLUDING REMARKS

This study quantifies the incidence of multiple auditors among the Scandinavian countries: 51% of the sample companies selected two auditors and 86% had a third auditor appointed. Those companies selecting more than one auditor tend to be younger, smaller entities. Multiple auditors are far less likely to be observed when one of the auditors for an entity is a Big Six firm. One interpretation of the evidence is that smaller companies "substitute" multiple auditors for the use of one Big Six auditor by larger entities. Beyond this pattern of auditor selection, the type of report issued is observed to vary, with two auditors being more likely to issue a clean report. A reward for clean audit reports, apart from how many auditors are engaged, is quantified as a 2.38% interest rate savings.

Since the sample size is small and other variables, such as mix of CPAs' services and auditor retention, could have effects on the observed relationships, the findings are tentative. Future research is needed to determine whether this preliminary evidence that the use of two to three auditors is more commonly observed when a Big Six firm is not an auditor can be generalized. Future inquiry would no doubt benefit from directing attention to larger samples, tracking similar detail, and being directed toward intricacies within specific industries, particular debt and equity markets, and varying ownership structures, lending further insight as to the magnitude of the cost of capital savings reasonably expected from audit-associated selections by individual companies. As capital markets have increased in their complexity with derivatives, hedging, debt-equity swaps, floating swaps, and plans for a European Union currency, means of relating reported financial numbers and market-based measures likewise increase in complexity. Some might argue that the selections of Big Six auditing affiliations relate to more sophisticated derivative strategies or enhanced global tax strategies aided in some manner by the professional service firm's consulting activities.

From a regulatory perspective, insight is gained as to when multiple auditors are likely to be observed, possible influence of auditor selection on report type, and the association of both with cost-of-capital components. As global markets grow,[9] the manner in which signals of auditor selection and report type are associated with cost of capital may help us calibrate the real return to lowering capital providers' information search costs. Regulators may wish to evaluate this evidence as they prescribe regulatory structures for multiple auditors and auditors' reporting practices, and companies' decision makers may wish to do likewise as they make selections from among the alternatives available within the existing framework.

APPENDIX

Table A.1. Dataset for the Evaluation of How Auditing-Related Choices are Associated with Various Financial Measures for Denmark, Sweden, and Norway

Variable	*Mean*	*Std Dev*	*Minimum*	*Maximum*	*N*	*Label*
COUNTRY	1.77	.68	1.00	3.00	64	1=Denmark 2=Sweden 3=Norway
BIG8	.19	.40	.00	1.00	53	1=Big 8 (Big 6) 0=Not Big 8 (Big 6)
TWOAUD	.51	.50	.00	1.00	81	1=Two Auditors Noted 0=1 Auditor Noted
THIRDAUD	.78	.42	.00	1.00	78	1=Two Auditors and Third Appointed
NOTBOILE	.47	.50	.00	1.00	49	1=Other Than Boilerplate Opinion
BOARDT	10.96	22.49	.00	200.00	81	Board Size:Total
BOARDD	11.27	4.02	5.00	23.00	84	Board Size:Directors
STKHLBD	8.83	5.76	.00	21	35	Stockholder Board Representatives
EMPLYREP	2.61	1.77	.00	6	28	Employee Board Representatives
GOVTREP	1.73	1.84	.00	6.00	37	Government Board Representatives
SOLICREP	.47	1.17	.00	5	19	Solicitors' Board Representatives
SALBDSPR	3.895E+10	2.2600E+11	.00	1.32E+12	34	Salary of Board and President
SALOTHER	16349.21	94250.16	2.58	581936.0	38	Salary for Other Employees
SOCIALCS	5928.95	22780.44	2.50	107788.0	22	Social Costs
NOLOB	3.57	3.20	1.00	15	44	Number of Lines of Business
MKTSHR	8.76	23.39	.01	100.00	34	Market Share
SICCODE	3549.26	2507.65	541	9673.00	19	SIC Code
NOEMPLOY	15840.00	38691.34	76.00	189493.0	38	Number of Employees
EMPLOCTY	5912.23	8057.97	.00	37943.00	48	Employees Located in Country
NOABROAD	5811.17	18347.76	.00	122823.0	47	Employees Located Abroad
AGEOFCOM	785.55	1389.38	.00	5013.00	31	Age of Company
NOOPERLO	46.93	83.12	1.00	390.00	42	Number of Operating Locations
NOCOUNTR	28.63	50.57	.00	241.00	55	Number of Countries of Operation
PERCFORS	4.55	7.23	.00	32.00	44	Percentage of Foreign Sales

(continued)

Table A.1. (Continued)

Variable	*Mean*	*Std Dev*	*Minimum*	*Maximum*	*N*	*Label*
PERNAMER	.34	.31	.00	1.00	39	Percentage of North American Sales
EXCHANGE	1343.95	6172.48	−122.00	30300.00	24	Exchange
SHRPRICE	207.25	161.52	36.00	710.00	19	Share Price
HIGHSHPR	231.91	135.45	62.00	715.00	27	High Share Price
LOWSHRPR	196.52	105.23	33.00	425.00	26	Low Share Price
GENINDXS	191.16	126.37	42.00	590.00	25	General Index
INTEREST	120.40	151.72	.08	465.00	23	Interest
MARGTR	.13	.08	.08	.36	11	Marginal Tax Rate
AVGTR	.42	.07	.36	.50	3	Average Tax Rate
EFFECTXR	.34	.04	.31	.36	2	Effective Tax Rate
BONUSES	8.10	16.98	.00	42.70	6	Bonuses
STKAPPRR	916.52	2101.29	.00	5200.00	6	Stock Appreciation Rights
STKOPTIO	19245429	30454537.1	.00	83890000	7	Stock Options
DIVPD	2798.95	7930.41	.14	31400.00	30	Dividends Paid
UNRESTER	5675.34	22309.40	−46.60	124393.0	46	Unrestricted Earnings
UNRRETEA	563950072	4034927275	−6.00	2.91E+10	52	Unrestricted Retained Earnings
BKVSTKHE	453696121	1529053998	13.30	9.31E+09	69	Book Value Stockholders' Equity
NETTANGA	338458879	1127911029	119.30	8.38E+09	68	Net Tangible Assets
GRFIXEDA	997084292	5822385873	41.80	4.89E+10	73	Gross Fixed Assets
NETPLANT	193252570	981057875	.90	8.16E+09	70	Net Plant
NETPLTEQ	93805305	532258153	5.90	3.76E+09	62	Net Plant and Equipment
INTANGAS	6.143E+09	2.1746E+10	.00	1.20E+11	73	Intangible Assets
TA	3.891E+09	2.2820E+10	.00	1.94E+11	81	Total Assets
CASH	611555501	3809574602	.20	3.24E+10	73	Cash
MKTSEC	45963780	209021289	.00	1.32E+09	53	Marketable Securities
LIQUIDAT	509612982	1433486901	.00	9.37E+09	70	Liquid Assets
CURASSET	331062711	1968052366	.00	1.57E+10	65	Current Assets

GOODWILL	268580804	650771658	.00	4.02E+09	66	Goodwill
CURLIAB	330278785	1874071556	.00	1.44E+10	59	Current Liabilities
CURINTBL	6072743.3	42540163.1	20.87	3.04E+08	51	Current Interest-Bearing Liabilities
STNP	15339255	106179790	.00	7.51E+08	50	Short-Term Notes Payable
LEASES	408104352	1214831095	.00	6.46E+09	35	Leases
LTDEBT	1.315E+09	5110782007	.00	2.62E+10	43	Long-Term Debt
LTLIABSU	61210.59	280893.20	.00	1614738	41	Long Term Liabilities Subsidiaries
OVERDRF	9833392.7	53859373.6	.00	2.95E+08	30	Overdraft
BONDDEBL	5.595E+09	1.9393E+10	.00	1.07E+11	53	Bond and Debenture Loans
TOTDEBT	302077173	1783723375	.00	1.30E+10	54	Total Debt
TOTBONDS	164285.50	582239.67	.00	2784301	46	Total Bonds
PREMBNDS	678.57	1432.88	.00	4225.80	12	Premium on Bonds
DISCBNDS	.00	.00	.00	.00	3	Discount on Bonds
CONVBDS	174662705	513989245	.00	1.90E+09	14	Convertible Bonds
PROVPENS	6824621.8	39202220.0	−85.00	2.25E+08	33	Provision for Pensions
PENSUNFL	25219.51	78701.42	.00	324368.0	23	Pension Unfunded Liability
PENPASTS	1347.43	2780.64	.00	8146.00	10	Pension Past Service
LOANCOMT	76.03	100.20	.78	285.60	9	Loan Commitment
COMMITFE	96500.25	136471.26	.50	193000.0	2	Commitment Fees
CONTRACL	Variable is missing for every case.					Contract Length
COLLATRQ	1.00	.	1.00	1.00	1	Collateral Requirements
INTERESR	.10	.02	.08	.12	9	Interest Rate
COUPONRT	1.60	4.24	.08	12.10	8	Coupon Rate
TERMD	5.07	8.60	.09	15.00	3	Term
ORIGAMNT	30.00	.	30.00	30.00	1	Original Amount
REMAINYE	2.00	.	2.00	2.00	1	Remaining Year-End
YLDTOMAT	Variable is missing for every case.					Yield-to-Maturity
SINKFUND	Variable is missing for every case.					Sinking Fund
TLADJCIV	108503.94	525609.75	−28588.0	2983634	32	Total Liability Adjusted for Cash & Inv.
MINORITI	154660.93	548975.68	−4491.60	2720289	45	Minority Interests

(continued)

Table A.1. (Continued)

Variable	Mean	Std Dev	Minimum	Maximum	N	Label
UNTAXRES	326161181	1922266997	.00	1.27E+10	44	Untaxed Reserves
COMEQTY	27989.81	120782.75	.00	705846.0	50	Common Equity Stock
PREFSTK	35147.36	142288.80	.00	700000.0	24	Preferred Stock
NOCLSSTK	1.76	.99	.00	4.00	29	Number of Classes of Stock
NOSHRS10	10339548	19137387.3	.00	79996178	31	No. of Shares Held by Largest 10 Shrh.
PERNOT10	4021673.4	8678892.25	.05	32998272	26	Number of Shares Not Held by Largest 10
WARRANTS	34756793	309833161	−7.2E+08	1.14E+09	20	Warrants
RE	856226952	4292744625	.00	2.91E+10	46	Retained Earnings
SE	315297778	1488367215	.00	1.05E+10	63	Stockholders' Equity
NONDISPC	91573629	245187986	48.14	1.53E+09	67	Non-disposable Capital
SHARCAP	179585517	684723912	.02	4.94E+09	68	Share Capital
SATUTORR	97109193	517812175	8.14	3.53E+09	52	Statutory Reserves
ONGNEWIS	47842.94	144462.45	.00	654475.0	24	Ongoing New Issue
TOTDISPC	5114.90	22021.78	.00	125280.0	32	Total Disposable Capital
SEUNTAXR	59187.42	264346.81	.00	1687462	53	Stockholders' Equity Untaxed Reserve@70%
OWNRISKB	95366.83	382348.94	.00	2420448	53	Total Own Risk-Bearing Capital
OWNRBCAP	1.017E+10	2.7081E+10	.00	1.20E+11	45	Own Risk-Bearing Capital Percent
LIABSE	7.918E+09	3.2621E+10	517.75	1.94E+11	39	Liabilities to Stockholders' Equity
CONTLIAB	326077.88	1304127.35	2.90	8349934	51	Contingent Liabilities
ASSETPL	14712.84	67567.83	.20	455000.0	48	Assets Pledged
NOSHRLHD	486309.51	2368462.84	12.00	15263000	42	Number of Shareholders
NOSHRSOS	35154623	55627698.6	.50	2.57E+08	38	Number of Shares of Stock Outstanding
BOOKEQPS	14788254	28401154.2	.02	1.22E+08	20	Book Equity Per Share
ADJEQPS	172082.04	687961.32	.12	2751937	16	Adjusted Stock Equity Per Share
RISKCAPS	187.28	104.80	63.00	390.00	10	Risk Capital Per Share
STKREPUR	4.159E+09	2785173266	1.02E+09	1.15E+10	20	Stock Repurchase Plan

TURNTS	1.701E+09	8977265533	1.00	6.84E+10	58	Turnover of Total Sales
OPERINCM	973143940	7332186669	−44.70	5.96E+10	66	Operating Income
ADVERTIS	24333108	69400713.5	19.40	2.82E+08	24	Advertising Expense
RDEXPENS	733109490	1903418269	57.13	9.13E+09	25	Research and Development Expense
INTEXPEN	438752055	1832796806	6.40	1.02E+10	33	Interest Expense
ISSUEEXP	105743882	468840410	−3.7E+07	2.43E+09	27	Issue Expense
CURRGL	17919582	120346851	−5.9E+08	3.26E+08	42	Currency Gains and Losses
TAXEXPEN	123127531	420773953	−1799000	2.86E+09	57	Tax Expenses
DEPREXP	121444435	698593789	−6793.00	5.14E+09	55	Depreciation Expenses
DEPLEXP	67031297	158399786	−2467000	5.96E+08	29	Depletion Expenses
PROFITAD	46978504	143622590	−9.0E+07	7.26E+08	33	Profit After Depreciation
PROFAFIE	148783715	1006088597	−37.60	8.24E+09	67	Profit After Financial Income & Expenses
EXTRAINC	56702213	210175554	.00	1.26E+09	61	Extraordinary Income
EXTRAEXP	1275438.1	5524701.08	.00	31009000	33	Extraordinary Expenses
GROUPCON	113579591	223629801	−9.0E+07	8.97E+08	34	Group Contribution/Shrhldr.
PROFBAPT	302324332	1506531039	.00	9.51E+09	40	Profit Before Appropriations and Taxes
APPROPRI	16250.63	68360.09	−1718.00	423397.0	45	Appropriations
PRFSHREM	101144003	344551640	−2.1E+08	2.29E+09	51	Profit-Sharing With Employees
NI	366764013	2188380365	−7742000	1.42E+10	42	Net Income
PPSAFI	25028.70	87417.91	−6.00	416604.0	24	Profit Per Share After Finan. Inc.&Exp.
PRFPSAST	10.63	8.75	.00	23.73	9	Profit Per Share After 30% Standard Tax
PRFPSAT	362.89	1338.18	.00	5200.00	15	Profit Per Share After Full Tax
EPS	14.03	10.76	.01	35.70	12	Earnings Per Share
YIELDPER	7.53	10.73	.02	29.60	8	Yield
PERATE	79.23	254.88	1.30	1000.00	15	Price Per Earnings Rate
DIVPERSH	6.61	5.88	.00	20.80	20	Dividends Per Share
DIVYLDCS	52727276	174876579	.90	5.80E+08	11	Dividend Yield Per Share of Common Stock
NETFDSFL	33593132	156645123	−3043.00	8.59E+08	31	Net Funds Flow
FUNDFOP	315579033	1798535704	−7567000	1.23E+10	48	Funds From Operations
WC	15138282	81889184.4	−111884	5.43E+08	51	Working Capital

(continued)

Table A.1. (Continued)

Variable	*Mean*	*Std Dev*	*Minimum*	*Maximum*	*N*	*Label*
FUNDPRIN	100848.73	571387.20	−582821	3787660	48	Funds Provided Internally
FUNDUSEI	72132.35	270364.70	−53.00	1604621	44	Funds Used Internally
TINTGEN	26434.79	140544.85	−749.00	919961.0	43	Total Internally Generated
FUNDPRIS	84666.90	389969.21	−1591.00	2300000	38	Funds Provided By Issuing New Shares
FINFUNDF	−1.80E+08	1079833353	−6.5E+09	5541.00	36	Financial Funds Flow
CHSTFINV	24894273.9	24894273.9	−3784.00	1.61E+08	42	Change in Short-Term Investments
CASHFLOW	102881533	358927316	−26399.0	1.95E+09	37	Change in Liquid Cash Flow
CAPEXPEN	3357322.75	3357322.75	−852.00	19000000	32	Capital Expenditures
CAPEXPFP	5848822.8	26017008.5	−39.10	1.35E+08	40	Capital Expenditures in Plant
CAPEXPEQ	62966321	130609788	.00	4.04E+08	22	Capital Expenditures in Equipment
INVFA	201200976	800163818	.00	3.92E+09	26	Investment in Fixed Assets
RESTSA	91509.45	286635.95	−39.10	997800.0	12	Restricted Sale of Assets
RESTDVP	Variable is missing for every case.					Restricted Dividends Payable
ATGROR	13.30	.	13.30	13.30	1	Accounting Rate of Return
RORNEWIV	14.40	.	14.40	14.40	1	Rate of Return on New Investment
ROREXAST	Variable is missing for every case.					Rate of Return on Existing Assets
ADJEQTY	47221.22	219696.86	.00	1229700	31	Adjusted Equity
RETPEQAS	144705.54	734111.05	−3.99	5172385	52	Ret. on Adjusted Equity After 30% Std.Tax
RETADJSE	9906226.9	47508547.6	.92	2.28E+08	23	Return on Adjusted Stockholders' Equity
OWNRBCP	3653979.9	19014952.2	.00	1.06E+08	31	Own Risk-Bearing Capital
RETRSKAT	5035303.3	17226466.9	.00	73336537	25	Ret. % on Risky Capital After Final Tax
RETABTX	5.69	7.79	.18	11.20	2	Return % on Assets Before Tax
RETCEBT	15.90	.71	15.40	16.40	2	Return on Capital Before Tax
RETCAPEM	20.24	11.41	.22	30.80	6	Return on Capital Employed
BETA	6.50	.	6.50	6.50	1	Beta
EQRATI	16.33	14.94	.22	31.00	4	Equity Capital I, Percent

EQRATII	17.15	17.16	4.00	42.00	4	Equity Capital II, Percent
RSKCAPP	16.10	9.76	6.10	25.60	3	Risk Capital Percent
DEBTEQRA	133813909	732928914	.00	4.01E+09	30	Debt/Equity Ratio
CAPITTUR	5.17	6.89	.00	33.38	22	Capital Turnover
GROSSMAR	17.40	.	17.40	17.40	1	Gross Profit Margin
PROFMAR	25.00	10.75	17.40	32.60	2	Profit Margin
INTCOVER	11.22	9.27	.04	26.10	6	Interest Coverage
RETEQB	31750008	63499994.5	1.98	1.27E+08	4	Return on Equity Before Tax
INVFAST	131000966	185260611	1932.00	2.62E+08	2	Investm.(excl.Fixed Assets in Ac'd Cos)
DEBTPC	13.40	46.59	.00	317.73	48	debtpc=totdebt/se
STEP1	.35	.65	.01	2.55	28	step1=debtpc*(intexpen/totdebt)
STEP1A	.32	.65	.00	2.55	26	step1a=debteqra*(intexpen/totdebt)
STEP1B	125.88	451.33	.03	1627.99	13	step1b=debteqra*interest
STEP1C	193.66	447.37	.00	1627.99	22	step1c=debtpc*interest
STEP2	.21	.39	.00	1.53	28	step2=step1*(1-.40)
STEP2A	.19	.39	.00	1.53	26	step2a=step1a*(1-.40)
STEP2B	75.53	270.80	.02	976.79	13	step2b=step1b*(1-.40)
STEP2C	116.19	268.42	.00	976.79	22	step2c=step1c*(1-.40)
STEP3	–127.92	461.74	–2474.43	28.16	29	step3=(1-debteqra)*retpeqas
STEP4	-47.76	101.93	–472.71	28.24	26	step4=step2+step3
STEP4A	-47.76	101.93	–472.71	28.24	26	step4a=step2a+step3
STEP4B	56.24	270.79	–78.36	953.53	13	step4b=step2b+step3
STEP4C	56.24	270.79	–78.36	953.53	13	step4c=step2c+step3

ACKNOWLEDGMENTS

The support of the KPMG Peat Marwick Foundation's Research Opportunities in Auditing Program is gratefully acknowledged. A number of research assistants at both Texas A&M University and College of William and Mary have assisted me in this inquiry; in particular, I appreciate the assistance of Scott Summers, now on the faculty at the University of Missouri—Columbia, and Mark Ruback, Brandon Steele, and John Walsh, alumni of the MBA program at the College of William and Mary.

NOTES

1. The historical Big Eight have gradually merged into the current Big Six auditing firms, which provide the structure used in this research for coding: Arthur Young and Ernst and Whinney merged in 1989 to form Ernst & Young; Deloitte, Haskins, and Sells and Touche Ross merged in 1989 to form Deloitte & Touche.

2. Specifically, "audit-related adjustments show an overwhelmingly *negative* effect on preaudit net earnings and net assets. The average aggregate adjustment reduces earnings and assets by two to eight times the minimum amount that would materially misstate the financial statements. Thus, the year-end audit is seen as directly reducing positive bias in pre-audit net earnings and net assets as well as improving the precision of measurement. This implies that, other things equal, if auditing had not been applied, then the financial reports of these firms would have tended to show materially inflated earnings and assets" (Kinney and Martin 1994, 149).

3. Admittedly, some studies are *inconsistent* with the notion of the Big Eight (now Big Six) auditors signaling higher quality, including Simunic (1980) lack of pricing differential and both Fried and Schiff (1981) and Nichols and Smith (1983) which did not find a positive abnormal return associated with switches from small to large auditors.

4. Specifically, Beatty (1989, 708) reports that the "hiring of a 'nationally known' audit firm is related to less underpricing of an initial public offering of equity securities." Of interest is Beatty's observation that "the widely used Big Eight/non-Big Eight classification may measure CPA firm reputation capital with error particularly for the smaller Big Eight and larger non-Big Eight firms" (p. 693—at that time, Laventhol and Horwath was the largest of the non-Big Eight considered).

5. Of course, as described in Palmrose (1991), the incidence of highly visible litigation cases, defined based on incidence of *Wall Street Journal* disclosures, clusters among the larger firms—for example, 41 of 52 cases (p. 62). This leads to a number of issues involving reputation effects of litigation.

6. These authors report evidence that price reactions observed at the disclosure of Laventhol and Horwath's bankruptcy appear attributable to the absence of the expected insurance coverage provided by auditors.

7. Raman and Wilson observe that "the GAO (1986, 21) noted that a higher percentage of smaller CPA firms performed substandard audits than did larger firms" (1992, 292)

8. There may be more incidences of English-language reports among respondents than the total population sampled, based on research in 1983 involving Swedish listed companies that found that for 100 companies, 58 had more than one version of their Swedish-language report: 58 in English, two in French, three in German, and two in Spanish. This same study reports that while 47 were complete translations, nine involved condensed text. (Auktoriserade Revisorers Serviceaktiebolag 1985, 74).

9. American holdings of foreign stocks by 1993 were $210 billion, more than double the level of 1990 (Frankel 1993).

REFERENCES

Akerlof, G., 1970. The market for "lemons": Quality uncertainty and the market mechanism. *Quarterly Journal of Economics* (August): 488-500.

Alberts, W.W., and G.L. Hite. 1983. The Modigliani-Miller Leverage equation considered in a product-market context. *Journal of Financial and Quantitative Analysis* 10(4, December): 425-437.

Alexander, G.J., R.D. Stover, and D.B. Kuhnau. 1979. Market timing strategies in convertible debt financing. *The Journal of Finance* 34(1, March): 143-155.

Ang, J.S. 1975. The two faces of bond refunding. *The Journal of Finance* 30(3, June): 869-874.

Antia, M.J., and R.L. Meyer. 1984. The growth optimal capital structure: manager versus shareholder objectives. *The Journal of Financial Research* 7(3, Fall): 259-267.

Antle, R. 1982. The auditor as an economic agent. *Journal of Accounting Research* 20(2): 503-527.

Antle, R. 1984. Auditor independence. *Journal of Accounting Research* 22: 1-20.

Arditti, F.D. 1973. The weighted average cost of capital: Some questions on its definition, interpretation, and use. *The Journal of Finance* 29(4, September): 1001-1007.

Arditti, F.D. 1975. Replies. *The Journal of Finance* 30(3, June): 889-892.

Auktoriserade Revisorers Serviceaktiebolag. 1985. *Survey of Accounting Practices in Larger Swedish Companies 1984.* Stockholm: Auktoriserade Revisorers Serviceaktiebolag.

Bailey, W.T. 1982. An appraisal of research designs used to investigate the information content of audit reports. *The Accounting Review* (January): 141-146.

Baiman, S., J. Evans, III, and J. Noel. 1987. Optimal contracts with a utility maximizing auditor. *Journal of Accounting Research* 25(2): 217-244.

Ball, R., R.G. Walker, and G.P. Whittred. 1979. Audit qualifications and share prices. *Abacus* (June): 23-34.

Balvers, R.J., B. McDonald, and R.E. Miller. 1988. Underpricing of new issues and the choice of auditor as a signal of investment banker reputation. *The Accounting Review* 63(4, October): 605-622.

Banks, D.W., and W.R. Kinney, Jr. 1982. Loss contingency reports and stock prices: An empirical study. *Journal of Accounting Research* (Spring): 240-254.

Baron, D.B. 1975. Firm valuation, corporate taxes, and default risk. *The Journal of Finance* 30(5, December): 1251-1264.

Beatty, R. 1989. Auditor reputation and the pricing of initial public offerings. *The Accounting Review* 64(4, October): 693-709.

Bell, T.B., and R.H. Tabor. 1991. Empirical analysis of audit uncertainty qualifications. *Journal of Accounting Research* 29(2): 350-370.

Ben-Shahar, H. 1970. On the capital structure theorem: Reply. *The Journal of Finance* 25(3, June): 678-681.

Biddle, G.C., and S.M. Saudagaran. 1991. Foreign stock listings: Benefits, costs, and the accounting policy dilemma. *Accounting Horizons* 5(3, September): 69-80.

Bloomfield, T., and R. Ma. 1975. The weighted average cost of capital: Some questions on its definition, interpretation, and use: Comment. *The Journal of Finance* 30(3, June): 887-888.

Blume, M.E., and D.B. Keim. 1987. Lower-grade bonds: Their risks and returns. *Financial Analysts Journal* (July/August): 26-33.

Boness, A.J., and G.M. Frankfurter. 1977. Evidence of non-homogeneity of capital costs within "risk classes." *The Journal of Finance* 22(3, June): 775-787.

Bowlin, O.D. 1966. The refunding decision: Another special case in capital budgeting. *The Journal of Finance* 21(1, March): 55-68.

Bradley, M., G.A. Jarrell, and E.H. Kim. 1984. On the existence of an optimal capital structure: Theory and evidence. *The Journal of Finance* 39(3, July): 593-609.

Brennan, M.J., and E.S. Schwartz. 1984. Valuation of corporate claims. *The Journal of Finance* 39(3, July): 593-609.

Brigham, E.F. 1966. An analysis of convertible debentures: Theory and some empirical evidence. *The Journal of Finance* 21(1, March): 35-54.

Brown, S.J., and P.H. Dybvig. 1986. The empirical implications of the Cox, Ingersoll, Ross theory of the term structure of interest rates. *The Journal of Finance* 41(3, July): 617-632.

Bublitz, B., and M. Ettredge. 1989. The information in discretionary outlays: advertising, research, and development. *The Accounting Review* 44(1, January): 108-124.

Buse, A. 1975. Reply. *The Journal of Finance* 30(4, September): 1141-1142.

Caks, J. 1977. The coupon effect on yield maturity. *The Journal of Finance* 32(3, June): 811-821.

Carleton, W.T., and J. Lakonishok. 1985. Risk and return on equity: The use and misuse of historical estimates. *Financial Analysts Journal* (January/February): 38-47.

Carleton, W.T., and I.H. Silberman. 1977. Joint determination of rate of return and capital structure: An econometric analysis. *The Journal of Finance* 32(3, June): 811-821.

Choi, F.D.S., and R.M. Levich. 1991. Behavioral effects of international accounting diversity. *Accounting Horizons* 5(2, June): 1-13.

Chow, C., L. Kramer, and W.A. Wallace. 1988. The environment of auditing. In *Research Opportunities in Auditing: The Second Decade*, eds. A.R. Abdel-Khalik and I. Solomon, 155-183. Sarasota, FL: American Accounting Association.

Chow, C.W., and S.J. Rice. 1982. Qualified audit opinions and share prices—An investigation. *Auditing: A Journal of Practice and Theory* (Winter): 35-53.

Cohan, A.B. 1960. Abstracts of doctoral dissertations—The price of underwriting services on corporate debt, 1935-1952. *Journal of Finance* 15(3, September): 407-408.

Conover, T.L., and W.A. Wallace. 1995. Equity market benefits to disclosure of geographic segment information: An argument for decreased uncertainty. *Journal of International Accounting, Auditing, and Taxation* 4(2): 101-112.

Conover, T.L., and W.A. Wallace. 1994. Two roads diverge. *Financial Executive* (May-June): 6.

Courtadon, G. 1982. The pricing of options on default-free bonds. *Journal of Financial and Quantitative Analysis* 17(1, March): 75-100.

Craswell, A.T., J.R. Francis, and S.L. Taylor. 1995. Auditor brand name reputations and industry specializations. *Journal of Accounting and Economics* 20(3, December): 297-322.

Davenport, M. 1970. Leverage, dividend policy and the cost of capital: A comment. *The Journal of Finance* 25(4, September): 893-897.

DeAngelo, L.E. 1981. Auditor size and audit quality. *Journal of Accounting and Economics* 3(2): 183-199.

Dhaliwal, D. 1978. The impact of disclosure regulations on the cost of capital. In *Economic Consequences of Financial Accounting Standards: Selected Papers*, 73-100. Stamford, CT: Financial Accounting Standards Board.

Dobrovolsky, S.P. 1958. Economics of corporate internal and external financing. *The Journal of Finance* 12(1, March): 35-47.

Dodd, P., N. Dopuch, R.W. Holthausen, and R.W. Leftwich. 1984. Qualified audit opinions and stock prices: Information content, announcement dates, and concurrent disclosures. *Journal of Accounting and Economics* 6(1): 3-38.

Dopuch, N.R., R.W. Holthausen, and R.W. Leftwich. 1986. Abnormal stock returns associated with media disclosures of "subject to" qualified audit opinions. *Journal of Accounting and Economics* (June): 93-117.

Dopuch, N.R., R.W. Holthausen, and R.W. Leftwich. 1987. Predicting audit qualifications with financial and market variables. *The Accounting Review* 62(3): 431-454.

Eichenseher, J.W., M. Hagigi, and D. Shields. 1989. Market reaction to auditor changes by OTC companies. *Auditing: A Journal of Practice and Theory* 9(1): 29-40.

Elliott, J.A. 1982. "Subject to" audit opinions and abnormal security returns: Outcomes and ambiguities. *Journal of Accounting Research* III(Autumn): 617-638.

Elliott, R.K., and P. Jacobson. 1994. *Costs and Benefits of Disclosing Information.* Report prepared for the AICPA Special Committee on Financial Reporting.

Estep, T. 1987. Security analysis and stock selection: Turning financial information into return forecasts. *Financial Analysts Journal* (July/August): 34-43.
Ettredge, M., and R. Greenberg. 1990. Determinants of fee cutting on initial audit engagements. *Journal of Accounting Research* 28(1, Spring): 198-210.
Firth, M. 1978. Qualified audit reports: Their impact on investment decisions. *The Accounting Review* (July): 642-650.
Fisher, F.M. 1988. Accounting data and the economic performance of firms. *Journal of Accounting and Public Policy* 7(4): 253-260.
Francis, J.R., and D. Simon. 1987. A test of audit pricing in the small-client segment of the U.S. audit market. *The Accounting Review* 62(1, January): 145-157.
Francis, J.R., and E.R. Wilson. 1988. Auditor changes: A joint test of theories relating to agency costs and auditor differentiation. *The Accounting Review* 63(4, October): 663-682.
Frankel, J.A. 1993. The internationalization of equity markets. Working paper 4590, National Bureau of Economic Research, December.
Fried, D., and A. Schiff. 1981. CPA switches and associated market reaction. *The Accounting Review* 56(2, April): 326-341.
Friend, I., and I. Tokutsu. 1987. The cost of capital to corporations in Japan and the U.S.A. *Journal of Banking and Finance* 11: 313-327.
Fung, W.K.H., and A. Rudd. 1986. Pricing new corporate bond issues: An analysis of issue cost and seasoning effects. *The Journal of Finance* 41(3, July): 633-644.
General Accounting Office. 1986 (March). *CPA Audit Quality: Many Governmental Audits Do Not Comply With Professional Standards*. Washington, DC: General Accounting Office.
Ghandi, J.K.S. 1966. On the measurement of leverage. *The Journal of Finance* 21(4, December): 715-726.
Gordon, M.J., and P.J. Halpern. 1977. Cost of capital for a division of a firm: Reply. *The Journal of Finance* 32(5, December): 1781-1782.
Haugen, R.A., and J.L. Pappas. 1970. A comment on the capital structure and the cost of capital: A suggested exposition. *The Journal of Finance* 29(3, June): 674-677.
Healy, P., and T. Lys. 1986. Auditor changes following Big Eight mergers with non-Big Eight audit firms. *Journal of Accounting and Public Policy* 5: 251-265.
Healy, P.M., and K.G. Palepu. 1993. The effect of firms' financial disclosure strategies on stock prices. *Accounting Horizons* 7(1, March): 1-11.
Hopwood, W., J. McKeown, and J. Mutchler. 1989. A test of the incremental explanatory power of opinions qualified for consistency and uncertainty. *The Accounting Review* (January): 28-48.
Huberman, G. 1984. External financing and liquidity. *The Journal of Finance* 39(3, July): 895-910.
Jang, H.J., and C. Lin. 1993. Audit quality and trading volume reaction: A study of initial public offering of stocks. *Journal of Accounting and Public Policy* 12(Fall): 263-287.
Jones, E.P., S.P. Mason, and E. Rosenfeld. 1984. Contingent claims analysis of corporate capital structures: An empirical investigation. *The Journal of Finance* 39(3, July): 611-627.
Kane, A., A.J. Marcus, and R.L McDonald. 1984. Capital structure. *The Journal of Finance* 32(3, July): 841-855.
Kim, H., J.H. McConnell, and P.R. Greenwood. 1977. Capital structure rearrangements and me first rules in an efficient capital market. *The Journal of Finance* 32(3, June): 789-810.
Kinney, W.R., Jr., and R.D. Martin. 1994. Does auditing reduce bias in financial reporting? A review of audit-related adjustment studies. *Auditing: A Journal of Practice & Theory* 13(1, Spring): 149-156.
Klein, B., and K. Leffler. 1981. The role of market forces in assuring contractual performance. *Journal of Political Economy* (Vol. 89, No. 4, August): 615-641.
Kwong, M.F.C., J.W. Munro, and K.V. Peasnell. 1995. Commonalities between added value ratios and traditional return on capital employed. *Accounting and Business Research* 26(1, Winter): 51-67.

Lee, C.F., and M. Gupta. 1977. An inter-temporal approach to the optimization of dividend policy with pre-determined investment: A further comment. *The Journal of Finance* 32(4, September): 1358-1361.

Lerner, E.M., and W.T. Carleton. 1966. Financing decisions of the firm. *The Journal of Finance* 21(2, May): 202-214.

Lewellen, W.G., and D.R. Emery. 1980. On the matter of parity among financial obligations. *The Journal of Finance* 35(1, March): 97-111.

Lewellen, W.G., and D.R. Emery. 1986. Corporate debt management and the value of the firm. *Journal of Financial and Quantitative Analysis* 21(4, December): 415-426.

Lindberg, E.B., and S.A. Ross. 1981. Tobin's q ratio and industrial organization. *Journal of Business* 54(January): 1-33.

Litzenberger, R., and C.P. Jones. 1970. The capital structure and the cost of capital: Comment. *The Journal of Finance* 25(3, June): 669-673.

Lynn, M., G.M. Zinkhan, and J. Harris. 1993. Consumer tipping: A cross-country study. *Journal of Consumer Research* 20(December): 478-488.

Magee, R., and M. Tseng. 1990. Audit pricing and independence. *The Accounting Review* 65(April): 315-336.

McCauley, R.N., and S.A. Zimmer. 1989. Explaining international differences in the cost of capital. *FRBNY Quarterly Review* (Summer): 7-28.

McConnell, J.J., and C.M. Sandberg. 1975. The weighted average cost of capital: Some questions on its definition, interpretation, and use: Comment. *The Journal of Finance* 30(3, June): 883-886.

McConnell, J.J., and H. Servaes. 1990. Equity ownership and corporate value. Working paper 286, University of Chicago, Graduate School of Business, Center for Research in Security Prices.

McKeown, J.C., J.F. Mutchler, and W. Hopwood. 1991. Towards an explanation of auditor failure to modify the audit opinions of bankrupt companies. *Auditing: A Journal of Practice and Theory* 10(Supplement): 1-13.

Melumad, N.D., and L. Thoman. 1990. On auditors and the courts in an adverse selection setting. *Journal of Accounting Research* 28(1, Spring): 77-120.

Mendelson, M. 1970. Leverage, dividend policy and the cost of capital: A comment. *The Journal of Finance* 25(4, September): 898-903.

Menon, K., and D. Williams. 1991. Auditor credibility and initial public offerings. *The Accounting Review* 66(2, April): 313-332.

Menon, K., and D.D. Williams. 1994. The insurance hypothesis and market prices. *The Accounting Review* 69(2, April): 327-342.

Monsen, N., and W.A. Wallace. 1995. Evolving financial reporting practices: A comparative study of the Nordic countries' harmonization efforts. *Contemporary Accounting Research* 11(Spring): 973-997.

Myers, S.C. 1984. The capital structure puzzle. *The Journal of Finance* 39(3, July): 575-592.

Myers, S., and N. Majluf. 1984. Corporate financing and investment decisions when firms have information that investors do not have. *Journal of Financial Economics* 13(2): 187-221.

Nantell, T.J., and C. R. Carlson. 1975. The cost of capital as a weighted average. *The Journal of Finance* 30(5, December): 1343-1355.

Nichols, D.R., and D. Smith. 1983. Auditor credibility and auditor changes. *Journal of Accounting Research* 21(2, Autumn): 534-544.

Nobes, C.W. 1992. *International Classification of Financial Reporting*, 2nd edition. New York: Routledge.

Nobes, C.W., and R.H. Parker. 1985. *Comparative International Accounting,* 2nd edition. Oxford, UK: Phillips Allan Publishers.

Palmrose, Z. 1986. Audit fees and auditor size: Further evidence. *Journal of Accounting Research* 24(1, Spring): 97-110.

Palmrose, Z. 1988. An analysis of auditor litigation and audit service quality. *The Accounting Review* 63(1, January): 55-73.

Palmrose, Z. 1991. An analysis of auditor litigation disclosures. *Auditing: A Journal of Practice & Theory* 10(Supplement): 54-71.

Peterson, P.P., and G.A. Benesh. 1983. A reexamination of the empirical relationship between investment and financing decisions. *Journal of Financial and Quantitative Analysis* 18(4, December): 439-453.

Pettit, R.R. 1975. The weighted average cost of capital: Some questions on its definition, interpretation and use: Comment. *The Journal of Finance* 30(3, June): 919-920.

Purvis, S.E.C., H. Gernon, and M.A. Diamond. 1991. The IASC and its comparability project: Prerequisites for success. *Accounting Horizons* 5(2, June): 25-44.

Raman, K.K., and E.R. Wilson. 1992. An empirical investigation of the market for "single audit" services. *Journal of Accounting and Public Policy* 11: 271-295.

Roberts, R.W., and G.W. Glezen 1990. Determinants of school district audit fees. In *Research in Governmental and Nonprofit Accounting*, Vol. 6, ed. James L. Chan, Editor, 127-147. Greenwich, CT: JAI Press.

Ross, S. 1977. The determination of financial structure: The incentive-signalling approach. *Bell Journal of Economics* 8: 23-40.

Ross, S. 1979. Disclosure regulations in financial markets: Implications of modern finance theory and signaling theory. *Issues in Financial Regulation* (New York, New York: McGraw-Hill) 177-201.

Rubin, M.A. 1992. Municipal selection of a state or external auditor for financial statement audits. *Journal of Accounting and Public Policy* 11(2, Summer): 155-178.

Salamon, G.L. 1988. On the validity of accounting rates of return in cross-sectional analysis: Theory, evidence, and implications. *Journal of Accounting and Public Policy* 7(4, Winter): 267-292.

Salamon, G.L., and R. Kopel. 1993. Accounting method related misspecification in cross-sectional capital market research designs. *Journal of Accounting and Public Policy* 12(3, Fall): 217-238.

Schwartz, K., and K. Menon. 1985. Auditor switches by failing firms. *The Accounting Review* (April): 248-261.

Scott, J.H., Jr. 1977. Bankruptcy, secured debt, and optimal capital structure. *The Journal of Finance* 33(1, March): 1-19.

Scott, J.H., Jr. 1979. Bankruptcy, secured debt, and optimal capital structure: Reply. *The Journal of Finance* 34(1, March): 253-260.

Simunic, D. 1980. The pricing of audit services: Theory and evidence. *Journal of Accounting Research* 18(1, Spring): 161-190.

Simunic, D., and M. Stein. 1987. *Product Differentiation in Auditing: Auditor Choice in the Market for Unseasoned New Issues.* Vancouver, British Columbia: The Canadian Certified General Accountants' Research Foundation.

Smith, C.W., Jr., and J.B. Warner. 1979. Bankruptcy, secured debt, and optimal capital structure: Comment. *The Journal of Finance,* Vol. xxxiv (1, March): 247-251.

Sougiannis, T. 1994. The accounting based valuation of corporate R&D. *The Accounting Review* 69(1, January): 44-68.

Spence, M. 1973. Job market signaling. *Quarterly Journal of Economics* 87: 355-374.

Tajika, E., and Y. Yuji. 1988. Cost of capital and effective tax rate: A comparison of U.S. and Japanese manufacturing industries. *Journal of Economics* 29(December): 181-200.

Tobin, J. 1969. A general equilibrium approach to monetary theory. *Journal of Money, Credit, and Banking* 1(February): 15-29.

Vickers, D. 1970. The cost of capital and the structure of the firm. *The Journal of Finance* 25(1, March): 35-46.

Wallace, W.A. 1980. *The Economic Role of the Audit in Free and Regulated Markets.* The Touche Ross & Co. Aid to Accounting Education Program (Rochester, New York: University of Rochester).

Wallace, W.A. 1981. The Association between municipal market measures and selected financial reporting practices. *Journal of Accounting Research* 19(2): 502-520.

Wallace, W.A. 1984. The effects of delays by accounting policy-setters in reconciling the accounting treatment of stock options and stock appreciation rights. *Accounting Review* (April): 325-341.

Wallace, W.A. 1987. The economic role of the audit in free and regulated markets: A review. In *Research in Accounting Regulation*, Vol. 1, ed. Larry M. Parker and Gary John Previts, Editors, 7-34. Greenwich, CT: JAI Press.

Wallace, W.A. 1995. *Auditing*, 3rd edition. Cincinnati, OH: South-Western Publishing.

Ward, D.D., R.J. Elder, and S.C. Kattelus. 1994. Further evidence on the determinants of municipal audit fees. *The Accounting Review* 69(2, April): 399-411.

Weston, J.R., and W.Y. Lee, 1977. Cost of capital for a division of a firm: Comment. *The Journal of Finance* 32(5, December): 1779-1780.

Whittington, G. 1988. The usefulness of accounting data in measuring the economic performance of firms. *Journal of Accounting and Public Policy* 7(4, Winter): 261-266.

Wild, J.J. 1992. Stock price informativeness of accounting numbers: Evidence on earnings, book values, and their components. *Journal of Accounting and Public Policy* 11(2, Summer): 119-154.

Wilson, E.R., and T.P. Howard. 1984. The association between municipal market measures and selected financial reporting practices: Additional evidence. *Journal of Accounting Research* 22(1): 207-224.

Yagill, J. 1982. On valuation, beta, and the cost of equity capital: A Note. *Journal of Financial and Quantitative Analysis* 17(3, September): 441-449.

PERSPECTIVE

INTERNATIONAL ACCOUNTING STANDARDS:

ONGOING PROGRESS SUGGESTS THEY MAY BECOME A REALITY

Arthur R. Wyatt

ABSTRACT

Interest in International Accounting Standards is growing rapidly as the International Accounting Standards Committee continued to make real progress in developing and refining its standards. Many barriers to widespread acceptance of IASC standards exist, but as the quality of the standards improves and as an effective interpretive mechanism for their maintenance evolves, these barriers are likely to lose signficance. With cross border trade growing at a remarkable pace, interest in international accounting standards will remain high. Acceptance broadly of international accounting standards during the next quarter century looks increasingly likely. To meet the ongoing needs for increasingly high quality standards, the structure of IASC itself is likely to change to improve its efficiency and the quality of its work product.

Research in Accounting Regulation, Supplement 1, pages 277-286.

ISBN: 0-7623-0338-7

INTRODUCTION

Today one finds increasing interest in international accounting standards. Some are interested because greater acceptance of international accounting standards will lead to pressure in the local country to enhance the quality of local financial reporting. Others are interested because greater acceptance of international accounting standards will lead to pressure for acceptance that, at least in the view of some in the local country, will lead to a lower quality of financial reporting. Still others are interested because the direction of the development of international accounting standards is fundamentally different from the type of standards currently used locally. The fact is that the closer we come to completion of a quality set of international accounting standards, the greater the level of interest in those standards around the world.

EVOLUTION OF INTERNATIONAL STANDARDS

One needs go back only 20 years to find that the topic of international accounting standards would have been of interest only to a subset of academicians and a few isolated professionals. The International Accounting Standards Committee (IASC)was formed in 1973 and embarked on a program of developing international standards. The objective was to enhance the quality of financial reporting around the world by obtaining agreement that similar events and transactions would be accounted for similarly regardless of governmental jurisdiction. The result would be increased understanding of financial statements and more efficient analyses of financial information. Early standards were characterized often by the acceptance of alternative procedures, mainly because IASC voting procedures often would require that the two most popular accounting procedures be accepted in order to garner sufficient votes for passage. While these efforts often did lead to the elimination of some less desirable accounting procedures, the end result hardly merited the label of standards. Thus, early progress was modest and led few to conclude that the internationalization of accounting standards was likely to occur in the near term.

In the mid-1980s, the IASC began work on a conceptual framework project. In part, frustration with the inability to narrow accounting procedures in an area to a single acceptable approach encouraged IASC leaders to seek agreement on a set of concepts that would then hopefully provide the basis for resolving disputes between existing acceptable alternatives in given practice areas. This framework was debated within the IASC Board and eventually adopted under the same stringent voting requirements that apply to the adoption of standards. The agreed upon framework was similar to those in place or under development in the United States, Canada, the United Kingdom, and Australia and embraced concepts that were quite different from those that supported accounting principles in, say, Germany and Japan. While the IASC conceptual framework that emerged from this effort was less than perfect, it has proved to be good enough to enable the IASC to reduce markedly the number of acceptable alternatives in its standards from those that existed 10 years ago.

As work on the conceptual framework evolved, the IASC began an active program to reconsider its existing standards, particularly those that contained two or more acceptable alternatives. This program was initially styled as its "comparability project" and later as its "improvements project." By the mid-1990s, the work was largely completed and more than 20 previously acceptable accounting procedures were no longer acceptable. Work continues to eliminate several of the remaining alternatives. Also, by the mid-1990s, the IASC had agreed, with significant support from the International Organization of Securities Commissions (IOSCO), on a work program that would initiate several new projects that, when completed along with the recently revised standards, would produce a core set of standards that would be acceptable to the IOSCO. The core set of standards would provide a basis for securities regulators around the world to begin to accept, from multinational companies desiring to enter nondomestic capital markets, financial statements prepared in accordance with international accounting standards.

Thus, with only modest success to show for its efforts in the mid-1980s, the IASC has progressed in the relatively short span of 10 years to near completion of a truly remarkable undertaking to reach acceptance on a core set of accounting standards that securities regulators around the world find acceptable.

REACTION TO CHANGING INVESTOR NEEDS

Clearly, this rapid progress by the IASC was motivated by more than the mere desire of a group of professionals that meets only three or so times a year to improve the quality of financial statements of multinational companies. In fact, the IASC's initiatives were a relatively rapid reaction to the developing needs of the world business community as capital markets became gradually more international in scope. Advances in communications and other technology made capital accessible in a far wider range of markets than formerly. As nondomestic companies undertook increasing initiatives to access foreign capital markets, lenders and securities regulators had to face the problem of evaluating financial information that was prepared by applying far different standards from those that the lenders or regulators were accustomed to in their individual domestic markets. Thus, the advances made by the IASC are more the result of changing market forces than of isolated desires of standard setters. These market forces have also been increasingly effective in altering long-standing cultural patterns as leading commercial and industrial countries want to become more effective players in the world economy.

One would expect in this changing environment to find that securities regulators in various countries would come together to try to resolve the problems that all faced in varying degrees. Of course, this did happen, and the IOSCO became an increasingly significant influence on the evolving standard-setting process. Surprisingly, the tensions between the private-sector standard-setters (IASC) and the securities regulators from various government sectors were modest and the degree of cooperation significant. No doubt, securities regulators recognized the accounting expertise within the IASC and the already existing standard-setting structure. In addition, even though the securities regulators were all governmental officials, not all governments operate in a uniform way.

Reliance on the private sector was a useful alternative to governmental group actions, while the IASC recognized the changing needs of the world business community and began its ambitious project to improve the quality of its existing standards, the IOSCO began working more closely with the IASC and effectively provided added incentive for the IASC to accelerate the timing of its work program.

During this same period, accounting standard-setting was moving forward locally in several countries. In addition, the European Commission developed a set of accounting directives that members of the European Union adopted. Several countries developed accounting conceptual frameworks, and these tended to be more similar to each other than they were different. Thus, economic activity in individual countries stimulated added interest in the quality of accounting standards at the same time that cross-border financing activities were generating pressure for a set of international standards that could be found acceptable across individual country borders.

ACCELERATED IASC WORK PROGRAM ADOPTED

In July 1995 in Paris, the IOSCO and IASC reached joint agreement on a work program for the IASC that would produce an agreed upon core set of standards that was of sufficient quality to be effectively useful across borders. IOSCO representatives would do their best in each of their countries to have local securities regulators accept financial statements prepared in accordance with international standards for purposes of meeting filing requirements in the country by companies desiring to raise capital in the country. Such a development would, of course, add efficiency to the workload of regulators by reducing, markedly in some cases, the number of accounting regimes that the regulators would have to understand.

Shortly after this accord was reached, the IASC announced an accelerated timetable that now specifies a July 1998 target date for the completion of the core set of standards. No doubt various pressures encouraged the IASC to accelerate its timetable, leaving it now with a very ambitious undertaking. While timeliness is certainly an important consideration, it is likely that the success or failure of the IASC undertaking will rest more on the quality of its core set of standards than on whether the July 1998 deadline is met. Experience in the United States and other countries suggests that writing accounting standards against a tight time deadline is not a very productive exercise, and the IASC may well find some slippage of its ambitious timetable.

The core set of standards agreed upon includes either new standards or revisions of existing standards in several controversial areas including financial instruments, income tax accounting, accounting for intangibles, accounting for pension costs, and accounting for provisions. The fact is that the IASC tackled some difficult, but relatively less controversial, topics during the latter 1980s and early 1990s, and the current agenda items may well prove to be particularly difficult to resolve under a tight time deadline. As recently as 1993, the IASC leadership had expected that standards in these new areas would require seven to 10 years to complete. Trying to force completion by mid-1998 will be a real challenge.

Even assuming that the current IASC work program is able to be completed on a timely basis, the expectation is that any country may elect to require a limited number of departures from such standards. For example, the core set of IASC standards could provide for the capitalization of certain development costs as assets. A given country could find this treatment unacceptable and require such costs to be expensed in financial statements filed with it. Or, a company may follow an IASC acceptable alternative—say, the revaluation of long-lived assets—and a given country could require restoration of historical costs in the accounts of the company before accepting its financial statements for registration purposes.

Of course, the greater the number of instances in which exceptions are required by any country, the less we have a true body of international accounting standards. Significant pressure can be expected to build over time for any country to eliminate its few special requirements, and such elimination will likely occur as time passes. For a few years after the agreement to use the completed set of core international standards as the basis for multinational company security offerings, however, we can expect to see some limited local variations as countries gain comfort in applying new approaches to old accounting issues.

INTERPRETATIONS OF IASC STANDARDS

Upon completion of the core set of standards agreed upon with the IOSCO, it seems highly likely that the IASC, at the urging of the IOSCO, will have to establish some type of relatively formal interpretive process before wide acceptance of the core set of standards will be achieved. Experience in several countries with more advanced processes of accounting standard-setting is that users of the standards do not always read the standard in the same way, or even in the way in which the standard setter intended. Experience also shows that when differing interpretations do arise, practice tends toward the least desirable interpretation, from the standard-setter's perspective—sort of a Gresham's law of standard-setting. Since the opportunity for differing interpretations seems enhanced when a standard is applied in a variety of countries, the adoption of some sort of interpretive process by the IASC seems a necessary and important step.

SUMMARY OF PROGRESS

In summary, the progress toward a more complete set of high quality international standards has been rather remarkable over the past decade. The motivations to move forward with these initiatives remain strong, and the resolve of those involved in the process remains high. Even so, it is still too early, in my judgment, to conclude that international accounting standards are currently good enough to, for example, replace the current body of GAAP in the United States, or probably the current body of accepted standards in those countries with reasonably well-developed accounting standards. A number of roadblocks, or potential roadblocks, exist that will have to be dealt with in some form or another if the developments over the last decade are to result in widespread use of a truly international set of accounting standards.

DIFFICULTY OF ADAPTING TO CHANGE

The IASC has made rapid progress toward development of its core set of standards over the past 10 to 12 years. Given that the standards adopted by the IASC differ in many respects from those found in a number of countries, this pace of change has been a troublesome factor for many countries. Changes in accounting standards previously had often been infrequent, and expectations of substantial continuity of existing standards have been high. Change in any area often creates a variety of concerns or even objections. In many cases, all that is needed to gain acceptance of the changes is additional time for interested parties to gain comfort with the new approaches. The accelerated IASC timetable tends to heighten these natural tensions and create an even more difficult roadblock than would exist under the earlier IASC timetable.

In other cases, a given accounting practice may be deeply embedded in a country and strong emotional reactions may arise in the face of efforts to change the practice. For example, the long-standing U.K. practice of not requiring amortization of goodwill has been particularly difficult for the U.K. representatives to overcome. With only modest support from others, such intransigence can become a significant barrier to evolving an acceptable standard.

One would hope that within the IASC, some sensitivity exists that change will be agonizing for some countries. While the pace of progress seems to have been a dominant concern of the IASC over the past few months, that pace of change is nowhere near as important as the quality of the standards produced and the achievement of a relatively high degree of acceptability among participants from leading countries.

PERCEPTION OF UNDUE U.S. INFLUENCE

Another potential roadblock is the perceived similarity between the standards being developed by the IASC and the standards issued by the FASB. Representatives from many countries find it emotionally difficult, if not impossible, to sell in their countries a set of accounting standards that critics can characterize as U.S. accounting standards. Of course, the fact is that the IASC standards are no closer to U.S. standards than they are to U.K. standards, Canadian standards, or Australian standards. In each case, the IASC standards depart in some measure from existing standards in those countries.

The perceived similarity in IASC standards to U.S. standards flows from the adoption by the IASC of its conceptual framework in 1990. The concepts that make up that framework were debated within the IASC over a three- or four-year period and eventually were adopted by the IASC following the same voting pattern that applies to the adoption of individual standards. That framework, while not identical to frameworks in place in the United States, the United Kingdom, Canada, or Australia, is similar to those other frameworks in many respects. The framework places emphasis on the needs of creditors and investors, focuses on assets and liabilities, and articulates clearly the role of full and open disclosure in the financial reporting process. The similarity of the IASC conceptual framework to those of the so-called Anglo-Saxon countries made the similarity of the IASC standards to those in these countries easily predictable.

The shape of the various conceptual frameworks currently in place reflects the high importance attached both to financial transparency and corporate stewardship by those societies having such frameworks. Both financial transparency and corporate stewardship are considered vital to the efficient functioning of the capital markets in those countries. Further, experience with the evolution of accounting in those societies relying on this perspective demonstrates that reporting entities benefit from the sharp focus on accountability and openness of disclosures. Managers manage better that which they are accountable for and that which they are required to make transparent in the reporting process. Since much of the impetus for the high level of current interest in international accounting standards flows from the globalization of capital markets and the broadened base of investor interest that this creates, it is understandable that the IASC conceptual framework is closely aligned with the conceptual frameworks of countries that have experienced similar forces in their domestic markets. The perceived strengths in the financial reporting process in the various countries with well-developed capital markets is not likely to be easily surrendered in the face of similar needs on a broadened global basis.

While critics focus their attention on the similarity of IASC standards to those found in the United States, such focus appears more emotionally oriented than substantive in nature. The fact is that the foundations of the IASC conceptual framework have often not been important in the evolution of accounting standards in many countries. Since the IASC standards flow from the conceptual framework in important respects, those in countries with different (even if unarticulated) underlying concepts should have recognized early on that IASC standards were likely to differ from their domestic standards. Given all the effort that has been expended to get the IASC core of standards to its present state of development, it would be most unfortunate if progress were stalled by emotional arguments that have some residual resentment against the United States at their base. Once the IASC voted to adopt its conceptual framework, the direction of future standards should have been apparent.

Somewhat related to the perceived similarity in IASC standards to those in the Anglo-Saxon countries is the relatively wide differences in those standards as compared to those in Germany and Japan, two other very important commercial countries. Even though accounting leaders in those two countries have been well aware for several years now that the thrust of IASC standards was moving in a direction that would lead to significant differences from their domestic standards, the time interval for those countries to become acclimated to the provisions of the new standards has probably been too short to expect any acceptable degree of buy-in. While Germany has recently made a substantial adaptation of its accounting policies, at least at the government level, to those of the IASC, for consolidated financial statements, such adaptation has been slower in Japan. In each case, many business and cultural influences underlie existing policies and practices, and these influences will persist, even if on a diminishing basis, over the next generation.

UNCERTAINTY ABOUT U.S. SEC POSITION

Another potential roadblock to the acceptance of the IASC standards lies with the possible nonacceptance of IASC standards by the U.S. Securities and Exchange Commission for nondomestic companies coming to the U.S. securities markets. While political forces in the United States are bringing increasing pressure on the SEC to be more accommodating, the SEC has a powerful track record of success to support its reluctance to accept any body of standards that it believes are of insufficiently high quality to protect the interests of investors.

The New York Stock Exchange would dearly love to have the chance to attract the 200 or more multinational world-class companies not currently listed on the Exchange, and it has been lobbying for relaxation in SEC listing requirements for some time. In some respects, the challenge at this point in the United States seems to be whether the IASC can achieve completion of its core set of standards with a sufficiently high degree of quality on a sufficiently timely basis to attain acceptance by the SEC before the political forces operating within the United States effectively cause the SEC to buy into a set of standards that could impair the investor protection policies that have long governed the work of the SEC.

PROSPECTS FOR ADOPTION OF IASC STANDARDS

Given this assessment of progress to date, the existing accelerated work program, and the number of potential stumbling points, what is the prospect today for the IASC to achieve its objective of acceptance of a set of accounting standards that could be used in all countries, at least for the purposes of cross-border securities listings and other financing? My view is that the IASC efforts are highly likely to be successful as long as quality is not sacrificed for undue haste in achieving an acceptable core set of standards. In the short run, I would expect IASC standards to be used primarily by multinational companies as they pursue their financing needs in various countries. Existing domestic standards would continue to be followed by non-multinational companies within various countries, and even by multinationals when reporting locally by some countries. While this dual approach might survive briefly in some countries, such as the United States, it could persist for an extended period in other countries, such as Japan and Germany. On a longer-term basis, I would expect the IASC standards gradually to gain acceptance as the principal basis of financial reporting in most, if not all countries.

Predicting the timing of expected events is, of course, much more tenuous than predicting the events themselves. Even so, I can see the IASC completing its core set of standards and putting in place an acceptable interpretive mechanism for those standards by the end of the century. I can see the major commercial countries accepting the use of international standards as the basis for financial reporting in cross-border transactions within a few years thereafter. Wider acceptability and use of international standards on a domestic basis will vary from country to country, as noted, but over time one would expect IASC standards to predominate, particularly if they are effectively maintained. Of course, this latter development is contingent on the total package of IASC standards, the ongoing development of standards to meet changing business needs, and the effectiveness of the interpretive mechanism in producing an increasingly respected basis for financial reporting.

Assuming that the IASC continues to make progress as it has over the past decade, I would expect the SEC to approve the use of international accounting standards by registrants, whether U.S. or foreign. That acceptance will arrive, however, only when the SEC is satisfied that the international standards are of sufficiently high quality, that the disclosure requirements in those standards are adequate for U.S. investor needs, that the IASC interpretive process is working in an effective manner, and that securities regulators in other countries are diligent in meeting their regulatory responsibilities. This latter contingency is, of course, a matter for IOSCO consideration and will, no doubt, be a significant challenge for the SEC to accomplish. I would expect SEC acceptance of IASC standards to be forthcoming only after a relatively high level of satisfaction has been reached that quality standards will be interpreted consistently and administered even-handedly around the world.

This is not to say that continuing tensions will be unlikely. Countries that have lost a battle with regard to a specific accounting standard that has been very important to them are likely to resurrect the issue after passage of a few years. Any significant change in the direction of capital flows might also be a cause for concern. On the other hand, should the broader use of international standards prove to be cost effective for cross-border financing arrangements and lead to an improvement in the efficiency of the world's capital markets, as is clearly expected, any pressures for undoing the acceptability of IASC standards will diminish.

THE STRUCTURE OF THE IASC: IS A CHANGE NEEDED?

Finally, we need to consider whether the current structure of the IASC is the most effective means of delivering high quality accounting standards on a continuing basis. THe IASC meets only three or four times a year, now has as many as 50 or more people sitting at the deliberation table, and has only a skeleton staff. While the accomplishments achieved with this structure are truly remarkable, a serious question exists as to whether this structure is adequate for the future. The size of the group appears to be unwieldy, the time commitments quite heavy for volunteer standard-setters, and the currently discussed structure for the interpretive group seemingly unworkable. The means of effecting any substantial change are difficult to envision, given the desire of all existing IASC Board member countries to continue to have a voice in the process and the desire of others to play a role. One can certainly build the case that the board is already too large and its meetings too infrequent to operate effectively, but geographical representation as well as the diversity of interests involved will make any change in structure difficult to achieve.

However, after the turn of the century, we may well see a smaller board of the IASC with one or more full-time members. Such a board would almost certainly be located some place in Europe, would have a non-U.S. chairman, and conceivably could be composed largely, or exclusively, of individuals who have been active standard-setters in their own countries. The trade-offs to achieve such a structure, assuming for the moment that it is desirable, are substantial. Many would view the resulting standards as being imposed by an "outside" body and, therefore, would see no need to buy into them. The trade-off of volunteers representing specific jurisdictions for professionals carrying no particular ties to any jurisdiction always creates concerns, if not suspicions. Even so, the history of accounting standard-setting in various countries indicates that the structure currently employed is not immutable to change. And, the direction of change has been toward smaller groups of professionals and away from larger groups of volunteers. Such a move is certainly possible for the IASC, and particularly so if its current work program achieves the success that many envision, a success that I view as very likely over the next decade or so.

IASC AND FASB STANDARDS:
DO DIFFERENCES MAKE A DIFFERENCE?

Carrie Bloomer

ABSTRACT

As the IASC nears completion of its core standards project, it is time to reflect upon the impact of the potential use of IASC standards by foreign issuers in U.S. capital markets. Use of IASC standards instead of various sets of national accounting standards is likely to increase comparability of financial reporting outside the United States. If the SEC accepts use of IASC standards instead of reconciliation to U.S. GAAP, that will likely lower the cost to foreign issuers listing in the United States. However, because IASC standards differ from U.S. GAAP in many areas, their use in U.S. markets can introduce noncomparability, which increases the costs faced by investors in comparing investment opportunities. The challenge to the SEC will be assessment of the credibility and integrity of IASC standards in areas that differ from U.S. GAAP.

Research in Accounting Regulation, Supplement 1, pages 287-294.

ISBN: 0-7623-0338-7

INTRODUCTION

Few can argue that there is an intensifying demand for a single set of accounting standards to be used worldwide for cross-border capital raising. The International Organization of Securities Commissions (IOSCO) has identified the core accounting issues that an acceptable body of international accounting standards needs to cover. The International Accounting Standards Committee (IASC) has committed to a work program for developing a body of "core standards" by March 1998. Many organizations and multinational corporations are pushing for recognition of accounting standards issued by the IASC as suitable standards for cross-border filings. Because requirements for listing in U.S. capital markets are perceived to be among the most stringent, pressure is focused on the Securities and Exchange Commission (SEC) in the United States to accept IASC standards for foreign issuers. The SEC has stated that once the IASC's work program is satisfactorily completed, the SEC will consider allowing foreign issuers to use IASC standards when offering securities in the United States. Differences between IASC standards and current U.S. generally accepted accounting principles (GAAP), which are issued primarily by the Financial Accounting Standards Board (FASB), may be cause for concern because of the noncomparability that would result from acceptance of both sets of standards in the U.S. market. However, the SEC has indicated that IASC standards "need not reproduce the words of U.S. GAAP" to be acceptable but "they must yield the same results, in terms of credibility and integrity" as those produced by U.S. standards (Burkholder 1996). Thus, while it is unrealistic to expect uniformity between the accounting standards of two vastly different organizations with different available resources and different missions, it is also unrealistic to believe that differences between IASC and FASB standards will not be a consideration in the SEC's assessment of IASC standards for U.S. markets.

INTERNATIONAL ACCOUNTING STANDARDS AND THE IASC

Without international accounting standards, financial statement users are faced with the costs of understanding the similarities and differences between financial statements prepared under different national accounting standards and making adjustments in order to compare investment opportunities and make optimal investment decisions. Some of the current problems are overcome if the capital seekers reconcile financial information to the standards of the country in which they are seeking capital or if they actually prepare their financial information based on those standards. As the demand for international capital increases, it seems that capital seekers are less willing to bear the costs of those alternatives, especially if it means reconciling to or preparing financial information based on U.S. GAAP. Some of that reaction may reflect national pride, but in many cases aversion to transparency of financial information and high preparation costs are cited as the reasons. Ideally, a set of international accounting standards would solve many problems. It would cut the costs of doing business and raising capital across borders, streamline the internal accounting and auditing functions for multinationals, increase efficiency of market regulation, and decrease the costs of international financial statement analysis and investment.

For the last 20-odd years, the IASC has been developing accounting standards with the objective of working "generally for the improvement and harmonization of regulations, accounting standards and procedures relating to the presentation of financial statements" (IASC Constitution, ¶2). The IASC can be commended for its part in the effort to reduce the number of differences between national accounting standards. Even as differences between national accounting standards continue, there is perhaps greater comparability of accounting standards and the resulting financial information than ever before due to different countries adopting, adapting, or enforcing compliance with IASC standards. It would seem that the IASC has in no small part met its mission statement and objectives.

In July 1995, the IASC reached an agreement with IOSCO that if it completed a set of high-quality accounting standards that covered a number of key areas, IOSCO would consider recommending those "core standards" for endorsement by its members for cross-border filings. The IASC has committed to completing its core standards by March of 1998. Through that agreement, the IASC has propelled itself to the forefront of a debate about whether its standards can meet the demands of the world's most sophisticated markets. And it has become clear that the IASC—with the support of many would-be cross-border capital seekers and stock exchanges in the United States that stand to gain from acceptance of IASC standards—has a particular target in mind: the United States.

IASC TARGET: THE UNITED STATES

To put the debate in perspective, many who clamor about the need for acceptance of international accounting standards as a broad, global issue are motivated by a fairly self-interested and pointed objective: entry by foreign multinationals into U.S. capital markets without incurring the cost of U.S. GAAP reconciliation. After all, Sir Bryan Carsberg, the present secretary-general of the IASC, is proud to proclaim that IASC standards presently are "already accepted in virtually all the stock exchanges"[1] with the exceptions of Canada, Japan, and the United States. That alone is quite an accomplishment. But multinational companies in Germany and Switzerland, for example, are not pushing to use IASC standards as a vehicle to access the stock exchanges in Mexico, Hong Kong, or even Canada. IASC standards are ultimately of little use to them if they are not accepted in the United States, where the sources and types of capital available are more abundant than in any other market in the world. In fact, were it not for the appeal of U.S.

markets and the seemingly high hurdles to listing on, for example, the New York Stock Exchange, one could argue that there would be much less support buttressing the current momentum for international standards and bolstering the IASC's image.

The FASB has been a leader in developing accounting standards for over 20 years. The international recognition enjoyed by U.S. GAAP is an acknowledgment (albeit sometimes grudging) of the perception that FASB standards are of high quality. It is a perception supported by the success of U.S. capital markets, of which FASB standards are a fundamental element. But perceptions change. Where meeting the requirements of the U.S. SEC once was a sign of world-class integrity, a prestigious badge of merit for foreign multinationals, those requirements are now seen as some of the greatest impediments to the unencumbered flow of capital to deserving market participants. The SEC is now often characterized as a rigid sentry, guarding its precious territory and forcing its costly and burdensome requirements upon those outside U.S. borders.[2]

The SEC takes its mandate for investor protection seriously. Whether FASB or IASC standards are used, there remains a need and a desire that the accounting standards and resulting financial information used in the United States be rigorous enough to withstand the expectations and demands of U.S. investors, U.S. regulators, and the litigious U.S. environment. It is no higher an expectation than that to be met by domestic registrants.

DIFFERENCES MATTER

A simple way to gain acceptance in U.S. markets would be for the IASC to produce standards that were exactly the same as FASB standards. However, the IASC is not, and does not intend to be, a rubber-stamping organization. To do justice to its mission and membership, it has to deal with myriad different national perspectives on accounting issues and seek international consensus. As a result—and not surprisingly—there are differences between IASC standards and FASB standards. And although they need not be the same to be acceptable to the SEC, the challenge to the IASC has been concisely summed up by Arthur Levitt, chairman of the SEC, who indicated that IASC standards "must be of high quality—they must result in comparability and transparency, and they must provide for full disclosure."[3]

Measuring the quality of an accounting standard poses difficulties. As a benchmark, it must be assumed that existing FASB standards are seen by the SEC as being of acceptable quality for U.S. markets. Consequently, where IASC standards and FASB standards are the same or very similar, IASC standards should be acceptable. It is where they are different that assessing quality will be the greatest challenge. While the SEC has not indicated the methodology by which it will assess the quality of IASC standards, existing and potential differences from FASB standards likely will be a consideration. Thus, even though the IASC may be banking on the SEC's assertion that the standards need not be the same, differences between IASC standards and FASB standards do matter.

In a recently published report, the FASB staff undertook a comparative study of IASC and FASB standards.[4] The report identifies 255 areas of similarity and difference ("variations") between FASB standards and the existing IASC standards that are part of the proposed set of core standards.[5] With a primarily domestic focus, FASB standards overall tend to be fairly detailed, responding to the complexities of the U.S. economic environment and a sophisticated financial statement user demand for reliable, high-quality financial information. IASC standards, on the other hand, are not developed with a focus on any particular economic environment and, thus, tend to be more general. As a result, while there are some similarities between the standards, there also are many differences.

The mere existence of differences between accounting standards is not sufficient as a measure of the quality or merit of any particular accounting standard relative to the other. Yet, certain types of differences—if we accept the premise that FASB standards are of sufficient quality for U.S. markets—may be seen as problematic. For example, the types of differences of greatest significance in assessing quality are likely to be in those areas in which: (1) an IASC standard is based on a different underlying approach to an accounting issue (22% of the areas of variations identified in the FASB report), for example, an IASC standard requires that an item be capitalized, while the FASB counterpart requires it to be expensed; (2) an IASC standard does not provide requirements or guidance for a particular topic or class of transactions within an accounting area covered by its FASB counterpart (14% of the areas of variations identified in the FASB report);[6] and (3) an IASC standard permits a choice between two or more alternatives in accounting for a similar transaction, whereas the FASB counterpart requires use of a single method (6% of the areas of variations identified in the FASB report).

Those differences can result in differences between the financial information reported under IASC standards and that prepared under U.S. GAAP. Some of those differences are: (1) an item may be expensed as incurred under one standard but capitalized and amortized under the other (for example, development costs are capitalized under IASC standards and expensed under FASB standards); (2) a similar item may be recognized in the financial statements under one standard and not under the other (for example, some leases that meet the criteria for capitalization under FASB standards may not be capitalized under IASC standards); and (3) the value of the same item may be measured differently depending upon which standard is followed (for example, IASC standards generally permit revaluations of assets and reversals of asset write-downs, neither of which is permitted in the United States). Those types of differences in reported financial information are very significant from both a conceptual and a practical standpoint. Issues related to whether to recognize and how to measure items in the financial statements are among the most fiercely debated by standard setters. For financial statement users, the types of differences illustrated above are likely to be some of the most difficult to compensate for because the information necessary to reconcile them may not be available.

Further, although the underlying objective of using international standards is to improve comparability, acceptance of IASC standards that differ from FASB standards actually will introduce noncomparability to U.S markets. Noncomparability is an issue of concern not solely to standard-setters and financial statement users but also to financial statement preparers. At a minimum, if foreign issuers were permitted to use IASC standards that are different from FASB standards, the playing field would not be level for domestic issuers competing with foreign issuers in U.S. markets. But of greater concern is the potential for domestic companies to lobby for the use of IASC standards. Many differences between IASC standards and FASB standards reflect areas in which the IASC and the FASB came to different conclusions, and one set of standards may be perceived as more flexible than the other in terms of permitted accounting for certain items. Although the SEC has stated that the option to use IASC standards would not be available to domestic registrants, the SEC's stance on that issue may be vulnerable if foreign issuers are allowed to use different accounting methods than domestic issuers, especially if IASC standards are perceived as being less onerous or less rigorous than FASB standards.

CONCLUSION

The internationalization of capital markets is a clear and measurable phenomenon, and it challenges all nations to face and accept change. The development of international accounting standards is an important part of advancing that process. Given the need for international standards and the apparent success of the IASC, there is a natural inclination to arrive by deduction in support of IASC standards for cross-border filings on all capital markets. The conclusion, however, demands serious consideration of the implications for U.S. markets.

In the U. S. capital markets, investors, creditors, analysts, and other financial statement users demand high-quality financial information so that they may make informed resource allocation decisions, have confidence in the system, and be protected from misunderstanding, abuse, and fraud. That demand has led to a complex set of interrelationships between users, accounting standard setters, regulators, preparers, and auditors, creating a market infrastructure that has led to the development of the largest, most liquid capital markets in the world. There is a desire to maintain those characteristics, including the value added by high-quality accounting standards to the capital allocation process.

Because IASC standards and FASB standards are not identical, it is reasonable to raise conceptual and practical questions about the suitability of IASC standards for use in U.S. markets. If IASC standards are found to be of sufficient quality to be acceptable for foreign issuers in the United States even though they are different from FASB standards, their use would remove some of the cost burden that foreign firms incur to list securities in the United States. However, with the introduction of noncomparability to the U.S. markets, the costs of bridging the gap between foreign and domestic financial statements would be shifted to the financial statement user. Just as with differences between various national accounting systems, financial statement users would need to learn to make adjustments for differences between IASC standards and domestic standards.

The true test of an accounting standard is whether it satisfies the demand for information in the environment in which it is intended to be used. Empirically, the IASC's past success generally has been the result of voluntary (and sometimes selective)[7] application and enforcement and a body of standards developed to accommodate a variety of accounting techniques. By contrast, FASB standards have been developed and tested in an environment where challenge and change are the norm. Thus, while differences between IASC and FASB standards may be acceptable, the decision to allow the use of IASC standards in the United States ultimately will be based on the quality of the financial information provided under IASC standards relative to the information currently provided under FASB standards. If accepted for U.S. markets, IASC standards would need to meet the same demands.

ACKNOWLEDGEMENT

Carrie Bloomer is a member of the staff of the Financial Accounting Standards Board. The views expressed in this paper are those of Ms. Bloomer and do not represent an official position of the FASB. Official positions of the FASB are developed only after extensive due process and deliberation.

NOTES

1. From IASC Home Page @ http://www.iasc.org.uk
2. In fact, the SEC has made a number of accommodations to foreign issuers to ease the requirements for listing on U.S. markets. For example, the SEC already accepts aspects of certain IASC standards that are not the same as FASB standards: IAS 7, "Cash Flow Statements;" IAS 21, "The Effects of Changes in Foreign Exchange Rates;" IAS 22, "Business Combinations;" and IAS 29, "Financial Reporting in Hyperinflationary Economies."
3. U.S. Securities and Exchange Commission Press Release 96-61, April 11, 1996.
4. The report, *The IASC-U.S. Comparison Project: A Report on the Similarities and Differences between IASC Standards and U.S. GAAP,* is available from the FASB Order Department, 401 Merritt 7, P.O. Box 5116, Norwalk, CT 06856-5116.
5. The IASC continues to work on its standards and plans to issue many new and revised standards. In any case, the FASB report covers 24 existing IASC standards, five of which are scheduled to be replaced as part of the IASC's work program and, therefore, were not included in arriving at the 255 identified variations. Four other IASC standards covered in the report are expected to receive only minor revisions, and the rest are expected to be presented to IOSCO in their present form. Therefore,

of the 255 variations identified in the FASB report, the vast majority will remain after the IASC's work plan is complete.

6. The 14% of variations of this type quantifies only those "core areas" identified by IOSCO for which an IASC standard exists. It does not include the many areas outside the core areas or where comparison to a FASB standard is not possible because there is no counterpart IASC standard—for example, specialized industry standards (such as insurance, financial, and rate-regulated enterprises) and specialized transactions (such as futures contracts and hedging, troubled debt restructuring, and employee stock compensation).

7. See, for example, the survey on financial reporting in Switzerland in *World Accounting Report*, March 1997, in which David Cairns and financial analysts look at Swiss financial reporting and how major companies apply IASC standards.

REFERENCE

Burkholder, Steve. 1996. SEC's Levitt sees continued role for FASB even if global standards adopted. *Securities Regulation & Law Report* 28(48): 1530-31.

International Accounting Standards Committee. 1997. IASC Constitution. In *International Accounting Standards* 1977 17-22. London: IASC.

THE DEVELOPMENT OF THE ACCOUNTING PROFESSION IN CHINA

Yunwei Tang

THE HISTORY OF THE ACCOUNTING PROFESSION IN CHINA

The development of the accounting profession in China can be divided into several periods: (1) the development before the founding of the People's Republic of China, (2) the period after the founding of PRC, and (3) the revival of the public accounting profession.

After the First World War, foreign capitalists came in succession to China to seek investment opportunity. National industry and commerce experienced a period of quick development. This era saw the appearance of some limited liability companies in which managers were separated from investors. During this period, some foreign CPAs came to China and started public accounting service. For example, Deloitte Haskins & Sells, Price Waterhouse, and similar firms set up branches to develop their business in Shanghai in this very early period. The then-Beijing government issued "Provisional Rules for Accountants" in 1918. First

Research in Accounting Regulation, Supplement 1, pages 295-312.

ISBN: 0-7623-0338-7

Chinese CPA designation was born soon after. The development of the accounting profession is reflected in the following laws and regulations:

- The "Rules of Certification for Accountants" was issued in 1928;
- The "Regulation for Accountants" was promulgated in 1930; and
- The "Law of Accountants" was enacted in 1945.

These rules, regulations, and laws stipulated the required qualifications, scope of services, responsibilities, and ethics of CPAs.

During this period, there were some famous CPA firms in China, such as the Zhengze CPA Firm, Xu Yong-zuo CPA Firm, Li Xing CPA Firm, and Gong Xing CPA Firm. These four CPA firms were called the "Big Four" in China. Le Xing CPA Firm (Xu-lun Pan) was well-known in Hong Kong, Singapore, the Philippines, and Macao. It had headquarters in Shanghai and branches all over the country.

For the purpose of promoting the CPA system, the Shanghai Association of Accountants was founded in 1925. Some local associations were founded successively. The Chinese Federation of Accountants was founded in 1946. In this period, the accounting profession developed steadily (Table 1).

At the beginning of the PRC (1949), the new government adopted a policy to provide support and guide the development of private enterprises. CPAs continued to render their services, check the accounts of private enterprises, present audit reports to boards of directors and other concerned parties, and handle other business affairs. From 1953, the government began to change private ownership into socialist public ownership. In the long period after that, China experienced a unique model of a planned economy. CPA firms, which are closely related to the market economy, lost ground and gradually disappeared from the economic society of China.

In 1979, the government promulgated the "Law of Joint Ventures in the People's Republic of China." This stipulated that the paid-in capital of all parties of joint ventures must be verified and that the annual financial statements and liquidation

Table 1.

YEAR	*THE NUMBER OF CPAS*
1918-1921	13
1922-1924	101
1925-1927	171
1927-1929	268
1929-1930	184
1931-1937	1,036
1938-1947	1,583

Table 2.

stage	period	CPA	CPA firm
re-establishment stage	1981-1986	500	80
initial stage	1986-1988.11	3,000	250
developing stage	1988-1993.10.31	10,733	700
leaping stage	1994.12.31	25,000	1,000
	1995.12.31	26,760	2,260
	1995.12.31	30,000 (auditor)	3,700 (auditor firms)

accounting statement of joint ventures would be valid only after being attested and verified by Chinese CPAs and after presenting certificates (Article 90, Executive Regulation). The "Detailed Rules and Regulations of the Law of Joint Ventures in the PRC," issued in December of 1980, also stipulated that the auditing reports made by CPAs registered in China would be required when they submitted tax returns and financial statements to the local taxation agencies (Article 20). The initiation of foreign investment enterprises and related requirements of the laws and regulations impelled the reestablishment of the CPA system in China. The first CPA firm established in Shanghai in 1981 signaled the start of a new era for the Chinese public accounting profession.

Soon afterwards, CPA firms mushroomed all over the country, and the Chinese CPA system began to develop step by step. The development of the accounting profession in this period is shown in Table 2.

In 1986, the State Council issued the "Regulations of the People's Republic of China on Certified Public Accountants" (RCPA), which prescribed the examination, registration, scope of services, rules of work, and establishment of CPA firms. There were two methods to obtain CPA qualification—examination and evaluation. In fact, people obtainned the certificate of CPA only through evaluation in the early stage because the unified CPA examination was not offered until as late as 1991. Practical experience and education are considered when finance bureaus issue certificates. Most of the CPAs thus approved were elderly senior accountants who had practical experience in public accounting service a long time ago. The issuance of the Regulation of People's Republic of China on Certified Public Accountants promoted the CPA system of the PRC, and a unified CPA examination started soon afterwards.

The establishment of the Chinese Institute of Certified Public Accountants (CICPA) in 1988 was a landmark event in the development of the CPA profession in China.

In 1993, the People's Congress approved and promulgated the "Law of Certified Public Accountants" (LCPA). CPAs as a profession gained deserved social status. The LCPA prescribed the examination and registration, scope of services, rules for CPA firms, the institute of CPAs, their legal duties, and so forth. It came into effect on January 1, 1994. It also prescribed that a candidate for CPA status must pass the

Table 3.

Year	CPA	Staff
2000	100,000	300,000
2010	300,000	1,000,000

national unified examination to obtain the CPA qualification. The adoption of the LCPA indicates that independent auditing is going to play an important role in China. The Leader of the State Council drew an ambitious blueprint for the CPA profession in China, shown in Table 3.

THE ORGANIZATIONAL STRUCTURE OF THE ACCOUNTING PROFESSION

The Ministry of Finance

The accounting profession in China is, to a certain extent, different from those in Western countries. According to the Law of Certified Public Accountants, the Ministry of Finance and local finance bureaus have the authority to supervise and guide certified public accountants, accounting firms, and institutes of CPAs.

The Chinese Institute of Certified Public Accountants

It is obvious that the finance authorities play an important role in the development of the accounting profession. The Chinese Institute of Certified Public Accountants is a semi-official organization under the close supervision of the MOF and has the delegated authority to self-regulate CPAs and CPA firms. The national institute is responsible for the self-regulation of CPA firms all over the country and for setting up auditing standards and by-laws. It was given the authority to organize the unified CPA examination. On behalf of the Ministry of Finance, it is responsible for the inspection of CPAs and CPA firms that are approved by local institutes, while the local institutes are responsible for the self-regulation of local CPA firms. Local finance bureaus approve CPAs and CPA firms.

There are eleven divisions in the CICPA. The major divisions are:

- *Division of Registration:* handles the registration affairs of CPAs and CPA firms (including branches), approves the appointment of CPA firms by listed companies, and approves CPAs' transfers among firms.
- *Divison of Standards:* responsible for setting up independent auditing standards and professional ethics, and for continuing education program and control of quality standards;
- *Division of Examination:* organizes nation-wide professional examinations.

- *Division of Training:* organizes professional training. Three training centers are going to be established in Beijing, Shanghai, and Guangdong.
- *Division of Field Work Supervision:* responsible for the annual review of CPAs and CPA firms and regular audit work to discipline the profession.
- *Division of Foreign Cooperation:* liaises with overseas professional accountancy bodies, such as AICPA (U.S.), ACCA (U.K.), CGA (Canada), ASCPA (Australia), and the Big Six, and organizes cooperative training with these organizations.

Accounting Firms

Accounting firms are members of the CICPA. Like CPA firms in Western countries, they are obliged to observe the charter of the institute and abide by the requirements of self-regulation and restrictions of the institute. The institute supports the legitimate activities of CPAs and CPA firms and protects their lawful interests.

A unique feature of the Chinese accounting profession is that many of the accounting firms were initiated by government organizations and other institutions and, thus, are financially related to them. This feature has been criticized for compromising the independence of CPA firms.

Certified Public Accountants

The qualification of certified public accountant is awarded through an examination or evaluation system, as described below.

Examination

A college graduate or a person with equivalent academic education who has worked in the field of accounting and auditing for three years may apply to take the professional examination. Currently, the subjects examined are financial accounting, auditing, managerial finance, taxation, and business law. When all requirements have been met, the candidate can request his or her employing firm to report to the MOF or the provincial finance bureau for approval and registration. If a CPA is approved for registration by the provincial finance bureau, the burueau reports this to the MOF for recording purpose. The MOF will prepare and issue a uniform CPA certificate.

Evaluation

The following persons may be exempted from examination if evaluation shows that they meet the required standard:

- Persons who are senior accountants, professors or associate professors of accounting, research fellows or associate fellows, and have some practical experience; or
- Persons who have a college or equivalent academic education or equivalent academic ability, and have pursued a financial or accounting career for over 20 years and have professional accounting expertise.

China started its first uniform CPA examination in 1991. In the following four years, over 400,000 candidates took the examination. More than 10,000 passed all the required subjects. The results of the uniform national examination in 1995 are shown in Table 4. Only 2.19% of the participants passed all the subjects at the same time. The intention of CICPA to control the quality of CPA is obvious. Starting in 1994, China permitted foreigners to take the Chinese CPA examination. So far, over 2,500 people from more than 10 countries and regions have participated. The results of foreigners who took the Chinese CPA examination in 1995 are shown below in Table 5.

Chinese CPAs cannot render service individually. A CPA must be a member of a CPA firm, and all services must be performed in the name of the CPA firm. If a CPA is negligent in his or her professional conduct, the finance bureau that approved the registration shall cancel it and revoke the CPA certificate and report to the MOF for recording. If a CPA violates the rules of work, resulting in serious consequences, the CPA firm is responsible for making an accurate report, and the finance bureau in charge imposes sanctions on the accountant, according to the seriousness of the case, that range from a warning or a fine to suspension from practice and revocation of the CPA certificate. A CPA who violates the criminal law is to be committed to the judicial authority for punishment according to the law.

These relations are depicted below:

The Ministry of Finance → CICPA → CPA Firms → CPAs

Table 4.

Subjects	*Number of persons sitting examination*	*Number of persons passing examination*	*Passing rate %*
Accounting	104,608	12,617	12.06
Auditing	64,773	6,834	10.55
Managerial Finance	83,265	9,697	11.65
Economic Law	76,215	13,619	17.87
Taxation	92,082	12,928	14.04
All of above subjects	35,176	772	2.19

Table 5.

Subjects	*Number of persons sitting examination*	*Number of persons passing examination*	*Passing rate %*
Accounting	1,222	334	27.33
Auditing	1,119	172	15.37
Managerial Finance	1,140	271	23.77
Economic Law	1,192	83	6.96
Taxation	1,192	118	9.90
All of above subjects	820	41	5.00

ISSUES AND PROBLEMS

At present, the number of CPAs has reached 55,000, not counting another 50,000 nonpracticing CPAs. The number of CPA firms has reached 7,000 (including audit firms, which were originally under the supervision of the State Audit Administration). The auditing service covered joint stock companies, joint ventures with foreign investment, and some state enterprises and private enterprises. The 1994 revenue of accounting firms exceeded one billion Yuan for the first time in the history. The average size and revenue per firm is very low.

Several difficulties have been identified by the Ministry of Finance regarding the development of the accounting profession in China. The CPA profession, both in the number of CPA firms and CPAs and in the quality of its service, can hardly satisfy the demand of an open socialist market economy. According to the plan of the Ministry of Finance, the number of CPAs should be increased to 100,000, and the total of practicing and nonpracticing CPAs should reach 200,000 by the end of the century. By then, there will be enough auditors to provide coverage for the majority of enterprises, as shown in Table 6.

A complete legal system has not yet been established. Security law, commercial bank law, and other relevant laws are yet to be written. The existing laws and regulations are not completely compatible with each other. More directly, the legal responsibility of CPAs has not been prescribed explicitly in the law. These shortcomings have created some difficulties in the development of the Chinese accounting profession.

The quality of CPAs must be improved. The common body of knowledge as presented in the subjects covered by the CPA examination is under development. A high percentage of CPAs were recognized through evaluation before the CPA examination started in 1991. Most of them are elderly and are not familiar with modern auditing concepts and techniques. Great efforts must be made to bring them up to a level compatible to their duties.

The internal management of most CPA firms is, generally speaking, rather weak. Except for a few major accounting firms, quality control does not usually exist within the firms. Unethical competition is not uncommon among these firms.

Table 6.

Enterprises with foreign investment	100% (70 currently)
State enterprises	80% (50% currently)
Other enterprises	50%

Note: Unusual measures must be adopted to train above mentioned CPAs.

The CICPA and its local branches have begun to check the quality of their service. To build a modern profession seems not to be an easy job and will take some time.

The external environment, especially government interference, impairs the independence of CPAs and their firms. At present, the majority of CPA firms in China are subordinated to government organizations such as tax authorities and financial bureaus, and many others are attached to line industries. Markets for the public accounting service are dominated by protectionism, and the existence of financial relationships between CPA firms and their clients is observable. Efforts against professional monopoly have been made to restore confidence of the public on auditors' credibility.

Relevant regulations have been announced to allow the establishment of CPA firms on a partnership basis. Recently, joint venture CPA firms between the Big Six international accounting firms and their Chinese counterparts were formed, and this is regarded as an important step toward enhancing the independence and quality of CPAs in China.

Accounting Standards

China does not yet have a complete set of accounting standards. Business accounting was in the past regulated by the MOF through a uniform accounting system. Large amounts of foreign investment introduced under the country's open policy and the establishment of a CPA profession have encouraged China to set accounting standards. This mission was taken up by the MOF, with input from the accounting profession and academics. A basic accounting standard was issued in 1993, and an exposure draft of around 30 detailed accounting standards has been widely circulated and is waiting final approval by the MOF.

Internationalization of Accounting Practice

From the outset of standard-setting, the MOF held an open attitude by encouraging the adoption of internationally recognized accounting practice. This is seen from the following aspects:

International accounting standards have been introduced gradually and firmly. With the acceptance of Chinese accountants in mind, the MOF first introduced some accounting concepts and practices recognized internationally into joint venture accounting regulation. The regulation departed from the traditional fund-based accounting approach and established the concept of accounting elements such as assets, liabilities, capital, revenue, and expenses. The concept of financial statements—that is, the balance sheet, the income statement, and the statement of changes in financial position—were adopted. The principles of historical cost, matching, consistency, and the distinction between revenue expenditure and capital expenditure were explicitly required.

In the second stage, the MOF introduced international accounting standards for domestic joint stock companies. In addition to those that are adopted in joint venture accounting regulation, the accounting practice related to stockholder's equity and other important concepts were also adopted.

After a period of digestion, Chinese accountants have gradually become familiar with international accounting practice. The MOF started a movement to set up accounting standards uniformly applicable to all kinds of enterprises. The internalization of accounting practice is still one of the main objectives of accounting reform and development.

Advice has been sought from the international accounting community. Within the Department of Administration of Accounting Affairs, a department of the MOF, an accounting standard-setting group was formed. Soon after, one of the Big Six international accounting firms, Deloitte Touche Tohmatsu, was appointed as a consultant. Accounting standards of different countries and their experiences in setting standards were introduced by Deloitte Touche Tohmatsu representatives to serve as references. Moreover, when the general standard and detailed standards were drafted, foreign experts including those from International Accounting Standards Committee and international accounting firms were invited to give their opinions. These opinions are being seriously considered during the revision course.

Attempt to form a framework. When China began its accounting standard-setting, the experiences of other countries, especially United States, in developing a conceptual framework were studied. American accounting standards have evolved for many years, and it was finally decided to develop a theoretical foundation of interrelated objectives and concepts that would lead to the establishment of consistent financial accounting standards. Despite its late start, China tried very hard to make use of this treasurable experience and started with a basic accounting standard, called the Accounting Standard for Enterprises. In this standard, basic accounting assumptions are addressed, users of financial accounting information are identified, and quality requirements of accounting information and general accounting principles are elaborated. Definitions are given to all accounting elements. Measurement and reporting issues are dealt with. This standard is expected to serve as the foundation on which detailed accounting standards can be developed.

The efforts of the Chinese accounting standard-setting body is praiseworthy. However, what it has provided is not in any real sense a framework. Some of the definitions are not stringent; inconsistency exists; logic is not always clear. One reason for this is that China has not much practical experience in this field. Many accounting concepts and practices are new to Chinese accountants and new to the members of the standard-setting group. Thorough understanding can hardly be reached without sufficient practical experience. A more important reason is that the theoretical research in China has not been designed to help develop a well-organized framework. Despite the framework's prematurity, it has made some contribution to the development of accounting standards. Besides, it is subject to review and, in due course, improvement is expected.

Impact of the social and economic environment. The adoption of international accounting practice resulted in great changes in accounting in China. Nevertheless, the social and economic environment in which accounting operates is different in China. Market mechanisms are still under construction. Laws and regulations which have accounting implications have not been completed. The development of a securities market is in its early stage. All these have a great impact on the formation of accounting standards in China.

Independent Auditing Standards

In 1994, the Chinese Institute of Certified Public Accountants (CICPA) was authorized by the Ministry of Finance to draft the Independent Auditing Standards. According to the Accounting Law, it will be approved and promulgated by the Ministry of Finance. An auditing standards drafting group was formed with representatives from the CICPA, major accounting firms, and academics.

In order to secure the quality of the drafted auditing standards, two advisory groups were formed. The Chinese advisory group consists of officials of relevant government departments and experts from accounting firms and universities. The external advisory group consists of representatives from accounting professional bodies of other countries, international accounting firms, and academics.

According to the CICPA's overall plan, Chinese auditing standards will contain three levels.

The first level is the basic auditing standard, which contains the basic requirements for certified public accountants and the basic rules of practice. The basic auditing standard serves as a base on which specific auditing standards, the practice bulletin, and performance guidelines are built.

The second level is specific auditing standards and audit practice bulletins. The specific auditing standards are related to audit field work and audit report, while the audit practice bulletins are specifically prepared for particular industries or for audits with a special purpose or of a special nature.

The third level is performance guidelines. These are prepared based on basic auditing standards, specific auditing standards, and practice bulletins and are intended to provide more detail and more specific operational guidance to audit work.

The following steps are followed by the CICPA in formulating auditing standards.

1. *Selection of topics.* Alternative topics are put forward first by the auditing standards group; then advice is sought from the advisory groups and other sources. Topics are approved by the Ministry of Finance before the standards group embarks on the drafting work.
2. *Drafting.* The auditing standard group drafts the standards based on research and investigation. Revision is made after listening to the opinion of advisory groups and others. An exposure draft is then submitted to the Ministry of Finance.
3. *Solicitation of comments.* The exposure draft is issued by the Ministry of Finance. It is circulated widely among local institutes of CPA, accounting firms, universities, and research institutes for comments.
4. *Final revision.* The auditing standards group, after considering the comments from public and advice from domestic and external advisory groups, makes the final revisions.
5. *Promulgation.* The Ministry of Finance approves and promulgates the standards.

During the preparation of auditing standards, internationally recognized standards from a few other countries were considered. This was so particularly for the basic auditing standard, which is divided into three components: general standards, field standards, and reporting standards. Specific auditing standards are planned for issues such as engagement letters, audit planning, audit sampling, audit evidence, working papers, and so forth, The basic auditing standard and first seven specific auditing standards were issued in December of 1995 and became operative from January 1, 1996. The other eight specific auditing standards are under final revision and are due to be promulgated by the end of 1997, according to the plan of the Ministry of Finance.

Several characteristics can be identified in the auditing standards passed so far. The objective of independent audit is to issue an opinion on legitimacy, fairness of financial statements, and consistency of accounting treatments. Legitimacy means that the preparation of financial statements must be in compliance with all regulations prescribed by the state concerning the financial statements and accounting standards.

The legal responsibilities of auditors are not defined clearly. According to the drafted audit standards, the responsibility of the auditor is to establish a complete internal control system, to protect the safety and integrity of assets, and to ensure the truthfulness, legality, and completeness of accounting information. It is the responsibility of the auditors to ensure the truthfulness and legitimacy of audit reports.

Truthfulness of audit reports means the audit report must reflect truly the audit scope, the audit basis, and the audit procedures followed and must be appropriate as the situation indicates. Legitimacy means the preparation of audit reports must be in compliance with the Law of Certified Public Accountants and the independent auditing standards.

The other indication of auditors' responsibility is that the audit opinion must reasonably assure the reliability of audited financial reports. Uncovering irregularity and management fraud are not mentioned in the auditing standards.

The auditing standards reflect the environment of the transition period toward a market economy. In the standard auditing report, the consistency of accounting treatments of auditors must be disclosed. According to international practices, this is no longer the case because "fair representation" contains the requirement of consistency and it is deemed not necessary to state separately. The situation in China, however, is different. State enterprises originally run by the government are now gaining autonomous power. Many of them are still under reconstruction, and some of them are seeking joint venture partners. Still others are issuing shares and changing into joint stock companies. With such drastic changes, the consistency of accounting treatments is a major concern of investors and the government. The preparers of auditing standards are aware of the current development of economy and have taken into consideration the current economic environment. They are trying to make the auditing standards more responsive to the economic reality.

A similar situation can be seen in other parts of the standards, which indicate in a number of places that special concern must be given to subsequent events, contingency, going concern, and so on. These are concepts that did not exist in the past or were neglected by many accountants. They are now considered to be very important in providing relevant information and are being given special attention.

Another unique feature of Chinese auditing standards is the verification of capital investment. Ownership structure is changing and will be changing for a fairly long time to come in China. State ownership in many places is being changed into the equity of joint ventures and shares of joint stock companies. There are cases where the managers of state enterprises are so eager to reach a joint venture agreement and raise the funds through issuing shares, that they are willing to devalue the enterprise's assets to make the deal. This has caused tremendous losses of state assets. On the other hand, investments from foreign partners have been found to be unchecked. Some of the invested capital is in the form of machinery and equipment, much of which has been found to be outdated or to have an overstated value. In other cases, the registered capital was found never to have been received. In order to protect the rights of enterprises as legal entities as well as state ownership, a special practice bulletin was designed called "Capital Verification" which elaborates on the procedures of capital verification, bases of measurement, and form of capital verification report.

Generally speaking, the coming auditing standards have adopted most of the content and format of international prevailing standards. Compared with current Chinese accounting standards, which are also under final revision, foreigners could find the new standards more familiar and easier to understand. Their successful promulgation and implementation will not only improve greatly communication with investors from abroad and at home but also increase the reliability of accounting information provided by Chinese enterprises.

Joint Venture Accounting Firms

International public accounting firms have taken a positive attitude toward developing business in China since the revival of the CPA system. In the early 1980s, all the Big Six firms established representative offices in the major cities of China. According to the regulations, statutory audits for Sino-foreign joint ventures and wholly foreign-owed enterprises are performed by Chinese CPAs. The representative offices are only allowed to provide consulting services in accounting and taxation to their overseas clients who invest or do business in China. The services provided to domestic enterprises are limited to information concerning foreign investors, international taxation, and training.

China opened its accounting market in early the 1990s to a certain extent. International accounting firms are allowed to form joint venture accounting firms with local CPA firms in order to provide statutory audits. The six largest international accounting firms quickly responded to the new opportunity and found partners in Beijing and Shanghai. Joint venture firms are accepted as group members of CICPA and are subject to the supervision of the MOF or its authorized local finance bureaus.

According to current regulation, international accounting firms cannot provide statutory audits in their own names or in the names of representative offices. In case the foreign investor of a joint venture requests a foreign CPA firm to audit the financial statements, all costs incurred are borne by the foreign investors.

Joint venture accounting firms are playing a very important role in auditing Sino-foreign joint venture and foreign companies, especially multinational giants. Auditing related to initial public offering is another important service they are providing. Three types of shares are currently issued by Chinese enterprises: "A" shares, which are denominated in Yuan and held only by Chinese nationals; "B" shares, which are denominated in U.S. dollars in Shanghai, and in Hong Kong dollars in Shenzhen, and are intended for foreign investors only; and other kinds of shares which are listed on foreign exchanges—"H" shares listed on the Stock Exchange of Hong Kong and "N" shares listed on the New York Stock Exchange, all of which are sold to foreign investors. Because "B" shares are listed in Chinese securities exchanges, the financial statements of their issuers should be audited by

Chinese CPA firms. If the overseas underwriter requests the financial report be audited by foreign CPA firms, the underwriter should pay for it, and the audit report is only valid abroad. For overseas listing, foreign securities exchanges usually require international accounting firms to do the audit, and they sign the audit report accordingly.

All Big Six joint venture accounting firms observe the standards applicable worldwide. Quality of service has been secured to a satisfactory extent. To avoid duplication of efforts in the case a company issues both "A" shares and "B" shares, joint venture firms, after completing the audit, may issue two audit reports, one for the international community in the name of the international firm, another for domestic use in the name of the joint venture firm.

The participation of international accounting firms exerts great influence in the development of the accounting profession in China. First, they bring in expertise in international accounting practice, which then spreads within the Chinese accounting profession. Second, they bring in well-developed professionalism, which is badly needed in China. Third, they bring in modern auditing techniques and internal management systems for accounting firms. Last but not the least, they have trained large numbers of Chinese accountants. All joint accounting firms follow the policy of localization, and a new generation of CPAs who are up to the international standard is being fostered.

A recent development has been for the MOF to encourage well-known international accounting firms to develop their member firms in different cities. The prerequisition is that the local firms they incorporated must first be changed into a real partnerships. This notion may create positive results in the sense that China is going to open more widely its accounting market to international community, and partnerships will become a predominant form of accounting firm.

EDUCATION AND TRAINING

CPA Courses in Universities

To speed up the provision of qualified CPAs, universities have begun to set up CPA specialization in the undergraduate accountancy programs. A set of textbooks has been specifically deigned to prepare the students to become professional accountants. These courses are:

- Intermediate Financial Accounting,
- Advanced Financial Accounting,
- Financial Management,
- Cost and Management Accounting,
- Auditing,
- Management,

- Taxation,
- Economic Law, and
- Computing and Computer Audit.

These courses use substantial Western textbook contents, particularly in subjects such as auditing, computerized accounting, and auditing.

Training Programs Provided by International Accounting Professionals and Accounting Bodies

Another aspect of the development of the accounting profession is the participation by international accounting firms and other accounting professional bodies.

Table 7. Training Programs Organized by International Accounting Firms for Chinese CPAs

Program	*Organizing Firm*	*Content*
Chief Accountant Training Course	Coopers & Lybrand KPMG Peat Marwick	CPA Firm-organization, staffing and recruitment, internal quality control system; preparation of working paper; risk avoidance measurement; promotion and audit strategy; requirements of CPA by administering institutes; CPAs responsibility and code of conduct; management of a CPA firm.
Audit of listing companies training course	Price Waterhouse Deloitte Touche Tohmatsu	Annual reports and disclosure requirements of listed companies; CPA's audit responsibility; comparative study of IAS and China's accounting standards; Difference in stock valuations, accounts receivable, fixed assets and investment arising due to application of different accounting standards; audit risk assessment and its impact on the audit scope; consolidated financial statements; accounting for associated companies; disclosure of accounting policies; contingent liabilities and post-balance sheet events; audit planning; audit sampling.
CPA training course	Arthur Andersen BDO Ernst & Young	Principles of accounting and financial statement analysis; principles of audit; interview technique; audit of financial statements; audit evidence and working paper; professional ethics and legal responsibility; special audit reports; audit planning; audit sampling.

During the years 1991 and 1992, all Big Six international accounting firms formed joint venture accounting firms with local counterparts. They not only brought to China accounting expertise in international accounting standards and auditing standards, but they also adopted a policy to localize their staffs. Some of the Big Six accounting firms established training centers in China to train their local personnel. Furthermore, in answering the requirement of the Chinese Institute of Certified Public Accountants, international accounting firms have provided numerous accounting training programs to Chinese public accountants. Major training programs conducted in 1994 are listed in Table 7.

As can be seen from the table, it is evident that these training programs have covered various aspects and catered for different levels of audit work. Experienced partners and senior managers of these CPA firms participated in conducting these training courses and compiling training materials. These programs were well received. Chinese CPAs, especially high- ranking officials of Chinese accounting firms, have started to apply what they have learned to their work. Internationally recognized accounting and auditing practices have spread widely throughout China.

Training Courses for Professional Examinations of International Accountancy Professional Organizations

In order to train Chinese professional accountants who understand international practices, the MOF, the Ministry of Foreign Trade and Economic Cooperation, and the State Audit Administration started in 1990 to work with the Chartered Association of Certified Accountants (ACCA) to organize courses for candidates taking the ACCA's professional examination. The ACCA formally established a training center in the SUFE in 1993. Spurred by the success of SUFE's training center, a number of training centers were established thereafter in other universities. The numbers of participants are shown in Table 8. The training program adopts teaching materials supplied by the ACCA. It has achieved great results, as evidenced by the results of participants who have taken the ACCA examinations, shown in Table 9.

In a similar way, the Canadian General Accountants (CGA) have also established training centers in China. The Chinese candidates outperformed candidates from the rest of the world in the CGA examinations. Some Chinese universities have even incorporated the materials provided by ACCA and CGA into their regular undergraduate programs.

CONCLUSION

After an interruption lasting more than 30 years, the public accounting profession re-emerged in China in the 1980s along with the economic reform and develop-

Table 8.

University	*Beijing*	*Tian-jing*	*Shang-hai*	*Wuhan*	*Guang-zhou*	*Shenz hen*	*Dalian.*	*Nan-jing*
The Chinese Association of International Exchange of Personnel	49							
SUFE			203					
Tianjing College of Finance & Economics		51						
Chung-Nan University of Finance & Economics				104				
Jinan University					75-100			
People's University of China	To be confirmed							
North East University of Finance & Economics							To be confirmed	
Nanjing audit College								To be confirmed
Motorola		30						
BDO	17							
Unilever			9					

ment of market economy. Despite its very late start, the profession is developing rapidly. Like any young profession, it faces numerous problems and difficulties.

The legal system in general is under construction in China. Some laws and regulations relevant to accounting practice, such as security law, are still absent. The legal liability of CPAs has not been defined explicitly. Interference by government organization impairs the independence of CPAs and CPA firms, especially when accounting firms are attached to such organizations.

Since a great number of CPAs were registered before CICPA started its uniform examination, their education and practical experience vary significantly, and many of them are not up to the standard of a qualified CPA. Reeducation and training is imperative in order to raise the standard of the accounting profession.

Accounting standards and auditing standards are the bases on which the accounting profession are built. They came very late in China. It is good, though,

Table 9.

Class	*Examination date*	*Examination paper*	*Worldwide passing rate*	*SUFE passing rate*
1993	Dec '93	Financial Accounting	34%	90%
		Cost Accounting	46%	95%
	June '94	Information Analysis	48%	71%
		Audit Framework	36%	75%
	Dec '94	Tax Framework	43%	94%
		Managerial Finance	42%	93%
1994	Dec '94	Accounting Framework	39%	72%
		Management Information	50%	96%

that since from the very beginning, the accounting regulatory body and accounting profession have accepted internationally recognized accounting and auditing practices and incorporated them into two local standards to a great extent. The implementation of the two standards will take some time, considering the current standard of Chinese accountants.

The participation of international accounting firms in public accounting service has created a condition favorable to the development of the Chinese accounting profession. Their experience is shared by domestic firms. They are making a contribution to the development of China's accounting and auditing standards. Their well-organized training programs are provided not only to joint venture firms but also to Chinese firms. In return, the Chinese government decided to open its market more widely to foreign firms. The internationalization of the Chinese accounting profession can be expected as a result.

CHINA'S ACCOUNTING REFORM PROJECT:
DEVELOPING DETAILED ACCOUNTING STANDARDS

Anne J. Rich, Richard M. Goligoski, and Gu Liang Tang

ABSTRACT

China culminated the first stage of its accounting reforms by issuing a conceptual framework titled Accounting Standards for Business Enterprises (ASBE) in November 1992. Accounting journals and other Chinese publications already provide several overviews of China's conceptual framework for accounting and the underlying rationale for its publication. The second step in the accounting reform project is the creation of detailed accounting standards. To date, China has developed 28 exposure drafts and issue one standard. This paper summarizes the accounting reform project and the process used by the Chinese Ministry of Finance to generate detailed accounting standards. In addition, this paper provides a summary of each of the standards currently proposed. If all of the standards are implemented and enforced, Chinese financial statements will look very much like those of the industrialized countries. However, the process has assured that China will have maintained its independent thought and its responsiveness to China's unique needs.

Research in Accounting Regulation, Supplement 1, pages 313-329.

ISBN: 0-7623-0338-7

INTRODUCTION

In the last two decades, the Chinese government's policy of economic reform has opened its markets and encouraged foreign investment. To support this change in economic policy, the government implemented major changes in the People's Republic of China's (hereafter, China) legal and accounting systems. The transformation of the accounting system, from a fund accounting orientation to an accrual-based financial reporting system, requires substantial thought. Chinese accountants researched international accounting concepts and many of these accounting concepts are integrated into the new Chinese accounting standards. As a result of the accounting reform project, Chinese accounting systems are experiencing great change.

The reform of its financial accounting standards is actually only a small part of a much larger reform project. Eventually, China will modify the entire accounting system, including government and not-for-profit organizations. However, recent attention has been directed at bringing Chinese financial reporting standards for

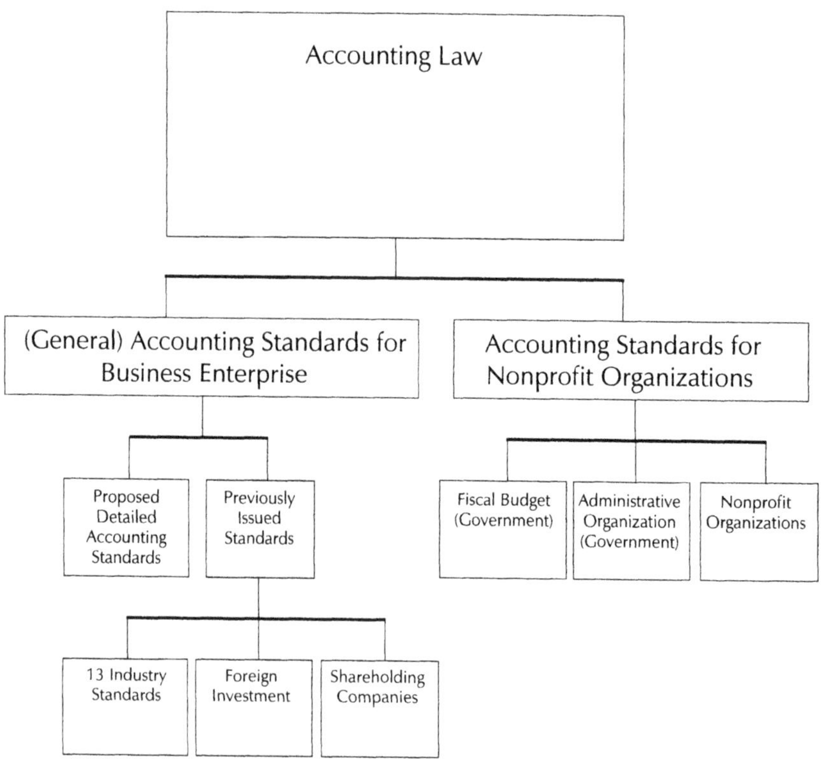

Figure 1. The PRC's Accounting Reform Project

business enterprises in line with international standards and developing the profession of public accounting. An overview of China's accounting reform project is presented in Figure 1. China successfully implemented the first steps in the accounting reform project with the issuance of its conceptual framework, "Accounting Standards for Business Enterprises" (ASBE), in November 1992. Winkle, Huss, and XiZhu (1994), Xiao et al. (1995) and Davidson, Felardi, and Li (1996) provide an overview of China's conceptual framework for accounting and the underlying rationale for its publication. The conceptual framework is just the foundation for significant changes in financial reporting standards. Recently, the Ministry of Finance drafted detailed accounting standards. Rarely do accountants and others interested in financial reporting have an opportunity to watch a very large nation completely revise its accounting standards in a relatively short period of time. The process used by the Ministry, as well as an overview of the standards, is summarized in this paper.

THE PROCESS OF DEVELOPING DETAILED ACCOUNTING STANDARDS

In China, the Ministry of Finance is responsible for issuing standards related to financial reporting. The task was assigned to Madam Feng Shuping, Director of the Department of Accounting of the Chinese Ministry of Finance. Chen YuGui headed the group that researched and wrote the standards. Until recently, Deloitte Touche Tohmatsu International, under funding from the World Bank, provided consulting support to the Ministry. The consulting firm researched accounting standards of the IASC, Hong Kong, France, Japan, the United States, and the United Kingdom, in order to provide feedback to the Ministry concerning accounting standards used elsewhere in the world. The Ministry decided that China would not simply adopt IASC standards or those of any country. Rather, the setting of accounting standards in China would reflect China's uniqueness. However, the standards would be acceptable by the international investment community.

The December 1995 newsletter of the International Accounting Standards Committee (IASC) provides an excellent description of the process followed by the Ministry of Finance in developing and issuing China's detailed accounting standards. One of the authors of this paper, Richard Goligoski, a partner in the firm of Deloitte & Touche LLP, who has previous experience working at the IASC and who served as the primary technical consultant to the Chinese Ministry of Finance, writes "an integral part of the Ministry's initiative is the holding of forums at which accounting and reporting issues can be discussed. The first such forum was held in Shenzhen in February 1992; the second in Shanghai in December 1994. Representatives of the International Accounting Standards Committee attended and presented at each of these forums, and the work of IASC received a great deal of attention." Throughout China, academics and practitioners were invited to discuss and debate the accounting standards.

The other two authors of this paper, Tang Gu Liang and Anne Rich, participated in a meeting of academics hosted by the Beijing Institute of Business in Beijing in October 1995. In addition, both Richard Goligoski and Anne Rich participated in a meeting of foreign experts with the standard setters within the Ministry of Finance which was held in Beijing in November 1995. This meeting included representatives from the World Bank, the Hong Kong and Australian Societies of CPAs, major accounting firms, and respected academic institutions. Participants were given the English translation of all accounting standards being discussed. (Understandably, those using the English version sometimes experienced translation problems.) These meetings were remarkably open and characterized by lively discussion. Thus, while the standards are being set by a government agency, the Ministry of Finance has engaged, and is expected to continue to engage, in the process Chinese and foreign accountants as well as academics.

Table 1. Detailed Accounting Standards Under Development (Proposed but not effective)

1.	Accounting for payables
2.	Accounting for receivables
3.	Inventory
4.	Investments
5.	Capitalized borrowing costs
6.	Form of the balance sheet
7.	Form of the income statement
8.	Fixed assets
9.	Intangible assets
10.	Research and development
11.	Long-term contracts
12.	Cash flow statements
13.	Basic banking business
14.	Owners' equity
15.	Foreign exchange transactions
16.	Revenue
17.	Accounting for income tax
18.	Consolidated financial statements
19.	Accounting policies and changes in accounting policies and estimates
20.	Subsequent events
21.	Employee benefits
22.	Contingencies and commitments
23.	Government grants and donations
24.	Liquidation accounting
25.	Commodity Futures
26.	Leases
27.	Business combinations
28.	Nonmonetary transactions

THE (PROPOSED) DETAILED ACCOUNTING STANDARDS

The (proposed) detailed accounting standards currently in existence follow the same format as the International Accounting Standards. The first section provides an introduction, followed by definitions, then the accounting rules and disclosure requirements. Drafts of the standards were widely exposed for comment in China. On April 28, 1997, China Daily reported that the "new standards that will enable China's enterprises to meet international accountancy criteria are in the final approval stage." The article reported that Zhang Youcai, Vice Minister of Finance, had announced that the new standards would be issued beginning May 1997. "He said the first of the 29 new accountancy codes will be issued in May followed one by one until all have been put into effect." Following this annoucement, the Ministry of Finance issued the first standard entitled "Disclosure of Related Parties and Related Party Transactions." The objective of this specific accounting standard is to prescribe the disclosure of related party relationships and transactions. Initially, only listed Chinese companies are required to implement this standard, which is effective beginning January 1, 1997 for financial statements issued for external reporting purposes. It is expected that when other standards are issued, they would be tested in select State enterprises and then institutionalized across the country. Codification of the new standards is expected to be completed by the year 2000. Table 1 provides an overview of the accounting standards currently developed but not yet effective. A detailed summary of the 28 exposure drafts and the one issued standard is found in the Appendix.

The Chinese have provided numerous definitions in their standards. Perhaps the most useful feature is the consistency of definitions across standards. Also, China has benefited from international discussions concerning the meaning of fair value, market value, replacement cost, and net realizable value. In the Chinese standards, fair value is defined as the value for which an asset could be exchanged, or a liability settled, between knowledgeable, willing parties in an arm's length transaction. This definition appears in the following standards:

- Accounts payable, notes payable and bonds payable
- Receivables
- Investments
- Fixed assets
- Intangible assets
- Owners' equity
- Government grants and donations
- Business combinations
- Nonmonetary transactions

Market value is defined as the value which is received or paid for on sale or acquisition of an investment in an active market and is found in the standard on investments. Replacement cost is defined as the amount that needs to be paid for the replacement of a fixed asset (or inventory) at current market price (or under the current condition) and is found in the standards relating to fixed assets and inventory. Net realizable value is defined as the remaining amount of the price of a salable property net of any necessary expenses directly related to the sale of such property, or the amount at which the property can be used to settle debt obligations. It is referred to in the inventory and liquidation accounting standards.

Another interesting feature is the amount of consistency in accounting treatments. For example, reciprocity is found in the accounting for accounts and notes payable compared with accounts and notes receivables, especially in debt restructuring situations.

ADVANTAGES OF THE CHINESE PROCESS

The process of developing detailed accounting standards in China has several strong points. China has the benefit of drawing upon international and national accounting bodies that have had a long history in the setting of accounting standards. In addition, the Chinese standard-setters have been able to take advantage of issuing a comprehensive set of accounting standards within a relatively short period of time. As a result, the definitions for all elements are consistently applied across all the standards. For example, fair value has only one meaning throughout all 29 standards. The Chinese accounting standards include guidelines on the content and format for all financial statements. In China, if one wants to know the specific format for the balance sheet and income statement, there will be an authoritative pronouncement to follow. The IASC has just developed international guidelines in its presentation of financial statements after many years of issuing accounting standards, and the United States still has no comprehensive guidance.

Another advantage of the Chinese accounting standard-setting process is China will have comprehensive accounting rules by topic rather than piecemeal in numerous standards. This comes as a result of developing all of the standards within a short period. In the United States, for example, many areas have several authoritative pronouncements that must be taken as a whole in order to fully understand the rules.

Reciprocal accounting may also be considered an advantage. Chinese accounting requires reciprocal accounting in such areas as accounts receivable and payable, debtor and creditor restructurings, revenue recognition, nonmonetary transactions, and leases between parties.

There is significant detail in some of the standards, and often there is guidance concerning such specificity as how to record a transaction. As a result, the standards provide some of the much needed education and training for accountants that will be needed for successful implementation. For example, the standard on depreciation provides calculations for depreciation under various methods.

China has been able to incorporate recent changes in international standards—for example, the cash flow statement—quicker than many other countries. While making great progress towards meeting international accounting standards, China's accounting standards reflect the unique legal rules relating to China, such as employee benefits and the rights of creditors during bankruptcy. In addition, the standards have largely ignored areas that are currently prohibited such as dealing with financial futures. Alternatively, the standard-setters have concentrated on relevant areas, such as commodity futures, in order not to overly complicate rules.

DISADVANTAGES OF THE CHINESE PROCESS

Some of the disadvantages provide a mirror image of the advantages. By having a required prescribed format for financial statements, companies are precluded from creating formats that may be more relevant and useful to users. In addition, because the standards provide great specificity in some areas, the professional judgment of accountants is significantly restricted. Finally, while some standards provide enormous details, others do not. There may be substantial differences in interpretations in some critical areas.

CONCLUSION

By looking at the process of setting standards in China, we are able to observe how eager China is to adhere to the international accounting standards. China's handling of controversial areas, such as amortization of consolidated goodwill and research and development, provide a peek into how future accounting issues may be resolved. Concerning amortization of purchased goodwill, China mandates a period of no less than ten years. Concerning accounting for research and development, China will adopt the same approach as the United States, namely, to expense R&D as incurred. Thus, China will clearly maintain its own unique accounting standards, selecting from alternatives that meet the needs of its stakeholders.

This paper has provided a progress report on the accounting reform project of China. Substantial progress has been made not only in developing a conceptual framework but also in developing detailed accounting standards. When implementation of all of the standards begins, Chinese financial statements will look very much like those in industrialized countries and China will have met its goal of bringing its financial accounting systems for business enterprises into line with international expectations.

APPENDIX: SUMMARY OF 28 DETAILED ACCOUNTING STANDARDS PROPOSED BUT NOT EFFECTIVE AND ONE STANDARD ISSUED

1. Accounts Payable, Notes Payable, and Bonds Payable (revised exposure draft) 8/28/95

This standard deals with the accounting for and disclosures in financial statements of accounts payable, notes payable, and bonds payable. It included definitions of cash discounts, purchase allowances, face value, premiums, discounts, nominal and actual rates, and fair value. Accounts and notes payable follow international practices. Amortization of premium or discount on bonds payable can be accomplished by using the straight line or actual interest method. The standard also provides the accounting for convertible bonds and bonds with attached warrants and debt restructures. It requires the debtor who transfers assets to a creditor to recognize the difference between the carrying value of the liabilities satisfied and the fair value of the asset transferred as income and recorded in the current profit or loss. Other provisions refer to the situation where some terms for settling the liability are changed and the amount payable in the future by the debtor is more than or equal to the carrying value of the liability prior to the restructuring. In this case the carrying value does not change but interest expense should be recalculated.

2. Receivables (revised exposure draft) 6/19/95

This standard regulates the accounting treatment for receivables for business enterprises. Definitions include recourse, discounted, cash discount, bad debt, fair value, equity security, and effective interest rate. A company may choose the allowance method or direct write-off method to account for bad debts. Bad debt losses may be estimated based on aging of accounts receivable or percentage of outstanding accounts receivable. The provision for bad debt is treated as an administrative expense. Criteria for write-offs are included in the standard. Rules for notes receivable include accruing interest and accounting for notes receivable that are discounted, with recourse and without. Also included are rules for debt restructuringand rules for the creditor similar to those in the notes payable standard. The standard provides accounting for prepayments and other receivables as well as disclosure requirements.

3. Inventories (revised exposure draft) 4/28/95

This standard deals with the accounting treatment and financial statement disclosure of an enterprise's inventories. It provides definitions including historical cost and replacement cost. The standard provides guidance on inventories that are included within the scope and those that are excluded. It identifies that historical cost is the initial measurement for inventories, however, at the period end, the company must carry inventories at the lower of cost or net realizable value. For inventories that are self-manufactured, the costs include direct materials, direct labor, other direct expenses, and allocated indirect manufacturing expenses. In addition, there are rules for donated inventories, inventories contributed by investors, and inventory overage. For inventory that takes more than 12 months to complete, the reader is referred to the capitalization of borrowing costs standard. Unusual losses and losses from abnormal spoilage should not be included in the cost of the inventory. Enterprises are free to choose specific identification, FIFO,

LIFO, and weighted average inventory cost flows. If the company changes methods, the reasons must be disclosed. Six specific disclosures for inventory are specified.

4. Investments (revised exposure draft) 7/25/95

This standard deals with accounting and financial statement disclosures for investments by enterprises (excluding such specialized investment enterprises as investment funds or securities companies). It defines investments, investment property, current investment, long-term investment, cost method, equity method, premium or discount of bonds, amortized cost, acquisition cost, market value, fair value, and unrealized gain or loss.

The standard provides for the timing in recording an investment, the value of an investment is recorded and valuation at the end of an accounting period. At year-end, current investments are valued using the cost method or the lower of cost or market (using the entire current investment portfolio aggregate cost method). Long-term investment in bonds is valued at amortized cost. Investment property is valued at fair value with unrealized gains and losses recorded as part of owner's equity. Long-term equity investments are divided into three classes: control, significant influence, and nonsignificant influence. Normally, control is achieved when direct and indirect ownership exceed 50%. Significant influence normally occurs when the direct or indirect ownership is beyond 20%. Nonsignificant control is normally when the investor has less than 20% ownership. When a controlling relationship exists between an investor and an investee, the investment should be valued using the equity method. When an investor has significant influence on an investee, the investment should be valued using the equity method; however, there are three situations where the equity method is specifically not allowed. When the investor has no significant influence over the investee, the investment should be valued using the cost method.

The standard provides accounting rules for permanent declines in the value of an investment, revaluations of investments, transfers of investments, disposal of investments, and disclosures.

5. Capitalization of Borrowing Costs (revised exposure draft) 9/15/95

This standard deals with the accounting for capitalization of borrowing costs. It defines borrowing costs and capitalization of borrowing costs and contains accounting treatments for recognition of capitalization as well as disclosures.

6. Balance Sheet (revised exposure draft) 7/20/95

This standard regulates the information to be disclosed by an enterprise in the balance sheet which is reported externally. It establishes periodic preparation and the use of the renminbi as the monetary unit normally used. Comparative balance sheets and disclosures are required.

7. Income Statement (revised exposure draft) 7/20/95

This standard regulates the information that an enterprise's income statement should disclose in external reporting. It includes extensive definitions including operating revenue, operating costs, operating taxes, other deductions, selling expenses, administrative expenses, financial expenses, and investment income. It establishes disclosures for extraordinary items which are items that are indefensible and unavoidable. It calls for reporting of discretionary reserves, distributed profit, and undistributed profit. Comparative income statement should be presented. A multi-step format should be used.

8. Fixed Assets (exposure draft) 9/15/95

This standard deals with the accounting for and disclosures in financial statements of fixed assets of an enterprise. It contains definitions for fixed assets, estimated useful life, estimated net salvage value, depreciation, net value of fixed assets, fair value, replacement value, and construction in progress. Accounting recognition is described. The cost of a fixed asset is presented, including rules for recording the cost of a self-constructed fixed asset. Assets subject to depreciation are listed as well as rules for calculating depreciation. Accounting for improvements, extensions, and repairs is specified. Treatment for fixed asset overage or shortage is specified. Rules for disposal of a fixed asset identify the treatment for gain or loss. Revaluation accounting indicates that any increase in the carrying value be posted to capital while any decreases are assigned to the period (with special rules for subsequent revaluations). Disclosure requirements are identified. The appendix provides calculations for straight-line, units of production, hours of operations, sum of the years digits, and double-declining balance methods, all of which are permitted.

9. Intangible Assets (exposure draft) 9/14/95

This standard deals with accounting treatment and financial statement disclosure for the intangible assets of the enterprise. Definitions include intangible assets, monetary assets, nonmonetary assets, fair value, goodwill, and identifiable assets. Intangible assets are recognized when the cost to obtain the asset can be measured reliably. Purchased goodwill is recognized. Negative goodwill is also recognized and amortized equally in no less than five years and recorded into the profit or loss of each period. Accounting rules are presented for all assets acquired from the outside, including land-use rights, patents, and trademarks. Amortization periods follow the law, if specified, or a period not to exceed 10 years except for purchased goodwill which is no less than five years. There are rules for transfer and writeoff of intangible assets. Revaluations are allowed. Maintenance and improvement are considered period expenses. Disclosures are also required.

10. Research & Development (exposure draft) 9/14/95

This standard deals with accounting for and financial statement disclosures of an enterprise's research and development activities. Research and development are defined. Detailed components of research and development expenses are identified. The costs of all research and development activities should be expensed immediately. If the government underwrites the cost of R&D, those funds should offset expenses. The enterprise should disclose the R&D expenses recorded in the current period.

11. Long-Term Construction Contracts (exposure draft) 9/15/95

This standard deals with the accounting for and financial statement disclosure of long-term construction contract. It defines long-term construction contracts, percentage of completion method, and completed contract method. It specifies the accounting for single contracts and combined contracts, defines contract revenues and contract costs, and provides the recognition criteria for contract revenue and contract costs. If the outcome of a long-term construction contract can be estimated reliably, the percentage of completion method must be used. Otherwise, the completed contracts method is used. The standard addresses recognition of expected losses, changes in accounting estimates, and items to be disclosed.

12. Cash Flow Statement (final draft) 10/l/95

This standard regulates the information that an enterprise's cash flow statement should provide in external reporting. However, it does not specify the information that should be provided by a consolidated cash flow statement and its preparation method. The standard defines cash and cash equivalents, operating investing and financing activities, and extraordinary items. In this standard, extraordinary items refers to the cash item of an enterprise that occurs infrequently, is of a special nature, and cannot be classified as operating, investing, or financing. Cash flows are classified as operating, financing, and investing. Interest disbursements are shown net after deducting revenues from deposits in banks and are classified as operating. However, capitalized interest expenses on investment borrowings are reflected in the cash flows for investing activities. Exchange rate translation differences appear in a separate section. The enterprise may prepare cash flows on the direct or indirect method. Significant investing and financing activities which do not relate to the current period's cash receipts and disbursement, but have an effect on the financial position of an enterprise or generate future cash flows of an enterprise, should be reflected and explained in the supplemental information of the cash flow statements or in the footnotes.

13. Basic Banking Business (exposure draft) 8/26/95

This standard deals with the accounting for and disclosures in financial statements of banks' deposits, loans, and settlement transactions. When non-bank financial institutions and other units conduct business operations of deposits, loans, and settlement, they should account for and disclose in financial statements those transactions according to the regulations in this standard. This standard includes accounting for collateralized and discount loans. In addition, off-balance-sheet transactions giving rise to contingencies and commitments are identified. Extensive disclosures are required.

14. Owners' Equity (exposure draft) 9/15/95

This standard deals with the accounting for and disclosures in financial statements. It provides definitions of owners' equity, share capital, paid-in-capital, convertible bonds, convertible preferred stock, cumulative preferred stocks, par value, stock dividends, and fair value. Accounting for donations and asset revaluations is specified. Numerous disclosures are required.

15. Foreign Currency Translation (exposure draft) 9/27/95

This standard deals with the translation of transactions that are denominated in a foreign currency and the translation of financial statements prepared in a foreign currency into ones expressed in the enterprise's recording base currency or the required currency. This is a comprehensive approach to accounting for foreign currency translations and transactions and is as complete as a chapter in an accounting textbook. Currency exchange rate differences are recognized in the current period.

16. Revenue (exposure draft) 9/8/95

This standard deals with the accounting for and the financial statement disclosure of revenue arising from the following operating activities: the sales of goods, the rendering of services, and the use of the enterprise's assets by others. Revenue is recognized when: (1) goods have been delivered and all other work necessary to be performed to obtain the revenues have been substantially completed, and (2) the consideration has been received or the right to receive the consideration has been obtained. Recognition of income related to the rendering of services, if estimated reliably, should follow the percentage of completion method. Alternatively, the completed contract method should be used. Interest revenue should be recognized and calculated periodically based on the principal outstanding. Royalty revenue should be recognized and calculated based on the time and method stipulated in the related contract or agreement, and dividend revenue should be recognized when the investor obtains the right to receive the dividends. The amount of revenue should be determined by the agreement between the enterprise and the buyer, or the enterprise and the user of its asset. An enterprise must disclose the accounting policies adopted for revenue recognition in the notes to the financial statements.

17. Accounting for Income Tax (exposure draft) 9/27/95

This standard deals with the accounting for and financial statement disclosures on the income taxes of an enterprise. It identifies timing differences (taxable and deductible) and permanent differences. An enterprise should recognize and measure current income tax expense (or benefit) according to the liability method. Deferred tax liabilities and deferred tax assets are recognized. Numerous items must be disclosed.

18. Consolidated Financial Statements (exposure draft) 9/27/95

This standard deals with the preparation of consolidated financial statements of an enterprise group. It defines parent, subsidiary, controlling power, minority shareholder, internal transactions, and consolidated difference. In general, consolidated financial statements must be prepared for an enterprise group unless a parent is itself a subsidiary wholly owed by another parent. A parent which prepares consolidated financial statements should include all of its subsidiaries conducting various types of businesses, foreign and domestic, with a few exceptions. Consolidated financial statements must include any investee with over one-half of its equity capital owned by the parent. Minority interest should be differentiated from the liabilities and owner's equity of the parent and presented separately. Numerous disclosures are required.

19. Accounting Policies and Changes in Accounting Policies and Estimates (exposure draft) 9/13/95

This standard deals with the significant accounting principles and treatments of accounting policies, changes in accounting policies, and accounting estimates applied in the preparation of the financial statements by an enterprise. Accounting policies must be disclosed and firms should adopt policies which will objectively reflect their financial positions and operating results. Policies to be selected are listed in the following categories: general accounting policies, asset items, liability items, profit and loss items, and other items. Changes in accounting policy require a cumulative effect of an accounting change calculation recorded in the current period. Changes in accounting estimates are recorded in the current and future period and no cumulative adjustment is needed. Numerous disclosures are required.

20. Subsequent Events (exposure draft) 9/13/95

This standard deals with the accounting for and financial statement disclosure of subsequent events of an enterprise. Subsequent events, adjusting event, and non-adjusting events are defined. The events occurring after the balance sheet date that provide new evidence to assist with the new estimation of amounts relating to conditions existing at the balance sheet date should be treated as adjusting entries. Both favorable and unfavorable adjustments can be made; however, there must be conclusive evidence to support realization, and footnote disclosure is required.

21. Employee Benefits (exposure draft) 10/20/95

This standard regulates the accounting for and financial reporting of employee benefits. It define employee benefits, social insurance, housing reserve fund, and other additional benefits. Each type of social insurance expenditure that an enterprise should pay should be recognized as expenses of the period in which the employees provide related services to the enterprises. Medical insurance expense paid by an enterprise for retired employees are recorded in the administrative expenses of the employer. It also specifies certain disclosures.

22. Contingencies and Commitments (exposure draft) 1/16/96

This standard regulates the accounting for contingencies and financial reporting for contingencies and commitments. The standard defines contingencies, commitment, and counter-claims. Contingent losses should be recognized as losses and charged to profit and loss of the current period if: (1) it is probable that future uncertain events will confirm that an asset has been impaired or a liability has been incurred at the balance sheet date, and (2) a reasonable estimate of the amount of a contingent loss can be made. The amount of contingent losses and counter-claims that have been recognized should be presented separately in the balance sheet. Any contingent losses not yet recognized should be disclosed in the notes. Commitments should not be recognized by a enterprise. Irrevocable commitments should be disclosed.

23. Government Grants and Donations (exposure drafts) 1/12/96

This standard regulates the accounting for and financial reporting of government grants and donations, and the financial reporting of other government assistance. It defines donation, government assistance, government grant, fair value, and replacement value. An enterprise that donates cash or other assets should treat the amount donated as a non-operating expense at the time the related assets are given away. An enterprise that receives cash or other assets as a donation should treat the donation as capital surplus at the time the related assets are received. Donations received are recorded at fair market value.

24. Liquidation Accounting (final exposure draft) 1/17/96

This standard stipulates the accounting for and financial reporting for an enterprise in the period of liquidation. It defines liquidation, bankruptcy liquidation, dissolution liquidation, revocation liquidation, right of lien, hypothecation right, mortgage right, and net realizable value. The enterprise should prepare a balance sheet and a statement of changes in net assets based on net realizable values. Assets should be classified into those used as collateral and ordinary assets. Numerous disclosures are required. A detailed model is provided in the standard.

25. Futures (exposure draft) 12/29/95

This standard regulates the accounting for and financial statement disclosures of commodity futures transaction. It defines margin, performance margin, strike price, settlement price, liquidation, delivery, cash delivery, commodity delivery, market-to-market, hedging for commodity futures, speculation, member qualification fee, seat occupation fee, annual membership fee, transaction service charge, futures clearing charge, risk reserve, and transaction loss reserve. Accounting rules are provided for future clearing houses and futures brokerage firms.

26. Leases (exposure draft) 9/22/95

This standard deals with the accounting for and disclosure of leases by an enterprise in the financial statements. Financing and operating leases are defined. Reciprocal accounting by lessees and lessors is required. Accounting for leverage leases and leasebacks is described.

27. Business Combinations (exposure draft) 1/19/95

This standard deals with the accounting for and disclosure in financial statements of business combinations. The standard provides the acquisition accounting treatment when one of the combining enterprises can control another combining enterprise. Alternatively, uniting of interests is required when the enterprises combined are a jointly controlled organization. Ten conditions are required for the uniting of interests method. When determining the fair value of the acquired identifiable assets and liabilities, the acquirer can use market value, carrying value, replacement cost, present value, estimated selling price, appraisal value, net realizable value, and so forth. Goodwill generally should be amortized using the straight-line method over a period not exceeding 10 years and should be recorded as an expense in each period. There are numerous required disclosures.

28. Nonmonetary Transactions (exposure draft) 1/17/96

This standard deals with the accounting for and the financial statement disclosure of reciprocal transactions of enterprises' nonmonetary assets. Definitions include nonmonetary transactions, fair value, productive assets, and nonproductive assets. In the exchange of similar nonmonetary assets, the carrying value of assets given up should be treated as the cost of assets acquired. Boot occurring in the exchange of similar nonmonetary assets should be treated according to different condition. The party that receives boot should take the net amount of the carrying value of the asset less the boot as the cost of the nonmonetary asset acquired. The party that pays the boot should take the amount of the net carrying value of the asset given up plus the boot as the cost of the asset acquired. Various disclosures are required.

29. Disclosures of Related Party Relationships and Transactions (Issued May 1997)

This standard regulates the financial reporting of related parties relationships and transactions. Enterprises controlled by the government do not have to disclose the transactions between them in their separate financial statements. In deciding whether a related party relationship exists, consideration should be given to the substance of the relationship, not merely the legal form. Numerous disclosures are mandated.

ACKNOWLEDGMENT

The authors gratefully acknowledge the comments of Dr. Chen Yu Gui, Ministry of Finance, PRC.

REFERENCES

Chow, L. M-y., G. Chau, and S.J. Gray. 1995. Accounting reforms in China: Cultural constraints on implementation and development. *Accounting and Business Research* 26(1): 29-49.

Davidson, R., A. Gelardi, and F. Li. 1996. Analysis of the conceptual framework of China's new accounting system. *Accounting Horizons* 10(1): 58-74.

Goligoski, R. 1995. The impact of international accounting standards in the People's Republic of China. *IASC Insight, The Newsletter of the International Accounting Standards Committee* (December). London, England.

Xiao, Z., D. Young, J. Dyson, and A. Pan. 1995. Development of accounting standards and conceptual framework in China. In *Advances in International Accounting*, Vol. 8, Timothy J. Sale, Editor 177-100. Greenwich, CT: JAI Press,

Winkle, G., H. Huss and C. XiZhu. 1994. Accounting standards in the People's Republic of China: Responding to economic reforms. *Accounting Horizons* 8(3): 48-57.

THE DEVELOPMENT OF ACCOUNTING REGULATION IN INDIA

R. Narayanaswamy

ABSTRACT

This paper describes important features of the regulation of financial accounting and disclosure in India. It examines the evolution of Indian financial reporting, highlights significant influences on this evolution, and presents the current state of financial reporting regulation. An attempt has been made to view these developments within larger theoretical frameworks: Choi and Mueller (1986), Puxty et al. (1987), and Gray (1988). The evidence presented confirms the predictions of these theories and offers new insights on the effect on accounting regulations of a country's economic, social, legal, and other systems. Comparisons with selected foreign jurisdictions are made. Given the increasing importance of India in global capital markets and the paucity of research on Indian financial reporting, the paper would help set the agenda for research in Indian accounting and disclosure regulation.

Research in Accounting Regulation, Supplement 1, pages 331-365.

ISBN: 0-7623-0338-7

INTRODUCTION AND BACKGROUND

This paper describes the development of accounting regulation in India, analyzes the factors that affected that development, explains the major differences between Indian and international accounting practices, and indicates the likely effect of the on-going economic reforms on reporting by Indian companies. It addresses the following basic research question in the Indian context: how does accounting regulation interrelate with economic, social, legal and political systems?

The research question assumes importance due to the recent opening up of India's economy. For about four decades, India had followed a centralized, inward-looking model of development that discouraged domestic competition and impeded foreign investment. In such a setting, the rest of the world was not concerned with Indian accounting systems and Indian companies had no incentive to keep pace with international developments in financial reporting. This resulted in the neglect of India in international accounting research. The sweeping economic reforms initiated by the government in the early 1990s significantly altered the picture. India is now regarded by many as an emerging economic giant. The country's sophisticated manufacturing base, skilled workforce and expanding markets are particularly fancied by large global corporations. The rise of India as a favored destination for foreign investment is bound to generate interest in the country's accounting systems.

The research question is important to many individuals and organizations including accounting firms, fund managers, brokers and analysts, investment banks, multinational corporations, foreign stock exchanges interested in listing Indian securities, Indian companies interested in foreign listings, standard-setters, securities market regulators, and academics. Financial reports are a product of the larger environment—corporation laws, securities markets, stock ownership, accounting profession, and culture—in which they are produced. Since the environment of financial reporting in India differs significantly from that in other countries, the aforesaid individuals and organizations would require a good understanding of the Indian accounting regulatory structure and processes so as to be able to deal effectively with the differences and the resulting problems. This paper analyzes the development of accounting regulation in India within three larger, well-recognized theoretical frameworks: Choi and Mueller (1986), Puxty et al. (1987), and Gray (1988). These frameworks provide multiple perspectives for investigating the research question.

Past research in Indian accounting or finance is meager, lacks methodological rigor, and is mostly based on small samples. There are very few papers on Indian accounting in reputed journals devoted to international accounting. Given these limitations, an attempt is made here to present prior literature that is relevant to this paper. The few available studies indicate that the quality of financial reporting in the country is generally low. In an early study by Singhvi (1967), corporate disclosure in annual reports in India was compared with that in the United States.

Using an index of disclosure consisting of 34 items, Singhvi found that the quality of disclosure in India was inferior to that in the United States at that time (1964-1965). Marston (1986) showed that disclosure in the United Kingdom was better than in India. Das Gupta (1977) concluded that most of the companies in India provided minimum information required by law. A study by the accounting profession, however, concluded that published reports gave more information than strictly required by law (ICAI 1981). Many of the companies covered in this study who had made voluntary financial disclosures were in the public sector. Chander (1992) found an improvement in the disclosure practices of a set of companies in 1984-1985 over 1980-1981, with disclosure by companies owned by government improving better than private-sector companies.

Indian business is apparently sensitive to the effect of accounting rules. For example, Narayanaswamy (1992) reported that companies with high leverage and low profitability are influenced by the off-balance-sheet financing nature of leasing and that the imposition of a lease capitalization rule could result in companies with high leverage purchasing rather than leasing assets. Sharma and Kennedy (1977) concluded that stocks on the Bombay Stock Exchange obeyed a random walk and were equivalent in this sense to the behavior of stock prices in the markets of advanced industrialized countries. Some unpublished doctoral dissertations indicate that the Indian stock market adjusts rapidly to the information releases such as the issue of bonus shares.

This paper is the first one in an international journal to provide a detailed analysis of the key features of the regulation of financial accounting and disclosure in India. It examines the evolution of Indian financial reporting, highlights significant influences on this evolution, and presents the current state of financial reporting regulation. International comparisons with Indian practices indicate the need for important accounting reforms.

The rest of this paper is organized as follows. The second section summarizes the political and legal institutions in India. The third section provides an overview of the country's economic and business environment. The fourth section relates the major influences on accounting development in India to that environment. The fifth section presents the framework of financial reporting including disclosure requirements and auditing. The sixth section analyzes the existence of several unusual disclosures in Indian financial reports in terms of the country's economic and social objectives. The seventh section discusses the constitution of the accounting profession; the education, training, and ethical requirements for its members; the state-profession relationship; and the challenges facing the profession. The eighth section examines the role of the government, the securities regulator, and the accounting profession in establishing accounting standards. The ninth section illustrates the case of a market-driven financial reporting initiative of an Indian software company. The tenth section summarizes the conclusions, contributions, and limitations of the paper.

POLITICAL AND LEGAL INSTITUTIONS

India has a very ancient and rich civilization going back more than 5,000 years. From the Indus Valley civilization that flourished around 3500 B.C. to the British Raj that ended in 1947, India and its various parts have been ruled by several kings, queens, and dynasties, native as well as foreign. Over 80% of the population are Hindus; the rest include Muslims, Christians, Sikhs, Buddhists, and Jains.

India became independent on August 15, 1947. The country's political and legal institutions are based on the Westminster model of parliamentary democracy. The Constitution of India adopted in 1950 envisages three tiers of government: central, state, and local. The central government comprises the President, the two Houses of Parliament, the Prime Minister, and the Council of Ministers. The President is the head of state and the Prime Minister is the head of government and chief executive. The revenues of the central government include income tax and customs and excise duties. State government comprises the Governor, the two Houses of State Legislature (one House in some states), the Chief Minister, and the Council of Ministers. The states derive revenues from their own taxes, such as sales tax, and receive a share of the revenues collected by the central government. Local government consists of a number of institutions including city corporations, town councils, and village councils. The revenues of the local bodies consist of property tax and octroi (entry tax) on goods, and funds allocated by the state government. India has an independent judiciary that has powers to rule on virtually all central and state legislation. The main sources of Indian law are the central and state statutes, custom and usage, and English common law.

ECONOMIC AND BUSINESS ENVIRONMENT

At the time of Independence, agriculture was the mainstay of the economy of India. Since then, there has been a conscious attempt to make the country a modern industrial power with a large manufacturing base. The government adopted the vision of a "socialistic pattern of society" as the guiding philosophy of the country's economic development. National priorities were laid down in five-year plans formulated by the Planning Commission. The goal was to become self-sufficient in every area of economic activity, and import substitution became an important means to achieve this goal. Private foreign investment was looked upon with suspicion because of fears of re-colonization. Growth with equity and abolition of poverty became the slogans of successive governments.

The state assumed a major role in determining the economic life of the country. A mixed economy system, with the state occupying the commanding heights of the economy and the private sector playing a supportive role, was put in place. State regulation extended to most areas of economic decision making; for example, detailed rules existed for matters such as capital raising, investment in specific

Table 1. Selected Indicators of India's Economy

Indicator	*1990-1991*	*1991-1992*	*1992-1993*	*1993-1994*	*1994-1995*	*1995-1996*
Panel A: Absolute values						
Gross domestic product at factor cost (at 1980-81 prices) Rs. billion	2122.53	2139.83	2248.87	2360.64	2510.10	2686.71
Index of agricultural production 1980-81 = 100	148.4	145.5	151.5	156.8	164.6	166.1
General index of industrial production 1980-81 = 100	212.6	213.9	218.9	232.0	253.7	284.2
Index of wholesale prices 1981-82 = 100	182.7	207.8	228.7	247.8	274.7	295.8
Consumer price index for industrial workers 1982 = 100	193	219	240	258	284	313
Money supply (M3) Rs. billion	2658	3170	3668	4344	5314	6018
Value of imports US $ million	24073	19411	21882	23306	28654	36370
Value of exports US $ million	18145	17865	18537	22238	26331	31831
Balance of trade US $ million	–5928	–1546	–3345	–1068	–2323	–4539
Foreign investment, net US $ million	—	139	555	4235	4895	4347
Foreign currency assets US $ million	2236	5631	6434	15068	20809	17044
Panel B: Percent change over previous period						
Gross domestic product at factor cost (at 1980-81 prices)		0.7	5.1	5.0	6.3	7.0
Index of agricultural production 1980-81 = 100		–1.9	4.1	3.5	4.9	0.9
General index of industrial production 1980-81 = 100		0.0	2.3	5.9	9.3	12.0
Index of wholesale prices 1981-82 = 100		13.7	10.0	8.3	9.7	7.6
Consumer price index for industrial workers 1982 = 100		13.4	9.5	7.5	10.0	10.2
Money supply (M3)		19.2	15.7	18.4	22.3	13.2
Value of imports		–19.3	12.7	6.5	22.9	26.9
Value of exports		–1.5	3.7	19.9	18.4	20.8

Source: *Economic Survey* (1995-1996), *Reserve Bank of India Bulletin* (September 1996).

industries and regions, import and export of goods, prices and distribution, size of industrial houses, receipt and use of foreign exchange, and remuneration payable to company directors. The state issued licences, permits, and quotas for a large number of industrial and consumer goods. During the period 1950-1990, the growth rate of the economy was below 4%.

Discontent with the low level of economic development began to rise in the 1980s, particularly in the wake of the success registered by other Asian economies. Some of these countries had been poorer than India until the early 1960s. The current phase of the economic reforms was forced on the country by the country's unprecedented economic crisis in 1991. That year, for the first time in its history, India was close to defaulting on its international commitments. India's international credit ratings were downgraded and external credit was completely denied.

The new government that assumed office in June 1991 took swift action to restore international confidence in the economy. A program of macroeconomic stabilization was initiated soon after. Simultaneously, the government undertook structural reforms in foreign trade, taxation and industrial policy. Many of the numerous controls on firm-level economic decision making were dismantled. Free floatation of the Indian rupee, permission to Indian companies to raise capital abroad, liberalization of the rules for foreign direct investment, and permission for portfolio investment by foreign financial institutions are particularly significant in the context of this paper.

Key economic indicators have showed improvement since the economic reforms began. Annual inflation has reached single-digit levels, foreign exchange reserves

***Table* 2.** Key Statistics for the Bombay Stock Exchange

Indicator	*1992-1993*	*1993-1994*	*1994-1995*	*1995-1996*
BSE Sensitive Index[1]	2280.52	3778.99	3260.96	3366.61
BSE National Index[2]	1300.4	1899.60	1534.57	1549.25
Trading volume(in rupees billion)	456.96	845.38	677.49	500.64
Market capitalisation (in rupees billion)[3]	2109.52	3984.32	4354.81	5264.76
Number of listed companies[4]	2861	3585	4702	5838
Price-earnings ratio[5]	35.51	36.35	28.96	17.18

Notes: [1]BSE Sensitive Index (1978-1979 = 100) is based on 30 shares. The values are as of March 31 at the end of the year.
[2]BSE National Index (1983-1984 = 100) is based on 100 shares. The values are as of March 31 at the end of the year.
[3]Market capitalization values are as of March 31 at the end of the year.
[4]Number of listed companies is as of March 31 at the end of the year. The number for 1995-1996 has been computed by adding the number of companies listed during the year to the number on March 31, 1995.
[5]The price-earnings ratio is for the 30 shares that comprise the BSE Sensitive Index.

Source: *The Stock Exchange Review* (various issues), *The Stock Exchange Official Directory* May 1995. Both are published by the Bombay Stock Exchange.

have gone up substantially, and the real gross domestic product recorded growth of around 7%.[1] Major indicators of India's economy are presented in Table 1.

The Indian capital market, even though classified as an "emerging market" by foreign investors, is in many ways different from other emerging capital markets and is closer to developed markets. It is over a century old, has a multi-million investor base and several thousand listed companies with decent accounting and disclosure practices. The first stock exchange in India was officially established in 1875 in Bombay. Key statistics for the Bombay Stock Exchange for the last four years are presented in Table 2. The Securities and Exchange Board of India (SEBI) was made a statutory body in 1992, broadly on the lines of the Securities and Exchange Commission in the United States, with extensive powers to regulate the stock exchanges and market intermediaries. In 1992, India's equity markets were opened to foreign institutional investors (FIIs), subject to limits. Furthermore, the government has allowed Indian companies to raise capital in international markets.

INFLUENCES ON ACCOUNTING DEVELOPMENT

Choi and Mueller (1986) have identified several environmental factors that have direct effects upon accounting development. These factors are: legal system, political system, nature of business ownership, differences in size and complexity of business firms, social climate, level of sophistication of business management and of the financial community, degree of legislative interference in business, presence of specific accounting regulation, speed of business innovations, stage of economic development, growth pattern of an economy, and status of professional education and organization. Financial reporting practices in India reflect, to a great extent, the influence of many of these factors.[2]

Legal and Political Systems

Indian legal and political systems evidence the significant influence of about two centuries of British colonial rule. Successive English Companies Acts and commercial law left their imprint on Indian company law, including requirements relating to accounting and reporting. Colonization has been identified as the most important vehicle for the transfer of accounting systems within the British Empire and Commonwealth (Briston 1978; Parker 1989). To quote Briston:

> In a number of countries...the British influence is very long standing, and almost all of the colonial territories in which any substantial degree of industrial development took place under British rule will have had imposed upon them a British Companies Act and the usual reporting and auditing requirements (Briston 1978, 107-108).

In India, the accounting profession and the business community are left with considerable flexibility in financial reporting, subject to the minimum legal framework. Radebaugh and Gray (1993) rightly include India among the countries that follow Anglo-Saxon accounting systems. In India, the securities legislation has not had a dominant influence on accounting practice. This contrasts with the position in the United States, where the securities laws of 1933 and 1934 have influenced the evolution of accounting and disclosure (Zeff 1972). Indian company law contains comprehensive accounting requirements for listed as well as unlisted companies. The securities regulators have, until recently, generally played a limited role in specifying accounting disclosures by listed companies.

Business Ownership

Nature of business ownership is a significant factor influencing the development of accounting. Widespread public ownership of corporate securities would lead to greater disclosure of information to the public, while large shareholdings by groups (e.g., financial institutions, families, etc.) would seem to limit sharing of financial information to the members of the owning groups. In India, extensive cross-holdings of shares and inter-locking of directorships by the members of families are fairly common. Further, government-owned financial institutions own a sizable number of shares in many companies and meet much of their credit needs. A study of 185 large and medium companies included in *CRISILCARD 1994* shows that the mean shareholding by financial institutions was 24.31%, the highest and the lowest being 59.94% and 0.11%, respectively. Also, on average, two out of 10 directors on the boards were nominated by the institutions.[3] However, public shareholding is set to rise with companies directly going to the capital market leading to improved financial disclosure.

Social Climate

The social climate in India may also have influenced the level of accounting development. For example, in sharp contrast to the United States, the social climate in India is highly conservative and therefore demands considerably less financial disclosure by large companies. Rising consumerism and awareness of environmental issues in India, for example, are likely to lead to demand for increased disclosure of financial and other information by companies.

Economic Development

The semi-socialistic, inward-looking model of economic development has played a significant role in the evolution of accounting. The introduction of cost audit and social audit requirements, disclosure of the remuneration of directors and highly paid employees, disclosure of information relating to foreign exchange earnings from exports and foreign exchange outgo on imports, royalties, and dividends are examples of the effect of the economic model on financial reporting.

Business Innovation

The relatively low speed of business innovations has also influenced accounting practice. For example, business combinations resulting in mergers or acquisitions have become popular in India only in the last few years. Equipment leasing is still in its infancy in terms of the volume of business, types of assets covered, and varieties of products. The level of sophistication of financial instruments is very low. Since there are few business transactions requiring complex accounting treatments, measurement and disclosure practices have remained fairly simple.

Accounting Profession

The existence of a well-trained group of accounting professionals clearly distinguishes India from other emerging markets. The systems of training, examination, and discipline of professional accountants are highly rated in the country. The accounting profession enjoys a high social status. Members of the accounting profession often advise the government on taxation, company law, and securities regulation, apart from accounting and auditing.

Degree of Globalization

Radebaugh and Gray (1993) suggest that as the degree of internationalization of the economy increases, financial reporting systems tend to move towards internationally accepted benchmarks. Since Indian companies have functioned for a long time in a closed economy, they have had little incentive to incorporate international advances from the 1950s in financial accounting and disclosure in their domestic financial reports.

Cultural Influence

Gray (1988) examines the influence of culture on the national financial reporting systems. He identifies the following four value dimensions:

- Professionalism versus statutory control;
- Uniformity versus flexibility;
- Conservatism versus optimism; and
- Secrecy versus transparency.

Professionalism refers to the scope for the exercise of individual professional judgment and the existence of a self-regulated profession, whereas statutory control involves compliance with legal requirements regarding accounting. The existence of an independent accounting profession that functions autonomously under a broad legal framework would suggest that India is closer to professionalism than to statutory control.

Uniformity emphasizes conformity to a standard set of accounting practices for all entities, as opposed to the flexible adoption of accounting practices to suit the needs of individual business organizations. In India, there is a great deal of flexibility in the choice of accounting and disclosure alternatives. There are few accounting measurements that have legal sanction. Conservatism emphasizes a cautious measurement approach. The attitude of Indian business towards measurement seems to vary. Closely held companies seem to prefer a conservative approach to income measurement, while widely held companies seem to be less conservative and may be even said to be optimistic. Furthermore, almost all large listed corporations have revalued their fixed assets above historical cost. On the whole, it would seem that Indian companies are closer to optimism than conservatism.

The secrecy versus transparency comparison relates to disclosure, not measurement. As stated earlier, the social climate in India is highly conservative, and many large corporations are owned by major family groups and/or financed by heavy borrowings from government institutions. As a result, capital market forces have had virtually no impact on the level of financial disclosure. Recent revelations of illegal acts by some major companies have reinforced the demand for greater transparency in corporate affairs.

THE FINANCIAL REPORTING FRAMEWORK

The Companies Act 1956 (CA 1956) was the first company legislation to be passed in independent India by Parliament and extends to the whole of India. It was enacted to meet the changing social and economic needs of the country and aimed at achieving the government's objective of a socialistic pattern of society, protecting the interests of stakeholders and helping companies to develop on healthy lines. CA 1956 has been amended several times, reflecting changes in government policy and business conditions.

Many large business corporations are incorporated as public companies who are allowed to invite capital from the public and their shares are freely transferable. Small companies are generally incorporated as private companies. They are not allowed to invite capital from the public and their shares are not freely transferable.

Basic Legal Requirements

CA 1956, the primary source of authority for corporate reporting, contains the following chief requirements relating to financial reporting:

- A company must keep proper books of account for its cash receipts and payments, sales, purchases, assets, and liabilities. These books have to be kept on accrual basis according to the double entry system.
- The board of directors of a company must lay at the annual general meeting of shareholders a balance sheet and a profit and loss account for the preceding financial year.
- The balance sheet shall give a "true and fair view" of the state of affairs of the company and has to be in the specified form. The profit and loss account shall give a "true and fair view" of the profit or loss of the company and shall disclose the specified information.
- Consolidated financial statements are not required. The financial reports of the subsidiaries must be attached to the balance sheet of the parent.
- The directors' report must cover, among others, the company's state of affairs and material changes and commitments that occurred after the end of the financial year.
- The balance sheet and profit and loss account shall be audited by a chartered accountant in practice.
- A copy of the balance sheet, profit and loss account, auditors' report, and directors' report must be sent to every shareholder before the annual general meeting.
- The balance sheet, profit and loss account, auditors' report, and directors' report of a public company shall be filed with the Registrar of Companies. These documents are open to inspection by any member of the public.
- The annual report of a government company—a company in which not less than 51% of the paid-up share capital is held by the central government and/or one or more state governments—must be laid before Parliament with a copy of the audit report and any supplementary report of the Comptroller and Auditor-General of India (CAG).

Auditor's Report

The auditor must state whether the balance sheet and the profit and loss account give the information required by CA 1956 and give a true and fair view of the company's state of affairs and profit. Also, the auditor must state whether:

- All the necessary information and explanations have been obtained by the auditor;
- Proper books of account have been kept by the company; and
- The balance sheet and the profit and loss account are in agreement with the books of account.

Over the years, the scope of the auditor's report has been expanded to cover a number of nontraditional areas.

Appointment, Qualifications, and Powers of Auditor

The shareholders appoint an auditor at each annual general meeting to hold office from the end of that meeting to the end of the next meeting. The existing auditor must be reappointed unless he or she suffers from any legal disability. Furthermore, the auditor cannot be removed without the previous approval of the government. These provisions are to protect the auditor's independence. The auditor can access at any time the company's records and documents and can require from the company's officers necessary information and explanations. The central government appoints the auditor of a government company.

An auditor must be a chartered accountant in practice. An individual or a partner of a firm can audit a maximum of 20 companies, out of which not more than 10 companies can have a paid-up capital of 2.5 million rupees or more. The ceiling on the number of audits was imposed in 1974 in place of the earlier proposal for rotation of audit among chartered accountants. The objectives of the measure were to improve audit independence, reduce audit monopoly, and improve opportunities for younger members of the accounting profession. The Joint Select Committee of Parliament made the following observations on rotation and ceiling:

> This [rotation] was done with a view to bringing about a dissociation of auditors from groups of companies so that they may not have any temptation to shield the shortcomings of the management from the shareholders. It was also done with a view to achieving a more equitable distribution of audit work amongst the different auditors so that the younger sections of the audit profession may have better chances of advancement in the profession.. The Committee have considered this matter in all its aspects and feel that a ceiling on the number of audits would achieve the objects which the Government had in view when the Bill was introduced (Joint Select Committee ¶30, 1974).

SPECIAL FEATURES OF FINANCIAL ACCOUNTING AND DISCLOSURE IN INDIA

The vision of a socialistic pattern of society has played an important role in the development of accounting regulations in India. The corporation was considered accountable to the society at large, and not just to its shareholders and creditors. This philosophy is reflected in the significant expansion of the scope of the financial report beyond conventional boundaries.

Disclosure of nonfinancial information was introduced in 1971 and extended considerably in 1973. The disclosure requirements continue to be in operation. Many of these items might be considered extraordinary elsewhere. An analysis of the major items of disclosure is presented below:

- *Licensed capacity, installed capacity, and actual production of manufacturing companies:* Production in excess of licensed capacity implies departure from the scheme of central allocation of resources as well as violation of capacity licensing regulations. On the other hand, a shortfall in the installed capacity or actual production in relation to licensed capacity may imply meant that the company was cornering licenses and benefiting from the higher prices resulting from the resulting shortage of goods.

- *Payments in foreign exchange:* Self-sufficiency is to be achieved through import substitution. Payments in foreign exchange are looked at as the company's inability to indigenize production causing drain of scarce foreign exchange reserves. The value of imports of materials and capital goods and the percentage of the value of imported materials consumed during the year to the total consumption provide a measure of the degree of import dependency. Self-sufficiency also means the use of local technology in preference to foreign know-how; hence, the requirement to disclose of expenditure in foreign currency on account of royalty, know-how, and professional and consultation fees. Shareholding by foreigners was discouraged because of the then-recent experience of colonization and exploitation. Hence, the need for disclosure of remittances in foreign currencies on account of dividends and interest in financial statements.
- *Research and development:* The disclosures in the directors' report regarding the company's research and development activities include the following: areas of research, benefits derived, future plans, and expenditure, technology absorption, adaptation and innovation, and foreign exchange outgo. This would give an idea of the efforts being made to improve technological self-sufficiency.
- *Earnings in foreign exchange:* Disclosure of earnings in foreign exchange is emphasized since the country has generally been affected by shortage of foreign exchange. The amount of foreign exchange earned via export of goods, royalty, know-how, professional and consultation fees, and interest and dividends is to be disclosed in financial statements. The total foreign exchange earnings must be disclosed in the directors' report.
- *Remuneration of "highly paid" employees:* Remuneration of employees should reflect their qualifications and experience, and it should not be too high in order to reduce income inequalities. Furthermore, it is important that individuals were employed by virtue of their competence rather than their being the kinsmen of the company's directors. In the background of rising unemployment, it was also important that the government was seen to be doing something to ensure fairness in employment. These factors explain the rule requiring disclosure of certain information regarding every employee who received a remuneration of 144,000 rupees per year (The current per capita income of India is about 10,000 rupees per year). The following disclosure is required for such employees: name, age, designation or duties, remuneration, qualification, experience, date of commencement of employment, last employment, and, if the employee is a relative of any

director, the name of such director. This report runs into several pages for many large companies.

- *Conservation of energy:* Since India produces only about a third of its requirement for crude oil, and imports of petroleum products account for about a fifth of the country's total imports, efficiency in use of energy is an important priority for the country. The directors' report describes the energy conservation measures taken by the company and provides information on the unit costs of energy generated or purchased by the company and the quantum of energy consumption.
- *Directors' remuneration:* In the past, besides an overall ceiling by way of a percentage of net profit, there were detailed guidelines for determining the remuneration payable to whole-time directors of companies. The disclosure of directors' remuneration covers payments made to the directors by the company, its subsidiaries, and any other person by way of remuneration, allowances, commission, and payment for retirement from office. Further, the net profit for the purpose of calculation of commission payable must be computed as specified in CA 1956 and the computation is shown in the financial statements. The purpose of the disclosure is to prevent directors from overpaying themselves at the expense of the shareholders.
- *Payments to auditor:* The company must disclose all amounts paid to the auditor as fees, expenses, or otherwise in the following categories: as auditor; as adviser in respect of taxation matters, company law matters, or management services; and in any other manner. The purpose of the disclosure is to provide information particularly about payment for non-audit services, since provision of such services by the auditor might be seen to have impaired the auditor's independence.
- *Minimum depreciation:* Distributable profit is computed after providing depreciation at minimum rates specified in Schedule XIV to CA 1956. The requirement for minimum depreciation was in response to a finding by a commission of inquiry in the 1950s that certain companies were distributing dividend out of capital by not providing adequate depreciation. The rates are given for the straight-line method and the written-down value method. Separate rates are given for major classes of assets. The depreciation method used and depreciation rates or the useful lives of the assets, if they are different from the rates specified in the Schedule, must be disclosed. Note that the depreciation rates for financial reporting are different from those used for tax reporting.

The expanded audit report (sometimes referred to as "social audit report"), required since 1975 and subsequently further extended, is a special feature of auditing in India.[4]

The enabling legal provision was introduced in 1965. Consequent on introduction of the report, auditors must comment on several matters including some not directly related to the numbers appearing in the financial statements. These reporting requirements are applicable to companies engaged in manufacturing, mining, processing, services, trading, financing, or investment. The matters on which additional reporting is required include the following:

- *Internal control systems:* Are there adequate internal control procedures for purchase of materials, plant and machinery, and other assets and for sale of goods? Does the company have an internal audit system commensurate with the size and nature of its business?
- *Related party transactions:* Are the conditions of loans taken by the company from group companies or from other parties in which a director is interested prejudicial to the interests of the company? Are the prices paid for materials purchased during the year from subsidiaries or other parties in which directors are interested reasonable as compared to the prices of similar items supplied by other parties?
- *Recovery of loans and advances:* Are the parties to whom loans have been given by the company repaying the principal amounts as stipulated and are regular in payment of interest? If not, have reasonable steps been taken by the company for the recovery of the principal and interest?
- *Fixed assets and inventories:* Does the company maintain proper records for fixed asses? Have the fixed assets and inventories been physically verified by the management at reasonable periods? Have any serious discrepancies noticed on such verification been properly dealt with in the books of account?
- *Revaluation of fixed assets:* In case any of the fixed assets have been revalued, the report must indicate the basis of revaluation.
- *Inventory valuation:* Is the valuation of the inventories fair and proper in accordance with the normally accepted accounting principles and is on the same basis as in the earlier years? If there is any deviation in the basis of valuation, the effect of the deviation, if material, is to be reported.
- *Remittance of employees' benefits:* Is the company regular in depositing Employees' Provident Fund dues and Employees' State Insurance dues with the appropriate authorities?
- *Remittance of taxes and duties:* Are there any undisputed amounts payable in respect of income-tax, sales tax, and customs and excise duties outstanding at the balance sheet for more than six months from the date they became payable?
- *Unsecured borrowings:* Has the company complied with the directives issued by the Reserve Bank of India and the provisions of CA 1956 relating to unsecured deposits accepted from the public?
- *Cost accounting records:* If maintenance of cost accounting records has been prescribed by the government, have these records been maintained?

- *Financial distress:* Is the company a "sick industrial company" within the meaning of the Sick Industrial Companies (Special Provisions) Act 1985? A company is defined as sick if its accumulated losses are more than the shareholders' equity.
- *Personal expenses in company accounts:* Have any personal expenses of employees or directors been charged to the company other than those payable under contractual obligations or accepted business practice?

The legal requirements for cost accounting records and cost audit are a unique feature of Indian accounting. In the licensing era, there was little incentive for companies to improve their efficiency and reduce costs. In the absence of competition, cost-plus was the basis for product pricing. It was important that companies did not make monopoly profits and pass on their inefficiency to the consumer. This is the background for the requirement to maintain records relating to utilization of material or labor or to other items of cost. An audit of the cost records of a company by a cost and works accountant was to serve as a check on the records as well as highlight areas of waste and inefficiency. Hundreds of companies have been directed by the government to maintain cost accounts and to get the cost accounts audited.

THE ACCOUNTING PROFESSION

The growth of the accounting profession in India was an outcome of the Indian Companies Act 1913, which prescribed for the first time qualifications for the auditor. The qualifying examination was the "Government Diploma in Accountancy," which was conducted by the provincial governments. Subsequently, the Indian Accountancy Board, constituted as a result of the Act of 1930, handled most of the matters pertaining to accountancy and auditing. Its main function was to advise the state on all matters pertaining to accounting and auditing and to help the state in maintaining high standards of qualification and conduct required of auditors. In 1949, the Institute of Chartered Accountants of India (ICAI) came into existence following the passage of the Chartered Accountants Act. The ICAI regulates the profession of chartered accountants. As of April 1, 1996, there were 74,352 chartered accountants including 45,222 in full-time practice (ICAI 1996).

The Chartered Accountants Act contains detailed provisions regarding membership, Council, committees, Regional Councils, professional misconduct, reciprocity and recognition of foreign accountancy qualifications, and powers of the government. The ICAI's affairs are managed by the Council, composed of 24 members elected by members of the Institute and six persons nominated by the government. The President and the Vice-President are elected by the members of the Council. There are three standing committees of the Council: the Executive Committee, the Examination Committee, and the Disciplinary Committee. Each of these committees consists of the President and the Vice-President ex officio, and three other members of the Council elected by the Council. In the case of the Disciplinary Committee, however, two shall be elected by the Council, and the third nominated by the government from among the nominated members of the Council.

The Chartered Accountants Act catalogs the various acts and omissions of chartered accountants that constitute "professional misconduct." The First Schedule to the Act deals with cases of misconduct by a chartered accountant that adversely affect other chartered accountants and require action by the Council. The following are some items of misconduct mentioned in the First Schedule:

- Soliciting clients or professional work;
- Advertising professional attainments or services;
- Accepting a position as auditor previously held by another chartered accountant without first communicating with the former auditor in writing;
- Charging professional employment fees which are based on a percentage of profits or which are contingent upon the findings or results of such employment; and
- Undercutting fees.

The Second Schedule to the Act deals with cases of misconduct by a chartered accountant that adversely affect the society at large and require action by a High Court. The following are some items of misconduct mentioned in the Second Schedule:

- Disclosing information acquired in professional engagement to any person other than the client;
- Failing to disclose a material fact known to the accountant which is not disclosed in a financial statement, but disclosure of which is necessary to make the financial statement not misleading;
- Failing to disclose a material misstatement known to the accountant to appear in a financial statement with which the accountant is concerned in a professional capacity;
- Being grossly negligent in the conduct of professional duties;
- Failing to obtain sufficient information to warrant the expression of an opinion, or the exceptions are sufficiently material to negate the expression of an opinion; and
- Failing to invite attention to any material departure from the generally accepted procedure of audit applicable in the circumstances.

The Council has powers to recognize foreign accountancy qualifications for the purpose of membership of the ICAI on the basis of reciprocity. In the past, accountancy qualifications from a number of countries, including the United Kingdom,

Australia, South Africa, and Pakistan, have been recognized. Recently, there has been some tightening of these arrangements.

The government has powers to direct the Council to make any regulations or to amend or revoke any regulations already made within a specified period. If the Council fails to comply with the order, the government may make the regulations or amend or revoke any regulations made by the Council.

The ICAI's system of examination and practical training is modeled largely on U.K. lines. The written examination covers a range of subjects including accounting, cost accounting, auditing, business law, tax law, economics, and management. The training consists of an articleship with a firm of chartered accountants for a period of three years. Apart from the value of practical experience, the training is designed to help aspiring accountants in developing qualities of integrity, independence, and objectivity which are considered essential for a professional accountant and auditor.

During World War II, there was a growing need for qualified cost accountants to investigate the cost structure of supplies by contractors and government-owned factories. As a result, the Institute of Cost and Works Accountants of India (ICWAI) was set up in 1944. After Independence, the industrialization of the economy resulted in an increase in the number of cost accountants. In 1959, the ICWAI was given statutory recognition with the passage of the Cost and Works Accountants Act, which is similar to the Chartered Accountants Act in most material respects.

The demands on the accounting profession will increase as a result of the ongoing program of economic liberalization and globalization that began in 1991. Financial reporting has come under considerable scrutiny following raising of capital by Indian companies abroad and inflow of foreign capital into the country by way of direct as well as portfolio investments. The market for audit and con-

Table 3. Top Ten Accounting Firms in India

Rank	*Name of the Audit Firm*	*Number of Clients*
1	A. F. Ferguson & Co.	97
2	Price Waterhouse	68
3	Lodha & Co.	37
4	S. R. Batliboi & Co.	36
5	Lovelock & Lewes	34
6	C. C. Chokshi & Co.	28
7	Fraser and Ross	27
8	Brahmaiah & Co.	26
9	S. B. Billimoria & Co.	26
10	Dalal & Shah	22

Source: "The Big vs Little Six" (1995).

sulting services, currently dominated by Indian firms, and the audit industry structure are likely to undergo significant changes with the entry of large international accounting firms. In 1985, the ICAI banned foreign audit firms from practicing in India on the grounds that countries where these firms were registered did not allow ICAI members to practice there. However, Arthur Andersen and Price Waterhouse escaped the regulation, having been established in the country before 1985. Other Big Six firms are currently operating in the country through their Indian associates ("The Big Six Set Up Shop" 1996). The names of the top 10 firms in 1992-1993 by number of clients are listed in Table 3.

India is a founder member of the World Trade Organization (WTO), which overseas arrangements for free trade in goods and services, and of the South Asian Association for Regional Cooperation (SAARC), a regional economic grouping. Furthermore, India has indicated interest in joining two other major economic groupings in the Asia-Pacific region, the Association of South East Asian Nations (ASEAN) and the Asia Pacific Economic Cooperation (APEC). Given that free trade in services is a matter of concern for the member countries of all these organizations, the Indian government and accountancy profession are bound to come under pressure to liberalize rules for establishing accounting practices in the country. Recognition of foreign qualifications, greater freedom in selecting firm name, and relaxation of the ban on advertising are some of the matters that require early resolution.

Accounting education in India is characterized by the absence of integration between professional courses and the university system. Radical changes were suggested by the special committee on education and training in the 1970s, but many of the recommendations have not been implemented. The Indian Accounting Association, based in Calcutta, takes an active interest in academic accounting. (For a detailed study of accounting education in India, see Banerjee 1994.)

ACCOUNTING STANDARDS AND STANDARD-SETTING IN INDIA

Modes of Accounting Regulation

Corporate financial reporting can be regulated in several ways. At one extreme, firms may be left to choose their own accounting rules; in this case, each company will be influenced by a number of considerations, including pressure from the capital market. At another extreme, the process may be entirely in the hands of an agency designated by the government; in this case, the regulatory body lays down the accounting rules to be followed by companies and enforces compliance. Puxty et al. (1987) visualize a continuum of modes of regulating accounting practices in advanced capitalist economies. "Liberalism," in which regulation is provided exclusively by the discipline of the market, and "legalism," in which accounting

Table 4. List of Accounting Standards Issued by ICAI and Corresponding Standards

ICAI		*IASC*	
AS 1	Disclosure of Accounting Policies	IAS 1	Disclosure of Accounting Policies
AS 2	Valuation of Inventories	IAS 2	Valuation and Presentation of Inventories in the Context of the Historical Cost System
AS 3	Changes in Financial Position	IAS 7	Cash Flow Statements
AS 4	Contingencies and Events Occurring After the Balance Sheet Date	IAS 10	Contingencies and Events Occurring After the Balance Sheet Date
AS 5	Prior Period and Extraordinary Items and Changes in Accounting Policies	IAS 8	Net Profit or Loss for the Period, Fundamental Errors and Changes in Accounting Policies
AS 6	Depreciation Accounting	IAS 4	Depreciation Accounting
AS 7	Accounting for Construction Contracts	IAS 11	Accounting for Construction Contracts
AS 8	Accounting for Research and Development	IAS 9	Research and Development Costs
AS 9	Revenue Recognition	IAS 18	Revenue Recognition
AS 10	Accounting for Fixed Assets	IAS 16	Property, Plant and Equipment
AS 11	Accounting for the Effects of Changes in Foreign Exchange Rates	IAS 21	The Effects of Changes in Foreign Exchange Rates
AS 12	Accounting for Government Grants	IAS 20	Accounting for Government Grants and Disclosure of Government Assistance
AS 13	Accounting for Investments	IAS 25	Accounting for Investments
AS 14	Accounting for Amalgamations	IAS 22	Business Combinations
AS 15	Accounting for Retirement Benefits in the Financial Statements of Employers	IAS 19	Retirement Benefit Costs

practice follows the letter of the law, represent the two extremes of the continuum. "Associationism" refers to the accomplishment of regulation through the development of organizations that are formed to represent and advance the interests of their members. In "corporatism," the government licenses organized interest groups as well as incorporating them into its own centralized system of regulation. Puxty et al. suggest that the United Kingdom has an associationist system of accounting regulation, whereas the United States is both legalist and associationist, with the latter being subordinated to the former.[5]

Applying the Puxty et al. framework to India (although India is by no means an advanced capitalist economy), it appears that the country is closer to the associationist system, with shades of corporatism, than to the other systems. Over the past several decades, the accounting profession has issued a number of statements, standards, and guidance notes describing desirable accounting practices. These recommendations have played persuasive role in shaping accounting practice, though currently they do not have any legal force. As can be expected, the level of compliance with the ICAI's standards has tended to vary; in particular, compliance has been low in the case of recommendations having an adverse effect on the likely tax position of companies, since companies have an apprehension that the tax authorities may take an unfavorable view of their tax position (although tax reporting is separate from shareholder reporting).

In 1977, the ICAI established the Accounting Standards Board (ASB) to harmonize the accounting practices in use in India. The ASB is constituted as a committee of the ICAI's Council, which issues the final accounting standards. As of March 1997, 15 standards had been issued, and compliance with all but two—inventories and funds flow statement—was mandatory for accounting periods commencing on or after April 1, 1995. Indian standards have been influenced significantly by the standards issued by the International Accounting Standards Committee (IASC). The ICAI's standards and the corresponding International Accounting Standards are listed in Table 4.

A major criticism of the ASB has been that it functions like a closed club consisting only of members of the accounting profession. In recent years, the ICAI has responded partly to this criticism by coopting onto the ASB outsiders representing financial institutions, regulatory bodies, academia, and others. The ICAI has made it mandatory for company auditors to ensure compliance with many of its standards. There have been doubts about the legal basis of the standards, given that the duty of the auditors is to report whether the financial statements give a "true and fair view." As a result, the implementation of the accounting standards program has been tardy. In 1993, the government introduced a proposal to require disclosure of all significant accounting policies adopted by a company and of material departures from ICAI's standards together with the reasons. It has been pointed out that there may be scope for conflict between the ICAI's standards and the instructions contained in the proposed law (Sarbadhikari 1993).

Regulatory Activism

In the recent past, the government and the SEBI have taken certain actions that could affect the future shape of financial reports. In 1995, through an amendment to the Income Tax Act with potentially far-reaching implications for financial reporting, the government was empowered to issue "accounting standards" for tax reporting purposes.[6] Although the scope of these standards is limited to the computation of taxable income, companies might consider adoption of the tax accounting standards for the purpose of shareholder reporting as well. The government has issued only a few standards so far.

Another development likely to precipitate accounting reforms is the role the securities regulator intends to play in financial reporting. Until now, the SEBI has restricted itself to improving disclosure in prospectus and other offer documents and has stayed away from financial reports. Of late, it seems to be getting more active in the financial reporting arena. For example, in May of 1995, it directed listed companies to publish cash flow statements. It may be noted that CA 1956 does not require cash flow statements. Again, the SEBI has required listed companies to send their shareholders full annual reports in place of the abridged reports currently being sent by many companies.[7] These actions are consistent with the SEBI's need to respond to its constituency of investors and with its mandate to protect investors from losses resulting from wrong or inadequate disclosure. The cash flow statement has been required following complaints that some companies have diverted the funds raised in the capital market to purposes other than those stated in offer documents.

Sometime ago, the Department of Company Affairs considered a proposal to delink the Accounting Standards Board from the ICAI and set up an autonomous body to formulate accounting standards ("DCA Planning Autonomous Body for Accounting Norms" 1995). The need for an autonomous body was felt following the involvement of some of the country's leading accounting firms in the audit of banks and companies affected by the securities scandal.[8] The proposal appears to have been given up because of opposition from the ICAI. Nevertheless, the question of raising the standards of Indian reporting to international levels still remains.

Indian Accounting Standards and International Benchmarks

The ICAI is a member of the IASC and has agreed to support its objectives. The ICAI (1979, ¶2.2) has stated that it will give due consideration to International Accounting Standards (IASs) and try to integrate them, to the extent possible, with its standards in the light of the conditions and practices prevailing in India. Information pertaining to the extent of conformity of Indian accounting standards with IASs is presented in Table 5.

Table 5. Conformity with International Accounting Standards

IAS		India	United Kingdom	United States	Australia	Malaysia
1	Disclosure of accounting policies	3	3	3	3	1
2	Inventories	3	3	3	3	1
4	Depreciation	3	3	3	3	1
5	Disclosures in financial statements	3	3	3	3	1
7	Cash flows	3	3	3	3	1
8	Unusual items	3	3	3	3	1
9	R&D	5	3	3	3	1
10	Contingencies	3	3	3	3	1
11	Construction contracts	2	3	3	3	1
12	Taxes	6	3	5	5	1
13	Current assets	3	3	3	3	1
14	Segments	6	5	3	3	1
15	Changing prices	6	6	3	4	1
16	Property, plant and equipment	3	3	3	4	1
17	Leases	6	3	3	3	1
18	Revenue recognition	3	4	3	4	1
19	Retirement benefits	4	3	3	6	1
20	Government grants	3	3	3	4	4
21	Foreign exchange	5	3	3	3	1
22	Businesss combinations	6	3	3	3	1
23	Borrowing costs	5	4	3	4	1
24	Related parties	6	6	3	3	4
25	Investments	4	3	3	4	4
26	Retirement plans	4	3	3	6	4
27	Consolidation	6	7	7	3	1
28	Associates	6	7	7	5	1
29	Hyperinflationary economies	6	7	7	6	6
30	Banks	5	7	7	4	1
31	Joint ventures	6	7	7	5	6

Notes:
1. IAS adopted as a national requirement.
2. IAS used as the basis for a national requirement.
3. National requirement developed separately and conforms, in all material respects, with IAS.
4. No national requirements but national practice generally conforms with IAS.
5. National requirement developed separately but does not conform with IAS.
6. No national requirements and national practice does not generally conform with IAS.
7. No information from the sources mentioned above.

Source: IASC (1988), Cooke and Parker (1994), and letter from ICAI to IASC (copy obtained from IASC).

Although British accounting has a strong influence on Indian accounting, there are important differences between the two systems. Highlights of major differences between Indian accounting requirements (imposed by accounting standards, ICAI's pronouncements, and CA 1956) and the requirements of the U.S. GAAP, U.K. GAAP, and IASs in selected areas of reporting are presented in Table 6. The

Table 6. Highlights of Differences Between Indian GAAP and U.S. GAAP, U.K. GAAP, and IASC GAAP

Area of Accounting	*India*	*United States*	*United Kingdom*	*IASC*
Business combinations, goodwill and intangibles	1. Pooling of interests method is required if certain conditions are met. 2. Purchase method is applicable where the use of pooling is not allowed. 3. Goodwill is recognized and amortized over a period not exceeding five years unless a longer period can be justified.	1. Pooling of interests method is required if certain criteria are met. 2. Purchase method is applicable where the use of pooling is not allowed. 3. Goodwill is recognized and amortized over useful life not exceeding 40 years. 4. Separately identifiable intangibles are recognized.	1. Pooling of interests is optional when criteria are met. 2. Purchase method is applicable where the use of pooling is not allowed. 3. Goodwill is charged against equity at acquisition. 4. Separately identifiable intangibles are recognized.	1. Pooling of interests is required if an acquirer cannot be identified. 2. Purchase method is applicable where the use of pooling is not allowed. 3. Goodwill is recognized and amortized using the straight-line basis over a period not exceeding five years, unless a longer period, not exceeding 20 years, can be justified.
Consolidation and equity accounting	1. Neither consolidation accounting nor equity accounting is required in primary accounts or supplementary statements. 2. Financial statements of subsidiaries are attached to the financial statements of the parent.	1. Consolidation accounting is required if the investor's shareholding exceeds 50% of voting interest. A change to 'economic control' is being explored. 2. Equity accounting is required if the investor's shareholding ranges between 20-50% of voting interest.	1. Consolidation accounting is required if investor's shareholding exceeds 50% of voting interest or where investment is integrated and managed as a single unit. 2. Equity accounting is required if the investor's shareholding exceeds 20% of voting interest where control is not deemed to exist.	1. Consolidation accounting is required for enterprises controlled by the investor. 2. Equity accounting is required for significant influence (usually 20% or more voting interest).

Foreign currency transactions and translations[a]	1. Monetary items denominated in a foreign currency are generally reported using the closing rate. 2. Non-monetary items other than fixed assets are reported using the exchange rate at the date of the transaction. 3. Exchange differences arising on foreign currency transactions (except those relating to fixed assets) are recognized as income or expense in the period in which they arise. 4. Exchange differences arising on repayment of liabilities incurred to finance fixed assets are adjusted in the carrying amount of fixed assets.	1. Financial statements of a foreign branch are re-measured using the temporal method. Re-measurement adjustments are included in net income currently. 2. Financial statements of a self-sustaining foreign entity are translated using the current rate method. Translation differences are reported as a separate component of shareholders' equity. 3. Transactions settled in the same accounting period are translated using the exchange rate at the transaction date. 4. Transactions not settled at balance sheet date are re-measured using the exchange rate at the balance sheet date.	1. Financial statements of a foreign branch are re-measured using the temporal method. Re-measurement adjustments are included in net income currently. 2. Financial statements of a self-sustaining foreign entity are translated using the current rate method. Translation differences are reported as a separate component of shareholders' equity. 3. Transactions settled in the same accounting period are translated using the exchange rate at the transaction date. 4. Transactions not settled at balance sheet date are re-measured using the exchange rate at the balance sheet date. Contract rate may be used if fixed by the terms of the transaction.	1. Financial statements of a foreign branch are translated using the temporal method. Translation adjustments are included in net income currently. 2. Financial statements of self-sustaining foreign entity are translated using the current rate method. Income and expense items are translated at exchange rates on the dates of the transactions. Translation differences are classified as equity. 3. Transactions settled in the same accounting period are translated using the exchange rate at the transaction date. 4. Transactions not settled at balance sheet date are re-measured using the exchange rate at the balance sheet date.

(continued)

Table 6. (Continued)

Area of Accounting	*India*	*United States*	*United Kingdom*	*IASC*
Lease accounting	*Lessee* 1. Lease rental on finance leases as well as operating leases is expensed over the lease term as it becomes payable. 2. There is no requirement for capitalization of finance leases in the financial statements of the lessee.	*Lessee* 1. Operating lease rental is expensed over the lease term as it becomes payable. 2. Asset and obligation relating to a capital lease are recorded in amount equal to present value at beginning of lease term of minimum lease payments, limited to the asset's fair value. 3. Asset is amortized over useful life if ownership is transferred or if lease has a bargain purchase option, otherwise amortized over lease term.	*Lessee* 1. Operating lease rental payments are expensed on a straight-line basis over the lease term, regardless of the actual cash payments. 2. Asset and obligation relating to a finance lease are recorded in amount equal to present value at beginning of lease term of minimum lease payments 3. Asset is amortized in accordance with normal depreciation policies and depreciable life generally limited to lease term, or if transaction is a hire purchase contract, the life of the asset.	*Lessee* 1. Operating lease rental payments are expensed on a systematic basis representative of the time pattern of the user's benefit. 2. Asset and obligation relating to a finance lease are recorded in amount equal to present value at beginning of lease term of minimum lease payments. 3. Asset is amortized over the shorter of lease term or useful life (unless reasonable certainty that lessee will obtain ownership) consistent with lessee's policy for other similar fixed assets.

Income taxes	1. Corporate income tax is levied and collected by the Central Government. 2. Current income tax payable is accounted for on accrual basis. 3. Deferred income tax is not recognized on timing differences.	1. Corporate income tax is levied and collected by the Federal Government as well the State Governments. 2. Current income tax payable is accounted for on accrual basis. 3. Deferred income tax is recognized on temporary differences using the liability method. 4. Comprehensive interperiod tax allocation is done.	1. Corporate income tax is levied and collected by the Central Government. 2. Current income tax payable is accounted for on accrual basis. 3. Deferred income tax is recognized on timing differences using the liability method. 4. Partial interperiod tax allocation is done.	1. Current income tax payable is accounted for on accrual basis. 2. Deferred income tax is recognized on timing differences. 3. Comprehensive or partial interperiod tax allocation is done.
Pensions[b]	1. Past service cost may be recognized immediately or allocated to future periods in which service is to be rendered. 2. Minimum liability is not recognized.	1. Prior service cost is amortized (straight line) over the average employees' remaining service lives. 2. Minimum liability is recognized based on unfunded accumulated pension obligation.	1. Prior service cost is normally amortized over remaining working life or average working life of plan participants, but method of allocation is not specified. 2. Minimum liability is not recognized.	1. Prior service cost is recognized systematically over a period approximating the average of the expected remaining working lives of participating employees. 2. Minimum liability is not recognized.

(continued)

Table 6. (Continued)

Area of Accounting	*India*	*United States*	*United Kingdom*	*IASC*
Fixed assets and depreciation	1. Fixed assets are generally recorded at historical cost. 2. Minimum depreciation rates are specified in the Companies Act and most companies follow these rates. 3. Depreciation is charged on a systematic basis using the straight-line or the written down value or other methods. 4. Revaluation of fixed assets is recognized and the difference between the cost and the revalued amount is taken to a Revaluation Reserve, not available for payment of dividends or issue of bonus shares. 5. Depreciation on revalued assets is (in effect) related to the historical cost.	1. Fixed assets are recorded at historical cost. 2. Revaluation of fixed assets is prohibited. 3. Depreciation is charged over the estimated useful life of the asset.	1. Fixed assets are generally recorded at historical cost. 2. Depreciation is charged on a systematic basis using the straight-line or the written down value or other methods. 3. Revaluation of fixed assets is recognized and the difference between the cost and the revalued amount is taken to a Revaluation Reserve, not available for payment of dividends or issue of bonus shares. 4. Depreciation on revalued assets is related to the revalued amount.	1. Fixed assets are generally recorded at historical cost. 2. Depreciation is charged on a systematic basis using the straight-line or the written down value or other methods. 3. Revaluation of fixed assets is recognized and the difference between the cost and the revalued amount is taken to a Revaluation Reserve, not available for payment of dividends or issue of bonus shares. 4. Depreciation on revalued assets is related to the revalued amount.

Segmental information	1. The Companies Act requires disclosure (physical and financial) of the production, sales and inventories of different classes of goods. 2. Disclosure of profits for the industry segments and for the geographic segments is not required.	Information about sales, profits, and net assets before tax in respect of each industry and each geographical area is disclosed.	Information about sales, profits, and net assets before tax in respect of each class of business and each geographical area is disclosed.	Information about sales, profits, and net assets before tax in respect of each class of business and each geographical area is disclosed.
Investments[C]	1. Current investments are carried at the lower of cost and fair value (often equal to market value). 2. Long-term investments are carried at cost. A provision for permanent diminution in value is made.	1. Marketable securities are valued at the lower of cost and market value. 2. Other investments are carried at cost (with a provision for permanent diminution in value), or as stated in the section 'Consolidation and Equity Accounting'.	1. Current asset investments may be written down to its net realizable value if it is less than its purchase price, but that write-down should again be reversed if the reasons for it cease to apply. 2. Other investments are carried at cost (with a provision for permanent diminution in value), or as stated in the section 'Consolidation and Equity Accounting'.	1. Current investments are carried at the lower of cost and fair value (often equal to market value). 2. Long-term investments are carried at cost. A provision for permanent diminution in value is made, or as stated in the section 'Consolidation and Equity Accounting'.

(continued)

Table 6. (Continued)

Area of Accounting	*India*	*United States*	*United Kingdom*	*IASC*
Cash flow statement	Listed companies are required to publish cash flow statements under amended listing regulations from accounting year 1995-96.	Cash flow statement forms part of the set of primary financial statements and is published.	Cash flow statement forms part of the set of primary financial statements and is published.	Cash flow statement forms part of the set of primary financial statements and is published.
Earnings per share	EPS information is not required to be disclosed.	EPS information is required to be disclosed.	EPS information is required to be disclosed.	Exposure draft on EPS information is being considered.

Notes: [a]In India, the accounting standard on foreign exchange rate changes was scheduled to come into effect in respect of accounting periods commencing on or after 1 April, 1995. Earlier practice was somewhat varied and differs significantly from the position stated in the table.

[b]In India, the accounting standard on pensions and other retirement benefits was scheduled to come into effect in respect of accounting periods commencing on or after 1 April, 1995. Previous practice was somewhat varied and differs significantly from the position stated in the table.

[c]In India, the accounting standard on investments was scheduled to come into effect in respect of accounting periods commencing on or after 1 April, 1995. Earlier practice was somewhat varied and differed significantly from the position stated in the table. Previously, all investments were generally carried at cost (with provision for permanent diminution in value) and the market value of quoted investments was disclosed by way of a note.

Source: Offer documents of Indian companies that have made Euro-issues, published reports of large Indian companies, U.S. GAAP compilations, Arthur Andersen & Co. et al. (1991).

purpose of the comparison is to give the "flavor" of Indian GAAP, with a focus on how it differs from internationally accepted benchmarks.

MARKET-DRIVEN FINANCIAL REPORTING: AN ILLUSTRATION

Infosys Technologies Limited, a leading Indian software company that earns the bulk of its revenue from abroad, has recently taken some significant financial reporting initiatives. The case of Infosys illustrates the differences between Indian practices and international benchmarks and explains the effect of internationalization of business on narrowing these differences (for a discussion of the case, see Narayanaswamy forthcoming).

Infosys was the fifth largest software exporter in India as of March 31, 1995. Its objective is to become a globally competitive information technology company. The company's clients include NCR, Xerox, Reebok, Nortel, Nordstrom, and BJ's Wholesale Club. The company's software products cover banking, retail store, and warehouse management sectors. The company's net revenue for the year ended March 31, 1996, was $26.60 million.

In 1995, the company voluntarily published U.S. GAAP financial statements and became the first (and up to now, the only) Indian company to publish a complete set of financial statements based on U.S. accounting principles. The statements have attracted considerable attention, even though they have not been audited by any Indian or U.S. accounting firm. A study of these statements highlights accounting differences between Indian and U.S. systems.

Deferred Tax Liability

The tax-payable method is followed in the company's Indian statements, since deferred tax accounting is not required in India. The U.S. GAAP statements were prepared using the tax-deferral method.

Depreciation

Until 1994, Infosys provided depreciation at the minimum rates required by CA 1956. From 1995, depreciation has been provided based on the management's estimate of the useful life of the assets. Identical estimates are followed in the Indian GAAP and U.S. GAAP statements. As a result of the revision of asset lives, there is an additional depreciation charge in 1995.

Cost of Raising Equity

Indian companies amortize the cost of raising equity over several years. But U.S. GAAP requires that the cost be expensed when incurred. Until 1994, Infosys amortized the cost of raising equity equally over a period of ten years. In 1995, the unamortized balance was charged to share premium account, which is permitted by Indian company law. In the U.S. GAAP statements, the amount of unamortized balance was charged to revenue.

Gains on Short-Term Investments

Infosys carries short-term investments at cost, as is the practice in India. In the U.S. GAAP statements, these investments are marked to market. As a result of the accounting change, unrealized gain has been added to retained earnings and the related deferred tax liability has been charged to retained earnings.

The after-tax profit reported in the Indian profit and loss account is 133,244,266 rupees (U.S.$4,352,965). The amount reported in the U.S. income statement is $3,512,432. The reconciliation of the two amounts is as follows:

Profit after tax per Indian profit and loss account		$4,352,965
Deduct:		
Deferred tax	$258,813	
Preliminary expenses	485,905	
Difference in depreciation due to translation difference	95,815	840,533
Net income per U.S. income statement		3,512,432

Discussions with the management of Infosys indicated that two factors would seem to explain the company's decision to produce U.S. GAAP statements. First, the company made a private placement of equity in October 1994 with foreign institutional investors, who are more comfortable with U.S. GAAP than any other system. Second, the company derives a very large part of its software revenues from the United States. For example, in both 1995 and 1994 about 73% of its revenues came from the United States, compared to about 52% in 1993. Although there was no request or suggestion from the company's customers to provide U.S. GAAP information, it seems that the benefits to the company of providing the information are likely to be high, particularly in negotiating long-term contracts. The decision to form a wholly owned software subsidiary (Yantra, Inc.) in the United States could be a related factor. Yet another explanation is the company's interest in seeking a NASDAQ listing in the future. No target date has been set for the listing, but the company intends to pursue this objective.

The Infosys case underscores the role of the international capital and product markets in improving financial reporting by Indian companies.

CONCLUDING REMARKS

This study of financial reporting in India has confirmed existing theories about the role of environmental factors in the development of accounting regulation in a country and has yielded some new insights. After Independence, India opted for a semi-socialist model of development that resulted in the birth of several new institutions. This paper has presented extensive evidence to show that accounting regulations were inspired by the new economic, social, legal, and other systems. Special disclosures in India include capacity utilization, foreign exchange payments, exports, research and development activities, energy conservation, employee and director remuneration, and payments to auditors for audit and non-audit services. Auditors are required to report on a number of specific matters including internal controls, related party transactions, and compliance with certain economic and employee legislation. The special disclosures and the expanded audit report indicate the contours of a comprehensive business report that provides both hard numbers and soft data for use by a company's shareholders, employees, and other stakeholders. This point deserves attention in the current Anglo-American discourse on corporate governance, which is constrained by the frame of reference of maximizing shareholder value.

Indian reporting does not have several of the features of reporting in other major jurisdictions, in particular the United States and the United Kingdom, because of India's inward-looking economic policy. Post-1947 international advances in accounting such as consolidated financial statements, segmental disclosures, lease capitalization, earnings per share, deferred tax accounting, and off-balance sheet liabilities have left India unaffected. Increasing integration of the Indian economy with the rest of the world will result in pressures to narrow the differences between current Indian accounting and disclosure practices and the relevant international standards of reporting.

The winds of change are blowing. The case of Infosys Technologies Ltd. illustrates the nature of the incentives available to, and the forces that operate on, firms that are globalizing and the kinds of differences between the Indian and U.S. accounting systems. Furthermore, the long-overdue proposal to modernize CA 1956, if and when implemented, is likely to effect major changes in financial reporting, including standard-setting arrangements. Also, increasing inflows of foreign investment into the country and joint ventures will expose Indian companies to the current practices in major accounting jurisdictions, with consequent improvement in the standards of domestic reporting. Finally, the entry of international accounting firms is likely to accelerate the pace of accounting reform as these firms have incentives to harmonize accounting practices worldwide and to improve the standards of reporting by their clients to protect themselves from legal liability as well as to enhance their professional reputation.

The level of Indian accounting research falls short of research in many other countries. From the researcher's point of view, India offers several unique and interesting institutional settings, as described in this paper. It is somewhat ironical that Indian academics who have made a mark in the United States have not published on Indian accounting issues. India is seemingly on its way to becoming an economic giant, and this is the right time to study financial reporting and capital markets in India. Since Indian laws and financial reports are published in English, the researcher's set-up time and cost are minimal.

ACKNOWLEDGMENTS

The author acknowledges the useful comments and suggestions of Sidney Gray, Claire Marston, Gary Meek, Raj Minhas, Jenice Prather, Philip Shrives, Hiroji Takao, Stuart Turley, and the two anonymous referees. Larry Parker, editor, provided valuable guidance and support throughout the project.

NOTES

1. All statistics given in this paper have been taken from the Government of India's *Economic Survey* 1995-96, the Reserve Bank of India *Annual Report* 1995-1996 and other economic reports. The fiscal year of the government is April to March.

2. The fact that Indians have themselves significantly influenced the course of accounting is not widely known. Mattessich (1994) records the development of negative numbers by Indian mathematicians as "a major accounting contribution to human culture." According to him, Indian mathematicians discovered the meaning of negative numbers "in social reality, namely in accounting where they noticed that debts are a kind of negative asset (e.g. '*negative* accounts receivable' or 'debts' as reducing total wealth)—and this was almost a millennium before the Europeans got used to negative numbers" (pp. 358-359).

3. *CRISILCARD* is an annual publication of Credit Rating Information Services of India Limited.

4. From Mikol (1995), it appears that in France, too, the auditor's report includes a few additional areas.

5. The United Kingdom has moved closer to "legalism" on the continuum of regulatory modes from liberalism to legalism since 1990 following the legal changes introduced from that year requiring compliance with the accounting standards issued by the Accounting Standards Board.

6. The government stated that a separate set of accounting standards for purposes of tax reporting has become necessary since the standards issued by the ICAI allow "flexibility."

7. CA 1956 gives a listed company the option of sending its shareholders an abridged annual report without the detailed schedules and notes to the financial statements. However, shareholders must be supplied at no charge with a full report on request.

8. The reference is to what is known in India as the "securities scam," which involved fraudulent and illegal trading in government securities by a number of banks (including some foreign banks) and other financial institutions. The scandal became public around mid-1992. A Joint Parliamentary Committee consisting of selected members of the two Houses of Parliament investigated the scandal and made adverse comments, among others, on the conduct of external audit by some accounting firms. Also, the Reserve Bank of India took action against some of the firms that had audited banks and other financial institutions affected by the scandal.

REFERENCES

Arthur Andersen & Co., Coopers & Lybrand, Deloitte & Touche, Ernst & Young, KPMG Peat Marwick, and Price Waterhouse. 1991. *Survey of International Accounting Practices*, USA.

Banerjee, B. 1994. *Accounting Education in India.* Calcutta: University of Calcutta.

The Big Six set up shop in India. 1996. *Business World* (February 7-20): 116-119.

The big versus the little six. 1995. *Business Today* (January 22-February 6): 86-93.

Briston, R.J. 1978. The evolution of accounting in developing countries. *International Journal of Accounting Education and Research* 14: 105-120.

Chander, S. 1992. *Corporate Reporting Practices in Public and Private Sectors*. New Delhi: Deep & Deep Publications.

Choi, F.D.S., and G.G. Mueller. 1986. *International Accounting*. Englewood Cliffs, NJ: Prentice Hall.

Cooke, T.E., and R.H. Parker. 1994. *Financial Reporting in the West Pacific Rim*. London: Routledge.

Das Gupta, N. 1977. *Financial Reporting in India*. New Delhi: Sultan Chand & Sons.

DCA planning autonomous body for accounting norms. 1995. *The Hindu Business Line* (August 28).

Gray, S.J. 1988. "Towards a Theory of Cultural Influence on the Development of Accounting Systems Internationally." *Abacus* (March): 1-14.

Joint Select Committee of Parliament Report. 1974. New Delhi.

International Accounting Standards Committee. 1988. *Survey of Use and Application of International Accounting Standards*. London. IASC.

Institute of Chartered Accountants of India. 1979. *Preface to the Statements of Accounting Standards*. New Delhi: Institute of Chartered Accountants of India.

Institute of Chartered Accountants of India. 1981. *Precedents in Published Accounts*. New Delhi: Institute of Chartered Accountants of India.

Institute of Chartered Accountants of India. 1996. Forty-seventh annual report and accounts. *The Chartered Accountant* (October): 73-112.

Marston, C. 1986. *Financial Reporting in India*. London: Croom Helm.

Mikol, A. 1995. The history of financial reporting in France. In *European Financial Reporting: A History*, ed. P. Walton. London: Academic Press.

Mattessich, R. 1994. Accounting as a cultural force: Past, present and future. *The European Accounting Review* 3: 354-374.

Narayanaswamy, R. 1992. Accounting for leases by lessees in India: Some evidence of economic impact. *The International Journal of Accounting* 27: 255-261.

Narayanaswamy, R. 1996. Voluntary US GAAP disclosure in India: The case of Infosys Technologies Limited. *Journal of International Financial Management and Accounting* 7: 137-166.

Parker, R.H. 1989. Importing and exporting accounting: The British experience. In *International Pressures for Accounting Change*, ed. A. Hopwood. London: ICAEW Research Studies in Accounting, in association with Prentice-Hall.

Puxty, A.G., H.C. Wilmott, D.J. Cooper, and A. Lowe. 1987. Modes of regulation in advanced capitalism: Accountancy in four countries. *Accounting, Organizations and Society* 12: 273-291.

Radebauagh, L.H., and S.J. Gray. 1993. *International Accounting and Multinational Enterprises*, 3rd edition. New York: John Wiley and Sons.

Sarbadhikari, A.R. 1993. The Companies Bill 1993: A critical review of the provisions of Schedule XIII. *The Chartered Accountant* (October): 273-277.

Sharma, J.L., and R.E. Kennedy. 1977. A comparative analysis of stock price behavior on the Bombay, London and New York stock exchanges. *Journal of Financial and Quantitative Analysis* 12(September): 391-413.

Singhvi, S. 1967. Corporate disclosure through annual reports in the USA and India. Ph.D. dissertation, Graduate School of Business, Columbia University.

Zeff, S.A. 1972. *Forging Accounting Principles in Five Countries*. Champaign, IL.: Stipes Publishing.

THE GLOBAL REGULATION OF ACCOUNTING EDUCATION:

RECIPROCITY AND THE IFAC INTERNATIONAL EDUCATION GUIDELINES

Belverd E. Needles, Jr.

ABSTRACT

This paper addresses the forces that underlie the increasing global regulation of accounting education with special emphasis on the qualifications of professional accountants as promulgated by the IFAC International Education Guideline (IEG) and their implications for reciprocity. It consists of five parts, covering the following issues: the ways in which the qualifications of accountants are regulated at the state, national, and international levels; the role of the International Federation of Accountants and its Education Committee; the importance of reciprocity under the General Agreement on Trade of Services (GATS) and the reaction of the IFAC Education Committee; the revised IEG No. 9, "Prequalification Education, Assessment of Professional Competence and Experience of Professional Accountants," as a basis for mutual recognition; and the potential ramifications of the developments presented in this paper.

Research in Accounting Regulation, Supplement 1, pages 367-391.

ISBN: 0-7623-0338-7

THE GLOBAL REGULATION OF THE QUALIFICATIONS OF PROFESSIONAL ACCOUNTANTS

Professional accountants are accountants who have a professional designation by virtue of the fact that they are members of professional bodies or are licensed by a governmental body. The qualifications of these accountants refer to the conditions that must be met for them to become members of the professional body or obtain the license. These qualifications, broadly conceived, usually include an education component and an experience requirement and typically require the passing of a test of professional competence. The subject of this paper is the regulation of these qualifications.

The qualifications of professional accountants are subject to regulation at many levels. The term *to regulate* is generally used to mean to control or direct according to a rule, law, or principle. Hence, regulation refers to the setting forth of a rule or regulation by a governmental or quasi-governmental body by which a specified group of individuals must abide in conducting a certain activity or holding themselves out as possessing certain characteristics. The consequence of not following the rule or regulation is the imposition of a penalty. The qualifications of accountants are also subject to indirect regulation when, for instance, an organization or group influences the qualifications of professional accountants simply by the power that it holds.

This paper addresses the forces that lie behind the increasing direct and indirect global regulation of the qualifications of professional accountants. It consists of five parts, covering the following issues: the ways in which the qualifications of accountants are regulated at the state, national, and international levels; the role of the International Federation of Accountants and Its Education Committee; the impact of the General Agreement on Trade of Services (GATS) and the reaction of the IFAC Education Committee; IFAC International Education Guideline (IEG) No. 9, "Prequalification Education, Assessment of Professional Competence and Experience of Professional Accountants" (revised) as a basis for mutual recognition; and the potential ramifications of the developments presented in this paper.

Regulation on, and influence of, the qualifications of professional accountants occurs at the state, national, and international levels. While the emphasis of this paper is on the international level, state and national levels are also addressed because they are important components in the overall understanding of this subject.

THE GLOBAL STRUCTURE OF THE REGULATION OF QUALIFICATIONS OF PROFESSIONAL ACCOUNTANTS

In some countries, the qualifications of professional accountants are regulated at the state and national levels. The United States is a prime example. In its 52 jurisdictions, state laws establish the right to practice as a professional accountant through a licensing procedure. In some cases, the specific qualifications that individuals must meet to become professional accountants are set forth in the law and in other cases the requirements are established by a rule-making body, usually a state board of accountancy. In all states, the state board of accountancy, or a similar body, administers the law and assesses penalties for noncompliance. In addition, most professional accountants are members of a state society, which sets membership requirements and rules of conduct that govern the actions of professional accountants.

These state societies not only have control of the qualifications of its member professional accountants but also have influence over the state laws that regulate the qualifications of its members. For instance, many state societies have formal lobbying organizations that take an active role in urging passage of specific legislative agendas. Currently, there are many differences in qualifications among the states in the areas of education, experience, examination, continuing professional education, use of the CPA title, and even on the definition of public accounting (Mednick 1996).

The United States does not have a national accountancy law, but there is some movement to address the problem of multiple jurisdictions. In 1990, a special AICPA committee on governance and structure recommended "a national qualifications service to establish and administer qualifications for individuals that the licensing jurisdictions could voluntarily substitute for their own licensing and relicensing requirements" (AICPA 1990, 33; see also Mednick 1988). The president elect of the AICPA recently renewed this call for a national licensure and regulation of the profession that would have a national uniform certification of individuals but leave the licensure of practice entities to the states (Mednick 1996). The AICPA now exercises indirect regulatory influence over the qualifications of accountants. For example, the qualifications of accountants are influenced by the AICPA through its membership requirements. Moreover, even though it is administered by each state or jurisdiction, the uniform CPA Examination is a national test constructed and graded by the AICPA. Accounting education is also subject to national regulation through the accreditation standards imposed by bodies such as the American Assembly of Collegiate Schools of Business in the United States. Finally, the National Association of State Boards of Accountancy (NASBA) is an organization of the state boards of accountancy and may be a vehicle for achieving a national certification. NASBA exercises considerable influence through its efforts to establish uniformity among the qualifications set by the various jurisdictions.

NASBA has worked cooperatively with the AIPCA to develop and support a Uniform Accountancy Act that serves as a model for state accountancy laws. Although implementation of the Uniform Accountancy Law has been very uneven, the Uniform Accountancy Act may take on greater importance in the future because of recent proactive steps taken by the NASBA and AICPA. In 1997, a joint AICPA/NASBA Committee on Regulation issued a report that contains a wide set of recommendations that, if implemented, will have great impact on the regulation of accountants in the United States. Two key provisions of the report that are especially relevant to the mobility of accountants are:

- The implementation of a substantial equivalency approach to facilitate the mobility of CPAs across state lines; and
- A one-tier licensing approach for all CPAs, with no experience requirement for licensure except for those individuals who provide attest services (NASBA 1997).

The paper calls for the NASBA and AICPA Boards of Directors to approve a revised Uniform Accountancy Act, encompassing the proposed recommendations, by July 1997, for an aggressive effort thereafter to pass the provisions of the act in the states.

The United States legislative and executive branches have the ability to exercise significant influence on the qualifications of accountants. For example, a congressional inquiry into several notable "audit failures" during the 1980s led to pressures on educators from the AICPA to include more emphasis in the curriculum on the auditor's responsibility for the detection of fraud and on the techniques of fraud detection. Congressional influence may also lead to greater emphasis on these topics on the CPA examination, which will, in turn, affect curriculum in the universities.

In other countries, the qualifications of professional accountants are often regulated at the national level through national laws, through national professional accounting organizations, or through both. Many countries have a national accountancy law which sets forth the qualifications of accountants. This is common in many European and South American countries. In some cases, the laws are administered or interpreted by professional bodies. In other countries, much discretion is left to the professional bodies. In the United Kingdom, for instance, the Companies Act requires public companies to be audited by a member of one of four private-sector bodies: the Institutes of Chartered Accountants in England and Wales, in Scotland, and in Ireland, and the Chartered Association of Certified Accountants. These bodies establish the accountants' education, examination, and experience qualifications.

Until recently, accounting education was subject to little regulation at the international level. However, for a variety of reasons (discussed below), increasing pressures have arisen for regulation at the international level. For one thing, regional professional organizations are taking a more prominent role. For example, the Federation of European Accountants (FEE) has become much more active as the European Union becomes a reality. The implementation of the Eighth Directive, which deals with the qualifications of auditors, has made cross-border comparisons of qualifications more important. In Asia, the Confederation of Asian and Pacific Accountants (CAPA) is becoming a stronger organization. While the

Inter-American Association of Accountants has not yet become active in this domain, the situation may change if NAFTA is extended from North America to the rest of the Americas.

The United Nations has asserted its influence, especially through the Intergovernmental Working Group of Experts on International Standards of Accounting and Reporting (ISAR), which has called for a worldwide accountancy qualification to be sanctioned by the IFAC. Although the IFAC has rejected this role and ISAR's parent group within the United Nations had discouraged it from proceeding, ISAR has continued to press the issue, most recently with the World Trade Organization (WTO). The WTO's Working Party on Professional Services has a draft paper titled "Guidelines for Mutual Recognition Agreements or Arrangements in the Accountancy Sector." Following on from these developments, a United Nations group, UNCTAD, is developing an international benchmark for professional qualifications to serve as an evaluation too for assessing national accounting credentials to assess whether they meet world standards (OECD 1997). Although, at the moment, it seems unlikely that a global qualification will come about, these efforts are aimed at liberalizing the cross-border recognition of accounting credentials on a worldwide basis.

In Australia, New Zealand, and other ASEAN countries, a number of developments are leading to the development of international influences on accounting education. For example, the Accountancy Market Access Committee (AMAC) was formed in 1994 under the Department of Foreign Affairs and Trade (DFAT) to work on GATS agreements as they relate to accountancy profession (see discussion below). AMAC has identified barriers to market access and set priority markets in such countries as Malaysia, Vietnam, Korea, Singapore, Thailand, Indonesia, and China. Relative to bilateral reciprocal recognition arrangements, the Department of Employment, Education and Training asked the National Office of Overseas Skills Recognition (NOOSR) to commence a research project on mutual recognition of skills and qualifications with ASEAN countries. The Australian government is committed to funding this project, and the Australian accounting professional bodies have agreed with the Hong Kong Society of Accountants to hold preliminary discussions regarding a mutual recognition agreement. Currently, the professional bodies rely on country profiles, produced by the NOOSR, to provide an assessment of the universities in each country (Johns). This initiative demonstrates the need for international accounting education standards, an area that is the province of the International Federation of Accountants.

THE ROLE OF THE INTERNATIONAL FEDERATION OF ACCOUNTANTS (IFAC) AND ITS EDUCATION COMMITTEE

The International Federation of Accountants (IFAC) came into being as a result of initiatives put forward in 1973 and formally approved at the International Congress of Accountants in Munich in 1977. The mission of the IFAC is the development and enhancement of the profession to enable it to provide services of consistently high quality in the public interest. It is a nonprofit, nongovernmental, nonpolitical international organization of accountancy bodies. Through cooperation with member bodies, regional organizations of accountancy, and other world organizations, the IFAC initiates, coordinates, and guides efforts to achieve international technical, ethics, and education pronouncements for the accountancy profession. The membership of the IFAC currently consists of about 110 bodies from 80 countries.

The IFAC is governed by an assembly which consists of one representative from each member accountancy body. The assembly elects a Council, which has the responsibility for implementing the work program of the IFAC. An Executive Committee is chosen from the Council to carry out policy and decisions. The work program of the Council is implemented primarily by smaller working groups, including the following standing technical committees:

- Education,
- Ethics,
- Financial and Management Accounting,
- International Auditing Practices, and
- Public Sector.

The IFAC Education Committee "establishes standards, guidelines, discussion papers and other information documents on both prequalification education and training of accountants and on continuing professional education for members of the accounting profession. In addition, the Education Committee is expected to act as a catalyst in bringing together the developed and developing nations and to assist in the advancement of accounting education programs worldwide, particularly where this will assist economic development." (IFAC, 1997, 511). The members of the Education Committee are nominated by the member bodies in the countries selected by the Council of the IFAC. Country representatives serve two-and-a-half years and may be reappointed for another two-and-a-half-year term. Currently, the 12-member committee consists of Austria, Brazil, Canada, France, Ireland, Italy, Malaysia, Netherlands, New Zealand, Pakistan, the United States, and Zambia.

The Education Committee issues three types of documents:

- *International Education Guidelines (IEG)*: International education guidelines set forth essential requirements for accounting education which have the potential for international recognition, acceptance, and application. They promote good practice in accounting education.
- *Exposure Drafts:* Exposure drafts are proposed guidelines.
- *Discussion papers:* Discussion papers explore in depth a topic that may become the subject of a guideline. Discussion papers set forth issues, alternatives, and possible solutions.

Since its founding around 1980, the Education Committee has issued 10 IEGs, and five are currently in effect, as follows:

- IEG No. 2, "Continuing Professional Education,"
- IEG No. 7, "Education and Training Requirements for Accounting Technicians,"
- IEG No. 9, "Prequalification Education, Assessment of Professional Competence and Experience of Professional Accountants (Revised),"
- IEG No. 10, "Professional Ethics for Accountants: The Educational Challenge and Practical Application," and
- IEG No. 11, "Information Technology in the Accounting Curriculum."

IEG Nos. 1, 3, 4, 5, 6, and 8 are not listed because they were consolidated into IEG No. 9 in 1992. A major effort of the committee has been the complete rewriting of IEG No. 9, which was reissued in 1996. This may appear to be a meager output for so long a time, and indeed, the Education Committee's output has been subject to criticism (Needles 1990). It has been suggested that "No one seems to pay attention to [the] guidelines," because "(1) they lack a general purpose or objective; (2) they are so minimal in some cases that most countries can meet them; (3) they include exceptions in other cases that allow countries that do not meet them to continue to do what they are doing; and (4) they are supported by little rationale or evidence" (Needles 1990, 21-23).

In the past three years, however, the work of the Education Committee has taken on a new substance, and its profile in global professional concerns has been raised. Three principal movements have contributed to this development. First, successful completion of the GATT Uruguay Round, and specifically, the General Agreement on Trade in Services (GATS), and the creation of the World Trade Organization (WTO) put pressure on the accountancy profession to minimize the barriers to cross border provision of services. Second, given these pressures for cross-border recognition, the need exists for a basis by which the qualifications of accountants may be evaluated. Third, the movement throughout the world for privatization, along with the rapid growth of "emerging" markets, is increasing the need for professional accountants and an accounting profession as such in developing economies. The following sections detail the reaction of the IFAC Education Committee to these issues.

GENERAL AGREEMENT ON TRADE OF SERVICES (GATS), RECIPROCITY, AND THE IFAC EDUCATION COMMITTEE

The Education Committee often becomes involved in issues critical to the profession that do not result in the issuance of an IEG. A good example of this circumstance is its work in relation to the General Agreement on Trade of Services

(GATS). GATS is important because it "launches the first systematic assault on government-imposed barriers to trade and it initiates the first worldwide cooperative effort by the profession and governments to globalize accountancy" (Heeter 1994). To understand why this is true, it is important to consider how the new agreements work. The General Agreement on Tariffs and Trade (GATT) governs merchandise trade among 124 countries and sets out rules of government regulatory behavior intended to promote free and fair trade. It also serves as a forum for conducting periodic negotiations among signatory countries to reciprocally reduce existing trade barriers. Tariffs have traditionally been the principal barrier addressed, but recently non-tariff barriers such as import quotas are also on the agenda. The most significant result of the negotiations, and the most relevant to accountants, is GATS, an entirely new agreement formulated as part of the Uruguay Round. The objective of GATS, like its cousin GATT, is to address regulatory obstacles to international trade and foreign investment in service industries, including the cross-border practice of accounting. The broad intent is twofold:

- To remove discriminatory obstacles to market entry and practice by foreigners; and
- To ensure that foreign or internationally affiliated service providers, firms, and professionals enjoy the same treatment as their domestic counterparts or competitors with respect to government regulations.

The ramifications of this multilateral agreement are also twofold: First, its provisions on domestic regulation require countries to administer their licensing or certification rules in a reasonable, objective, and impartial manner, and forbid using them as disguised barriers to trade. To carry out this broad mandate, the agreement envisions the development of more specific binding disciplines in the future. Countries are also required to establish procedures for verifying the competence and credentials of professionals from other countries. Second, the agreement encourages countries to recognize other countries' qualifications, either autonomously or through mutual recognition agreements. It further sets out guidelines to assure that such agreements are not used simply to discriminate against professionals from countries that are not party to them.

To achieve its objectives, GATS adopts a very complex structure of rules and exceptions, schedules and annexes, special instructions and new institutions. The essence of the system is that most of these rules are valid only when nations apply them to specific service industries and professions as indicated in individual country schedules attached to the agreement. Once a commitment is made, not only does it bind the regulatory authorities to follow the rules, but it also binds state and provincial authorities and nongovernmental bodies acting in a regulatory capacity. In this latter category would fall professional institutes with regulatory powers and authority recognized by government.

Two of the GATS rules have particular relevance to the accountancy profession, although they apply to the full range of service industries and professions and not just to accountancy. These are Article V1 on domestic regulation and Article V11 on the recognition of qualification and licenses.

Article V1 on domestic regulation is one of the rules that apply only in cases where individual governments have made specific commitments in their schedules. It contains three important features:

1. Governments agree to apply regulations affecting service industries and professions in a reasonable, objective, and impartial manner so that they do not act as barriers to trade;
2. Qualification requirements and procedures, technical standards, and licensing requirements should not constitute unnecessary barriers to trade in services. Further disciplines or rules shall be developed on a sector-by-sector basis to ensure that such measures are based on objective and transparent criteria, are not more burdensome than necessary to ensure the quality of the service and, in the case of licensing requirements, do not in themselves serve as restrictions on the supply of the service. International standards should also be taken into account in determining compliance with these principles; and
3. All countries must have adequate procedures in place to verify the qualifications of professionals from other countries seeking the right to practice within their jurisdictions.

Article V11 on registration of qualifications and licenses applies across the board to all services and professions in all signatory countries regardless of whether specific commitments have been made. Like Article V1, this article has three features relevant to the accountancy profession:

1. Countries may choose their own approaches to recognizing foreign qualifications and licenses, through unilateral recognition, bilateral reciprocal arrangements, or international harmonization;
2. There is no obligation for a country to enter into any such arrangements. However, if a country decides to do so, whatever approach is chosen must be applied in a consistent, objective, and fair manner to all other countries seeking recognition of their professionals; and
3. Countries are encouraged to cooperate with intergovernmental and non-governmental organizations toward the establishment and adoption of common international qualifications and standards of practice.

Prior to GATT, the Education Committee identified reciprocity as an issue that deserved attention. It began addressing this issue in August 1991, when the committee member from India presented a draft paper on reciprocity and proposed that the committee adopt reciprocity as a project. This project was approved by the IFAC Council and, in May 1992, the Council asked that a point outline be developed that:

- Distinguishes clearly between reciprocity of practice rights and of membership;
- Draws up general guidance on how to compare the essential ingredients of a professional qualification (basic education, syllabus of exams, and practical experience); and
- Recognizes that any agreements on reciprocity can only be negotiated on a bilateral basis.

Based on this guidance, a draft guideline was developed and went through several versions over the following two years, by which time the GATS agreement had placed new urgency on this issue. In March and April 1994, due to the imminent formation of the World Trade Organization, with its commitment to the elimination of artificial barriers to trade in services, the IFAC Council was urging the Education Committee to give stronger support to the elimination of artificial barriers. What the Council required was a framework of multilateral rules that could be used in bilateral negotiations on mutual reciprocity, based on educational qualifications and licensing requirements; however, this would not necessarily mean reciprocity of professional membership. In the fall of 1994, a new draft of the document was prepared for presentation, not to the Council but to the GATS Advisory Task Force, which took over authorship of the framework, and a final document was released in 1995.

It is important to note that, under GATS, recognition need not be granted automatically to accounting professionals from other countries. However, each country is expected to have a methodology for comparing professional qualifications, which must be applied in a fair and consistent manner for all applicants. It may be helpful to examine how this principle is being applied in Europe and North America.

The legal foundation for the philosophy of mutual recognition was the 1957 Treaty of Rome, but nearly three decades passed before the enactment of the Single European Act 1986, which enshrined the philosophy of mutual recognition. The general system of mutual recognition of diplomas permits professionals in the EC to circulate more freely from one member state to another. This system concerns only individuals, and it ignores firms, even though they may be part of the relevant profession. In addition, the directive relates only to the establishment-based provision of services and does not address the question of the cross-boarder provision of services. The purpose is to honor the right of the professional to practice his or her profession in the host member state or to provide services there under the same conditions as those to which professionals in that country are subject. The progressive implementation of the eighth directive in member states and the effective organization of local knowledge examinations for the accountancy profession should result in a significant increase in the number of accountants benefiting from the mutual recognition of diplomas.

More recently, in North America, the North American Free Trade Agreement (NAFTA) established basic rules and obligations to facilitate cross-border trade in services. While recognizing the need for regulation, NAFTA encourages broader market access by providing that licensing requirements must be based on objective and transparent criteria, such as professional competence, and must be no more burdensome than is necessary to ensure the quality of service provided.

In 1991, the CICA, the AICPA, and the NASBA enacted an agreement, which became effective in some, but not all, states in November of 1993. This agreement, which establishes an International Qualifications Appraisal Board (IQAB), provides that a holder of one designation may qualify for any other by passing local knowledge examinations and by meeting certain experience requirements. Candidates for reciprocal recognition who qualify by passing the local knowledge examinations of one of the bodies are exempted from the obligation to write the final qualification examination of that body (AICPA/NASBA 1995). By 1997, reciprocity agreements had been reached by IQAB with Canada and Australia and an agreement with the United Kingdom was in its advanced stages. Furthermore, Mexico was developing a test of professional competence for its licensing procedure as a step toward a pact for recognition with the United States.

PREQUALIFICATION REQUIREMENTS: THE BASIS FOR MUTUAL RECOGNITION

Under GATS, the basis for mutual recognition is founded on the qualifications for professional accountants. These qualifications usually include specifications as to education, tests of professional competence, and experience, areas that fall under the province of the IFAC Education Committee. Up until 1996, the Committee's positions on these subjects had been specified in the original IEG No. 9, "Prequalification Education, Tests of Professional Competence and Practical Experience of Professional Accountants," which was a compilation of prior IEGs dealing with these topics. As seen above, these guidelines were subject to several valid criticisms and led to a comprehensive revision of IEG No. 9 by the Committee. Initiated in 1992, this review resulted in a discussion paper issued in June 1994 titled "2000 and Beyond: A Strategic Framework for Prequalification Education for the Accountancy Profession in the Year 2000 and Beyond." The paper takes a radically different approach to the qualifications of accountants than that followed under the original IEG No. 9, focusing more on the process of developing accounting education and on skills and knowledge requirements than on the academic courses that should comprise an accounting education. In forming this approach, the Committee relied on the work of the Accounting Education Change Commission in the

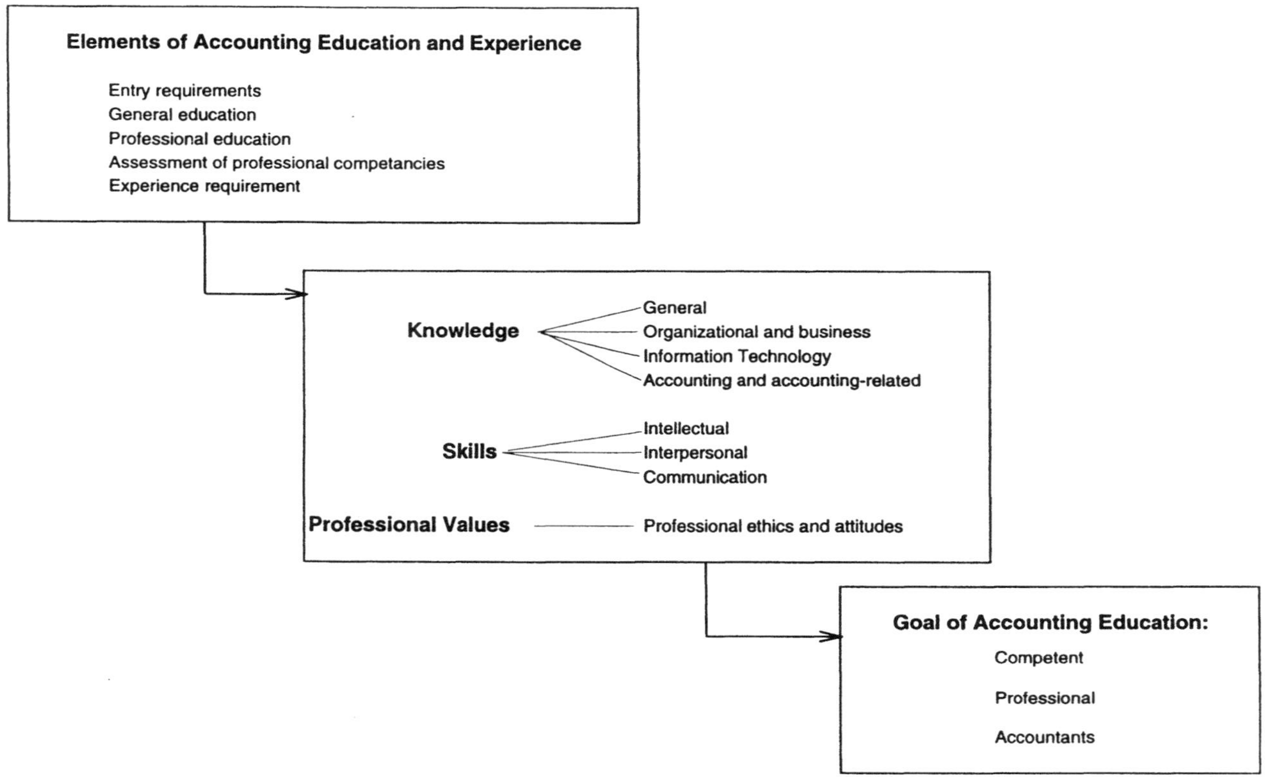

Figure 1. Goal and Structure of Prequalification Education and Experience of Professional Accountants

United States and the Australian and New Zealand professional bodies (Birkett 1993).

In the following year, the Committee developed a working document for a revision of IEG No. 9. This document, titled *Prequalification Education, Assessment of Professional Competence, and Experience Requirements of Professional Accountants,* was reviewed and approved for release as an exposure draft dated November 1995. Responses were to be made by May 31, 1996. The revised IEG No. 9 was approved by the Education Committee in September 1996. The following sections describe the content of revised IEG No. 9, which may form the basis of bilateral recognition agreements under GATS and be used as a model by many nations.

The recommendations in revised IEG No. 9 are directed toward establishing:

- The goal of accounting education and experience; its components of knowledge, skills, and professional values; and the elements on which education and experience for all professional accountants must be founded;
- The minimum benchmarks of professional education and experience that professional accountants must meet in order to obtain membership in their professional body and to exercise their profession; and
- The criteria for the assessment of professional competence.

The parts of revised IEG No. 9, which are discussed in the following sections, are organized according to: (1) the goal of accounting education and experience; (2) the knowledge, skills, and professional values necessary to achieve that goal; and (3) the elements that underlie the education and experience of professional accountants. The relationship among these sections is shown in Figure 1. In each section, the requirement is stated, and then discussed. All quotations in the sections that follow are from revised IEG No. 9 and all references to IEG No. 9 refer to the revised guideline unless otherwise noted.

Goal of Accounting Education and Experience

IEG No. 9 sets forth the goal of a program of accounting education and experience for professional accountants "to produce competent professional accountants capable of making a positive contribution over their lifetimes to the profession and society in which they work (para. 7) ." This goal addresses the need to maintain professional competence in the face of the changes that accountants increasingly encounter and requires that an attitude of learning be developed and maintained. It implies that a broad body of knowledge, skills, and professional values will provide strategies by which accountants can continue to learn and adapt to change throughout their professional lives.

The Committee believes that the predominant characteristic of the future in all cultures will be an environment of significant change, which will require a high standard of professional education and experience. This conclusion means that:

> A program of accounting education and experience must go beyond the traditional approach to accounting education, which has emphasized "transfer of knowledge," with learning defined and measured strictly in terms of knowledge of principles, standards, concepts, facts, and procedures at a point in time. Emphasis must be placed on a set of knowledge, skills, and professional values broad enough to enable adaptation to change. Individuals who become qualified professional accountants should be characterized by a constant striving to learn and apply what is new (para. 8).

Because professional accountants work in diverse cultural, political, and economic environments, the goal is to promote flexibility in the development of accounting education and experience. It holds that the focus of accounting education and experience should be on the knowledge, skills, and professional values needed for working in professional environments, such as public, managerial, or government accounting. Standards for accounting education and experience should place emphasis, first, on the desired output, and then, on the process necessary to achieve that output. This process, which will be carried out in an unstructured environment, is an important part of the concept of learning to learn. Moreover, the guideline says that a key objective of accounting programs should be to teach students to learn on their own. To achieve this objective, educators may need to be trained and must be encouraged to use a broad range of teaching methods, including:

- Use of case studies and other means to simulate actual work situations;
- Working in groups;
- Adapting instructional methods and materials to the ever-changing environment in which the professional accountant works;
- Pursuing a curriculum that encourages students to learn on their own;
- Using technology creatively;
- Encouraging students to be active participants in the learning process; and
- Using measurement and evaluation methods that reflect the changing knowledge, skills, and values required of professional accountants.

Knowledge, Skills, and Professional Values

In IEG No. 9, the Committee supports programs of accounting education and experience centered on outputs that are appropriate to the country or the professional organization to which they apply. This approach should make possible the development of measurable competency standards, which should form the basis for the monitoring and assessment that can lead to improvement in the quality of accounting education and experience.

The Committee contends that methods should be adopted to assess the potential of students for providing a positive lifelong contribution to the profession and society. These assessment methods should focus on developing competency standards to evaluate the knowledge, skills, and professional values required of professional accountants.

The Committee also asserts that to achieve the goal of providing a foundation for lifelong learning, a program of accounting education and experience must offer a grounding in an essential body of knowledge, skills, and professional values which would form the basis for competency standards. The professional bodies in each country must identify the knowledge, skills, and professional values relevant to their environments and develop the related competency standards. The Committee has identified the following sets as a basis for establishing these standards.

Knowledge

Prior to qualification, an individual should acquire information about the world in which the professional accountant works, covering knowledge in general, organizational and business areas; information technology; and accounting and accounting-related subjects. The content of these areas is as follows:

- *General knowledge:* Broad-based individuals, who think and communicate effectively and who have the basis for conducting inquiry, carrying out abstract logical thinking, and undertaking critical analysis must have a good foundation of general education. This foundation enables them to place decisions in the larger context of society, to exercise good judgment and professional competence, to interact with diverse groups of people, and to begin the process of professional growth.
- *Organizational and business knowledge:* Organizational and business knowledge provides the context in which professional accountants work. A broad knowledge of business, government, and nonprofit organizations; how they are organized, financed, and managed; and the global environment in which they operate, is essential to the functioning professional accountant.
- *Information technology knowledge:* Information technology has transformed the role of the professional accountant. The professional accountant not only must use and evaluate information systems but also play an important role in the design and management of such systems.
- *Accounting and accounting-related knowledge:* Accounting and knowledge provides the strong technical background essential to a successful career as a professional accountant (para. 12-15).

Skills

Whereas the knowledge set may be most directly identified with the information content of the curriculum, the skill set identified by the Committee is more oriented toward attributes that will result in the successful use of the knowledge set. They are not usually acquired from specific courses devoted to them but from the total effect of the educational program and professional experience. This set consists of three kinds of skills—intellectual, interpersonal, and communication, as enumerated below.

- *Intellectual skills:* Intellectual skills enable the professional accountant to solve problems, make decisions, and exercise good judgment in complex organizational situations. Capabilities that collectively comprise an individual's intellectual skills are:
  - The capacity for inquiry, research, abstract logical thinking, inductive and deductive reasoning, and critical analysis;
  - The ability to identify and solve unstructured problems in unfamiliar settings and to apply problem-solving skills in a consultative process;
  - The ability to select and assign priorities within restricted resources and to organize work to meet tight deadlines; and
  - The ability to adapt to change.

- *Interpersonal skills:* Interpersonal skills enable professional accountants to work with others for the common good of the organization. The components of interpersonal skills are:
  - The ability to work with others in a consultative process, particularly in groups, to organize and delegate tasks, to motivate and develop people, to withstand and resolve conflict, and at appropriate times to lead them;
  - The ability to interact with culturally and intellectually diverse people; and
  - The ability to negotiate acceptable solutions and agreements in professional situations.

- *Communication skills:* Communication skills enable the professional accountant to receive and transmit information, form reasoned judgments, and make decisions effectively. The components of communication skills are:
  - The ability to present, discuss, and defend views effectively through formal and informal, written and spoken, language;
  - The ability to listen effectively, including a sensitivity to cultural and language differences; and
  - The ability to locate, obtain, organize, report, and use information from human, print, and electronic sources (para. 17-19).

Professional Values

Professional values comprise the attitudes that identify professional accountants as a members of a profession. They are essential to making a continuing contribution to the development of the profession and the society in which it operates. The attributes which collectively comprise the values and attitudes of professional accountants are:

- A commitment to act with integrity and objectivity and to be independent under applicable professional standards;
- A knowledge of the standards of professional ethics of the member body to which an individual aspires;
- A concern for the public interest and sensitivity to social responsibilities; and
- A commitment to lifelong learning (para. 21).

Flexibility of Knowledge, Skills, and Values

By focusing on the outcomes of knowledge, skills, and values, the guideline recognizes that professional accountancy bodies, regulatory agencies, and educational systems across the world have adopted a variety of practices to ensure that candidates possess the educational background and intellectual qualities which, together with appropriate experience, are necessary for admission to membership. Differences in these practices result from differences in several other areas, including long-established preparation for the profession, educational systems, views on the role of prequalification education and the merits of practical experience, the organization and role of the profession, the influence of government, cultural outlooks, and economic conditions.

Elements of Accounting Education

Whereas a program's output will be specified by the foregoing goals and knowledge sets, the processes leading to that output will be determined by the elements of accounting education and experience. These elements include entry requirements, general education, professional education, assessment, and experience requirement.

Entry Requirements

Because of considerable variation in the entry requirements for entering a program of study for professional accountants, IEG No. 9 sets a minimum standard of the education that an individual must bring to the program of education and experience. This minimum standard states that "for an individual seeking to begin a program of study leading to membership as a professional accountant in an accountancy body should be at least equivalent to that which would entitle one to admission into a recognized university degree program or its equivalent (para. 26)." While in some countries, this standard may not seem minimal, it represents an improvement on the original IEG No. 9 in that it is a firm requirement not allowing for exceptions. It recognizes that the quality of a profession cannot be maintained and improved if the capability of the individuals that enter it do not meet high standards.

General Education

Because the Committee believes that a broad-based general education is critical, it proposes that general education "must focus on the development of general knowledge, intellectual skills, interpersonal skills, and communication skills through a broad range of subjects that provide students with a grounding in arts, sciences, and humanities." Although general education requirements vary greatly from program to program and from country to country, a broad-based general education is critical to lifelong learning and provides the foundation on which to build professional and accounting studies and should provide students with

- An understanding of the flow of ideas and events in history, the different cultures in today's world, and an international perspective;
- Basic knowledge of human behavior;
- A sense of the breadth of ideas, issues, and contrasting economic, political, and social forces in the world;
- Experience in inquiry and the evaluation of quantitative data;
- The ability to conduct inquiry, carry out abstract logical thinking, and understand critical thinking;
- An appreciation of art, literature, and science;
- An awareness of personal and social values and of the process of inquiry and judgment; and
- Experience in making value judgments (para. 29).

Professional Education

IEG No. 9 states that "the professional education component must consist of two or three years of full-time study (or the equivalent) and must build on and develop further the intellectual, interpersonal, and communication skills provided in general education (para. 31)." Professional education consists of the:

- Organizational and business knowledge core;
- Information technology knowledge core; and
- Accounting and accounting-related knowledge core.

The aim of the professional education component is to identify the subject areas which should be covered, but it does not necessarily suggest actual courses that would be taken, because the subjects identified are covered under different descriptions in different parts of the world. It is also recognized that some bodies require a greater range of subjects, while others place greater emphasis on some subjects in order to meet the purposes for which their students are being trained. The level of understanding required may also vary in different professional bodies and over different time periods. An important determinant of the curriculum should be the knowledge, skills, and professional values relevant to a particular country or professional body.

- *Organizational and business core:* The organizational and business knowledge core must include coverage of the following subjects:
  - Economics,
  - Quantitative methods and statistics for business,
  - Organizational behavior,
  - Operations management,
  - Marketing,
  - International business (para. 32).

These core subjects are intended to provide the prospect professional accountant with:

  - A knowledge of the activities of business, government, and non-profit organizations, and of the environments in which they operate, including the major economic, legal, political, social, international, and cultural forces and their influences and values;
  - A knowledge of macro- and microeconomics;
  - The application of quantitative methods and statistics to business problems;
  - An understanding of interpersonal and group dynamics in organizations, including the methods for creating and managing change in organizations;
  - An understanding of personnel issues, operations management, organizational strategy, and governance and marketing;
  - A basic knowledge of international trade and finance and the ways in which international business is conducted; and
  - An ability to integrate the above components in accomplishing strategic objectives (para. 33).

- *Information technology core:* The information technology core requirements for professional accountants are addressed in IEG No. 11, "Information Technology in the Accounting Curriculum." It may be obtained in a variety of ways, including in separate courses and by integrating the subject into the organizational and business core and into the professional accounting core, but should provide students with the knowledge and skills they need to use and evaluate information technology and systems and to provide input into the design and management of those systems. It also provides the prospective accountant with a knowledge of the process of identifying, gathering, measuring, summarizing, and analyzing financial data in the contemporary environment, including:
  - The basic concepts of information systems and technology;

  - Skills in the use of current software such as spreadsheets, word processors, graphics packages, database systems, electronic mail, accounting packages, and similar programs;
  - The concepts and principles of information system design;
  - The concepts and principles of information system evaluation; and
  - Use of information technology for competitive advantage, organization, staffing, planning, budgeting, and control.

- *Accounting and accounting-related core:* The accounting and accounting-related core identifies the subject areas to which all accountants should be exposed and provides students with the technical accounting knowledge and professional ethics and values sufficient to pursue careers as professional accountants. It must include coverage of at least the following subjects:
  - Financial accounting and reporting,
  - Management accounting,
  - Taxation,
  - Business and commercial law,
  - Auditing,
  - Finance and financial management, and
  - Professional ethics.

These core subjects should provide the prospective professional accountant with a knowledge of:

  - History of the accounting profession and accounting thought;
  - Content, concepts, structure, and meaning of reporting for organizational operations, both for internal and external use, including the information needs of financial decision makers and a critical assessment of the role of accounting information in satisfying those needs;
  - National and international accounting and auditing standards;
  - Financial management including managing resources, planning and budgeting, cost management, quality control, and benchmarking;
  - Environmental factors, including the regulation of accounting;
  - Ethical and professional responsibilities of an accountant;
  - The concepts, methods, and processes of control that provide for the accuracy and integrity of financial data and safeguarding of business assets;
  - Taxation and its impact on financial and managerial decisions;
  - The nature of auditing and other attest services and the conceptual and procedural bases for performing them in manual and electronic environments; and
  - A knowledge of finance, including financial statement analysis, financial instruments, and capital markets, both domestic and international (para. 43).

Specialized studies should be pursued only after a student has received a foundation in the organizational and business core and the professional accounting core. The IFAC Discussion Paper, "Specialization in the Accounting Curriculum," is devoted to this subject.

Assessment of Professional Competencies

Assessment of competence is an important element in any educational process. Public confidence in the profession depends, to some degree, on the adequacy of professional examinations. IEG No. 9 strengthens considerably the examinations element by stating that:

> A required component of the assessment process for individuals seeking to become A final examination, administered by, or with substantive input from, the professional body or regulatory authority. The examination must be comprehensive, require a significant portion of responses to be in writing, and be administered near the end of the educational and, where appropriate, experience requirement (para. 44).

The original IEG No. 9 addressed the need for tests of professional competence but did not require them. The Committee has determined that assessment of competence in the form of an examination of professional competence is a required element for several reasons. First, professional organizations, particularly those that are self-regulatory, have a responsibility to ensure that their members have the competence expected from them by society. Second, individuals who assume responsibility for certain aspects of the well-being of others need to demonstrate their ability to discharge them in a competent manner. Third, the well-being of society and the credibility of the profession is enhanced by preventing those who do not meet its competency standards from holding themselves out as professionals.

The Committee also believes that an examination of professional competence should measure more than just theoretical knowledge. For example, candidates should be able to demonstrate that they:

- Have a sound technical knowledge of the specific subjects of the curriculum;
- Have an ability to apply technical knowledge in an analytical and practical manner;
- Are able to extract from various subjects the knowledge required to solve integrated problems;
- Can identify information relevant to a particular problem by distinguishing the relevant from the irrelevant in a given body of data;
- Are able, in multi-problem situations, to identify the problems and rank them in the order in which they need to be addressed;
- Appreciate that there can be alternative solutions and understand the role of judgment in dealing with these;
- Have an ability to integrate diverse areas of knowledge and skills;

- Can communicate effectively to the user by formulating realistic recommendations in a concise and logical fashion; and
- Have knowledge of the ethical requirements of the profession (para. 48).

The overall thrust of this requirement is to place more emphasis on the assessment of competencies as opposed to knowledge. This is an approach that is already being tried in some countries. For example, countries in Southern Africa are working on the possibility of a joint examination and the work on competency standards in Australia, New Zealand, and other southeast Asian countries has already been cited.

Experience Requirement

To ensure that professional accountants have attained the necessary level of professional competence in their application of knowledge, skills, and values, an appropriate period of relevant experience in accounting practice is recognized as a component of most prequalification programs. The period of experience may vary due to differences among the environments in which professional accountants offer their services. Differences also exist among countries, as well as professional bodies, as to the length and nature of such experience.

IEG No. 9 addresses the issue of these differences by stating that "this period should be long enough to permit prospective accountants to demonstrate they have gained the knowledge, skills, and professional values sufficient for performing with professional competence and for continuing to grow throughout their careers (para. 49)." Although the guideline falls short of specifying a minimum period of experience, it does state, "This objective cannot normally be met in a period of less than three years (para. 49)." This period is greater than the experience requirement in some countries, such as the United States, where the trend has been toward a shorter experience requirement.

Another issue that the Committee found difficult to resolve is the nature of relevant experience. The term "relevant experience," as used in the guideline, refers to participation in work activities in an environment appropriate to the application of knowledge, skills, and professional values. IEG No. 9 states that prospective professional accountants should receive their relevant experience in accounting positions deemed "appropriate by the professional body to which they are applying." For those who intend to work in public practice, the most relevant experience would be gained in public practice. For professional accountants who will work in another field, such as industry, commerce or government service, or in a specialty, such as auditing and insolvency, experience in the relevant area may be required by a regulatory or professional body.

POTENTIAL RAMIFICATIONS OF THE GLOBALIZATION OF QUALIFICATIONS OF PROFESSIONAL ACCOUNTANTS

At least three potential ramifications of the heightened attention at the international level to the qualifications of professional accountants may be identified. One ramification is that the process of setting qualifications will become more political. The fact that the IFAC represents so many different organizations, some of which do not perform the attest function, influences the process of decision making. For instance, a number of organizations are concerned primarily with managerial accounting or governmental accounting and may not have a history of tests of professional competence or experience requirements. In the past, the Education Committee has tried to take these attributes into consideration in setting education guidelines. The result, however, was to weaken the guidelines and not provide definite guidance for use in countries which were endeavoring to develop an accounting profession. The revised IEG No. 9 is a major step toward setting firmer standards that provide benchmarks for all organizations and countries. This action on the part of the Education Committee, however, implies that some organizations and countries will not meet the standards and may be unhappy as a result. It may also be anticipated that there will be increased pressure from organizations such as the ISAR, the WTO, and UNCLAD for an international accreditation of accounting credentials. Also, as reciprocity agreements—such as the one between the United States and Canada and Australia—are made, there will be pressure for agreements with other countries such as Mexico. There will also be pressure for regional solutions to the reciprocity issue and, hence, regional associations of accountants will become more important. This is particularly true now in Europe but is also a key issue in other parts of the world, such as Asia and Africa. It may also become increasingly important in Latin America.

Another ramification of the global discussion of the qualifications of accountants is that global associations of accounting academics will become more important. This phenomenon is already manifested in the growth of regional academic organizations. For example, just a decade ago, the European Accounting Association was a small group of accounting educators mostly from the United Kingdom and a few other Northern European countries. Now, it is a large organization with active participation from most European countries and with a lively journal. The growth of the Asian Pacific Conference on International Accounting Issues in the last six years is more evidence of this trend. Perhaps most indicative of this global trend is the formation and growth of the International Association for Accounting Education and Research (IAAER). Consisting of fewer than 50 members just seven years ago, the organization by 1995 had almost 600 individual members from more than 50 countries and 34 institutional members. Approximately half of the institutional members are academic organizations and about half are professional accounting organizations. The IAAER has observer status on the IFAC Education Committee and works closely with the IFAC by coordinating activities through joint meetings of the respective Executive Committees and by holding joint conferences with the IFAC for institutional members. The Journal of Accounting Education has become the official journal of the IAAER and will bring an international perspective to research in international accounting education.

A third ramification of these developments is an increased demand for guidance about the qualifications of professional accountants from emerging countries in all parts of the world. Two principal forces are leading to this demand. One is increased trade by these countries with the developed world, especially through the moving of operations from developed countries offshore. The second is the global movement toward privatization. Throughout the world, there are countries without established accounting professions and without the infrastructure to establish accounting, auditing, and educational guidelines. The high demand for qualified accountants in these countries is making the establishment of indigenous accounting professions with appropriate standards a high priority, and these countries are looking to organizations such as the IASC and the IFAC to assist in establishing guidelines. For example, the IFAC Education Committee works with developing countries to support them in obtaining grants from international bodies, such as the World Bank, for accounting education and for the development of professional bodies.

REFERENCES

American Institute of Certified Public Accountants (AICPA). 1988. *Report of the Special Committee on Governance and Structure.* New York: AICPA.

American Institute of Certified Public Accountants and National Association of State Boards of Accountancy. 1995. *International Qualifications Appraisal Board (IQAB) Procedures.* New York: AICPA/NASBA, April.

Birkett, W.S. 1993. *Competency-Based Standards for Professional Accountants.* Sidney: Australia and New Zealand Societies of Accountants.

Burns, J.O., and B.E. Needles, Jr., eds. 1994. *Accounting Education for the 21st Century.* Oxford, UK: Pergamon.

Heeter, C.P., Jr. 1994. The GATT treaty: Issues and implications for accountants. Remarks presented at the International Conference on Research and Education Agendas, New York City, August 10.

International Accounting and Reporting Issues. 1992. New York: United Nations Centre on Transnational Corporations.

International Federation of Accountants. 1991. *International Education Guideline No. 9: Prequalification Education, Tests of Professional Competence and Practical Experience of Professional Accountants.* New York: International Federation of Accountants.

International Federation of Accountants. 1994a. Bilateral reciprocal recognition arrangements for accounting in the ASEAN region. In *IFAC Education Network.* New York: International Federation of Accountants, June.

International Federation of Accountants. 1994b. 2000 and beyond: A strategic framework for prequalification education for the accountancy profession in the year 2000 and beyond. Discussion paper of the Education Committee, IFA.

International Federation of Accountants. 1995. The United States-Canada bilateral agreement on reciprocity from a US perspective. *IFAC Newsletter* New York, (March).

International Federation of Accountants. 1996. International Education Guideline No. 9: Prequalification Education, Assessment of Professional Competencies, and Experience Requirements of Professional Accountants. IFAC Education Committee, October.

International Federation of Accountants. 1997. *IFAC Handbook: Technical Pronouncements.* New York: International Federation of Accountants.

Johns, A. 1994. Australian government initiatives. Notes from a presentation at the Conference on Education and Research Agendas, New York, August 10.

Mednick, R. 1988. Our profession in the year 2000: A blueprint of the future. *Journal of Accountancy* (August), 54-58.

Mednick, R. 1996. Licensure and regulation of the profession: A time for change. *Journal of Accountancy* (March), 33-38.

National Association of State Boards of Accountancy. 1997. NASBA board reviews joint committee's proposals. In *State Board Report*, March.

Needles, B.E., Jr. 1990. Standards for international accounting education: A consideration of the issues. In *Comparative International Accounting Educational Standards.* Urbana, IL: Center for International Education and Research in Accounting.

Needles, B.E., Jr., and V.K. Zimmerman, eds. 1990. *Comparative International Accounting Educational Standards.* Urbana, IL: Center for International Education and Research in Accounting.

Organization for Economic Cooperation and Development (OECD). 1997. World trade organization promotes trade in accountancy services. *Accounting Information Network* (February).

Rinke, D.F. 1994. Comparative analysis of the credentialing processes of professional public accountants in the European Community. In *The New Europe: Implications for Accountants and Accounting.* Champaign/Urbana, IL: Center for International Education and Research in Accounting.

EDITOR'S NOTE

ACCOUNTING: CULTURAL ARTIFACT AS TRUTH:

PERHAPS MORE TRUTHS ARE BETTER

Larry M. Parker

During a final quick read of the papers for this 10th Anniversary Special International Edition, I found myself with a sense of concern about the direction of the internationalization of accounting standards. I have been a supporter of changes in accounting worldwide (e.g., Parker 1989). I was never a fan of "standardization" of accounting. It seemed to assume that there would be a superior accounting culture which would lead the world to a superior form of accounting—almost a Friedrich Nietzsche approach to international accounting. Harmonization has appealed to me. It has the sense of a "salad bowl" view (as opposed to a "melting pot"), which always had an intuitive attraction for me during my time as a human relations instructor. So harmonization was not what was bothering me. As I struggled to decide what was disturbing me, I also decided it was not directly related to the unnecessary limitations or definitional boundaries that so inhibit what accounting can or should be (Parker 1996).

Research in Accounting Regulation, Supplement 1, pages 395-397.

ISBN: 0-7623-0338-7

I finally realized that I was fascinated by the impact of culture, in the broadest sense, on accounting standards, reporting, and ethics. And it came to me that I really do not want accounting systems, again in the broadest sense, to be very similar. I would like the accounting of the Peoples' Republic of China to be culturally different from that of Sweden, and Sweden to be different from Australia, Australia different from the United States, and so forth. This is not because of some nostalgia or whim. I would like to keep a strong dynamic tension in the inherently difficult relationship between cultural artifact and truth in accounting.

Even the pre-Socratic philosophers—Milesians, Pythagoreans, and Eleatics—delved into the difficulties of reality, perceptions of reality, and interpretations (beliefs or theories) of reality. To the extent that our interpretations represent underlying realities, the interpretations are "truths." The interpretations must be communicated through math, language, or some combination of math and language. Math and language, of course, are developed based upon some set of belief systems. It seems fitting to me that accounting, as the oldest known form of written communication, should perhaps accept that differences among cultures might help keep a tension or interplay alive that may be useful in the continuing attempt for accounting to represent underlying realities—truth.

Of course, accountants have occasionally discussed truth in accounting. MacNeal (1970[1939], vii) wanted to "bring every accounting rule in line with the proven principles of economics and logic." In the 1960s, a number of scholars wished to make accounting more scientific, hoping to bring more rigor to the truths expressed in accounting. Such efforts are understandable, even commendable, but foolish and in vain in my opinion. Accounting, I believe, is an applied social science, and nothing is proven or scientific. Accounting's search for truth(s) probably needs to be as diverse as are the societies, however global or provincial, accounting serves—developing and improving as societal belief systems change.

It is understandable that some of us idealize the search for truth and would wish accounting could be as precise as, say, natural science. But natural science itself struggles in its communication of realities. My favorite example is the search by physicists for what may be the "ultimate" building blocks of matter (matter, of course, comprises a significant portion of what most consider reality)—quarks. I particularly like the difficulties of juxtaposing math and language to attempt to communicate the reality of quarks. Competing theories of quantum physics attempt to be consistent enough to bar the possibility of "pathological variants," and describe superstrings that exist in a point of zero dimensions. Quantum chromatics attributes the colors red, green, and blue to quarks that are colorless. But I find the names given to quarks the most fascinating. Most theories seem to agree there are six quarks. The first three to be found were "up," "down," and "strange." Next were "charm" and "beauty." The last quark, to the best of my knowledge, has not yet been found. It appears that the last quark, currently designated as "t," will, when found, be called "truth." When scientists find "truth," the last of the ultimate building blocks of matter or physical reality, I suspect I shall be a little saddened.

However, the good news is that accountants can continue to search for truth (and beauty and charm and strangeness—whatever). And we can do it without the horrible communication machinations of the poor unfortunate physicists, who may or may not know "truth" when they "see" it.

The point is this. We need not and should not seek or envy someone else's truth as our own. The Spanish philosopher Julian Marias explained that no belief system can claim an exclusive and absolute view of truth. We accountants are fortunate to have our very own search for culturally different truths—we should be glad of it. With any luck, that search will be not only never-ending, but ever-expanding.

Many years ago I read this quote from Voltaire.

> There are truths
> which are not for all men,
> nor for all times.

Ain't it the truth.

REFERENCES

MacNeal, K. 1970[1939]. *Truth in Accounting.* Houston, TX: Scholars Book Co.

Parker, L.M. 1989. Medieval traders as international change agents: A comparison with twentieth century international accounting firms. *The Accounting Historians Journal* (December): 107-118.

Parker, L.M. 1996. Burning the old skins: Tearing down the profession's intellectual and professional constraints; building a new structure. In *Research in Accounting Regulation,* Vol. 10, eds. J Previts, L.M. Parker, and R. Eskew, 215-220. Greenwich, CT: JAI Press.

BOOK REVIEWS

A Report on the Similarities and Differences between IASC Standards and U.S. GAAP

Based on a Study by the FASB Staff
Edited by Carrie Bloomer
(Norwalk: Financial Accounting Standards Board, 1996; $25 paperback, 426 pp.)

Reviewed by **Kevin Carduff**

The internationalization of accounting standards is currently one of the largest concerns for the accounting profession due to the globalization of the capital and manufacturing markets. Not only are foreign companies, such as Daimler-Benz, applying to enter the U.S. capital markets, but U.S. firms are continually developing divisions overseas. As a result, foreign firms are willing to amend their financial statements to conform to U.S. GAAP, and U.S. firms are facing consolidation concerns with foreign divisions. The Financial Accounting Standards Board (FASB) amended its mission in 1991 to include the definition of international standards to aid investors. This joint project between the FASB and the International Accounting Standards Committee (IASC) attempts to compare the similarities and differences not only among the separate accounting standards but also between the methodologies and missions of the individual organizations. This is an important feature because standards might differ in scope and implementation, not only because of the needs of individual users but because of the purposes of the respective standards boards.

This project is one of the first studies on the differences between the IASC core standards and U.S. GAAP. The book is divided into two parts. The first part

Research in Accounting Regulation, Supplement 1, pages 401-403.

ISBN: 0-7623-0338-7

describes the individual organizations, the IASC and the FASB, and their missions, their methodologies, and their sponsoring organizations. The project starts by describing the organization of the two boards. The IASC is comprised of 116 different entities who represent the securities boards of 87 different countries, while the FASB is comprised of seven board members (nominated by the Financial Accounting Foundation) who come from the disciplines of academia, finance, industry, and public accounting. Additionally, the book describes the structures and processes of the organizations, including the different standards, the individual sponsoring boards, and the frameworks and nominating processes they use. This background establishes a basis for the next section, which analyzes the 32 standards accepted and implemented by the IASC.

The second section of the book is the analysis of the individual standards set by the IASC. These standards were studied by staff members of the FASB and then reviewed by panels to ensure completeness. The reviewers looked for similarities and differences in standards, based upon scope, definitions, recognition, measurement, display, and disclosure. Also, the reviewers had to determine the influence each of these differences would have upon interpretation and guidance for other analysts, academics, and accountants.

While this the most comprehensive analysis of the international standards to date, the study is still biased towards the FASB's interpretation of accounting standards. The internationalization of accounting standards should not lead to the gentrification of individual practices and methods. The project analyzes each standard the IASC has produced and compares the similarities and differences between the two standards. While the review recognizes the validity of the international standards for analysts as well as other considerations, it still expresses the importance and completeness of the FASB standards.

This is the most complete statistical analysis of the differences between U.S. GAAP and the IASC's effort to date. The book tries to express the international standards in GAAP terms. However, the two efforts are not comparable. The IASC is attempting to develop acceptable standards for a set of core accounting issues relevant to all firms, while the FASB is attempting to develop standards for all accounting issues relevant to U.S. capital markets.

There will never be a complete compatibility between standards until it is realized that U.S. standards will not totally translate overseas, and that the attractiveness of our capital markets is too overwhelming for foreign companies. The stock market is growing by impossible leaps because of mutual fund investing and foreign investment. There will never be total comparisons between standards. The U.S. accounting standards are the most comprehensive in the world; however, they were designed for our capital markets and our culture, while the international process must respect the cultures of all nations. Even though the FASB has established comprehensive standards, the rest of the world's standard-setting bodies will not universally accept these standards. As a result, the IASC must respect the requests of all the countries. While foreign companies are required to amend their financial statements in order to enter the U.S. capital markets, we need comparative standards and statements to analyze annual reports accurately. There needs to be greater cooperation between the FASB and the IASC to generate standards while satisfying the needs of all the constituents involved.

This book provided me with a much clearer definition of the roles and missions of the two standard-setting bodies, and the work done by them, than I had previously. While the FASB has done an outstanding job in analyzing the two organizations and it recognizes the need for harmonization, it still expresses the significance of its standards. This is the only weakness within the book. The expanding global economy demands the need for comparable international standards. The FASB does recognize the need for international compatibility; however, it feels that U.S. principles should be the standard. While differences in applying standards is important, an understanding that different cultures and foreign businesses follow different practices is more important.

Responsibilities and Liabilities of Accountants and Auditors: Proccedings of a Forum

Report by the Secretariat of the United Nations Conference on Trade and Development

(New York and Geneva: United Nations Conference on Trade and Development, 1996; ISBN 92-1-104451-0)

Reviewed by **Mark A. Segal**

The proceedings of the conference is composed of a Preface, Presentations by panelists, Questions and Comments from the ISAR Experts, Summary and Conclusions, a Select List of Publications of the Division on Transnational Corporations and Investment, and a Questionnaire. This report examines the preface, presentations, questions and comments, and summary and conclusions. Participants in the proceedings included:

- Roger Lawrence, Director in Charge, Division on Transnational Corporations and Investment, United Nations Conference on Trade and Development, author of the Preface;
- Richard H. Murray, Director of Claims and Risk Services, Deloitte Touche Tohmatsu International;
- Werner Ebke, Professor of Law, University of Konstanz, Germany;
- Carl D. Liggio, former General Counsel, Ernst & Young, New York;
- C. Ch. Mout, Partner, law firm of Nauta Dutilh, Amsterdam, Netherlands;

Research in Accounting Regulation, Supplement 1, pages 405-409.

ISBN: 0-7623-0338-7

- Bernard P. Germond, member of the Executive Committee, International Federation of Accountants;
- David Darbyshire, Partner, Arthur Andersen and Co., Vice President, Federation of European Accountants;
- James K. Loebbecke, Professor and Associate Dean, David Eccles School of Business, University of Utah;

The presentations make it clear that concern with accounting litigation is not restricted to the United States. Claims against accountants, particularly auditors, have been raised in some 80 countries. These countries include developed and undeveloped countries, as well as countries with civil and common law legal systems. The presentations indicate that accountant litigation has been of greatest concern in developed countries that have a common law tradition. Similarities seem to exist in the rationale and legal structure with respect to audit services, the factors contributing to the litigation crisis, and how these elements should be dealt with.

Preface. The preface, written by Roger Lawrence, provides a brief introduction to the proceedings and the themes which dominate the presentations. It notes the role of the media and corporate bankruptcies in the growth of accounting litigation. The expectation gap widely cited in the accounting profession is mentioned, as is the need for concern over the inelasticity of audit fees and the constraints placed on auditors in detecting fraud and irregularities. Hope is expressed that the ideas presented will be useful in the development of relevant rules and regulations.

Richard F. Murray. According to Murray, the liability crisis warrants concern about the survival of the larger accounting units and the ability of the profession to attract those best suited to meet its service expectations and professional responsibilities. Murray notes that accountants have been spared the full brunt of substantial judgments and settlements, due to insurance coverage. This coverage is increasingly scarce and expensive. As a result, should litigation problems continue, the profession will have to absorb an increasingly greater percentage of the payout. As providers of professional service, accountants cannot look to external investment to help soften the financial impact. Issue is taken with placement of responsibility upon accountants and auditors. In Murray's estimation, accountants are generally held responsible because they have deep pockets. It is not they who cause the loss but rather their clients, through negligence or irregularity, or other parties through negligence or assumption of the risk. The legal establishment and media have fostered an environment that contributes to the litigation problem. Failure to take ameliorative action will have drastic effects on economic competitiveness and capital formation.

Werner Ebke. Despite the substantial body of case law concerning auditor liability, a fundamental legal issue remains about what constitutes the scope of the duties of an independent auditor to the auditor's clients and third parties. In resolving this question, Ebke states that this is but part of a larger policy question involving what should be the role of the auditor in corporate governance. The discussion is targeted at providing guidance to emerging economies that have to contend with the issue. Ebke contends that all countries should adopt an established body of rules corresponding to GAAP and require that publicly held companies be subject to audit by an external properly licensed independent accountant. In order to avoid the expectation gap, there is a need to make users of financial statements and those who purportedly rely on the work of accountants, aware of what has truly been performed.

The comment is made that countries with a highly developed civil law tradition have far less accounting litigation than those with a common law tradition. In part, this is attributed to the lack of pre-trial discovery, rules regarding the burden of proof, and the recovery of legal costs. Rather than suggest a particular approach, Ebke calls for a balancing of auditor and third party interests. Concern is voiced over the need to keep auditor liability within reasonable limits and take into account the fact that frequently the plaintiffs in these cases are sophisticated business people.

Carl D. Liggio. Liggio begins by conceding that the accounting profession may justifiably be held responsible where committing negligence or fraud, and that the profession has been slow in making changes and improvement. Liggio then focuses his presentation upon a litigation system gone awry—a system characterized by juries that resolve cases based upon emotion rather than the word of law, an attitude that all wrongs merit compensation even if from one who did not cause the injury, and a society increasingly represented by people unable to take responsibility for their own actions and all too anxious to place the blame on others. These are but some of the factors contributing to the litigation crisis. Consistent with the presence of an expectation gap, Liggio mentions that a problem exists in the difficulty of laypersons to accept that the audit services provide reasonable assurance and reflect professional judgment but are not a guarantee of results. In order to remedy this situation, judgmental type decisions should be recognized and distinguished from those considered nonjudgmental. Another factor in need of increased attention is the establishment of causation both of the transaction and the loss. Transaction causation may be defined as existing where "but for" the improper conduct, the activity would not have been engaged in by the plaintiff, and loss causation as existing where the loss was caused by the conduct of the defendant. A problem contributing to the growth in litigation is the failure of courts to adequately explore both causation issues. Liggio concludes with excerpts of different standards regarding judgment and proposed language for a causation statute.

C. Ch. Mout. Mout, in a brief presentation, warns against the establishment of legislation as a means to resolve problems. According to Mout, stiff legal standards would constitute a barrier to the development of standards and would limit the flexibility of the courts. Mout concludes that the establishment of a rule that can be reasonably complied with is a complicated task.

Bernard P. Germond. Germond explores important issues relevant to the escalation in accountant liability and litigation. These issues include: Who are the users of the financial information prepared by accountants? What are their expectations? Who are the different groups of persons involved in the preparation of accounts? What are their qualifications? What are the lessons learned from litigation against accountants? And, what paths should be explored in order to meet the challenges?

In addressing these issues, Germond notes that there are numerous interested third parties and that several regulatory bodies exist to protect the rights of these third parties with respect to publicly held corporations. A basic problem noted in litigation is that the public tends to overlook the fact that management is responsible for the preparation and endorsement of financial statements. Statutory auditors have a duty to provide reasonable assurance as to whether accounts are a true and fair view of what they represent. A clean certification is not a guarantee of correctness. Recognition should be made that the auditor is vulnerable to being defrauded by management. Contributing to the accountant liability problem is the existence of common law, the large numbers of attorneys in many areas, and the presence of joint and several liability. Care must be taken so that auditors are not overly oppressed in light of the national and economic good they serve.

David Darbyshire. Darbyshire stresses the need for an increased understanding of the role of auditors. He mentions that in order to faithfully carry out this role, the cooperation of the client is needed, and that regulators should review legal systems to assure that reasonableness of regulations. In addition, he indicates that it should be the responsibility of companies to bolster risk management. Regulation should be appropriately modified to recognize the role of judgment in the audit process, and guidelines adopted to recognize the importance of GAAP and its equivalent.

James K. Loebbecke. Loebecke notes certain major issues in the laws regarding accountant liability. Emphasis is placed on the author's experience in litigation. According to Loebbecke, it is not the audit process as prescribed by professional standards which is at fault but professionals who, through inadequate professional skepticism, experience, planning and implementation of those standards that result in litigation where warranted. Changes in audit process are noted and approved. A particular problem which must be faced is the lack of sufficient processes and internal control by clientele. Loebbecke neither advocates nor criticizes legislative reform.

Questions and Comments. The questions and comments elicit several interesting observations. Liggio notes that despite the dominance of a small number of firms, the accounting profession does not operate as an oligarchy. Difficulty has arisen in developing improved engagement letters, with firms viewing each other as rivals rather than acting cooperatively. Some restraint on losses may have emerged from a greater willingness to engage in arbitration and alternative dispute resolution. A dilemma for the auditor is how to serve the conflicting objectives of the users of financial statements. Others note that auditors should be protected as long as they make a reasonable effort to collect evidence and exercise reasonable judgment. Differences are voiced over whether auditors are helped by the establishment of standards. Liggio notes that standards help auditors in that they provide a specific standard that can serve as a duty of conduct. Others note a need to bolster penalties on clients who lie or mislead. Consideration should also be given to having auditors work with regulators in the development of appropriate standards. Excessive finger pointing is noted and risk to capital markets and the firms providing audit services from the cost of litigation mentioned. Model statutory language is also provided.

Summary and Conclusion. In closing the proceedings, stress was placed on the vital role of auditors in facilitating the provison of credible financial informationion. It is desirable to alleviate the continuing expectation gap, consider legislative reform, emphasize to management the importance of internal control, and emphasize also that management is primarily responsible for the validity of the finacial statements. In addition, auditors must proceed with a skeptical mind and bolster the use of audit tests, procedures, and analysis of evidence.

International Accounting: A Global Perspective

by M. Zafar Iqbal, Trini U. Melcher, and Amin A. Elmallah (South-Western College Publishing, 1997; 610 pp.)

(New York and Geneva: United Nations Conference on Trade and Development, 1996; ISBN 92-1-104451-0)

Reviewed by **Lorraine L. Gilbert**

The collapse of the communist economic system in the former Soviet Union and the realization of the North American Free Trade Agreement (NAFTA), the European Union (EU), the General Agreement on Tariffs and Trade (GATT), and the Asia-Pacific Economic Cooperation (APEC) are all examples of global economic transformations that influence our lives. In this era of worldwide operations, global economy, and international capital markets, shifts in economic power bring changes in international commerce that increase the importance of international accounting.

International Accounting: A Global Perspective is a text that focuses on this world of international accounting. The text is concerned with accounting issues that are important to those directly and indirectly involved with accounting and financial control in firms with international operations. Sophisticated knowledge of accounting is not necessary to understand the contents of this book because the text contains both basic concepts and more advanced international accounting topics. The text introduces the fundamental concepts of international business and monetary affairs as a background for understanding the more complicated international accounting topics such as currency translation.

Research in Accounting Regulation, Supplement 1, pages 411-414.

ISBN: 0-7623-0338-7

International Accounting: A Global Perspective is written from a multinational business perspective rooted in accounting. The text was written for advanced undergraduates or graduate students. It is clearly written and is very understandable and concise. Extensive footnotes and chapter bibliographies provide additional readings for those individuals who want to further their knowledge about the subject matter that was introduced in the chapter. Real-life examples are used throughout the text in order to reinforce the student's comprehension of the concepts. At the end of each chapter are chapter summaries which highlight the key points for those who only have time to skim the chapter. In addition to discussion questions, exercises, and problems that definitely have an accounting orientation, each chapter includes at least one case that integrates, and sometimes extends, the material discussed in that chapter. Furthermore, at the end of each chapter is an unique attribute called "Notes to Students" which informs students of the literature to read to keep pace with developments in chapter topics. This innovative feature also discusses the emerging career opportunities in various accounting disciplines. The text also introduces a number of classic works such as Henry *Sweeney's Stabilized Accounting* (Chap. 5) and Mautz and Sharaf's *The Philosophy of Auditing* (Chap. 12).

Another interesting characteristic of this text is that the entire focus of the book is based upon the comparative practices of 11 different countries representing different regions of the world. These 11 countries are: Australia, Brazil, Canada, France, Germany, Japan, Mexico, Netherlands, Nigeria, the United Kingdom, and the United States.

Chapters 13 and 14 of the book discuss the problems and challenges that face developing countries (Argentina, Bangladesh, Brazil, Chile, China, Hong Kong, India, Indonesia, Malaysia, Mexico, Nepal, Pakistan, Peru, Singapore, South Korea, Sri Lanka, Taiwan, Thailand, and Vietnam) and the Eastern European countries (Hungary, Poland, the Czech Republic, and Russia). Specifically, Chapter 13 discusses free market economies, with a special emphasis on the role of accounting in privatization and economic reforms of Third World countries. Due to privatization and economic reforms, trade between developing countries and industrialized nations has increased. Arising from this economic growth and industrial development are major problems such as pollution and natural resource depletion. Chapter 14 begins with a discussion of socialist accounting. It examines the political, economic, legal, and social systems in Eastern European countries after the breakdown of communism. The chapter's primary focus is on financial statement practices and trends in the four selected Eastern European countries.

In addition to these features, the text also contains typical financial and managerial international accounting issues. The first seven chapters deal with financial international accounting issues and Chapters 8–10 deal with managerial international accounting issues. Chapters 1 and 2 examine the development of financial accounting practices as they relate to a global economy. Similarities and differences in global financial accounting are reviewed. The diversity in accounting that exists among the various countries discussed in the text has given rise to institutional influences that will harmonize these differences. Chapter 2 specifically introduces the work of many international and regional organizations and discusses the involvement of the United Nations in the development of accounting and financial reporting guidelines. Chapter 3 discusses environmental accounting issues and summarizes some innovative and voluntary disclosures that come from Europe, such as value-added disclosures. Chapter 4 examines the various ways that multinational corporations report to financial statement users. Specifically, it surveys the bodies that are responsible for accounting standards and the types of financial statements that are used. It also describes consolidation issues and segment information disclosure requirements. Overall, the chapter gives a comparison of the standard-setting process in the 11 selected countries mentioned above. Chapters 5-7 provide a comparative study of current practices in the featured 11 countries in regard to issues such as accounting for changing prices (current value accounting), foreign currency (foreign currency transactions and translations), and specific reporting issues related to consolidations, research and development, and pension and postretirement benefits. The authors' clarity make consolidations and foreign currency translation, conceptually difficult topics, manageable.

Chapters 8 and 9, the first managerial accounting chapters, examine organizational strategic planning and control issues, with specific attention given to cultural matters. Performance criteria in control systems of multinational corporations are also investigated. Accounting information systems in multinational corporations is discussed. Issues such as the impact of technological advances, with emphasis on compatibility with international accounting standards, are also examined. In addition, capital budgeting, product costing, and foreign exchange risk management are also presented. Finally, Chapter 10 discusses multinational transfer pricing and international taxation issues.

The subject of Chapter 11 is international financial statement analysis, a very important issue due to the increase in international trade and cross-border investments resulting from the worldwide movement toward the privatization of public enterprises and the liberalization of trade, investment, and currency policies. The chapter addresses the perceived problems associated with the availability of financial information such as reliability, timeliness of information, and so forth. The diversity in disclosure practices makes international financial statement analysis a very difficult subject. However, the authors handle the topic very eloquently. Finally, Chapter 12 discusses internal and external auditing issues associated with the reliability of accounting information. Environmental factors influencing both internal and external audit functions are also examined. Internal auditing is a management function whose objective is to determine whether management and accounting controls are in place and are effective. It also ensures that assets are safeguarded and used efficiently. Comparatively, the objective of external auditing, performed by public accountants, is to determine if financial statements are properly prepared. It is essential that the auditor knows both the accounting and auditing standards of each country. The chapter addresses the trend towards worldwide harmonization of auditing standards, paying particular attention to three organizations that are trying to harmonize these standards: the International Federation of Accountants (IFAC), the International Organization of Securities Commission (IOSCO), and the European Union (EU).

Overall, the book is very well written, thorough, and current. If there is a shortcoming, it would be the lack of discussion about the relevance of technology, such as the Internet, to international accounting. A new edition might incorporate a discussion of the World Wide Web as it relates to international accounting.

The Nature and Determinants of Disclosure Adequacy: An International Perspective
by Ahmed Riahi-Belkaoui

(Connecticut and London, England: Quorum Books, 1997; 223 pp.)

Reviewed by **Pei-Gin Hsieh**

International accounting has become more and more important since the flow of resources between countries became a crucial factor for successful operation of many businesses. However, differences in accounting objectives, standards, and techniques across countries has led to disclosure adequacy differences between these countries. Disclosure adequacy measures the quality of disclosures in covering all relevant information. In this book, Belkaoui examines the nature and determinants of the differences in disclosure adequacy internationally. Understanding such differences will help in further harmonization of accounting standards, principles, and techniques.

The first chapter explores: (1) disclosure adequacy proposals in the United States and (2) disclosure adequacy in the context of international comparative financial accounting research, and further proposes (3) an international accounting contingency framework which identifies the main determinants for differences in disclosure adequacy based on cultural relativism, linguistic relativism, political and civil relativism, economic and demographic relativism, legal and tax relativism, and religious relativism. The author provides explanations, measurement criteria, findings, and progress of accounting research with regard to each type of relativism.

Research in Accounting Regulation, Supplement 1, pages 415-417.

ISBN: 0-7623-0338-7

This chapter provides excellent overall guidance for researchers. In addition to the above discussion, the exhibits provide reviews of international accounting literature, a framework for cross-national accounting research, types of international comparative accounting research, and independent variables used in previous research studies. Discussions on disclosure adequacy proposals in the United States help accounting practioners and students within the United States develop a better understanding of possible disclosure requirements in the future, and help current and potential standard-setters outside the United States in setting their own disclosure standards. Those interested in understanding the determinants disclosure adequacy will benefit from this chapter.

Each of the remaining five chapters provides an example of empirical research published after 1989. These studies, using countries as the unit of analysis, support the propositions made in the first chapter by confirming that economic growth; country return and risk; managerial, academic, and professional influences; human development; political and civil indicators; and cultural dimensions lead to different social environments, which create differing levels of disclosure adequacy across countries. Each of these studies includes the development of hypotheses, measurement method for determinants of disclosure adequacy, empirical models, sample countries, empirical results, and implications for future research. However, all but one of the studies were undertaken by the author. Therefore, the perspective provided is largely limited to that of one researcher.

The content of the book is relatively different from the introductory international accounting books already on the market, which give broad, brief coverage of different topics in international accounting. The book is probably more valuable to researchers, teachers, and Ph.D. students than to the broad audience that the author mentions in the preface. Accounting practitioners, business executives, and general business students may find Chapter 1 and some of the explanatory parts in Chapters 2-6 to be useful.

The text might have been more useful to a broader audience had the author, based on prior literature on disclosure adequacy and the current disclosure development in various accounting clusters, provided synthesis, discussions, and practical recommendations to accounting practitioners, accounting standard-setting agencies, government agencies related to capital markets, investors, and business executives. The prior literature to be used as the basis for discussions would include not only those which use countries as the unit of analysis, but also ones which use countries as the object of research and as the context for research, and those studies that are transnational in character (Wallace, Olusegun, and Gernon 1991).[1] These would comprise all four types of studies on disclosure adequacy as categorized in international comparative financial accounting research.

In sum, this book provides a good overall guidance to international disclosure adequacy, particularly for researchers, and sheds light on the fact that research in this area is still in its infancy. Teachers familiar with the more traditional international accounting books may find some freshness in this text.

NOTE

1. Studies that are transnational in character treat countries as components of a larger international system (Wallace et al. 1991).

REFERENCE

Wallace, R., S. Olusegun, and H. Gernon. 1991. Frameworks for international comparative financial accounting. *Journal of Accounting Literature* 10: 222.

www.ingramcontent.com/pod-product-compliance
Ingram Content Group UK Ltd.
Pitfield, Milton Keynes, MK11 3LW, UK
UKHW020229290926
15470UKWH00002B/434

9 780762 303380